An Illustrated History of

DERBY

Dedication
To Carole and Cornelia

An Illustrated History of

DERBY

Maxwell Craven

breedon **books**
PUBLISHING

First published in Great Britain in 2007 by
The Breedon Books Publishing Company Limited
Breedon House, 3 The Parker Centre,
Derby, DE21 4SZ.

ISBN 978-1-85983-555-5

Printed and bound by Cromwell Press,
Trowbridge, Wiltshire.

CONTENTS

ACKNOWLEDGEMENTS

A startling number of people have contributed to this book. By listening attentively to those of all ages while lecturing over the past 33 years I have learnt much. In my former position as keeper of antiquities at Derby Museum and subsequently as a columnist for the *Derby Evening Telegraph*, I have learnt more, and my colleagues and readers have frequently been kind enough to share their own expertise with me. Foremost among these have been my former head of department the late Roy Hughes, my longstanding former colleagues David Fraser – the nation's foremost authority on Joseph Wright and his circle – Judy Anderson, who presided over the porcelain collections, Brian Waters and Mark Higginson, authorities on Rolls-Royce and railways (and much more) respectively and my old and valued friend Mick Stanley. Then there have been my colleagues who worked with me in the former Antiquities Department, especially those who ran the City Survey for me in the 1980s, Joe Lachowicz and James Darwin, the latter still enormously helpful in his present role as senior caseworker for the Georgian Group. I was much aided in trying to make sense of early Derby by Chris Drage of the Trent and Peak Archaeological Trust and, since publication of the first edition, by the research of John Heath, Jane Steer, and Joan d'Arcy.

The work carried out by Dr David Roffe in making sense of early Derby, most of which was never published except second hand in the pages of the first edition of this book, was undertaken at the instigation of the County Museum Service, who funded a comprehensive re-evaluation of the Derbyshire Domesday survey by him. His detailed analysis of the evolution of Derby was largely omitted from the two published articles arising from his work, but itself has not been subsequently academically challenged. I am also most grateful for the time Professor Martin Biddle took to go through my analysis of Roffe's conclusions, to which he was able to make some valuable additions. Nor can I let this opportunity pass to mention my debt to David Jones, now at the University of St Andrews, who first began a programme of research at Pickford's House in Friar Gate. He was aided by Jane Steer, whose subsequent work on mediaeval Derby has been of enormous help, and by the redoubtable Edward Saunders, whose *Joseph Pickford of Derby*, with which I had the honour to be associated, was published by Alan Sutton in 1993.

I have also relied heavily on the Derby Local Studies Library, and my warmest thanks go to all who have worked there past and present for years of tolerance and help. Don Farnsworth, who prepared many of the photographs, the late Cliff Burton, Richard Osborne and Dr Andor Gomme have been of enormous assistance too, and I owe an especial debt of gratitude to the late Clifford Harpur for allowing me to read and quote from his ancestor Samuel Harpur's MS *Journal*.

In the first edition, too, I was able to acknowledge the help of over 40 others in the footnotes. Without being able to name them all in this short space, I would like to thank them for their help, as well as very many more people who have shared their knowledge with me subsequently, most especially the loyal readers of my twice-weekly *Evening Telegraph* articles, to all of whom I am extremely grateful even for the smallest tit-bit.

Since 1988 I have acquired other colleagues, of whom it would be invidious of me to fail to mention my three successive *Evening Telegraph* editors: Keith Perch, Mike Norton and Steve Hall, especially the latter who very kindly agreed to co-sponsor this book, making available over 100 previously unpublished photographs. This involved the help and forbearance of Carole Seal and her colleagues (and predecessors) in the newspaper's library, which has been much appreciated.

Likewise, the sponsorship of the city council is gratefully acknowledged, especially the efforts of Steve Dunning and Phil O'Brien in facilitating this arrangement; their support is something of which to be immensely proud, and I would like to think that this book does Derby credit.

Similarly, it would be true to say that without Steve Caron and his hard working colleagues at Breedon Books this edition would never even have got off the ground; their support and tolerance has been exemplary and greatly appreciated. In other cases, I have tried to acknowledge photographs where appropriate, and I hope that those who have kindly lent me such images will find this adequate recompense. To those many others, named nowhere in particular, I owe an enormous debt.

I cannot close this note without acknowledging the hours of patient and uncomplaining help freely given by my wife, Carole, who compiled indices, lists and photographic captions hour after hour for the first edition and has not stinted her assistance for this one, either, even to the curtailment of our social life. This book is as much the fruits of her labours, as of all those mentioned above, as it is of mine. I only hope it is worthy of them.

In conclusion, I would point out that all mistakes are my own.

INTRODUCTION

To attempt to write the history of a city is to undertake a heavy burden of responsibility. One has to be at one and at the same time readable, reasonably comprehensible, and as thorough as is consistent with the other two elements, while staying within the parameters laid down by one's publisher. An additional burden is that this is a second edition, revised and updated, some 20 years after the first. Expectations have changed, new presentation is considered desirable and such changes have to be done without depriving the book of its authority. Nevertheless, I have attempted to deliver and add 20 rather packed years of the city's history without making the book significantly longer. It will be for the reader to judge how successful an attempt it is.

The author also admits having one or two bees in his bonnet. One is that, as an incomer to the city (albeit of long standing), he has become a convert to Derby's merits and thus is fired by a convert's proselytising zeal. Thus, this book is written from the standpoint that Derby is a place of the utmost interest, vastly underrated by a significant element of its inhabitants, and a place which, over its history, has nurtured events of the foremost national importance. By this I refer to that upsurge of intellectual and scientific enquiry and excellence which burst forth in the second half of the 18th century. We are all familiar with the achievements of Josiah Wedgwood, of the Strutts and the Arkwrights, even of Charles Darwin and the Industrial Revolution, but few of us were aware – at least before the first edition of this history was published and the author's subsequent efforts to emphasise it – that Derby was the true cradle of much of this unique flowering. I mention Charles Darwin, for in the copious philosophical outpourings of his grandfather, Erasmus, were in embryo many of the ideas which he developed and which are still generally considered valid today.

Another facet of Derby is that, despite its girdle of industry and subsequent damage to its built environment, it is still one of the finest Georgian towns of its size in the region, if not further afield. It does not overload the intellect to recognise that architecture is a life-enhancing discipline that is all too often overlooked as one of the fine arts, and hence an attempt has been made to incorporate an acknowledgement within these pages of Derby's architectural history.

Yet the physical appearance of a city and the nature of people who dwell therein are the two elements which make a settlement, whatever its size, what it is, give it its ambience and imbue it with its *genius loci*. Hence, there is also emphasis upon the people who have lived in Derby down the ages, from those who have come into the area from the time of the Belgic tribes in the first century BC, through the Saxons, Normans and later migrants from Europe, to those from many other disparate parts of the world in more recent times. Thus, with people and the buildings in which they lived and worked, the two millenia of vigorous continuity weave their way in and out, rising into our consciousness with events, before dropping out of sight.

While a fairly chronological narrative has been attempted, some facets of everyday life in Derby have had to be treated in a relatively thematic way, and the liberty has been taken to pause awhile from time to time in the course of the narrative to consider them as they arise and pursue them through to their termination or current state. While mention is made of what Derby historian William Hutton called 'Eminent Men', it has been thought more important to dwell only on those whose careers had a direct bearing on the city's history and not on those whose fame lay ultimately elsewhere; most of them in both categories have been dealt with in *Derbeians of Distinction* (Breedon 1998).

It was also thought right not to describe such things as social life in general, or in a national context, as some previous histories have done. This aspect of life has been adequately covered elsewhere, and is only highlighted where examples can be drawn directly from exemplars in Derby. Likewise, such things as 'donkey flying' and other events, described in detail and at length by Hutton, have been alluded to only. Those curious to know more will have to read the original, for this revised edition of *Derby – An Illustrated History* has had to be shorn of its footnotes in the interests of space. The reader may rest assured, however, that no fact has been quoted without having been tracked to its source, a process which has led to the elimination of more than a few old chestnuts concerning the history of the city long repeated from one work to another.

One aspect of the city which has not been given its due is the history of the suburbs. Space has not permitted the luxury of tackling this in detail, although numerous references have been made to these communities. Reference can be made, however, to the companion volume, *The Illustrated History of Derby's Suburbs*, published by Breedon in 1996, further supplemented – for those whose appetite for micro-history is paramount – by *Street by Street: Derby* in 2005.

The 1988 introduction of the first edition of this book rashly declared that 'Those who feel a sense of shock when they read of the atrocious tide of destruction which has enveloped the city over the past 60 or so years should not take it too hard' and 'That this trend has in general eased'. Unfortunately this is no longer true. The imposition of 17.5 percent

VAT on the restoration of existing structures while retaining new build as zero-rated, has been burden enough for those keen to preserve the built environment of the city. On top of that has been the problem of the Office of the Deputy Prime Minister in 2000 declaring urban gardens to be within the definition of a 'brownfield site' and thus available for preferred development and by effectively imposing housing quotas on local authorities by *fiat*. This has given *carte blanche* to developers great and small to virtually print money, sweeping away perfectly respectable unlisted buildings – in Derby's case even in conservation areas – and replacing them with meretricious blocks of flats, designed in many cases straight from their architects' CAD packages with little attempt to enhance the surrounding environment. This has been compounded by changes in the rules concerning the listing of historic buildings and the constraints, some of them implicit rather than statutory, placed by the government since 1997 on English Heritage, to the point where applications to add buildings to the statutory list are being refused as a matter of course. I might add that those who feel concerned about these ever-present threats are recommended to consider joining the very active Derby Civic Society.

Nevertheless, Derby remains as fine a city as one could expect to find anywhere, and its people are among the friendliest in these islands. It is to be hoped that what follows will reinforce this reality in the reader's mind and will emphasise the considerable significance of the history of the city through the ages.

Maxwell Craven
Derby
October 2006

I

ORIGINS

PREHISTORY

I N a sense, Derby may be said to have had two foundations, one Roman and another late Saxon. In fact, the Roman settlement, called by the Romans *Derventio* and by us Little Chester, was a separate entity which had decayed into a rural hamlet by the end of the first millennium of our era, to be later absorbed by the expansion of Derby proper. Yet certain enigmatic facts suggest that the two settlements can legitimately be viewed together. To set either of these foundations in context, it is, however, important to stand back from the city itself and view it from a wider standpoint.

Derby's position is a strategic one in terms of communications. Situated on the north flank of the Trent Valley on the lowest crossing point of its tributary, the Derwent, the site commands communications east to west along the former and north to south along the latter. The Trent affords a route of penetration into the West and North Midlands from the North Sea, and the Derwent Valley was a main route connecting the upland area of Derbyshire, the Peak District, with the Trent, and thus all points south, west and east. Further, the Trent forms not only an artery of communication but also a barrier dividing southern and northern England. Despite this, it has rarely been a border; its value as a route has been such that command of both banks between Trent Bridge (Nottingham) and Burton has been sufficiently important to have overridden its obvious advantages as a line of demarcation.

This was even so before the coming of the Roman Empire to Britain. While it would appear inappropriate to enumerate all the peoples and cultures which ranged across the site of Derby or *Derventio* before the foundation of either, the last Iron Age group which inhabited the area needs to be briefly discussed in the light of the subsequent history of the settlement.

An excavation at Willington, a few miles south west of Derby, carried out in 1970–72, established near continuous occupation of the rural landscape in the

Swarkestone Bridge - the causeway looking south, 2004. (Peter Billson)

9

Trent Valley from the Neolithic period on into the middle Saxon: that is, some 1,500 years of uninterrupted settlement. Furthermore, in the words of the excavation's director, 'The ten miles of the middle Trent Valley between Willington and Shardlow was an important focus of Neolithic and Bronze Age activity.'

Excavations between 1938 and 1976 have revealed information about sites at Aston-on-Trent, Findern, Twyford, Swarkestone Lows, Stenson and Shardlow. These sites have included one, perhaps two, *cursi* – highly elongated earthworks about which almost nothing is known – several barrows, burials, settlement features and at least one possible henge. Another habitational site was examined at Melbourne in 1976 and subsequent excavations have highlighted the extraordinarily rich concentration of Bronze Age finds from the area. Indeed, Richard Davis has recently written that 'The Trent is second only to the Thames in Britain in the recovery of metalwork from a riverine source.' The finds of mainly late Bronze Age material from gravel workings in and around Elvaston over the last 30 years have been astonishing, and the stretch of the northern bank of the Trent is especially rich in traces of early peoples.

All this goes to emphasise the intensive nature of settlement in the Trent Valley and its environs from well into prehistoric times. That even earlier material has failed to survive is probably due to acidic soils, shifts in the river's course and the sheer intensity of subsequent land use, rather than being an indication that very early cultures were never active in the area. In the Derbyshire Peak, subsequent land-use gradually tailed off into non-intensive subsistence farming; on the other hand, many more vestiges from these early periods have survived in the preserving peaty soils.

Such settlements were served by mendicant craftsmen, such as smiths – an elite in prehistoric times – traders and even priests. Thus adequate communications were necessary. Much research has been done into the ancient trackways and portways of Derbyshire, and it was astride one of these that the Saxon town of Derby seems to have been founded. This route ran north to south through the site of the later town. It followed the Derwent Valley north, deep into the Peak District. In the other direction it ran across the Trent through the later settlement of Melbourne to the Soar Valley and thence to the south.

In crossing the Trent there can be little doubt that it employed a causeway of the sort uncovered 30 years ago on the Somerset levels from the same late-prehistoric period. There appears no other obvious candidate for a trackway leading south from the Middle Trent and the Derwent Valley, and the surmise must be taken as being a secure one. Today's received wisdom that Swarkestone Bridge is a mediaeval feature rests upon an examination

of the surviving fabric. But this unique monument surely has its origins firmly planted in the pre-Roman Iron Age or before. Further, there is now good reason to suppose that the Romans used this route too. A glance at a map of Roman communications shows that, according to conventional wisdom, to go south a Roman would have been forced to travel south west to Wall (*Letocetum*) and beyond, or south east to Willoughby-on-the-Wolds via Sawley. These facts are based on archaeology and upon the Roman sources: Ptolemy's *Geographia*, the *Antonine Itinerary* and the *Ravenna Cosmography*. Yet, as will be demonstrated, *Derventio* and *Ratae Corieltauvorum* (Leicester) lay in the same basic tribal cantonal area under the Roman Empire, and a direct way between them would have been essential. The fact that the ancient sources do not mention one need not detain us overmuch; they are at best incomplete in the data they reveal. Lesser prehistoric tracks have also been identified within the area of the modern city; the best preserved is the Portway at Allestree.

Thus, in the last millennium BC, we have the Trent Valley intensively settled on its northern side (and thus on its south-facing slopes) with river and road communications extending both north to south and east to west. That there were undoubtedly neolithic and later settlements nearer the subsequent site of Derby than those proven at Findern or Stenson may furthermore be inferred from relevant chance finds made in the modern city area. There have been seven neolithic finds from the Allestree estate area alone; four in Chaddesden and seven between Boulton and Osmaston. One of the latter is probably early Bronze Age, but this period is much more thinly represented within the city: only eight are recorded, although a Bronze Age cremation cemetery was discovered on the alignment of Roman Rykneld Street at the top of Pastures Hill, Littleover, in 2003. Most recently there has been the discovery of a much earlier artefact, a cordiform middle Paleolithic hand-axe at Mickleover in 2003, now in Derby Museum.

Even less well represented are Iron Age artefacts, for while all these periods are heavily represented along the excavated sites of the Trent Valley, especially Willington and Swarkestone, only two are recorded as chance finds in Derby. One is from the site of the first Roman fort; the other, a gold coin of the Iron Age kingdom of the Corieltauvi, was recovered from the site of the Osmaston Park Road sports ground.

Mention of the latter, an uninscribed type adopted by most of the last Iron Age invading peoples – the Belgic tribes – and modelled on the Macedonian *stater*, brings us to the edge of recorded history. The coin dates from the last generation of the last millennium BC and was struck by the rulers of the Corieltauvi, a people who inhabited a poorly defined region stretching from the Humber to

A fine view of Derby's prehistoric through route as seen from the cathedral tower in June 1973: Iron Gate, Rotten Row, Corn Market, St. Peter's Street, The Spot and, in the far distance, Osmaston Road. (*Derby Evening Telegraph*)

Burton-upon-Trent in the west, Market Harborough in the south and the Lincolnshire coast in the east. Its axis would be represented by a line drawn down the Valley of the Lower Trent from its confluence with the Humber through Leicester.

What is unclear is how much of the Peak District was included and thus how much of West Derbyshire north of the Trent. It would be reasonable to assume that the uplands of the White Peak may have formed the boundary as it appears to have done later, in the Dark Age. Another gold stater of this tribe from Boylestone, while inconclusive on its own, might suggest that the territory stretched at least to the lower Dove, to some extent confirmed by Dr Roffe's ideas underlying the origins of Northworthy as outlined below. Thus Derby's thinly-populated site was then located securely within the tribal area.

The Corieltauvi were culturally akin to those Belgic tribes – like the powerful Catuvellauni immediately north of London, whose ruler Cunobelinus achieved a measure of immortality as Shakespeare's *Cymbeline* – with coinage, pottery and metalwork all of allied design. Beyond, northward from the Corieltauvian area, was the less advanced Celtic tribe of the Brigantes, later to be a thorn in the flesh of the Romans, and allied to the Belgic tribes only by virtue of their common Celtic origins and strategic self interest.

The fact that a single Iron Age object was found during excavations in Belper Road, Derby – site of Derby's earliest Roman settlement – means only that the two cultures, Corieltauvian and Roman, overlapped on the site in the 40s or 50s. Indeed, the Celtic peoples we call the Corieltauvi were (on Roman evidence) still there when the Roman government collapsed almost four centuries later.

Corieltauvian gold stater (South Ferriby type) found beside Long Lane in the 1950s. (The late R.G. Hughes)

Thus Derby has its ultimate roots in this Celtic tribe, even if they left no vestige of a settlement beside the spinal route they doubtless inherited from their more ancient precursors and which, even today, divides the modern city north to south.

What the Romans did for Derby

The Roman invasion of Britain, which began in AD 43, progressed fairly quickly to a line from the Humber to the Severn estuary, which, because it included the kingdom (strictly the *territorium*) of the Corieltauvi, suggests that the tribe swiftly submitted to Aulus Plautius, the Roman Commander-in-Chief, or else offered ineffectual resistance.

Within as few as perhaps six years of the invasion, the Romans had established a fort on the high ground immediately to the west of the Derwent, astride the present Belper Road. The earliest positive evidence for the fort is in fact datable to *c.*AD 54/60, although an earlier date is possible, but the fact remains that it was early and its purpose was undoubtedly to control the then lowest crossing point over the river from the high ground on its west. Further, this fort, with others on Corieltauvian territory at Littleborough and Broxtowe, Nottinghamshire, Pentrich and Sawley, Derbyshire, and Templeborough, Yorkshire, may have served the dual supplementary roles of policing the newly-submitted Corieltauvi and as a deterrent to the turbulent and as yet unsubdued Brigantes immediately to the north.

This fort – if fort it was – at Strutt's Park is of unknown size. From the scattered area of finds on both sides of Duffield and Belper Roads, it may turn out to have been quite significant. Unfortunately, it is almost entirely covered by late 19th and early 20th-century villas and only during garden works do any artifacts crop up. Where there have been untouched areas, as the garden of 192 Duffield Road, where a limited archaeological investigation was done in 1990, subsequent building has sealed the site for several generations to come in order to satisfy the rapacity of developers, in this case despite two public enquiries in 2001 and 2002. Indeed, even after the focus of Roman activity transferred across the Derwent, the old fort site may have retained some importance, as a rescue excavation in August 1998 uncovered what appeared to be ribbon development of fairly substantial timber-framed houses of a late second-century date built alongside Duffield Road to the south of the probable fort. This establishes Duffield Road – at least south of Five Lamps – as of at least Roman origin and confirms the 'north-south trackway' theory of communication in the area.

Doubtless the move to a new fortified site helped the Roman army weather the tempests of the uprising of the *Iceni* under Boudicca – Boadicaea in Latin – in AD 60 and that of the Brigantes under the previously pro-Roman Queen Cartimandua nine years later. Both these tribes bordered on the territory of the Corieltauvi, so the area may well have seen some alarums and excursions.

By this time, too, the Corieltauvi had been recognised in their *territorium* by the Roman administration and established with a capital at Leicester (*Ratae Corieltauvorum*), where evidence of late Iron Age occupation suggests there was already a settlement. The Roman *civitas* of the tribe thus consisted of the entire tribal area and capital, probably subdivided into districts (*pagi*), one of which may have included the Derbyshire section of the Trent Valley between the Dove and the Erewash. The evidence for the latter is highly inferential but persuasive.

Nevertheless, renewed Roman military activity under the Flavian Emperors (AD 69–96), and especially associated with the governor Cn. Julius Agricola, led to the establishment of a much more ambitious Roman fort at

Derventio in the presumed north western Corieltauvi*an pagus o*n the east bank of the Derwent.

DERVENTIO, the Roman name applied to the place we now call Little Chester, is of Celtic origin and was undoubtedly taken from that of the River Derwent. It occurs for this location only in the Ravenna Cosmography, an early mediaeval copy of an original Roman map, the name there appearing as DERBENTIONE, in the dative and with the 'v' mutated, as is common, into a 'b'. The name is made up of the Celtic elements *daru/deru [Welsh, derw = oak]* + *vent (later Welsh wen* = white); thus: 'place of the white oaks' or 'river in the oak wood'. Note, though, that the river name from which the place name is derived is common, with eight others: three other Derwents, Darwen, Darenth and three Darts. Not only that, there are five other places in Roman Britain called *Derventio*! It contributes the first syllable of the modern name Derby, too.

This fort was established on the lower ground opposite the previous one, which was probably

Excavations on Parker's Piece, Little Chester, in 1924 reveal what is presumed to have been a baths complex. Note the hypocaust floor supports towards the rear of the site. The wall extended well over 35 feet, disappearing under the GNR embankment, behind. (*Derby Evening Telegraph*)

Stone bas relief of a deity from Little Chester, thought to represent Apollo. (Derby Museum)

decommissioned and, after about AD 96, dismantled. The exact size of this new establishment is as yet far from clear, but a reconstruction in the Antonine period (*c.*AD 138/180) created a fort which was probably large enough to house a *cohors equitata milliaria*, a unit of about 1,000 infantry, some auxiliary cavalry and 'B' echelon ancillaries. As no official inscriptions have ever been found here, we cannot do more than guess the type of unit from the presumed size of the fort and any remains. It was rectangular in plan and enclosed roughly seven acres, with the usual approximately cruciform street plan, part of which survives on the Old Chester Road-City Road axis in modern Little Chester, the successor settlement.

The bounds of the fort were demarcated with a 15ft-high palisaded rampart, beyond which lay two deep ditches spaced 100ft apart. The interior of the fort doubtless contained a headquarters building, administration block, parade hall, a shrine, strongroom, commandant's house, granaries, sick bay, armory and, of course, linear barrack blocks for the soldiers

Roman-British 'Derbyshire Ware' pottery from Little Chester, photographed on site by R.G Hughes. The largest pot is almost 10½ inches high and weighs 5lb. © The late R.G. Hughes

themselves. Several wells were provided for fresh water, two of which were excavated and restored in the 1970s and for many years from 1980 were dressed by the local parish at a May ceremony, since discontinued due to repeated vandalism.

Excavations in 1987–88, near the south-east corner of the fort, revealed two quite large and sophisticated buildings, the functions of which are as yet unclear. The date is late first to early second century. One was equipped with underfloor heating and boasted walls decorated with painted plasterwork. Some parts of the associated building extended outside the bounds of the early fort and were enclosed later.

The presence of soldiers stationed at *Derventio* indicates that the need for 'service industries' and support of other kinds swiftly arose. Hence a civil settlement (*vicus*) undoubtedly congealed around the defences of the garrison. Indeed, a probable baker's shop was uncovered at the side of the road going north in excavations in 1926: the first known Derby tradesman.

Possibly the first named local citizen also appears on a graffito found hereabouts: PRI[VATUS], who must have lived in the mid-second century. Another, SENILIS, appears in a similar context suggesting the same period.

As time went by, an industrial settlement grew up on the side of the road which ran south east from Derventio towards Sawley. Activities here included the manufacture of the distinctive coarse Derbyshire Ware pottery, known from its 'goose pimply' exterior surfaces, smelting of metals, mainly lead, and other trades like tanning essential to the maintenance of soldiery. Although the pottery making appears to have diminished during the mid to late second century, the smelting continued, the element being quite probably an important trans-shipment point for the movement of lead from the Peak, mined under Imperial control, although so far no Roman lead pigs have turned up at *Derventio*. The crucial element appears to have been the as yet unlocated settlement of *Lutudarum*, lying probably to the north west. Wirksworth would appear to be a good candidate for it, being associated with the supply of lead as early as the seventh century, being close to a river called Ecclesbourne (see below) and having a dedication to St Helen, the mother of Constantine and discoverer of the True Cross in AD 324.

Communications being good, trade undoubtedly burgeoned accordingly, over and above those transactions which solely resulted from the needs of the army. One strange contrast to the present day is highlighted by the large quantity of oyster shells recovered here in the Roman strata, as indeed at other Roman settlements in Britain. Today, with the demise of Roome's fishmonger's, a fresh oyster is virtually unobtainable in Derby!

Little Chester. Looking west along the alignment of the road running east from Derventio: Vivian Street looking towards Old Chester Road) 1990. (M. Craven)

THE ROMAN ROADS

The communications system imposed by the Romans acted as a complement to that used previously by the Corieltauvi and their predecessors: the postulated north-south trackway, the so-called portways and the rivers. The most important highway of Roman origin was undoubtedly that subsequently known as Rykneld Street. This ran from the south west via Wall, Staffordshire (Roman *Letocetum*), to *Derventio,* where it appears to have skirted the fort to the south and east before turning north to continue through the Roman stations of Pentrich, Chesterfield and Templeborough to Doncaster *(Danum),* beyond the borders of the *civitas* of the Corieltauvi.

The other main artery ran from Chester *(Deva)* via Chesterton and Rocester (Staffordshire) to *Derventio,* the main part of the latter stretch being today marked by Long Lane and associated features. Unfortunately, it is quite unclear what alignment it took between Brun Lane (Mackworth) and Little Chester. The evidence suggests that it turned south or east and perhaps down the present Kedleston Road, or near it. The route of Rykneld Street on the other hand is quite well defined by the A38 road from Wall to Littleover and thence by vestiges to a point just south of the earlier Roman fort in Strutt's Park. Whether or not the course of the road was radically changed in

order to bring it across the river at a more amenable spot when the later fort was built at Little Chester is difficult to say.

Certainly, there are likely to have been two Roman bridges across the Derwent, for William Stukeley recorded the remains of one on the Rocester-Little Chester (Long Lane) alignment in 1719, of which the Derby historian Hutton, writing 72 years later, said '...the foundations are yet seen in clear water; I have felt them with the oar'. Research by divers in 1986–90 strongly supported this evidence, although final proof is still elusive. The bridges were probably of timber on stone cutwaters, pieces of the latter having been recovered in 1987.

Minor roads undoubtedly led off this and other more important arteries. Furthermore, at least two subsidiary settlements have been located within the area of the present city. Surface finds of coarser pottery wares appeared when the preparatory work was being made for the building of the new Oakwood suburb between Breadsall Hill Top and Chaddesden in 1982. These finds, allied with other features, suggest that a native rural settlement of a fairly extensive nature existed there. At the same spot, mediaeval pottery and other items, including house platforms and a possible moat, suggest that the site was revived and became the village of Breadsall Nether Hall, later again deserted. At Mickleover School, in 1988, prodigious amounts of Roman pottery, including pieces of the more refined Samian ware, were revealed during the building of an extension. Positioned at the upper edge of a south-facing slope, it is even possible that the site might have been that of a villa of some kind; a type of Roman site yet to be securely identified in Derbyshire, although excavation at Littlehay Grange near Ockbrook in 1994–97 revealed a rather modest aisled homestead, although it was probably no more than a better sort of working farm.

The Long Lane alignment continued on from *Derventio* (which it appears to have skirted on the northern side of the defensive ditches of the fort) east for a few hundred yards into the area of the present Racecourse Playing Field, where the industrial part of the civil settlement of *Derventio* lay, before swinging south east to Sawley, following for much of its course the line of the old Nottingham Road. At Sawley it crossed the Trent, although whether by bridge or, as seems more likely, by ferry, is not clear, and continued on to join the Fosse Way near Willoughby-on-the-Wolds, Nottinghamshire.

It was along the side of this road as it crossed the Racecourse Playing Field that from 1978 the remains of a number of plinth tombs were excavated and a later walled cemetery *(columbarium)* measuring 46sq ft identified close by. The latter – a feature not otherwise known so far north in the Empire – was in use by the mid-to-late second century but was used both for inhumations and the bestowal of cremated remains until at least the middle of the fourth century; a total of 61 burials were identified. It is thought that this was either a family burial site, in use for over 200 years and with six members for each of 10 generations, or a burial club plot, in which case, again, the burial club must have been remarkably long lived. One is inclined to favour the former suggestion over the latter. According to Roman law, burials had to be beyond the settlement boundary, so these finds define the eastern limit of *Derventio*. Moreover, plinth tombs are relatively rare in Britain, but were derived from the very monumental and architectonic ones, remains of which line the *Via Appia* out of Rome to this day. The local ones were erected around AD 100 when military occupation was at a premium, and the people whose memorials they were must have been either officers or civilians from the *vicus* of considerable status. If the latter is the case, then the civil settlement at *Derventio* must have become a more affluent and significant place at this date than previous writers have allowed.

An increase in affluence combined with changing strategic requirements might also lead us to conclude that the military presence will have given way to civilian life and increasing commercial prosperity. Evidence from the fort suggests that by late in the second century a unit of lesser status was introduced, presumably auxiliaries. After the campaigns of Septimius Severus in the north, early in the century following the barrack blocks were dismantled. Additionally, one of the two buildings excavated in 1988 near the south-east fort angle was rebuilt partly in stone at about this time. Plainly *Derventio* was able to flourish perfectly well without the presence of free-spending soldiers and, judging from the tombs, to flourish very well. Yet, by and large, the third century was one of stagnation for *Derventio* followed by a strong revival from the time of the tetrarchy.

Another factor, which may have had a bearing on the status of the town (for such we must now call it), was the granting of full Roman citizenship to all citizens of the Empire by Severus' son Caracalla in AD 217. Previously, only officers, time-expired soldiers, officials and certain migrants from the continent will have enjoyed full civil rights, as we might term them, at *Derventio*. Most of the native Corieltauvian British had not previously enjoyed full citizenship and the privileges that accompanied it. Henceforth, they could trade freely under the protection of the law, hold Imperial office and set up their own local government.

Although the town had no known Imperial status – either as a *Municipium* like St Albans, a *Colonia* like Lincoln or a *Civitas* capital like Leicester – we may be sure that a council of citizens *(decuriones)* ran the town and quite possibly a large area round about. Some evidence has been adduced, for instance, to suggest that the neighbouring and directly comparable settlement of Wall controlled a considerable *territorium* or *pagus,* a subdivision of the *Civitas* of the *Cornovii* in which the town lay. Likewise *Derventio,* as the most substantial settlement in the north west of the Corieltauvian area, may have controlled the *pagus* of its own region, perhaps even extending across the Trent. Nobody knows exactly how ancient the southern boundary of the county is and evidence of continuity of land units is continually growing.

Undoubtedly, much secular building was going on in the third century at *Derventio,* as archaeology has strongly suggested, and much of it was outside the old fort wall, indicating that, even without the military, the settlement was expanding. Nationally there is little evidence that the anarchy within the Roman Empire in the middle of the century seriously affected life. Nevertheless, many settlements acquired massive new

Little Chester, Derby racecourse excavations, 1978: tomb bases beginning to appear. (M. Craven)

Little Chester: two members of Derby Museum staff excavating a plinth tomb base on the racecourse, November 1978. (M. Craven)

defences, and the late third century – roughly about the time of the British-based Imperial usurpers Carausius and Allectus (the latter overthrown by the father of Constantine the Great) – is the time that some, including those at Little Chester, appear to have been built.

The new stone walls, 9ft thick at the base (suggesting a total height of some 20ft), seem mainly to have been built into the original earth rampart of the old military fort. Bastions may have been added at this time, or more likely during the century following, to enable defenders to enfilade the walls and to carry artillery-pieces *(ballistae)* on top, although the archaeological interpretation of the Little Chester bastions presents some very thorny problems.

A large building, probably dating from this later period and occupied into the last quarter of the fourth century, with a hypocaust (underfloor heating) – perhaps the bath-house of a substantial dwelling, less likely of a public building – was found in 1924 on Parker's Piece, a field by the river south of the fort at Little Chester. Such tantalising pieces of evidence suggest continuing affluence and expansion of *Derventio* into the fourth century, in any case a prosperous time in Roman Britain. That affluence and importance was now part of the story of *Derventio*, however, is attested by the excavation in 1988 of an architecturally pretentious building close to the east wall of the fort which also sported a hypocaust, decorative wall-plaster, carved masonry and a courtyard apparently with ancillary buildings. This dated from *c.*AD 120. A coal heap found elsewhere at Little Chester suggests that this fuel was imported from local sources for heating such things as hypocausts and strikes an almost contemporary note. There seems little doubt, too, that coal was used for manufacturing purposes, like farriery, craft metalwork and so on. Interestingly, unconfirmed reports in 1988 suggested that a section of mosaic was found when a hole was dug, immediately north of the fort, to erect a goal-

Two Roman bronze clothes pins (fibulae), one incomplete, from Little Chester. (The late R.G. Hughes)

post. Apparently, it was swiftly cemented in and no report was made to the proper authorities, nor a record made. It suggests, however, that further sophisticated buildings may lie in this part of the *vicus*.

Vast quantities of fourth-century coin have also been found at Little Chester, the sequence only ending with a bronze of the Emperor Theodosius I (AD 379–395), and a well-worn one at that, indicating a circulating life of some 15 years. It was a later issue and suggests the continuation of the money economy at least to AD 400–410, if not later.

DARK AGE DERVENTIO

The decline of the money economy introduces the problem of the decline and abandonment of Roman *Derventio*. Archaeological evidence tends to suggest at least a partial abandonment of the settlement in the third quarter of the fourth century. The reason for this is that no positive evidence remains from which to argue to the contrary, excepting the coin mentioned earlier and a more recently found one from the reign of Valentinian II, who died in 392. Nevertheless, the central problem is lack of surviving evidence.

The late Roman and later (and thus uppermost) layers – allowing for the evolution of the mediaeval and modern settlement of Little Chester – have probably just vanished. What pottery, typical of the late-fourth century, that there was – and it was by no means all that plentiful anywhere – does not show at Little Chester. Yet many parts of the settlement have had their archaeological levels destroyed and more await investigation; the evidence may yet emerge. On the other hand, there can be little doubt that the Racecourse Playing Field industrial settlement had declined in the mid-fourth century. This may, for instance, only be due to a shift of population of the *vicus*, or a change to other means of subsistence on other parts of its area.

Much evidence gleaned during recent excavations suggests that standing Roman buildings may have survived well into Saxon times, perhaps adapted and in crude re-use. Certainly, there seems to be evidence of Roman walling as later boundaries. The subsequent anomalies concerning the status of the successor settlement of Little Chester in mediaeval times rather suggest that an entity of some kind survived, even if a whole way of life was beginning to change.

We have already seen that the early settlements at Willington, on the Trent, served a whole series of different cultures but maintained a degree of territorial integrity. In the same way, it is hoped that a continuity of the possible Corieltauvian *pagus* around *Derventio* and its successor settlements can be demonstrated. For instance, there is no real reason why, given evidence from elsewhere in Britain, that the *territorium* – the immediate area – of *Derventio* should not have survived intact as a unit too.

It is quite unclear what the situation was in the Trent Valley–Derwent Valley part of the former Corieltauvian tribal area after the decay of the Roman administration. What is clear is that in some parts of Britain life continued in its Romanised way, and archaeological evidence at such places as St Albans, Gloucester and Wroxeter confirm this. Literary sources suggest that post-Roman Britain fragmented into a patchwork of Celtic principalities, and there is some evidence to suggest that some of these at least corresponded to some extent with the *civitates*, the old tribal areas, of Roman Britain. Unfortunately, internecine strife appears to have been a major preoccupation of these successor entities and further fragmentation seems to have taken place in an atmosphere of material decline, severe outbreaks of plague and incursions by incomers with no stake in the *status quo*, especially from Ireland and the Continent. Nevertheless, it is not until the sixth century that evidence of Anglo-Saxon occupation appears in Derbyshire, at first in the Trent Valley.

As a consequence of this, there is a gap in our knowledge of the area in which Derby lies for at least a century, probably a century and a half. Admittedly, the record for the half century before the collapse of Roman hegemony and for the century and a half after, to *c.*AD 560 (the likely date for the coming of the Saxons to the area), is scanty enough by any account. Nevertheless, in the critical century or more, not only is the archaeological record unhelpful, but almost every other source from which evidence might be adduced is equally silent or grotesquely misleading.

Bearing in mind that the vital archaeological levels have often been ploughed to destruction long since, other evidence of this type may have been destroyed by cellar-making on the site of the present Little Chester, and there may well be sites as yet undiscovered in the area.

However, it is clear from Dark Age sites elsewhere in Britain – especially cemeteries, the commonest intelligible type in many ways – that to disentangle Germanic from Celtic evidence is highly problematic, the fact being that materially the two were very similar, although, interestingly, DNA evidence recently gathered over a very wide sample of living people of English descent points to an enormous preponderance of genetic material indicative of Teutonic origin. Intermarriage there may well have been – there certainly was at *elite* levels – but the incoming element, although initially very small, ultimately prevailed. There is little doubt that a degree of ethnic cleansing, as it is today termed, was inflicted on the Romano-British population. The lamentations of Gildas and old Welsh tales of migrations may well be closer to the truth than was until recently considered likely.

Other elements are equally inconclusive. The study of place names has proved a fruitful field in some parts of Britain. However, few clues remain in the Derby area. The river name Ecclesbourne certainly implies from its first element (from Latin *ecclesia*/Welsh *eglwys)* a pre-Saxon church, perhaps at Wirksworth, itself, as we have seen, a credible candidate for the site of the Roman lead-producing settlement of *Lutudarum*. The Wirksworth slab is also likely to be early Saxon and very sophisticated, influenced by continental late antique forms. Studies elsewhere have established this assumption as a reasonable one.

In this case, while we can be fairly sure that Christianity – enshrined by the emperor Constantine through the Edict of Milan in AD 312 – survived in the area, the question of exactly where must remain an open one. In Kent, about AD 597, the Saxon King Aethelbehrt 'allowed Christians to build *or repair* churches in all places', plainly emphasising that Christianity in the area, even under pagan Saxon domination, must have survived, complete with associated buildings, relics and rites. In the case of Wirksworth, the late Roman-Christian nature of the subject matter and composition of the famous Wirksworth stone (in the Parish Church), while it is of Saxon and perhaps seventh century or later origin, has suggested a local continuity of tradition to some commentators, but only the cosmopolitan nature of Saxon Christianity to others. The cult of St Helen (mother of Constantine) at Derby, Wirksworth and Darley Dale may conceivably support this contention. Furthermore, Bede tells us the missionaries from Northumbria found, in the Peak country, Christians who had preserved their faith from generation to generation. *Eccles* names, moreover, are also found at Hope, Tideswell and Chapel-en-le-Frith.

History without personalities is ever an arid study, and so far the history of Derby has been starved of names, let

Number 83 Old Chester Road in 1963. Excavations in 1988 suggested that there was clear evidence of continuity on the site, from Roman to mediaeval successor structure. It was demolished in 1964. (M. Craven)

Wirksworth: established by the Saxons as a lead-trading centre by the seventh century and possibly the site of Roman Lutudarum, 1992.

alone personalities. Yet the only hint of political organisation among the Roman-British or re-emergent Celtic population for this period, strangely enough, concerns names. In the Peniarth MS, the *Achau Brenhinoedd*, is a passage that translates as 'These are the men of Glastonbury who came from *Letocetum* to the fort that even at this hour (about AD 1260) is called Aldud,' and names some names. An earlier MS, probably compiled in AD 954, names a prince called Iudnerth as one of a group of men at Glastonbury 'who came from the town which is called *Loytcoyt*'. *Loytcoyt* is the same as *Letocetum*, the next settlement south west down Rykneld Street from *Derventio* and also in the Trent Valley. Cadfan Llwytcoed is in both cases named as a prince of that place, apparently driven out by the Saxons and who sought refuge at Glastonbury in the seventh century. It is possible that this or a similar Principality included the *pagus* of which *Derventio* had once been part, although evidence suggests that the realm of Cadfan Llwydcoed was limited to the eastern parts of the Cornovian *civitas* centred on Wroxeter, Shropshire. A similar situation may well have pertained in the Derbyshire Trent Valley. Alternatively, *Llwydcoed* (= 'grey wood') could even have extended as far as *Derventio* itself.

Later evidence, including a probable Northumbrian presence as far south as Derby, has even suggested that one of the Northern British Princes may have held sway in the Lower Derwent Valley. Evidence from the surviving Welsh MS concerning these northern princes certainly implies that rather than submitting to wholesale conquest, the Principalities they ruled merely passed into Saxon domination through dynastic marriage with British heiresses. Deira, Bernicia (component parts of Saxon Northumbria) and Elmet (South Yorkshire) all appear to have fallen to Saxon domination in this way, with military victory acting as midwife. The third Saxon King of Lindsey (centred on Corieltauvian Lincoln) was Caedbad – a partly British name. Chris Sparey-Green, endorsing this point in his report on excavations at Little Chester, also draws attention to similarities with Dark Age Catterick (Roman *Cataractonum*, British *Catraeth*). The same may well be true of whoever ruled the former Corieltauvian *pagus* or district in which the by this time decayed settlement of *Derventio* lay.

The Saxon settlements in the Trent Valley range from the early to mid-sixth century at Swarkestone, King's Newton, Stapenhill (near a Roman-British rural settlement known to have endured to about AD 400), Brizlincote and Drakelow. All are pagan and thus early. Others at Borrowash and Wyaston may possibly have included Christian burials and if so would be either mid or late-seventh century Saxon, or even conceivably fifth or sixth-century British. A mid-sixth-century horse's head cruciform Saxon brooch was also found at Duffield along

with a female skeleton, which may have been part of a Saxon tumulus burial on the castle mound.

At *Derventio,* the skeletal remains of a group of pagan Saxons were buried in a decayed late-Roman building at the point outside the east gate of the fort where Rykneld Street passed. Again a comparable burial has emerged at Catterick. Some men – two of the total of 17 – were buried with their shields and spears; their six womenfolk with their personal ornaments. These few must represent the new settlers there, whose leaders or their successors doubtless wrested from their British predecessors control of a far wider area and under whose protection they were mingling with those elements of the British population who had not fled, marrying their daughters and putting down new roots. What really did not change were the units of land and the style of life, for one of the reasons why it is so difficult to tell Celt from Saxon in Dark Age deposits is that they had more of everyday things in common than things that divided them. What had changed since Roman times, though, was the appearance of Little Chester itself.

Assuming that with the collapse of the Romano-British cash-based economy most inhabitants were thrown back on a pastoral system fortified by barter, it would be reasonable to suppose that, within say two or three generations, the Roman settlement would have become mainly derelict, aided by the stripping of removable stone, timber and metal from the buildings for re-use elsewhere. It might be possible to visualise a smithy or similar surviving, but with only a few permanent inhabitants in the ruins within the shelter of the walls. Certainly the Roman building into which the 17 Saxons were interred was quite ruinous in *c.* AD 550.

When excavated too, the wells were found to be filled with refuse and, no doubt, other services had also ceased to function. Only the walls remained, as they were, to a considerable extent, when William Stukeley visited and mapped the tiny hamlet of Little Chester in 1719–21. These must have been impressive for they doubtless gave the name to the croft adjoining the Manor House at Little Chester in a later age called 'Castle Yard'. The then Manor tenant, Robert Hope, was in 1648 obliged to 'reserve to the Mayor of Derby or his steward to hold his (manor) courts there'.

It is quite likely that in turbulent times cattle and other stock, not to mention the more vulnerable members of the community, were able to take refuge behind the walls, and there is persuasive evidence to suggest that the whole site was reused later by the Norse. The basic cruciform pattern of the roads inside the fort area has survived through some kind of use (however occasional). Elsewhere, the line of the main Roman roads mainly fell out of use, many being later used as parish boundaries.

II
TRANSITION

THE FORMATION OF MERCIA

It is common to assume that the Saxons who settled around the site of Derby were Mercians. Yet in the seventh century, with Penda of Mercia (625–654) in frequent conflict with the Kingdom of Northumbria, the latter seems to have established hegemony for a time as far south as the Trent. This area might well have been later re-established as a Northumbrian fief at times of weakness in the Mercian body politic, as after Penda's death in 654 to c.660 or even c.716, and again at the end of the eighth century.

The cult of St Alkmund, a Northumbrian prince killed at the end of the latter period, was strong in the area, with dedications at Derby and Duffield. When Mercia was strong, on the other hand, the northern border of that kingdom extended to Dore in the extreme north east of the county, which agrees well with the edges of the Corieltauvian *civitas* of earlier ages, and which itself may have endured, absorbed as a kind of province by the Mercian kings after a century and a half of shadowy existence under the sway of anonymous native princes.

The chronology of Penda and his ancestors agrees quite neatly with what we know of Saxon pagan settlement in the Trent Valley. 560 is the date given by the Mercian Register of the *Anglo-Saxon Chronicle* when Creoda, grandfather of Penda, landed and began to carve out a patrimony for his sons. Pybba, one of them, reigned (we are told) from 593 to 615, and was father to Penda. He had been preceded as king by Ceorl, a cousin, whose only daughter had married the powerful Edwin, who forged the Kingdom of Northumbria from two smaller entities. It was thus probably to counter a potent Northumbrian claim on the burgeoning Mercian realm that sent Penda on to the warpath in league with his British ally, Cadwallon, King of Gwynedd, whose own territory at that time seems to have stretched from North Wales to the Staffordshire Peak, west of the Dove. Penda was also a lifelong pagan, like Aethelberht of Kent for instance, but the latter was persuaded to receive St Augustine in AD 597.

Consequently, it was not until his death in 654, in the battle at *Winwaedfeld,* that his son Peada, under irresistible Northumbrian influence, was able to allow the Christianisation of his realm. It cannot have been long after this that a monastery was established at his capital. The most significant thing for the history of

Derby is that this capital was then Repton, on the south bank of the Trent, some seven miles from the site of the future town of Derby. The name of Repton itself is important, being, in Professor Cameron's words, '…the only really archaic name in the county', deriving from a tribal name *Hrype,* or *Hreope* and *dun* (hill or fortification) thus 'The hill of the *Hreope*'. This otherwise unknown Celtic tribe could have been northern, for their name forms the first syllable of Ripon too. Were, perhaps, the *Hreope* the group which controlled Derbyshire and southern Yorkshire after Roman rule collapsed, or do they represent a portion of the Brigantian nation before the Corieltauvi established themselves in the first century AD?

A striking portrait, very much in the late antique tradition, of Aethelbald, King of Mercia, part of a Saxon highcross and excavated at Repton by Martin Biddle and Birthe Kjølbye-Biddle in 1979. (Professor Martin Biddle)

Repton's Royal Saint, Guthlac, founder of Croyland Abbey, being ordained by Hedda, Bishop of Winchester. (M. Craven)

The Saxon Crypt at St Wystan's Church, Repton, built in 1815, from S. and D. Lyson's *Derbyshire*. (M. Craven)

REPTON: CRUCIBLE OF MERCIAN CHRISTIANITY

The traditional founder of the Abbey at Repton was St Werburgh, a daughter of Peada's successor King Wulfhere (657–674). In reality, the monks of Breedon-on-the-Hill, just across the later border in Leicestershire, probably founded it. It was a double house – that is, for both monks and nuns – and it guarded the burial places of several Royal personages. Among them was Merewald, allegedly a brother of Penda, the only royal interment known from this era. He was later joined by Kings Aethelbald (d.755), Wiglaf (d.838), the latter's wife and son, St Wystan (Wiglaf's grandson murdered in 840) and a brother of Sigeberht, King of Wessex, a cousin. Aethelbald is probably the king depicted on one of the two faces of the Repton Stone, the upper stage of a high cross that once stood outside the first abbey church. He is shown with a round targe and long hair, just like the contemporary Merovingian Kings of France.

The most famous early Abbess was Eadburga, an East Anglian Princess who sent St Guthlac off from Repton to found Croyland Abbey and to whom her successor granted a coffin of Wirksworth lead. The crypt under the east end of the present church at Repton is one of

St Werburgh's Churchyard, c.1902. (M. Craven)

the most spectacular pieces of surviving Anglo-Saxon architecture in the country. Again, continental influences are apparent in that the spiral twisted stone columns which support the sophisticated vaulted roof seem to have for their inspiration late antique examples, as in the baldachino of old St Peter's, Rome.

St Werburgh is an important figure, for she founded abbeys on Mercian soil at Trentham, Hanbury and Weedon before her death in 699. That three churches near Repton were dedicated to her – Blackwell, Spondon and in Derby – testify to the strength of her cult and perhaps to the early date of their foundation. The St Werburgh's Church in Derby is the most interesting for it brings us back, at last, to the quest for Derby's origins. In AD 700 or thereabouts Derby still did not exist, yet we may, with reasonable certainty, postulate the existence of one of its churches from the early eighth century. How can this be?

It seems that the Derby Church of St Werburgh was the focal point of a separate settlement and, as usual in those days, was doubtless built by its lord. The survival of the name Wardwick, applied to the street in which the church now lies, is the clue. In the Darley Abbey charters of the late 12th and early 13th centuries, it is clear that Wardwick was a more general name. Indeed, there was even an important Derby figure in the late 12th century who took his name from it, and Wardwick (in Saxon: Walda's settlement) was undoubtedly the name of the community. It was absorbed by the late-Saxon *burh* of Derby so quickly after the latter's foundation that it lost its separate identity as a place quite early. Yet it was a part of the great manor of Mickleover in the 12th century and had certainly once been a distinct village.

All over the countryside bounding the Derbyshire Trent in the area of the former Corieltauvian *civitas*, settlements with Saxon names can be identified. Some revealed by archaeology were even then very old, like the site at Willington. Others were newer, although many may be renamings of older settlements which have left no trace behind. At this time, too, they were generally

scattered settlements, not exclusively grouped around the Lord's house or hall and the church (where such may have existed); this tendency to nucleation came much later. Their boundaries were in many cases undoubtedly the edges of earlier personal estates, taken over by the settling Saxons lock, stock and barrel. Others were carved from woodland by 'assarting', although we now know from aerial photographic evidence obtained during the very dry summer of 1976 that far more forest clearance had been done by the Roman period than had previously been thought. That assarting in forested areas for the enlarging of pasture and settlements was necessary merely suggests that the decline in population after the Roman period was far more serious than most commentators had realised and that the woodland reasserted itself extensively during the so-called Dark Ages for want of men to till or graze the established land to keep it in check.

THE COMING OF NORTHWORTHY

This area around the eventual site of Derby was carefully pieced together by Dr David Roffe through close analysis of the Derbyshire section of the *Domesday Book* (compiled 1086) and other evidence. It stretched from Little Eaton in the north to Potlock (south of Findern) in the south and from Mickleover in the west to Alvaston in the east. Certainly, it was considerably larger than the modern city of Derby and originally constituted a single (royal) estate.

It bore the name Northworthy, meaning Northern estate or enclosure. Roffe, followed by Sparey-Green, suggests it was 'north' in relation to Repton, with which it plainly had a relationship. It may also, in even earlier times, have been part of a larger whole extending east west from the Dove to the Erewash and north to Duffield or Milford.

Some time before the Viking invasions, this estate had become the personal fief of some Saxon lord, or even prince. It is possible, indeed, that it was the estate of the Mercian Ealdorman of Berkshire, Aethelwulf, killed on Mercia's southern borders fighting the Danes in 871 and buried in the minster church of Northworthy. The *Chronicle* entry recording his burial is the first to record the name Northworthy and as such points to its having been culled from a pre-Danish source: 'The body of the aforesaid Ealdorman was stealthily removed and taken to the province of the Mercians to the place called Northworthy but in the Danish tongue, Derby'.

It is probably the sarcophagus of this magnate which was, in 1967, excavated from the site of this minster, later dedicated to St Alkmund, and which now has pride of place in Derby Museum's archaeology gallery. The death

Dr C.A. Raleigh-Radford pictured with the interlace Anglo-Norse sarcophagus found beneath the later structures of St Alkmunds in 1967. It was almost certainly the tomb of the Ealdorman Aethelwulf. (*Derby Evening Telegraph*)

and burial of Aethelwulf, a possible proprietor of the great Northworthy estate, brings us on to the foundation of the minster church within the area. This plainly occurred after the succession of King Peada in 655 and before St Alkmund's burial there in *c*.802. The late Dr C.A. Raleigh Radford, who excavated the site in 1968, considered that the evidence to support an early date was very flimsy. All one can say is that such a date is about the earliest it may have been established, although of course it does square rather neatly with the evidence of the *Anglo-Saxon Chronicle* relating to Mercian Christianity

in its earliest phase. Indeed, the foundation of the Abbey of Repton at this period might well immediately presage the foundation of a minster church within the Northworthy area, especially if the latter had a close relationship with the former.

Either way, by about 800 a minster church had been established within the Northworthy estate, on a ridge west of the Derwent just south of Little Chester and with its west end abutting the spinal road, which appears to have run north–south through the area from time immemorial. That this spinal road, in mediaeval times

St Alkmund's Church: Dr Raleigh-Radford showing the newly discovered Anglo-Saxon sarcophagus to Derby Civic Society in 1968. (Civic Society)

the *via regia* ('King's Road', later King and Queen Streets), now jinks west and north around the precincts of the former church rather suggests that the tiny settlement which sprang up around the Saxon minster – where lived the missionary priests (canons) who served it and their staff – caused the diversion of what was then still an important track-way, and that this small community was the real nucleus of what was later to become Derby.

St Alkmund's Well, corner of Well Street and Duke Street, February 1993, after restoration. (M. Craven)

This church was endowed with lands by its anonymous founder and housed six canons. They, using the church as a base, ventured forth into the surrounding countryside converting the pagan Saxons and even perhaps ministering to those of the local population who had managed to keep Christianity alive from the end of the Roman period. These would probably (assuming they did exist) have been people of partly British ancestry – the heirs of the Corieltauvi – and evidence relating to the Saxon kingdom of Lindsey certainly suggests a similar survival of Christianity there. This possibility emerged from work done in the 1980s by my former colleague Kevin Leahy on the Church of St Paul-in-the-Bail, Lincoln.

It was this church that, in about 800, became the burial place of the Northumbrian Prince Alhmund (now spelt Alkmund). He was believed to be a son of King Alhred (i.e. Alfred), killed in a palace *coup* led by King Eardwulf. After his death, miracles centred on him and, due to the hostile political climate in his native kingdom, his remains eventually came to rest in the Northworthy minster church, which was eventually re-dedicated to him. (Its previous dedication, of course, if this church is earlier than *c*.800, is quite lost to us.)

This fact alone goes to support other evidence that periodically Derbyshire north of the Trent had been subject to Northumbrian influence, if not control. There seems to have been a sort of fluctuating dynamic tension between the two polities since the mid-seventh century when King Cadwallon allied with Penda to invade the north-eastern kingdom. Even church dedications seem to reflect this, once Penda's successors had converted (under Northumbrian influence), with dedications to the Northumbrians Alkmund (Derby and Duffield), Cuthbert (Doveridge), Oswald (Ashbourne) and Wilfrid (Barrow-on-Trent, Egginton and West Hallam), contrasting with those to Mercian saints like Chad (Barton Blount, Longford and Great Wilne), Werburgh (noted above) and Wystan (Repton and Bretby). Allowing for Northumbrian weakness around the time of Alkmund's death – it was fast becoming something of a banana republic politically, with internal weakness stemming from constant palace *coups* ultimately making it easy meat for an early Viking take-over – it is likely that St Alkmund's burial took place in a sympathetic part of Mercia rather than in an area then under direct Northumbrian control. Soon, though, a shrine was built for the Saint, so that pilgrims – mainly, we are told, from Northumbria – could come and pray to him and touch his relics.

In the 18th century, the then vicar, Revd Henry Cantrell, wrote to the Derbyshire antiquary Samuel Pegge, '…it has been commonly said that the North Countrymen inquire [*sic*] for this tomb and rest their packs upon it.' Indeed, taken at face value, this passage rather suggests that, even after the destruction of the shrine at the Reformation, vestiges of the Saint's resting place may have remained, or at least knowledge of its site, and that this knowledge may only have been lost when the mediaeval church was taken down in 1841–42. This also diminishes the likelihood that the relics of the saint were translated in the 11th century to Lilleshall in Shropshire, a contention that Professor Biddle has dismissed as a later fiction. Apparently, too, the old well dedicated to St Alkmund was anciently dressed, a ceremony revived on Whit Tuesday, 1870, although the Saint's day was on 19 March. This custom was discontinued again in 1939 and enjoyed as brief revival in the 1990s. The well itself, restored in 1987 under the Better City of Derby scheme after years of cruel neglect, once enjoyed curative properties. As late as the end of the 18th century, its waters are said to have cured the then vicar of St Werburgh, William Lockett, of consumption. Today the residents of the adjacent tower block, Rivermead House, still fill up two-litre plastic bottles of it in preference to the substance which emerges from their taps.

For the reason that the early Geordie pilgrims had expected to actually touch the relics of their Saint, a closed sepulchre is unlikely, which is why the lidded and finely carved sarcophagus eventually found beneath the Victorian church must be considered as most likely that of Ealdorman Aethelwulf or someone of his status. Ultimately the church, damaged during the Viking occupation and rebuilt later, must have been quite impressive. Saxon carvings and fragments of several high crosses have survived from it and are now also in Derby's Museum.

Thus, we have a picture emerging of the core of the northern part of the former Romano-British Corieltauvian district or *pagus* surrounding *Derventio* surviving as Repton (the early Mercian capital and first seat of its Christianity), its region – doubtless stretching to the allied Mercian monastic house, founded not long before at Breedon-on-the-Hill – and the large personal estate of Northworthy lying, as the name might lead one to expect, on the northern bank of the Trent.

The latter then acquired a fairly central minster church, doubtless surrounded by a mini-settlement to service the requirements of the six missionary priests, which is what the canons in effect were. Thus, what emerges is a region in which Christianity and the Mercian ruling caste had a considerable stake and which they controlled, still perhaps as an overall unit within the Kingdom of Mercia.

The fact that in about 664 St Chad removed the fledgling Mercian see to Lichfield, to be followed by the Mercian Royal House to Tamworth not long afterwards, merely serves to suggest that an ancient, perhaps Dark

Age, hegemony of *Letocetum* had also existed and was being revived or strengthened. The move might, on the other hand, represent the Mercian reaction to the final exile of the British sub-kings of Wall, for the date of their exile as calculated from their pedigrees lines up remarkably well with Chad's foundation of Lichfield. The name Lichfield, too, is virtually a translation of *Letocetum* in its Welsh form *Lwydcoed* and is only two and a half miles from the Roman settlement and at a place which must have lain securely within its sphere of influence – its *territorium*.

But because *Letocetum* was almost certainly an eastern extremity of the *civitas* of the British tribe of the Cornovii, centred on *Viroconium* (Wroxeter, Shropshire), it is more probably necessary to look on Chad's move as a Mercian expansion, crossing traditional boundaries, and less probably as a restoration of a Dark Age statelet.

ENTER THE VIKINGS

The *Anglo-Saxon Chronicle* is wonderfully matter-of-fact about what must have been a series of traumatic events. Concerning the irruption into this part of Mercia by the invading Danish Great Army, it says, under 874:

'In this year the army went from Lindsey to Repton and took up winter quarters there, and drove King Burghred across the sea… and they conquered all that land.'

It was historically an occasion of the first importance. Not only did it lead to the dismemberment of the powerful Mercian kingdom, but also set in train events which were to change the district completely and lead directly to the establishment of the borough of Derby.

We know all too little of the Danish settlement in our region, which began in earnest from 877, except that which is suggested by archaeology and implied by place names. Archaeology, thanks to a decade and a half of successful work at Repton by dedicated and endlessly enthusiastic husband-and-wife team of Martin Biddle and Birthe Kjølbye-Biddle, has revealed the fine detail of the events surrounding the 'Great over-wintering' at Repton of 874–75 (actually thought to be winter 873–74) and, thanks to their friend and colleague the late Dr Harold Taylor, much information about the church. What has emerged are two Royal mausolea and the great Abbey of Mercian Repton. Archaeology has also thrown further light on the Viking burials nearby at Heath Wood, Ingleby (itself a Danish place name – 'the place of the English'), some of which their excavator thought were post 874 arrivals direct from Scandinavia. Further excavation by Julian D. Richards in 2001 has reversed the picture somewhat, suggesting that here were cremation burials of warriors killed on the assault on Repton in 874

An early (pagan) Saxon cremation urn found on the site of Willington Power Station in the 1950s. (The late R.G. Hughes)

and on subsequent campaigns; the 'war cemetery of the Viking Great Army'.

What has not been revealed is anything more than the slightest hint of events within the Northworthy estate area. Place names suggest, however, that Danish settlement was fairly intense, as does evidence culled from study of the *Domesday Book* as it relates to the administrative structure of the later Shire of Derby. Further, one or two local gentry families, emergent after the Norman conquest, stem from recorded men with Danish names, e.g. the Okeovers of Okeover from one Orm and the Knivetons of Kniveton from one Haslac. An important Derby burghal family, that of Hugh de Derby, of which more later, had an early member, A[n]ghemund, bearing a Danish name, as do some of the moneyers of the later Saxon mint in the town.

The only written evidence really relates to the moment that Danish power in the area was broken by Aethelfflæda, widow of the Wessex-appointed Mercian Ealdorman Aethelred, effectively King of Mercia from 884, when he was put in charge of London by King Alfred and issued charters under his own name, establishing his sovereign status, denied him in later Wessex-friendly annals. He died *c.*910 and his campaigning against the Vikings – a veritable Mercian *reconquista* – was carried on by his Queen, Aethelfflæda, a daughter of his ally Alfred of Wessex. The crucial event, as far as Northworthy was concerned, occurred in 917 (or 920, depending on which version is consulted) under which date the *Anglo-Saxon Chronicle* states that the Mercian Queen,

'With the help of God, before Lammas obtained the borough *which is called Derby* with all that belongs to it,

and there also four of her thegns who were dear to her were killed within the gates.'

This passage poses a number of challenges, especially as it is reasonably contemporary with the events it describes.

The first is that the name Derby implies that a place bearing this name had come into existence by 917–20. The second is the last phrase, '...killed within the gates'. It is beyond serious doubt that Derby as a unified settlement owes its foundation to the period immediately following Aethelfflæda's dislodgement of the Danes. It is also beyond doubt that Derby never had gated defences as such. Thus, we must ask if the Danes had a camp or fortified place within Northworthy and, if so, did it have gates?

It was certainly the case that the Vikings set up a strongpoint in Northworthy as they had at Repton, in the latter case incorporating the Saxon church as part of their ramparted enclosure, and using the south bank of the Trent, too. Plainly, the Danes were sensible enough to use pre-existing structures to save themselves work where they could. Thanks to Dr Roffe, we also now know that the establishment of the Federation of the 'Five Boroughs' (Derby, Leicester, Lincoln, Nottingham and Stamford) was credited retrospectively (and wrongly) to the Danes, but were actually part of a post-Danish administrative and defensive infrastructure of the East Midlands.

Thus, in the Northworthy area, the Danes plainly had a fortified military (and probably administrative) base, but had not as such founded a town. This base may have come into being between 910 and 917, when the Vikings, having begun to suffer some military reverses, began to fortify East Midland sites. Candidates for this base which have been suggested are the shadowy earthworks believed to have once been a castle on the line of Albion Street, Derby (suggested by Hutton in 1791), the Roman fort at Little Chester and the appropriately named settlement of Normanton, a mile or so south of Derby town centre, the latter suggested solely by the name ('the place of the northmen').

Of these, the second suggestion is entirely convincing. Here was a generous area, in a reasonable strategic position, surrounded by a stone wall nearly 20ft high with defensible gates. All the Danish contingent needed to do was repair the walls, replace the gates and a secure camp was obtained with minimal effort. As it happens, archaeological evidence rather suggests that at Little Chester the Danes did rather more. When the former Great Northern Railway line embankment was removed in 1968–70, underneath was found a large corner extension, as Chris Sparey-Green appropriately calls it, added to enable defenders to enfilade the walls with various missiles. Yet this

A view westwards up the town ditch. Bridge Gate in the early 1920s, showing how the buildings higher up the street towered over it, clearly suggesting its defensive origins. (*Derby Evening Telegraph*)

structure was not keyed into the Roman wall behind it, and beneath the rubble base were found crushed sherds of Saxon pottery. Clearly it had been built not by the Romans, but long afterwards, and the Danes are the most convincing candidates. Subsequent events go some way to confirm this.

If the hypothesis advanced above, and supported by Dr Sparey-Green's excavation report, that the Danes did indeed re-fortify Roman *Derventio,* is correct, then the explanation for the death of Aethelfflæda's four thegns 'within the gates' is also to hand. He also cites London, Cambridge, Exeter and Cirencester – to which may be added the examples of Leicester and Lincoln – as examples of Danish re-fortification of Roman town walls. Clearly Aethelfflæda's army were by that time skilled in the technology of the siege.

Little other evidence of the Viking presence in the Northworthy area has come to light. Apart from a bone comb and a page-marker bearing a Runic inscription translating, 'Possessions increase respect for Hadda who wrote this', from the King's Mead area of Derby found in 1884, only Raleigh Radford's analysis of the vicissitudes of the minster church of St Alkmund need claim our attention. He pointed to evidence of damage to the fabric and reduction of the area in use as being from the (pagan) Danish occupation.

If so, then the Danes may have partly sacked the church and then restricted its canons' activities so that only a token Christian presence survived. In the Viking levels, a penny from the Norse Kingdom of York was found, but little can be read into one find.

As for the name Derby – in its earliest form *Deoraby* – this appears to be a Danish name, as the '-by' (= place) suffix suggests. But nothing is as simple as it seems.

The name may have evolved under the Danish occupation of the Northworthy area to describe not the as-yet-unbuilt town but the re-fortified Roman settlement of *Derventio,* as the Anglo-Saxon Chronicle entry implies. The 'Der-' element in Derby in this case may actually be a contraction to a single syllable of the (Celtic) river name or (Roman) place name, to which the Danes, out of habit, added '- by'.

This carries much more conviction in the light of modern advances in place name studies than the traditional explanation that the first element was a mutation of the Danish word *djur* (= deer) plus '-by', making 'place of the deer'. Apparently, the extension by Danish usage into two syllables of *deor-* does not necessarily imply derivation from *djur* at all.

Thus, our Derby is more like a contraction of 'Der[ventio]-by', giving the name a sound 2,000-year evolutionary pedigree.

The Emergence of Derby

With the Danes thrown out of the immediate area, measures had to be taken to ensure that the Saxon *reconquista* held. The minster church of St Alkmund was being rebuilt and fragments of the first Saxon church on the site were being incorporated into the new fabric. Embellishments were being added, however, to replace at least one interlace-work high cross destroyed in the Danish period, and these included more carved stonework with the clear imprint of Danish influence, including part of a fine Norse hogback grave cover.

Not long after the death of Queen Aethelfflæda at Tamworth on 12 June 918 (921), her daughter and heiress Aelfwyne, effectively the last Mercian princess, was deposed by Edward of Wessex (d.924) to leave him a free hand to complete his aunt's work. On her death, then, '...all the people who had settled in Mercia, both Danish and English, submitted to him'.

It is to Edward and his successors, Aethelstan and Edmund, that the emergence of the county and town of Derby can be attributed, and also the temporary military expedient of the creation of the loose Midland federation known as the Five Boroughs. Sometime around 921, one of those five boroughs, the present city of Derby, was created as a fairly typical defensive Saxon urban settlement known as a *burh.* The settlement would be an administrative and market centre, with its citizens, their loyalty ensured by grant of a plot, able to contribute to defence when required.

At Derby – we can be sure that the name evolved at *Derventio* under the Danes was transferred to the new site, even if it had not already included St Alkmund's – the site was defensible on three sides, by the Derwent to the east and the Markeaton Brook to the west and south, this minor watercourse being marshy for much of its course. To the north – immediately beyond St Alkmund's and just south of another holy well dedicated to St Helena, mother of the emperor Constantine, a typical dedication for an early religious site – a ditch was dug to connect the neck of high ground between river and brook, probably ramparted to the outside as a viable defence. This was the later Town Ditch vestiges of which survived a line of hedgerows extending west from Bridge Gate to the 18th century. Vestiges of it were uncovered by an archaelogical excavation early in March 2007, near the former marble works.

Meanwhile, in 937–39 King Aethelstan defeated a confederation of Danes and Strathclyde British, attempting to re-conquer Mercia, at the unidentified battle site of *Brunanburh.* Then, three years later, his brother Edmund:

'...over-ran Mercia, as bounded by Dore, Whitwell Gate and the broad stream the river Humber and the

A view along Queen Street towards the early Christian enclave around St Alkmund's Church from the northern end of the spinal road, alongside which the Saxon *burh* was built. Until the 18th century Queen Street was part of King Street, called the Via Regia in the 13th century. (*Derby Evening Telegraph*)

Five Boroughs, Leicester, Lincoln, Nottingham and likewise Stamford and also Derby, for a long time in bonds of captivity to the heathens…'

This passage emphatically suggests the emergent *burh* endured three years of renewed Norse domination, and is one of the passages which has given rise to the belief that the Five Boroughs were a much earlier Viking Confederation and, *in extenso,* that Derby was thus a Viking foundation. But the statement is not nearly so specific for, as David Roffe has demonstrated, the Confederation of the Five Boroughs was the creation of Edward and Aethelstan, consolidating Mercia in the 920s. The passage, written in the 940s, merely refers to them in the way which they were by then known, before they were re-taken for a time by Olaf II, King of Dublin, and his allies in 937–39, but finally regained by the Wessex kings – now kings of All England – at *Brunanburh* in 941, the event to which the passage refers.

The Saxon origin of the boroughs – not mentioned as such and with all five named until 942, as Dr Hall

pointed out 30 years ago – is also to some extent confirmed by the existence of Morcar 'thegn of the Seven Boroughs' who had land in north-east Derbyshire and was murdered in 1015. These Seven Boroughs consisted of the original five plus York and Torksey, all of which 'submitted to Swein, King of Denmark' in 1013. Edmund the Atheling re-took them, including Derby, after Morcar's murder. It was at precisely this juncture, Dr Roffe suggests, that the shires of Derby and Nottingham emerged, *replacing* the Five Boroughs Confederation, set up (and found rather wanting in the longer term) when the Wessex *reconquista* freed the East Midlands. The effect of this on Derby, however, was unlikely to have been very great. Furthermore, Derby and Nottingham both were founded as *burhs* in the 920s, each as the administrative centre for their newly-created attendant shires, and although in contrast the latter had existed as a settlement long beforehand (Asser quotes its Celtic name, *Tiggouocobauc* – 'Cavy dwelling', and the Vikings had built an enclave there as at Little Chester) Derby certainly did not. All that existed was Northworthy – a great Royal or aristocratic estate, dotted with minor settlements – a minster church serving it with its small associated settlement and a refurbished Roman fort used by the Danes as an administrative headquarters.

DERBY, THE NEW BURH

The new *burh* was laid out either side of the ancient spinal road, by this time slightly re-routed to the west of St Alkmund's Church in order to leave the small ecclesiastical community surrounding it inviolate. The streets off it form an approximate grid: to the west, Walker Lane and St Mary's Gate; to the east, St Michael's Lane, Full Street and Amen Alley. The whole was undoubtedly, as elsewhere, on land belonging to the king, and his officials divided the defensible area – at Derby the whole no doubt – into plots called *ma(n)surae* in the *Domesday Book* but later called burgage plots.

These took the form of long narrowish areas of land laid end-on to the edge of the street, which were tenanted for rent and occasional service by traders, all of whom became personally free thereby. Indeed, it is to this status by right of tenure in the borough to which we probably must look for the origin of the borough 'freeman', now an hereditary right falling rapidly into desuetude, yet in past ages conferring considerable benefits on the holder under the restrictions imposed by successive Royal charters. The burgage plots, although much amalgamated by later sale, are still easily picked out on the ground in Derby and even more easily spotted on larger-scale maps. Furthermore, as new streets evolved, at least up until the conquest, such plots were laid out along them, too.

At the south end of the new *burh* was founded a brand new minster with a whole new constituency of pagan Danish settlers to convert, dedicated to All Saints and served by a dean and six canons – one more than St Alkmund's – thus marking it out as the premier institution. This church was endowed directly by the Crown with the former settlement of *Derventio* (by this time Little Chester) still a stronghold and probably reserved to the Crown after its capture by Aethelfflæda in 917.

All Saints' was in fact a Saxon Royal Free Chapel. The dean and the six canons each had a holding at Little Chester, varying considerably in size and not all provided with a residence. The income from each was assigned to their support. These farms or prebends may well have been established on pre-existing holdings there, perhaps traceable even from the earliest Roman years of the settlement. Quarndon, which, like Little Eaton, endowed the canons of St Alkmund's, was also a

All Saints', Derby's second minster church, as rebuilt in 1968–71, seen from Stuart Street, 2005. (M. Craven)

piece of the old Northworthy estate, which now began to be broken up and distributed to newer, lesser lords, no doubt in return for services rendered to the crown. Thus, the fragmenting parts came to take the names of the vills (settlements) within them, and the name Northworthy no longer referred to a single entity, falling from use, ultimately becoming defunct and largely forgotten. Meanwhile, the new Saxon *burh* held on to its Danish name, which we have suggested had been coined for the re-fortified *Derventio* (Little Chester), transferred to it, and became, for the first time recognisably, Derby.

DERBY MINT

One of the chief purposes of a Saxon *burh* was trade (after a measure of defence), and the lifeblood of the Saxon trade was coin. Offa of Mercia (reigned 757–796) had re-introduced the small silver coin – derived from the Roman *denarius* – the penny. It swiftly became the universal English (and later also Norse) medium of exchange. Each *burh* had a mint, a few, like York,

London, Winchester and Canterbury, being of considerable importance, others less so. To these lesser mints, dies were distributed from either York or London for the striking of the Royal coinage, done by local mint masters who additionally placed their names and that of the *burh* on the coins. They were responsible to the Crown for the volume of coin, the quality of the striking and the purity of the metal, and were men of considerable consequence. A mint was established in the new *burh* of Derby under Athelstan (925–939) and immediately began to strike coin under no less than 11 named moneyers, whose names appear on the coinage of Athelstan from 924, although they were unlikely to have been all working at the same period.

The list of its mint masters constitutes the earliest body of named Derby citizens known to us, a valuable record. Thirty seven or 38 individuals are named, although one other could be added, Rathulf, a Danish moneyer striking in the period in which Derby was again briefly under the control of the Danish Anlaf, King of York, one of whose coins was found in the destruction layer of the first church on the site of St Alkmund's; he may have been sent from York and be an interloper. Not every reign is represented on a Derby silver penny: there are no known coins from the reigns of Edmund I (939–946), Edwig (955–959) or from the two Danish kings who followed Cnut, Harold I and Harthacnut (1035–42), not to mention Harold II.

The names are almost exactly evenly split between Norse and Saxon, neatly summarising the likely racial balance in Derby during its formative years and explaining the long usage of Danish linguistic forms. The only exception is Martin (924–950), whose Roman name completely disguises his extraction. There is also some evidence that the last moneyer Walchelin, whose name is Norman, was the son of his predecessor Brun (under Henry I) and the same may go for others. The last mint master, Walchelin (under the Anarchy), was a man of considerable substance and, with his wife Goda, left much property to the newly-founded Abbey of Darley, and has been unconvincingly claimed as founder of Derby School.

The mint was probably situated in the parish of All Saints' and most likely was conducted as a 'cottage' industry insofar as the striking of coin was done at the moneyers' houses rather than in a dedicated building – a hypothesis that archaeological evidence from York tends to support.

At this stage, although a borough (it being time the spelling was modernised) and defended by watercourses and the Town Ditch, with a mint, minster churches and doubtless a burgeoning population, Derby seems to have had little formal local government. True, there was a Royal official, a reeve, and a moot, a meeting place. The latter was called the *portmannemot* by the 12th century and undoubtedly survived from Derby's earliest times. The term, recorded in the Darley charters, tells us a great deal. *Port* was the Anglo-Saxon term for a trading centre, originally defended, to ensure security for merchants' wares. Thus *portmenn* were 'townsmen'. That a moot existed for them to meet implies at least some degree of corporate cohesion. Elsewhere, this was the borough Moot, or *burhgemot*, which met thrice annually, also acting as a court of law to settle disputes. It has been suggested that the erection of the Shire Hall towards the bottom of St Mary's Gate (1659–60) may well have made use of an early site of this nature. Likewise, the site may have been east of Iron Gate (behind the present No.7) where the Moot Hall was built *c*.1610, which still, miraculously, exists, albeit in seriously mutilated form.

By the 11th century, too, most of the churches of which we know were probably extant. From analysis of the *Domesday Book* and later sources we can identify as many as eight parish churches; the two collegiate churches and the presumed early Northworthy settlement church of St Werburgh – itself probably not in *Domesday* – have already been mentioned. All bar the latter were grouped along the line of the north–south spinal road. From north to south these others were St Helen's (later the nucleus of the abbey of Darley), St Michael's, St Mary's (vanished), St James's (later the core of a Cluniac Cell of Bermondsey Abbey, allegedly on the site of the later Kings' Head Inn), St Peter's and possibly St Leonard's – the original 'Luda's church', which gave Derby its extra urban settlement of Litchurch, first named in the *Domesday Book*. There may have been others in this very early period, but if so they vanished or were transformed very early on.

Silver penny of King Stephen, minted by Derby's last moneyer, Walchelin. (The late R.G. Hughes)

These churches all seem to have had outlying estates attached and, indeed, Margery Tranter in 1989 suggested that St Michael's, sandwiched in between All Saints' and St Alkmund's, might have originally been the mother church of outlying St Peter's, on its hill half a mile south, which later developed a parish of its own and acquired its own outlying chapelries. Whether one accepts that or not – and the evidence is far too patchy to be sure – it rather supports the supposition that Litchurch and St Peter's were not, in fact, connected in a similar way, as Professor Saltman has suggested.

ANOTHER LOST CHURCH?

There is circumstantial evidence for another early Derby church, probably dedicated to St George, a popular saint from the time of the first Crusade (1099). This would have stood a little back from Iron Gate, and its existence is hinted at by the presence of George Yard, long thought to have taken its name from the 17th century George Inn, but long pre-existing the pub, being recorded in an early charter as *Judkinlonne,* Judkin being a diminutive of George, a name absent from any Derby record at that date. The shape of the lane, the topography and the oddly truncated nature of some of the nearby burgage plots combine with irregularities in the early parish boundaries to make the notion very plausible. The naming of the later coaching inn, recorded from 1648, may merely be coincidence. Against the idea, one could argue that a complete lack of written record tells against the theory, but then St Mary's only occurs once by name in an official record and once – discovered serendipitously – in a local will.

The lesser churches were undoubtedly founded by secular lords as private chapels to serve their land holdings, and this fact is supported by the existence of later churches in the surrounding countryside linked to urban parishes. A similar phenomenon, but based on early Royal endowments, may account for the links of St Alkmund's and All Saints with Quarndon, Little Eaton and Little Chester; the first two certainly boasted early chapels-of-ease. Was there ever one at Little Chester, where a significant and organised group of east west burials dated to the early middle ages was uncovered by C.B. Sherwin in 1926 inside the west wall of the Roman small town?

By the period immediately before the Norman Invasion then, Derby covered the top of the isthmus on which it lay from the brook to the river and from present Irongate to St Alkmund's. It had a mint and something over eight parish churches, of which two were collegiate and one a Royal Free Chapel. It had also a moot and swiftly growing trade: by 1066 there were 243 burgesses

or free townsmen recorded. That this represents less than the whole is beyond doubt, for the *Domesday Book* deals mainly with those burgesses who were tenants of the king and who rendered to him their 'customs' – rents and tolls on their trade. By 1066, however, a third of this income accrued to the local Earl – Edwin, son of Aelfgar of Mercia – and he and other grandees held many tenements from the king which were sublet to burgesses who rendered their custom to them instead. It is likely that not all of these were counted, nor can we tell how numerous they were. Any estimate of population based on the number of burgesses mentioned in 1066 is thus likely to be an underestimate.

Some great lords, like Earl Aelfgar, had property in the town linked to their country estates (Weston-on-Trent in Aelfgar's case). Others are named as holding prominent positions before 1066 in the *Domesday Book.* As emerges later, among the burgesses there was at least one complex and powerful grouping who may well have had familial links with country landowners before 1066 and are known to have had them in the century following.

The town had also acquired its first suburbs from the break-up of the old Northworthy estate and as a result of the Viking occupation: Little Chester, at this time still replete with the relics of antiquity; Wardwick, across the brook to the west; St Peter's parish south of the brook and Litchurch. Other shadowy settlements lurk, half discernable in the sparse documentation: *Doggelowe* (Doglow) between Rowditch and the Bramble Brook, on the line of Rykneld Street, still an important thoroughfare, and The Haye, on or near the site of Little City, where some bizarre boundaries could once be traced, of which one at least survives on the ground.

The scene is set for the events of 1066, the upheavals that followed and the rapid increase in documentary evidence to aid our understanding of subsequent events.

Excavations of the site of the lost church of St Mary, 1925. (*Derby Evening Telegraph*)

III

MEDIAEVAL

DOMESDAY DERBY

Nationally, the consequences of the Norman Conquest are well known if not so well understood. A vigorous, reforming, land-hungry Norman *elite* began to impose themselves and their system of government upon the population, in Derbyshire at least, a rich mixture of people of Saxon, Norman and even recognisably Celtic descent. Thanks to the *Domesday Book*, the effects in Derby after 20 years, that is 1066–86, the dates the document contrasts throughout, can be to some extent gauged, although what the *compilation* does not mention is of equal significance to a study of the town's history.

For many reasons, it is clear that Derby was subordinate to Nottingham. Nevertheless, it was an important royal borough. Yet Nottingham was administratively, legally and militarily pre-eminent, a vestige of which being that the counties of Derby and Nottingham – formed *c.*1016 in succession to the Confederation of the Five Boroughs, the initial and somewhat flawed post-Viking arrangement – were governed under a single Sheriff until 1566. Nevertheless, Derby was commercially superior; even in the *Domesday Book* Nottingham is recorded as having only 173 burgesses compared with 243 for Derby, and the town's income was but £18 compared with Derby's £24. Even a head-count of their respective moneyers allows this point to emerge, not to mention a higher estimated population in 1066.

Derby itself had, by 1086, suffered a serious setback. The most likely reasons for this are the Northern Rebellion of 1069–70, the Stafford Rebellion of 1073 and the process by which pre-eminence in the Honour of Tutbury passed from Hugh d'Avranches, Earl of Chester, to Henry de Ferrers between 1070 and 1086: that is to say, unrest must have hit trade, and this may well have been exaggerated by proscription and even strife. It is likely, too, that the importance locally of Hugh may have extended to Derby, yet had become diminished by 1086, by which time he held two urban properties to de Ferrers's three and had had his Derbyshire land holdings reduced to Markeaton, Mackworth and Allestree, to de Ferrers's 115 manors. Indeed, the Earl's 'third penny' from the customary dues may well have been Earl Hugh's in the 1070s and have been transferred to Henry in a subsequent administrative shake-up.

In 1086 the number of burgesses had dropped from 243 to 140, with 103 tenements *(mansurae)* empty; there were four fewer mills (10) and, for all we know, even the number of such things as churches may have diminished. In the section of the *Domesday Book* which deals with parts of the town not under the king's control, we find a jumble of useful information which, unfortunately, does not give us the whole picture. The Abbot of Burton had a mill and three plots of land, over two of which the king had jurisdiction. There is no mention of St Mary's Church, however, although we know he held that, too, although in 1066 it had doubtless been the king's. William I had donated Mickleover, Littleover and various holdings in Derby, including the church, to the Abbey prior to 1086. The two churches held by Norman de Lincoln and Edric son of Coln probably had no manorial connections with the surrounding countryside and were perhaps those dedicated to St Helen and St James, both of which were in the hands of burgesses in the following century when they were given to monastic orders. As to which of the other two was which, we have no means of telling; both proprietors in the 11th century had non-Norman names.

At this date, Derby seems hardly to have expanded beyond the confines of the late Saxon *burh* founded some 140 years before. Archaeology has established that settlement did not begin on the north side of the later Market Place (that nearest the *burh)* until after *c.*1100. Indeed, a disincentive to expansion appears to lie within the charter granted to the town by Henry II between 1154–55 and 1160. In this the balance of trade and the restrictions placed thereon weigh heavily in the favour of Nottingham. The town at this time had a head-man: a *prepositus (*analagous to the ecclesiastical 'provost'), an appointee of the Earl who, as we have seen, received a third of the revenue from the town. Several other clauses in this charter, such as the limiting of dyeing to Nottingham and the right to hold markets there for both Nottingham and Derbyshire, seem to run contrary to Derby's interests. This period also marked the closure of Derby's mint – the last coins were minted in the name of King Stephen (1137–1154) – which must have been a further blow to prestige. Nevertheless, Walchelin, the last mint master of the town, continued to play an important role in its affairs.

A further charter, sought by the burgesses and granted by King John on 5 October 1204, rather put matters to rights. The burgesses had some control of their revenue, could elect yearly a pair of bailiffs (instead

A view north along Queen Street showing All Saints' Church (right, with original gate piers and Bakewell gates), the site of St Mary's (left), St Michael's and, in the distance, St Alkmund's, all grouped beside what was once the prehistoric spinal road. Photograph taken by Richard Keene, 1866. (M. Craven)

of the *prepositus*) and had their ancient legal body – the *portmannemot* (Latin, *curia*) – embodied in the charter. From various other documentary mentions, it is also plain that this body had a permanent building or place, as was touched upon above. Another concession was the right to a merchants' guild, and to house this a building separate from the *portmannemot* was undoubtedly established: the first guildhall. By the Reformation it is clear that a building called the Moot Hall existed behind Irongate, north of the Market Place, and that the Guildhall stood in the Market Place itself, where one of its successors, demolished in 1730–31, was recorded by Hutton.

As a rule, charters were renewed, in exchange for a handsome fee payable to the exchequer, at the beginning of each reign, although this does not appear to have been entirely consistent. Nevertheless, various extra corporate privileges were obtained over the years, such as the right to have a prison for the borough (1330), to appoint a Recorder, a form of legal officer, from 1446 and a town clerk – or common clerk – from 1611. From the 14th century, the assizes were held quarterly in each county, too, Derby hosting three of Derbyshire's from 1328 and Chesterfield one, usually the spring session. This continued until 1971.

THE RISE OF RELIGIOUS HOUSES

In mediaeval Europe, religion was, with work and family life, the most important element of everyday existence. People feared for their immortal souls and, if they could afford it, founded monasteries or gave land or chattels to them in order to aid their consciences and to ensure that the monks and nuns who lived in them would pray for them, their families and their departed. It did not take long for this to result in vastly increased wealth and thus power for the religious houses. In Derby, once they were established, their influence was, until the Black Death at least, all-pervading. Furthermore, it was an age quite unlike our own, in which nobody had the least doubt about their Christian faith.

In 1086 the only monastic establishments in Derby were the two collegiate churches of All Saints' and St Alkmund, along with some fairly extensive property belonging to Burton Abbey, whose tenants and agents were present in the town. Yet before long several others were to come into being, and their influence on the everyday life of the borough was very considerable. Further, they acted as property owners, engaged in litigation, received grants of land, undertook commercial operations and administered churches.

Robert de Ferrers, 6th Earl of Derby, from his seal. He was entitled to one third of the borough's revenues. (M. Craven)

The combined college itself continued as an independent body within its Royal Free Chapel only until a date generally reckoned to be 1107, when Henry I granted it to the dean and chapter of Lincoln Cathedral. Being from then on under the Dean of Lincoln, the head of the college in Derby was then or subsequently regraded from dean to sub-dean, the status his successors enjoyed until the Dissolution. It is, however, possible that the dean of the college retained his original style for another two generations, for this would explain the appearance of two powerful Derby men, both styled 'Dean of Derby': Hugh and Robert de Derby, father and son, the bar on clerical marriage then not being generally in force. The surviving records held at Lincoln are unfortunately not detailed enough to prove this theory, but previous suggestions lack conviction – one cannot, for instance, imagine anyone as powerful as Hugh de Derby being 'some kind of rural dean' as both Dr Cox and Professor Saltman suggest; no other holder of such office can be adduced. Nevertheless, it gave Lincoln an important toehold in the borough which, strangely, was not exploited as much as one might expect.

The first important new foundation following the Conquest was that of the convent of St Helen, north of the Town Ditch. The impetus for this was no doubt the uncertain tenor of the times caused by the seemingly endless civil war between Empress Matilda and King Stephen which, as we shall see, may well have spilled over into Derby. In or about 1137 a burgess named Towy, 'with others', established an oratory dedicated to St Helen 'on his own patrimony' to be served by Augustinian Canons. From this we may infer that Towy

Detail of the ancient house, 126 Nuns' Street, showing the early Tudor stone doorcase to what was probably built as a farmhouse by the Convent of St Mary de Pratis. It was carefully restored in 1997 by the university. (*Derby Evening Telegraph*)

was the proprietor of the church of St Helen and perhaps the heir of Edric son of Coln, rather than Norman of Lincoln (Towy is not a Norman name), both proprietors of town churches 50 years previously. This foundation was confirmed by Robert de Ferrers, Earl of Derby.

One of the burgesses associated with Towy, Hugh de Derby, the man styled Dean of Derby, some decade afterwards gave the convent all his land at Little Darley 'above the meadows by the Derwent', along with St Peter's Church, of which he was then the patron: by what process he succeeded to St Peter's is, however, lost. All one can say is that Hugh appears then pre-eminent among his fellow citizens. Within a few years the foundation had moved to its new property at Darley and re-established as the Abbey of St Mary, the most important house in the county. By 1159 the monks had also acquired control of the churches of St Michael and St Werburgh in Derby, six others and an oratory in the county and another in Staffordshire. As time went on,

they were also endowed with land, including much in Derby itself, mills and tenements, by men fearful for their eternal souls. Their local power swiftly increased and again Robert de Ferrers confirmed the grants of others in such a way as to suggest that he had personally established the Abbey. By about 1160, too, the original foundation at St Helen's had become a hospital, subordinate to Darley Abbey.

The St Helen foundation had been contemporary with another minor house, which began in 1140. In this year, a burgess, clearly of Danish descent, called Waltheof son of Swein, patron of the church of St James, which was situated in all likelihood in the north-west angle of the junction of Cornmarket and St James's Street, gave the church to the Cluniac monks of Bermondsey, who immediately established a small priory (cell) on the site. By 1229 they too had added a hospital. Thus, this house too, its foundation confirmed by King Stephen, was the product of the same uncertain and turbulent age that had seen St Helen's founded and grow into Darley Abbey.

The next two foundations, however, took place in the long and relatively settled age of Henry II (1154–1189). The first of these, and the town's third monastery, was the Priory of King's Mead. This arose out of the Abbey of Darley needing to establish a sister house for nuns. Hence Albinus, first Abbot of Darley, seems to have founded a Benedictine Priory of nuns in the parish of St Werburgh on the north west of Markeaton Brook, where lay some water meadows, hence the alternative name, St Mary de Pratis – St Mary of the Meadows, the old synonym for which was 'mead'.

Walter Duredent, the locally-born Bishop of Chester, acknowledged the foundation and Albinus's role therein in a charter of *c*.1160. The Priory became quite independent from *c*.1250, at which date the patronage of St Werburgh's Church nearby was transferred from the abbey. Little record of the buildings survive, although a pretty brick edifice, perhaps an associated farm house, built on a stout stone plinth with a plain early Tudor arch for an entrance, survives on Nuns' Street today, meticulously restored by the University of Derby in 1996. In February 1825 some foundations and a stone coffin containing a female skeleton were unearthed on Nuns' Street by men preparing ground for building on behalf of the Improvement Commissioners who had acquired the site from the Mundy family. Nearby was also found a floor 9ft x 4ft made up of coloured tiles three inches square. A contemporary opinion that this find was Roman seems unlikely in view of the size of the tiles. Also found were some 'arch stones', no doubt also from the nunnery.

Shortly after this, before the end of the reign of King Henry, a leper hospital was founded, almost certainly

All that survives of Derbyshire's largest monastic house, Darley Abbey – the 14th-century domestic building, converted into a pub in 1979, photographed in 2002. (M. Craven)

under a charter from the king himself, dedicated to St Leonard. Its site was, as might be expected from its role, outside the town, in Litchurch, somewhere on the west side of what is today Osmaston Road and in those days on the main route to Swarkestone Bridge and to London. Its exact location is uncertain, but the 19th-century Leonard Street may approximate to its site, which was surrounded by some of the borough's open fields: Wallfield, St Leonard's flat, Littledale and the Haye. A church, not necessarily bearing the same dedication, although it was extremely popular from the 11th century, may have formed the nucleus of this foundation as well as at the leper hospital founded at a slightly earlier period in Abbey Foregate in Shrewsbury.

The final foundation in 1224–38 was that of The Friary, on the south side of the road to Ashbourne. It is worth noting that later, from this foundation, the street was renamed Friar Gate, the continuing Norse vernacular in using 'Gate' for 'Street' suggesting a healthy Norse element in the town's population which, even then, had not lost either its identity or language. Once again, the uncertainty of the times – the minority of Henry III in this case – may well have been the catalyst which inspired the founder, William de Verdun of Foremarke. The site, 16 acres, was probably the urban fee of the Foremarke estate, perhaps, again, equipped with a residence and pre-existing chapel. Interestingly,

The cell of the Cistercian Abbey of Bermondsey at Derby, dedicated to St James, lay behind and to the right of this 1855 view of St James's Lane before widening. It also gives a good idea of a mediaeval side road! Nevertheless, it contained two coaching inns before widening in 1867–71. Richard Keene photograph. (M. Craven)

some 500 years later Sir Robert Burdett of Foremarke had land very close by on which he built a town house. It was given to the Dominican Friars Preachers, otherwise the Black Friars. It certainly incorporated a church after its foundation and associated buildings, which themselves seem to have been grouped between where today the Heritage Gate office development stands and Friary Street. The friars also dammed the Bramble Brook, a tributary of the Markeaton Brook flowing from Mickleover, on the south west, to make fishponds.

DERBY'S EARLY TOPOGRAPHY

The original Anglo-Scandinavian *burh* had, by about 1204, expanded considerably. The Market Place had come into being (it is first mentioned in a charter *c*.1210 and archaeology gives it another century) and the essential pattern of streets which still persists led thence southward along the spinal road to St Peter's Church. The latter is likely, as with Wardwick, to have been an original Northworthy settlement expanded into a flourishing suburb, although its name is lost, unless the surviving name of Morledge – akin to 'Morley' – is significant.

St Peter's is a very large parish and may be of early creation; in more recent times, Normanton, with Cottons (originally Codinton), Boulton and Osmaston

Corner of St Peter's Churchyard, spring 1882. The mediaeval post is now in Derby Museum; Richard Keene photograph. (M. Craven)

Cockpit Hill and the probable area of the castle, foreground. The churches are, left to right, St Werburgh's, All Saints' and St Michael's. (The late R.G. Hughes)

were hacked out of it to make separate parishes. Interestingly, the ancient ceremony of beating the bounds was still flourishing as late as May 1844. The ritual lasted, of necessity, all day, children following the incumbent, the churchwardens and choir, carrying wands, afterwards being treated to 'buns and ale'. Early street names are found hereabouts: Bag Lane (now, prosaically, East Street, first mentioned *c*.1220), St Peter's Street (*c*.1240) and Copecastle (1085) for instance. These lead us to be able to assign at least a pre-Conquest date to the enclave around St Peter's. Bag Lane led due east towards the Derwent where lay another early part of the settlement, Copecastle (which translates as 'Market Castle' or area), the name of which was recorded a year before *Domesday*. As the Market Place did not then exist, and only St Peter's Street connected this area to the infant *burh* (as a portion of the spinal road), we must conclude that the area was originally a separate settlement perhaps going back to the Northworthy period, with Copecastle perhaps as a trading area. Copecastle, adjacent to the two Castle Mills (so recorded by name later, but undoubtedly among those extant in 1066) is a puzzle. The name 'Castle' has been ever since lurking in the area in various forms, and several later writers refer to a castle as a certainty, mentioning vestigial earthworks, notably along the line of the present Albion Street.

The enigmatic site at Cockpit Hill connects with Bag Lane via a street called The Morledge, a name not recorded until some time after the 12th century. Nevertheless, its Saxon name is undoubtedly of pre-Conquest origin, and it can be presumed to have existed at this period: indeed, a Morledge surname appears in Derby early on.

Other early Derby streets help us to understand some of the trades and crafts of the early town: Irongate (1318, Smiths); Saddler Gate (*c*.1248, Saddlery); Leather Lane (leatherworking or glove-making, attested elsewhere);

The Shambles (butchery), Bold Lane (bolt or arrow making) and Walker Lane (c.1263, fulling). It was long thought that Full Street (13th century), suggestively sited beside the Derwent where fulling must indeed have been carried out, was named after that trade, as was Walker Lane from the 'walkers', the men who trod the natural oils from the fleeces. However, one of the older forms of the name suggests that it actually translates as 'foul-street': a place of noise-someness and squalor.

The name 'Castle Gate' as applied to East Street (Bag Lane) appears to have been a red herring arising from a mistaken quotation in Camden's *Britannia* (1610) and should not be included among the circumstantial evidence for a castle at Derby. A release of a house and land in 'a place or lane called Castle Gate otherwise called Bag Lane' of 1647 is evidence of the celerity with which the suggestion of a rather grander name for the street was taken up locally. A later annalist even tells of traders demanding that a Bag Lane contemporary take down a sign reading 'Castle Gate' from his shop. The fact that this name is not found used for Bag Lane prior to Camden's publication is proof enough of its spuriousness. Nevertheless, no word of a castle appears in any state record, yet any *official* structure of this sort would inevitably find itself on the written record somewhere. As a result, many commentators have taken the path of caution and let the matter lie as not proven.

Others have suggested – on the basis that Copecastle (in its later guise as the Cockpit Hill) is shown as a strange little structure actually on a mound – that a natural feature inspired the epithet of Castle, as elsewhere. This does not explain the earthworks, if we are to trust Hutton, and, if not a chimaera, could represent a quite separate phenomenon like early or civil war defence works. As they apparently ran north–south, rather than the tactically sensible east–west, these suggestions appear untenable.

The discovery of an 'adulterine' castle (i.e. one built without licence from the Crown) beside the Danish defences at Repton, however, suggests that at Derby, too, such a strongpoint might well have been established. The builder of that at Repton was Ranulph, Earl of Chester, on his own manor. It has already been suggested that Ranulph's grandfather, Hugh Lupus, 1st Earl of Chester, had a more dominant position in the *burh* of Derby before *Domesday*. Having taken the initiative on behalf of the Empress Matilda against King Stephen, winning a considerable victory at Lincoln in 1141, Ranulph seems to have re-established control in the Trent valley in the process of trying to realise his ambition to connect his Palatine County of Chester to his extensive Lincolnshire estates with a chain of strongpoints from sea to sea. Indeed, in 1149 Ranulph was granted 'the town of Derby and what belonged to it', confirmed in 1153. If such was

the case, no official record would remain of any hastily constructed castle, and, unlike Repton, most archaeological traces would also have vanished beneath the later town. Its position would most likely have been at the south end of Cockpit Hill, where 18th century topographical evidence suggests some bizarre hedge and plot patterns.

If the foregoing was the case, then the edifice, almost certainly a wooden structure, its chapel and its earthworks, would have been razed when Henry II ended the conflict and re-asserted control. Indeed, the *Anglo-Saxon Chronicle* for the period (1137) says that 'For every great man built him a castle and held them against the king; and they filled the whole land with these castles…'

The Darley charters and other written sources also help us to people early mediaeval Derby with identifiable characters, although only down to the level of shopkeepers and artisans; as usual, those at the bottom of the heap rarely surface on the record. The racial admixture by this time was largely a blend of Anglian and Scandinavian, to roughly equal proportions, unlike Lincoln where it is thought that the latter element predominated. Passage of time, however – more than 500 years – was sufficient for any hint of a Celtic racial element to have been subsumed in the subsequent social realignments.

Of other elements, only the Normans and the Jews can be discerned, neither, however, to any great extent. Norman names were rapidly taken up by native Derby families, as the charters amply demonstrate. At this stage Norman blood was confined to members of the *elite*: mainly the Barons, Knights and their kin. In 1086 only Norman of Lincoln, a proprietor of a church, was undoubtedly a Norman inhabitant of the town. The other Norman names are of county magnates, not townsfolk.

DERBY'S JEWISH COMMUNITY

We also know a community of Jews lived in Derby through three pieces of information: the burgesses, during the second Barons' War (1257), paid the exchequer 10 marks (£3.33) for 'having a certain charter granted to them that no Jew or Jews should reside in Derby' with the consequence that all Derby Jews were expelled and relieved of their non-portable assets at the same time; the Darley charters speak of a Jews' cemetery, and in 1290 the burgesses again obtained a licence to expel all the Jews from the town – probably the 1257 charter had been revoked. The story that Jury Street is a corruption of 'Jewry' is contradicted by the minutes of the Third Improvement Commission, which pitched it

Norman house of Aaron the Jew, Lincoln. Derby's Jewish quarter would have had similar houses in the 13th century. (M. Craven)

in 1796, naming it after the legal element of the adjacent Shire Hall.

It is estimated that at most some 15–25 households were affected. Regrettably, the loss of the bulk of the borough records in a fire at the Guildhall in 1841 means that few names of any Derby Jewish residents from that period have come down to us, although the Darley charters do record Solomon, the 13th-century lessee of Twigrist Mill on the brook opposite the bottom of St Mary's Gate, although his two sons bore Norman names, perhaps in an effort to blend in and avoid proscription.

In the early Middle Ages, only the Jews were congenital town-dwellers, and the only people to build in stone to any extent, their houses acting as secure places to store luxury goods or specie, with sophisticatedly divided-up living quarters above. A famous example of one of these houses exists at Lincoln, and others can be found elsewhere. Stone ensured their survival as among the very earliest English urban dwellings, and such houses must surely once have graced Derby; unfortunately, we do not know whereabouts.

Ravenshoe, Burton Road (now divided). In the early 20th century this house was Derby's synagogue, although it was built in the 1870s for T.C. Simmonds, first principal of Derby College of Art. (*Derby Evening Telegraph*)

In 1290 all the Jews in England – about 3,000 are estimated – were expelled and not allowed back until 1655. The first Jewish residents recorded in Derby after that date occur in the 1820s and the first synagogue in the city since 1290 was established in the outbuilding of 33 Harriet Street, owned by tailor Harris Levy in 1898. In 1913 the local community bought Ravenshoe, Burton Road, the fine villa of Thomas Simmonds, first principal of the art college, and converted part of it into a synagogue which flourished until 1985, since when Derby's few Jews have been obliged to travel to Nottingham.

DERBY PEOPLE

In the late-12th century and beyond, Derby was controlled by one very powerful grouping of inter-related families, headed by Hugh the Dean, already encountered as a founder of Darley Abbey and a patron of St Peter's. He was a figure who flourished from the civil wars through to the 1170s; he was dead by 1179. Unfortunately, the name of his father is lost to us, but the fact that his brother was called A(n)ghemund suggests a Scandinavian origin. His wife is thought to have been Cecilia, a daughter of Henry Touchet of Markeaton, Mackworth and Allestree, one of the powerful lords whose lands, carved out of the old Northworthy estate in earlier times, surrounded the town, giving them great influence within it. They also held land in Cheshire, and their paramount lord in all these estates was none other than the castle-building Earl of Chester.

The rise of the Touchets and the influence of Hugh were thus probably linked to the primacy of the Earls of Chester over Derby in the 12th century at the expense of the Earls of Derby. Hugh's family connections were of Byzantine complexity and included – it is not clear exactly how – Walchelin, the last moneyer, whose daughter Quenilda was, by 1202, married to Ingeram de Wardwick, and their son Peter later married Hugh's granddaughter and ultimate heiress.

Between them, between c.1150 and c.1280, Hugh's connections accounted for one Abbot of Derby, two deans, at least two high civic dignitaries, eight or nine major holders of land, 12 other ecclesiastics (with a couple of lay patrons of churches not included in other categories), at least 13 burgesses, including several lawyers, Members of Parliament and a mint master. Yet the decline of the power and influence of this local 'mafia' began in the middle of the civil war of c.1240–68, and by the next century we lose sight of the descendants of most of the progeny of Hugh the Dean and Walkelin the Moneyer. They and their influence were probably decimated by the Black Death, 1347–49.

Of the descendants of Walchelin, one was reduced to the status of a shoemaker. Walkelin himself, however, carries added significance in a donation he made with Goda his wife to the Abbey of Darley of some property in the town, of which 'the hall shall be converted into a school for clerks and the chambers above (in the same house), serve as a hostel for the master and clerks'. This has been taken by many authorities as the definitive foundation of Derby School. However, another charter suggests that this provision was never put into effect and the entire incident as related to the post-Reformation foundation of Derby School should be treated with extreme caution. Certainly, however, a school did exist under the aegis of the abbey in the later Middle Ages, for charters allude to such, and, in 1406, one Stephen Bell is described as 'magister scolarum de Derb', (schoolmaster of Derby) and William Roche appears in this position in 1481 – with only the slip of the pen of a parish clerk one might claim him as the ancestor of the homonymous actor who became a fixture on TV's *Coronation Street*, the scion of three generations of Ilkeston doctors!

Only the Touchets, supported by extensive holdings of land, weathered the storm of the Black Death. In 1386, indeed, they inherited the right of Summons to the House of Lords by marrying the heiress of 4th Lord Audley of Heleigh, another family nurtured in the bosom of successive Earls of Chester. Indeed, the present (26th) Baroness Audley is a direct descendant of this Domesday family. So numerous were the posterity of Hugh and Walkelin, indeed, that one might well expect to be able to establish at least one line of descent to the present, yet so total was their eclipse that it does not appear possible. Yet in Derby one other family, the Allestreys, are more or less traceable to the present day.

AN EXTRAORDINARY CASE OF CONTINUITY

The Allestrey family emerge in the late-12th century as humble villeins of the Abbot of Darley and took their surname from the then vill of Allestree immediately north of the town, over most of which the Touchets of Markeaton were lords. Sometime between 1248 and 1261 'Elias son of William de Allestreey, Felicia his wife with all their brood and chattels' were granted, with the land on which they toiled in Allestree, to the abbey, by the then head of the Touchets. A later charter acknowledges that Abbot Walter and the Canons of Darley 'have liberated' Elias, whose grandfather (we learn elsewhere) was one Thomas of Allestree, a villein living 1175–1215. Strangely, there were cousins then living who were free men, and it is conceivable that Elias's grandfather fell into villeinage through misfortune and was not born into it. Yet it was Elias's second son, Henry, who by 1307 had become 'Lord of Allestrey', an astounding case of social mobility.

Elias's descendants through another of his three sons are clearly traceable for a further century to William, holding land in chief at Allestrey and Alvaston, but thereafter the detail of the descent becomes obscure for three generations until Thomas de Allestrey is discovered as MP for Derby in 1466 holding the same parcel of land in Alvaston.

From him the male line survives at Alvaston Hall to the beginning of the 18th century, and thereafter through several female lines to the surviving Moults (formerly solicitors and including the immortal Ted) and several other local residents of today. Junior branches of the Allestreys were reduced to being tenant farmers in Morley and Ambaston in the 19th century.

This evidence of continuity is both convincing and exceedingly rare, and may, indeed, be unique in respect of an English town the size of Derby. Nevertheless, thanks to the litigious nature of mediaeval life, briefer pedigrees of quite humble townsmen have come down to us through contemporary documents.

The beginnings of surnames are seen at this time and these too furnish us with some clues as to the occupations of the ordinary townsfolk. As social mobility was such a rare phenomenon, those noted during the time up to, say, 1400, can be taken to some extent as reflecting local life. Between the 12th and 14th centuries no less than 21 distinctive surnames occur in the local charters, although at first often expressed by the Latin equivalent, like the earliest, Hereward Parmentarius (tailor) in a Darley charter of Henry II's reign, along with Simon Tinctor (dyer) 1233, Radulfus Molendarius (miller) of c.1270, William Olearius (oilman) c.1190, Hugo Sellarius (saddler – in Sadler Gate, naturally) c.1250 and so on. English equivalents are surprisingly early on the scene, too, though, like John le Irernmonger of c.1250, but many others first appear in Norman-French, as with Hervey le Vacher (cowkeeper) of 1240 and Peter le Prentice (apprentice) of 1345. Some of these names have not survived, but most represent the beginnings of some well-known modern surnames, like Taylor, Lorimer, Carpenter, Draper, Lister, Scrivener and Faber (Smith), all of which first occur in Derby at this period.

Many of the documents carrying mention of the humbler folk centre on the Abbey of Darley's holdings called the Newlands. These were an urban part of a country fee, the Serjeantry of Sandiacre, given to the monks by Peter de Sandiacre, one of the lords of the estate. The Newlands seem to have come to the Sandiacres at the beginning of the 13th century in a series of exchanges orchestrated by the king, perhaps to augment the land available to the town for possible expansion prior to the grant of the new charter in 1204.

This shake-up also affected Litchurch and other areas. The Newlands would appear to have comprised an extensive tract of no less than 212 acres, running from the west edge of the Wardwick to the boundary of *huver* (either Mickleover, Littleover or [Rough] Heanor) in the west, along the southern edge of Bramble Brook and south to Green Lane. It also bounded Rowditch, another interesting area, at one time part of the Touchets' estates, which eventually became attached to the Manor of Walton-by-Chesterfield. The Newlands themselves were divided up into tofts, with some strip-farming in between, and most of the holdings were small, held by quite unpretentious citizens who paid such rent as a few pence, or a cockerel, once a year on a fixed date to the abbot. As one of the open fields of the borough, it became a common in the 16th century which survived until after 1603, from which date the local inhabitants began to enclose these, although not without conflict.

By far the commonest mediaeval archaeological finds in the city are green-glazed (and occasionally unglazed) pottery sherds of *c*.1250–1350, mainly parts of pitchers with narrowish long necks and decorated handles. These appear to have been made at a site immediately to the north of the city boundary, but within the mediaeval parish of St Alkmund, at Burley Hill. Here a kiln was discovered in 1862, and later four others were discovered by ploughing, which were excavated by R.G. Hughes and S.O. Kay in 1957. Some vessels are decorated with horseshoe motifs, well known in other contexts as the canting heraldic badge of the Ferrers, Earls of Derby, although in this context the horseshoes are, in the main, unheraldically deployed, upside-down. Yet, given the proximity of the Ferrers' stronghold of Duffield Castle, this connection could conceivably be a valid one. It is worth noting, too, that late in Henry III's reign the significantly named Alan the Potter held half an acre in Burley Fields near the stream 'which is the boundary

Ancient market areas: Cornmarket, 1929, postcard. (M. Allseybrook)

between the fields of Burley and those of Allestree,' from the abbey's tenant William de Burley. The description of Alan's holding in the rubic of the charter matches closely the site of the kilns.

DERBY'S MARKETS

In mediaeval times, beast markets were held at the western end of Friar Gate and the road still widens out to demonstrate where they were accommodated. This was replaced in 1861. Mainly commestibles and fish were sold in the Market Place and the Cartulary of Tutbury Priory records such activities in the early 12th century. This continued until 1933 and is still occasionally used for stalls. Grains were sold in the Corn Market, also a road which funnels out towards the south and its crossing of the Markeaton Brook at St Peter's Bridge. Latterly, the various grains were measured into basins raised on pedestals, called stoops. This was replaced by the Corn Exchange in 1861. A subsidiary market area grew up in the widest part of The Morlege with a market for durables on Cockpit Hill. While the former was moved in 1933 to the new open market, the latter was suffered to survive until 1970.

As trade increased, so the wealth of the burgesses grew. They in turn petitioned each new monarch – for example in 1330 Edward III, in 1377 Richard II, in 1422 Henry VI, in 1460 Edward IV and Richard III in 1483 – for extensions of their privileges, including fair days and market rights.

DERBY'S FIRST BRIDGE AND ITS CHAPEL

At this period, the commercial power of Nottingham was also increasing, and it is reasonable to assume that communications between the two had to be improved. The route then lay down the old Nottingham Road (the Roman route to Sawley) south east to the Trent and then north east up to the neighbouring town. Crossing the Derwent at first was achieved via a ford, called, rather obviously, Stoneyford or The Causey, itself reached via St Michael's Lane. On the latter stood an inn called the Nottingham Castle, which goes a long way to confirming that this was indeed the route east from the town, as several English towns have inns named after the next settlement along the way. This establishment survived, with much late mediaeval timber-framing, until it was inexplicably demolished in 1965; had it survived it would have been a wonderful attraction to the tourist and local people alike in the new age of leisure.

The Causey – recorded as a 'crossing' of the Derwent in the town charter of 1229 – must have been made

Chapel of St Mary-on-the-Bridge, c.1954, as restored 23 years previously. (Derby Museum)

largely redundant by the construction of a stone bridge over the Derwent some time before 1326, in which year an Act called a *Pontage* was obtained to raise money for its repair. A Darley charter dateable to between 1233–48 refers to Bridge Gate as a street leading to a *magnus pons* – a great bridge – so the building of the first bridge can be pinned down to the period between 1229 and 1248. The bridge appears, from observational and archaeological evidence, to have had nine arches including the two abutment springers.

It had been, probably from the start, graced by a chapel dedicated to St Mary, which mercifully survives as one of Derby's six grade I listed buildings and one of only seven such chapels remaining in England. Its fabric dates largely from *c.*1450, albeit since 1968 dwarfed by a great concrete motorway bridge beside it, mockingly named 'Causey Bridge', and shaken by the constant vibration of the traffic.

Architectural and charter evidence suggests an original date for this pretty building is *c.*1275, if not a fraction earlier, and this must more closely date the creation of the first bridge – on this site at least. In the mid-14th century a cell for an anchorite was added and, in the century following, this part was occupied by a so-called hermit, John Shelton, and his wife. They collected tolls and did odd jobs. The chapel itself was secularised at the Reformation, taken back into religious use in the late 19th century and purchased by the Derbyshire Archaeological Society from the Whalley family, which had owned a boilermaking foundry beside it for much of the 19th century. With generous support from the wife of Herbert Ham, first Provost of Derby Cathedral, and her brother Eric Haslam, it was restored in 1930 by Percy Currey, FRIBA, in memory of their father Sir Alfred Haslam. It was then vested in trustees who still care for this precious building. Attached to the Cathedral, it is used regularly for services and is open to the public two afternoons a week.

Mediaeval Derby's appearance

It is difficult to be sure just by how much the town increased in size in the later mediaeval period. It is safest to assume by very little. Indeed, by 1204 Litchurch, one of the Northworthy settlements hitherto part of the borough, was granted by the Crown to Peter de Sandiacre III, an independent Lord with important holdings in the borough, whence it had passed by 1231 to William de Dunston, a Northamptonshire grandee. It then lay within the Parish of St Peter, its whilom importance attested by the fact that it had previously given its name to an Anglo-Norse administrative district, the Wapentake (later Hundred) of Litchurch,

Proof that behind the later façades of numerous less pretentious Derby buildings lies genuine antiquity. The cruck-framed rear portion of an unlisted shop in East Street stands exposed by modernisation in the mid-1970s. (*Derby Evening Telegraph*)

subsequently attached to that of neighbouring Morleston. Derby did not recover control over this area until as late as 1877.

As to population, the Lay Subsidy Roll of 1377 gives the number of laymen at 14 or over and thus liable for tax (i.e. owners of moveable property worth more than 5s [25p]) as 1,076. This excludes monks and priests, paupers, women and children and a theoretical total might be, say, 3,500, which would probably represent a substantial increase on 1086.

The buildings of the town at this time were mainly timber framed, or wattle and daub. Most were placed on burgage plots, the origins of which, as we have seen, go back to the Saxon *burh*. Because of their long narrow shape, most houses were placed gable end on – at right angles – to the road, as is clear from the first map of the whole town drawn by John Speed in 1610. Even grand houses up to the 16th century tended to be built in this way, although encroachments – usually on the public road – were constantly being made and the expansion of trade and population caused this to happen ever more frequently. As early as 1269 a man had built a porch on to his house fouling the 'King's highway' to the tune of 72sq ft. Three others and even the vicar of St Peter's had built parts of their houses (usually solar chambers, a sure sign of affluence) either encroaching the road or jettied excessively over it.

The listed and timber-framed Nottingham Castle Inn dated largely from the 16th century (with earlier core) and stood on St Michael's Lane, the original route to the very town after which it was named. It was, however, demolished in 1965, the site remaining as a car park for some 30 years. (*Derby Evening Telegraph*)

The 15th-century timber-framed merchant's house immured behind Newcastle House, Market Place, photographed 13 years before it was exposed by demolition on 16 June 1949. It was finally re-erected, shorn of its ground floor and with non-authentic fenestration, in Old Blacksmith's Yard, in 1980.

Hugh de Morley of Morley, a county magnate whose town house, called Morley Hall after his country seat, is the first such recorded in the town, was found to have encroached a foot onto Bridge Gate (where this edifice stood) and over a frontage of no less than 20ft. This means that he must have acquired at least two burgage plots in order to build such a wide house. Indeed the impression gained is of increasing sophistication of life as reflected in the more opulent buildings in town. Also, men like Hugh de Morley, and later the Portes, Babingtons and Poles, were erecting town dwellings in addition to their country seats in order to more effectively control their economies, attend civic and legal functions and acquire supplies.

Surviving fabrics from the age are today, of course, practically non-existent, yet until 1948 a house known latterly as the Old Mayor's Parlour, in Tenant Street, survived. It was large, with five gables, timber framed, and in order to fit a slightly curving burgage plot running down to the edge of the River Derwent it was built at a right angle to the street, its façade following the shape of the plot. Architecturally it was late-15th century in date and at the time of its wanton and unnecessary destruction was the largest urban residence of its type and date in England. Unfortunately, we do not know who built it, but it was probably a county magnate building a town house, rather than an opulent burgess. Later it was divided into two, one half being lived in for almost 50 years by Percival Willoughby (1596–1685), the aristocratic pioneer 17th-century obstetrician.

Apart from the Bridge Chapel and some fabric of St Peter's Church, very few mediaeval buildings survive today in Derby except parts of Stone House Prebend at Little Chester and the 15th-century merchant's house discovered embedded in the back of Newcastle House, on the north side of the Market Place, in 1971. The latter has been reconstructed after a fashion in Old Blacksmith's Yard off Sadler Gate.

Other mediaeval fabrics may survive, but only as fragments embedded in standing buildings. Until the present era, it was common practice in Derby (as elsewhere) to refront a house, to keep abreast of fashion as well as to increase its amenity, but to leave the rest. A pair of crucks survived in a house in East Street until the 1970s and early timber framing remains in several buildings in unwidened Sadler Gate. Beyond these, only surviving accounts, engravings and early photographs give us clues to actual buildings in mediaeval Derby. The best recorded are the gentry town houses; that of the Babingtons of Dethick seems to have been in existence before 1500; another in St Peter's Street belonging to the Portes then existed, and Every House on the east side of the Market Place may have had mediaeval origins: like Babington House it is known to have had a separate

gatehouse shielding a recessed courtyard behind. Another more modest structure with a splendid carved dragon post – preserved in the Museum's collections – stood at the south-west corner of St Peter's Churchyard until 1882. (See illustration on page 40.)

Of the 'lost' parish churches, that of St Mary had entirely ceased to exist by the mid-16th century and as a parish since c.1250. The last reference to it is in a will of 1516. Fragments of its remains reappeared in 1925 when the Halifax Building Society offices were being erected in connection with the widening of Queen Street (see page 34). The other extant churches were all rebuilt at various times up to the 1890s.

borough or common seal of Derby of 1446. (M. Craven)

LATER MEDIAEVAL DEVELOPMENTS

The later mediaeval period was one of subtle change. The influence of religion had begun to wane since the Black Death, and new families had replaced those decimated by the plague. Prosperity, despite the civil wars in the middle part of the 15th century, had risen to new and unprecedented levels.

From this time (1446) the borough seal has survived, which introduces the Buck-in-the-Park symbol for the first time. Seal matrices being durable objects, it is likely that this date marks the earliest corporate seal, and the uncertainty of the times may have led to its introduction. The symbolism is lost, for it pre-dates the theory the name Derby was from the Scandanavian for deer; indeed, its existence may have inspired it! A number of English towns bear deer in their iconography from this period. Nor was the device intended then to be heraldic;

it only became so in later usage, by placing it on a shield. Legitimate authorisation through the College of Arms was not, however, obtained until May 1939, when crest, motto and supporters were added, as befitted a county borough.

The privilege granted to the burgesses of having a gaol, granted under the 1330 charter, may have caused the rebuilding of the Guildhall into the form which was recorded by Woolley in 1713, by Hutton in 1791 and which was pulled down in 1730. This was a stone gaol-house, with a timber-framed guild-chamber above, approached by an outside covered staircase. The surviving Guildhall at Aldburgh, Suffolk, must closely resemble it. The style fits the date and no doubt the burgesses had met in a simpler timber hall previously. This Guildhall – usually known to Derbeians as 'The First Guildhall', although it must have been at least the second – stood proud at the southern edge of the Market Place, the street between being called *Bredelepes* – an area occupied by bakers. Indeed in 1540 there were seven bakers' shops there, mainly let at a rental of 1s 4d (7p) per annum.

The period, too, saw a decline in the stranglehold which the religious houses had on the town. One or two, indeed, may have vanished altogether at this time, like the hospital of St Leonard, along with the Church of St Mary. One problem is that from the 15th century their records become very scanty, but this does not necessarily mean that places such as St James's Priory or St Leonard's had ceased to operate. Indeed, a charter of 14th-century date suggests that the monks of St James's controlled the bridge over the brook connecting St James's Lane to the Wardwick, from which it might be possible to suggest that they had it built or built it themselves. Other bridges existing at this time may well have included St Peter's Bridge (rebuilt in 1787), Sadler Gate Bridge (rebuilt in 1786) and one connecting The Morledge with Tenant Street (Tenant Bridge); indeed there were probably more as Thomas Cox tells us there were no fewer than nine in 1730. A ford seems to have existed further west connecting Friar Gate with King Street, probably an integral part of the main route from Derby to Ashbourne at that time. A further ford may have existed on the former course of Rykneld Street where Nuns' Bridge was built in 1848.

TUMULTS

Derby's history has ever been punctuated by tumults. There is nothing new about the sanguinary excesses of football hooligans which occurred near the Baseball Ground. In 1344, for instance, 'a large body of men' from the town broke into the grounds of the Friary – an establishment by then important enough to have twice played host to the king not 20 years before – 'cut down trees and carried off goods and chattels to the alleged

value of £60 [a hefty four-figure sum today if not more] and beat, wounded and ill-treated the men and servants'. Apparently 44 people were identified from the raiding party, and their number included two priests, linen-drapers, grocers, skinners and shoemakers. The outcome and its cause are difficult to assess. The records are silent regarding the former, and only the tension to be expected from a rising mercantile class over which the religious houses exercised a control out of all proportion to their numbers and interests can be adduced as explanation.

Yet only a year later a party of locally-raised archers, *en route* to Southampton to fight in the war against France, were set upon by 'divers malefactors' in Derby and several of their number killed. Nor were these incidents isolated. Given a period of civil strife, like that of the century following, lawlessness became rife in the county and violence spilled over into the town. The Wars of the Roses split the county gentry fairly evenly. The vast holdings of the Duchy of Lancaster demanded from its servants and tenants allegiance to the Crown of Lancastrian Henry VI. The Protector, the Duke of York, head of the opposing faction, also exercised much *de facto* power in the county and held Assizes in Derby itself. Before him appeared Nicholas Longford who, with over 100 crudely-armed men, also entered 'with the force and arms aforesaid into a dwelling place of... Sir Walter Blount in the house of the Order of Friars Preachers in Derby'. Plainly, the Friary was under siege yet again. The miscreants were 'in manner of war arrayed, to wit, with cloaks of defence, iron caps, longswords, billhooks, lances, halberds, bows and arrows.'

Mostly, in the instances cited, the miscreants got off remarkably lightly, pardons and fines being the order of the day, even for murder and grievous bodily harm. Even treason could be atoned for by the submission of the guilty parties to the king for pardon. It was only with the advent of the unrelenting Tudors that judicial murder became the more usual result. On the local scale, how-ever, petty felons were treated more harshly than erring gentry, most often being consigned to the gaol beneath the Guildhall, while cases for trial tended to go to Nottingham, where criminals from both Derbyshire and Nottinghamshire could be tried and, when necessary, incarcerated. This system, a continuation of the semi-amalgamated arrangements between the two counties which had existed since their formation in the 10th century, continued until the middle of the 16th.

THE BLACK DEATH & LATER PLAGUES

Another cause of distress and unrest was undoubtedly the Black Death, which hit Derby in 1349. There are, however, no contemporary accounts of the course of this terrible scourge in Derby, but the fact that the local commission of the peace was particularly active in the 1350s suggests that there came in its wake a considerable amount of unrest.

Mostly, in context, only inferential evidence can be drawn upon. In the present city there are two place names which are suggestive. One, east of the London Road near Osmaston Park and in a marshy area, is Deadman's Lane in the area now called Wilmorton. In the 14th century this was on the boundary of the town and well away from people. The other, in Spondon, is Lousy Graves Lane, lying between the village and the estate of the then leper hospital of St Lazarus at Locko on the north side. Local authority inspired mealy-mouthedness at one time allowed this interesting survival to become mutated into Louise Greaves Lane (it is now Lousie Greaves Lane, a bizarre compromise). Unless these mass burial sites – for such, we must infer, they were – arose from a later plague in Derby, it must be to the Black Death that their origin be assigned. Later plagues in 1593 and 1637 are better documented, yet if these places were created at either of these dates, one might expect to find reference to them in official sources.

The Black Death also explains the ultimate disappearance of the descendants of Derby's first governing clique: the de Derbys, their descendants and their kindred. Careful analysis of the records show that

Deadman's Lane, Wilmorton. Probable route to the 1347–49 plague pits. (M. Craven)

other names vanish from sight at this time and new ones make their first appearance. Indeed, with the near total extinction of families and family groupings among the landowners and burgesses, a golden opportunity arose for new families to acquire land or goods at knock-down prices and rise to prominence. Certainly this was so in the countryside; well over half the English landed families existing today with mediaeval roots have their first recorded ancestor from this period. Only the Allestreys seem to continue, along with neighbouring and allied families outside the borough, like the Touchets and the Curzons of Kedleston.

TRADING AND THE TRADING ELITE

Nevertheless, trade continued to flourish. By the 15th century several Derby merchants had a base in the capital too. Although condemned for restrictive practice, the Merchants' Guild plainly enabled local trade the chance to flourish free from more than half-hearted competition. Only Nottingham overshadowed Derby in trade in the region. In the charter of Henry III it is obvious that there was then conflict with the merchants of Melbourne, but that document seems to give to the Derby burgesses the right to collect tolls from traders crossing the Trent at Swarkestone and at this earlier period from Doveridge too. It is the control over the bridge at Swarkestone which undoubtedly bestowed a later right, claimed by the Corporation of Derby, to a freedom from competitive markets within a radius of six and three quarter miles from the town centre. In the later 1980s this amusing piece of arcana was being invoked by the city council to strangle at birth privately sponsored markets or 'car-boot sales' at King's Newton and Barrow-on-Trent, and even the now defunct Derby Environmental Week was asked for a fee to have stalls at an event nearby. Indeed, an eight-mile jurisdiction was claimed in the former case. Plainly this privilege, if it really existed at all, must have been superseded in the Municipal Corporations Act of 1835 (if not before). By the passing of the 1973 Local Government Act such niceties must have become a dead letter, along with aldermen and the high steward.

That Derby's prosperity was able to provide a suitable base from which to make a fortune in a national or international context is exemplified by the career of William Shore. It is not clear for how long this family had been in Derby, but Robert Shore, William's father, was a merchant or tradesman of All Saints' parish by the 1430s at the time of William's birth. The family are recorded in the town as prosperous burgesses from the later 14th century. Thomas Shore was MP for the borough in 1396 and 1410, and Ralph served in the same capacity in 1418 but died before 1442, when his widow Isabel and son John were living. John, indeed, may have been William Shore's elusive uncle.

Robert had sufficient funds to apprentice his son to John Rankyn, citizen and mercer of London, and it may be that he, too, was a mercer and, having the means, decided to apprentice his son in London rather than at home in Derby in order to give him a head start. Further, when William came to set himself up in business in 1458 or 59, considerable capital would have been needed to acquire a stock of the luxury fabrics (silk, linen, worsted etc) in which London mercers chiefly dealt. By 1463–64 he had become a Liveryman of the Mercers' Company and shortly afterwards had acquired a house at Bergen-op-Zoom, in Flanders, where much of his trade was negotiated. He married the daughter of a fellow London mercer in the early 1470s. She was Elizabeth (known as Jane), daughter of Alderman John Lambert. Unfortunately the marriage produced no children and was exacerbated by the sexually hyperactive king (Edward IV) taking a shine to young Mrs Shore, and she became his mistress. A divorce on grounds of barrenness was obtained in 1476 and as a convenience she was then married off to the king's legal advisor, Thomas Lynam. None of this deflected the rise of Shore, however. He was shipping wine into England by 1480 and trading out of Hull (to Iceland) and Ipswich shortly afterwards.

Despite all this, however, Shore never lost contact with Derby, inheriting two houses there and buying a third. Of these, one was 'newly built' in St Mary's Gate and another (in which he appears to have lived when in the town) in Iron Gate. His sister had married into the county gentry in the person of John Agard of Foston, bringing connections with the Wolseleys of Wolseley (Staffordshire), the Stanleys and the Ferrers of Tamworth. Indeed, an Agard cousin, Thomas, had also served as MP for the borough in 1450, a fact which may have benefitted Shore at the outset of his career, especially when combined with the connections of his own family with Parliament.

As far back as 1464 one of Shore's own apprentices, a disaster-prone fellow called John Salford, was a protégé from a Derby family whose descendants were still wealthy London merchants as late as Queen Elizabeth's time and beyond. A cousin, Richard Stringer, was a Derby grocer and Salford's executor; a descendant was Bailiff of Derby in 1539 and 1548. Other descendants, George and Robert, served in Parliament in 1553 and 1571–88. One of Stringer's sons went into the church. Stringer had been Bailiff of Derby in 1494, 1496 and 1452. It is possible that Salford's father, Shore's father and even Shore himself were also town bailiffs at some time or other, but unfortunately the list

of bailiffs is quite incomplete before 1513, so we cannot be sure.

On his death at the Agard's house in Scropton in 1495, Shore left a vast amount of money and property. Much went to the Guild of the Holy Trinity at All Saints', Derby, including his house in Irongate with its garden and 'fish house' – probably a fishing pavilion on the banks of the Derwent nearby, as can still be seen in the Bucks' East View of Derby of 1728, lining the river bank in great variety and profusion; they may well also have had mediaeval origins.

These related families, with their inter-relationships and consistent hold on important offices, reflect to some extent the pattern set three and a half centuries earlier by Hugh the Dean and his posterity. The difference is that while the Shores, Stringers and Salfords were richer by far, their hold on the administration of the borough was not nearly so tight, nor so exclusive. Nor was it unique to the period, for in the late-14th century the Stokes or Stocks family enjoyed international trading connections and constant high office. John Stokes was MP for Derby in the Parliaments of 1386, 1389, 1394, 1399 and 1404. He was a merchant of the Staple of Calais, his fortune coming from the export of wool. Some 120 years earlier an ancestor was but a humble baker, William Stokes, having premises in Walker Lane. His son and grandson followed him as MPs to the mid-15th century.

DERBY'S FIRST MPS

This semi-dynastic representation of the borough in Parliament was a development not available to the immediate descendants of Hugh the Dean, yet was valuable insofar as election to serve in a Parliament, to each of which the borough sent two burgesses. It gave those selected a chance to make contacts in London both social and, more importantly, in business. As Shore's career shows, the two were inextricably intertwined.

The first two burgesses were sent to Parliament in 1295, and in 1380 the burgesses from Derby asserted that their borough was:

La meilloure ville du dite countee
(The best town in the said county)

and indeed, Derby was the only Derbyshire town which sent representatives to Parliament for a very long time, a reflection of its primacy within the county, but at the same time a reminder that the county as a whole was a relatively poor one.

Between 1295 and 1588, a period of three centuries, the borough sent 132 different individuals to Parliament, drawn from 102 different families. Of these, only 20 were established as county gentry families, about 18 we are uncertain and one was a mercantile family with its commercial base in Chesterfield. This leaves 63 families, forming a core of those putting forward candidates, originating in Derby or from parishes contiguous to the borough, mainly old Northworthy townships. Eighteen of these families sent more than one member to Parliament and, of these, four sent three MPs and one even sent eight. Some of these borough MPs served a considerable number of times: eight men served more than thrice, top honours going to a descendant of Hugh the Dean, one Thomas de Tutbury, who was elected eight times over the 33 years between 1328 and 1361.

It is valuable to have a more or less complete list of Derby's representatives to Parliament, not only because it provides us with names, when names are in short supply due to the appalling paucity of local records, but also because the list of bailiffs up until 1513 is extremely fragmentary. However, it is reasonable to suppose that the bailiffs would have been drawn from the same coterie of families and that this pattern of interlinked *burghal* families dominated the life of the borough in the late-Middle Ages, just as Hugh the Dean's had done in the early period and as many better known ones predominated in the centuries up to the Municipal Corporations Act in 1835 and even beyond. Indeed, it is the pervasiveness of these incestuous commercial groupings that in many ways shapes the entire history of the town, and to understand them is to understand many of the events and developments which flowed therefrom.

IV

TUDOR CENTURY

THE MONASTERIES DISSOLVED

The Dissolution of the Monasteries marks the Tudor period. This process, rather more drawn-out than we often realise, marked the end of the influence of the Church in the affairs of the town and thus was of momentous importance. In addition, once dissolved, the land and properties of the religious houses of the town afforded scope for the making of fortunes, for 'redevelopment' and for the reapportionment of incomes from land and property. Only the later 20th century has witnessed such far-reaching changes.

The monasteries were dissolved in two, almost three, stages. The first *tranche* consisted of all those with incomes of less than £200 per annum: St James's, St Leonard's Hospital and King's Mead, their annual incomes being respectively £11 15s 11d [£11.80], unknown [but about £10] and £18 6s 2d [£18.31]. They were closed in 1536, their contents auctioned and their sites sold.

Two years later it was the turn of the more prosperous institutions, chief among which locally was Derbyshire's largest house, the Abbey of Darley, with an income of £258 13s 5d (£258.67). The Friary, whose income is not recorded (but which may have been assessed differently anyway as Dominican Friars were not allowed, by the rule of their Order, to own property other than their house itself), was closed a year later in 1539. This left the combined College of All Saints' with St Alkmund. These collegiate institutions, being primarily churches serving a community rather than closed orders, were allowed to survive by Henry VIII, but under the more fanatical rule of Edward VI's first 'Protector', the Duke of Somerset, they too were wound up, without any provision for the continuing needs of the congregations of the two churches.

Together, the Derby monasteries accounted for a combined yearly income of £3,377 9s 6d (£3,377.47), which represented an impressive slice of real estate. Consequently, the Dissolution locally made some considerable impact. Generally, the Superiors and their brethren received adequate pensions; only where a closure was resisted – celebrated instances like Glastonbury spring to mind – was the treatment meted out by the Crown Commissioners harsh. Thomas Gainsborough, prior of St James's, was put out to grass on a pension of £7 per annum, actually a mark (6s 8d [33p]) more than the abbot of the far more powerful and prestigious Abbey of Darley, Thomas Page, who only received £6 13s 4d (£6.67). The latter's brethren got between £5 and £5 6s 8d (£5.33).

Only the Master of St Leonard's Hospital seems hard done by, being pensioned with a paltry 5s 6d (27p) per annum.

We do not know what happened to the sites of St Leonard's and St James's; the former may have been quite a humble abode in the first place and may have become a farm. Possibly it formed the nucleus of William Woolley's '….few poor houses called Knock-a-down' immediately south of the borough in the Osmaston Road. Then it was on the road to London, for the present London Road was not created until turnpiked much later. However, Woolley also adds 'London Road [meaning Osmaston Road again]… at the top of which *is* St Leonard's formerly a religious house…' St James's, though, came into the hands of the borough, being occupied by Nathaniel Hallowes (Mayor 1657) as successor of the ruined Royalist Sir Andrew Kniveton of Bradley Hall.

This may represent a trend noticeable in the conversion of local monastic properties, in that Kniveton used his residence as a town house. Nevertheless, the church (described as a free chapel) survived for some time, being recorded on a plan drawn in the 1630s. King's Mead was also converted into a gentleman's town house. Its income in 1535 was low and it had debts of 20 marks (£6.75). It seems that it had functioned for a considerable time as an upper-crust boarding school for young ladies of county families. Of its prioresses, two had been Curzons of Kedleston, two from the great Lancastrian house of Stanley, a Beresford of Beresford (Staffordshire), a Touchet of Markeaton, an Ireland of Yeldersley, a Mackworth of Mackworth and a Yorkshire Cholmeley. Plainly the sisters and superiors had been the unmarriageable scions of gentry families, and as their property, like the patronage of St Werburgh's Church (40s [£2] per annum), brought in very little, most of their income was doubtless derived from teaching and boarding fees. The only item of note is that part of the shirt of St Thomas of Canterbury was kept at King's Mead as an object of veneration.

In dissolution, King's Mead passed rapidly from Crown middlemen to the Earl of Shrewsbury in 1541, who sold it the following year to Thomas Sutton of Over Haddon (MP for the borough in 1553), who adapted the prioress's lodging as a town house. After a chequered history, the property was purchased by the Mundys of Markeaton, who swept away all but the much-reconstructed late-mediaeval building which survives on Nuns' Street to this day (see page 38). Hutton tells us that the original institution stood 100 yards north west of

The sub-dean's house at Little Chester, now called Stone House Prebend, in November 1977. It was probably the oldest domestic property in Derby and one of the prebendal farms which were allocated to the College of All Saints' at its foundation to support the canons. (*Derby Evening Telegraph*)

Nuns' Mill and 20 yards north of the bed of the old brook, on the west side of the Green, which took its name from the nuns and became the town's first 'public open space', as it would be termed by a modern planner.

Darley Abbey consisted at sale of a church (with two organs, clock, the usual furniture and fittings), cloister, chapter house, *frater*, vestry and abbot's residence. The latter had 14 rooms apparently. Robert Sacheverell (a younger son of Sir Henry, of Morley) received it on behalf of the Crown in 1538 and made a deal of money out of the materials. Two years later, the site (and whatever remained thereon) was granted by the Crown to Sir Thomas West, who adapted the abbot's residence as a seat. His house eventually came by purchase to the Allestreys and then to William Woolley, who pulled it down and replaced it with one designed by Francis Smith of Warwick in 1727. The one surviving building, of 14th-century date, ended as four cottages but was imaginatively converted into a public house in 1978.

Having mentioned the tradition of a school attached to this abbey, whether or not it was that founded by Walkelin the moneyer, it is worthwhile recording that a pension of 26s 8d (£1.33) per annum was granted at the Dissolution to Thomas Tutman, schoolmaster, presumably a lay appointment and whose name probably unscrambles from the MS source as Tantum. Thus, until 1536–38,

Derby plainly had two schools, one for girls at King's Mead and one for boys at Darley.

Part of the abbey, of course, was the old hospital of St Helen. This was sold to William Berners but soon passed to the Foljambes of Walton-by-Chesterfield. Parts of the original monastic fabric survived apparently, including the entrance and the church itself, in a 17th-century house demolished in 1800. In 1753, when it was the FitzHerbert town house, it was in the birthplace of the diplomat Alleyne FitzHerbert, 1st Lord St Helens (d.1839), and later the painter Joseph Wright lived there from 1772 to 1793.

The 16-acre site at the Friary was surrendered on 3 January 1539 and let to one John Sharpe at a yearly rent of 54s (£2.70). A year later he acquired a 21-year lease of the land and the house (i.e. the building in which lived the prior and around 30 monks, most of whom had been withdrawn at the Dissolution by their order to Scotland, Ireland or Flanders, leaving only six requiring pensions). The rest, including the church, was reserved to the Crown and was sold for the materials. It has already been observed that the Friary suffered plunder by disgruntled townsfolk and history appeared to repeat itself on 18 January 1544, when one Richard Camerdaye of Derby, a labourer, entered the church and house on a personal reformation and forcibly removed marble, lead, iron, glass and timber to the value of £4. The whole

Friary site was purchased in the 1560s by William Bainbrigge (thrice town bailiff and MP) who erected thereon a large, many-gabled timber-framed house.

The dissolution of All Saints' College had slightly different effects. The entire estate was sold to Thomas Smith and Henry Newsum for £346 13s 4 (£346.67), less some miscellaneous property in the town – including the Angel Inn, once the oldest pub in Derby – the income of which was retained to upkeep only the fabric of the two churches. No money was made available at all to support a priest to minister to the spiritual needs of the parishioners of either All Saints' or St Alkmund's. The Dissolution also ended the Guild of the Holy Trinity and the Bridge Chapel.

Messrs Smith and Newsum also received the Little Chester estate, which included the seven prebendal farms. Three were very small with acreages of 10, four and two respectively with rentals of but 13s 4d [67p] compared with the others which yielded £2 each or more and had acreages of 120, 100, 40 and nearly 18, the figures being valid for 1832 but not necessarily the same as 284 years earlier when the college was dissolved – or 1554 when these properties were restored to the Corporation. Indeed, the largest of these holdings was let at a rent of £63 17s 10d in 1729, the next two largest being then held at a rental of £61 8s 9d and £59 4s 10d, the latter two including other land attached at that time, which suggests that by 1832 the houses had been largely shorn of their land. Of these farms, the biggest, 'Le Subdeens Farm' or Stone (House) Prebend (page 55), survives as the oldest domestic building in Derby, immediately north of Parker's Piece on the east bank of the Derwent at Little Chester. Parts of the fabric are mediaeval, including a massive exterior chimney breast, the remainder being of late-16th or, more likely, early-17th century date on a very much earlier base.

Opposite this splendid building, which was sold for restoration by the Corporation after a superficially disastrous fire in the early 1970s, stands a pretty 17th-century farmhouse (Derwent House or City Farm) with traces of an earlier great hall, largely built of decorated brickwork including a blind arcade. It was built over a vaulted stone cellar, thought to have been of Roman origin but filled up with concrete by the city council, which then owned the listed building, in the late 1970s. The surviving cellarage is contemporary with the house, which was sold and restored as a private residence in 1990.

Derwent House had much in common with another former prebendal farm, known as the Manor House, being listed grade II and situated on the south side of Old Chester Road (formerly the *via decumanus* or *principia* of Roman *Derventio*). It, too, had a similar blind arcade and both seem to have been the work of the

same Jacobean mason. The latter was destroyed in 1964 being, inevitably, replaced by a filling station. It overlay one of the largish Roman buildings, excavated in August 1988. Evidence of an ancient boundary wall built straight on to Roman footings on the east of its curtilage suggests that the prebendal farms might well have been established on existing agricultural units, providing fascinating evidence, if the hypothesis of the excavator Chris Drage is correct, for some element of continuity from Roman times.

Smith and Newsum also acquired the college itself, a substantial dwelling immediately on the north side of All Saints' Church and within which had dwelt the sub-dean and the six canons. This, however, survived as a town house and was rebuilt several times later.

The Dissolution also secularised the Chapel of St Mary on the Bridge and doubtless led to the loss of the relics of St Alkmund from the ancient church which bore his name. No longer could the place be the object of pilgrimage of pious Geordies from the Saint's native climes. Indeed, the paucity of its endowment may have been the cause of the vicar, John Marriott, hanging himself 'in a bell-rope' in 1557; the poor fellow had already suffered the loss of his lucrative post as priest of the Wakebridge Chantry in Crich Church at the Dissolution, so the underfunded incumbency of St Alkmund may have come as the last straw.

THE HEADLESS CROSS

In Friar Gate, near Brick Street, is what looks like a pile of roughly-hewn stones. This is the base of the Headless Cross, the topmost stone of which is all that is left of the original preaching cross, those below it being 19th-century replacements, provided when Joseph Strutt removed it from near this spot to the safety of the Arboretum in around 1840. John Speed's map shows one in the Market Place and another on Nuns' Green, in this very Friar Gate area, both intact. It is also known that there was a third – the White Cross – near the borough boundary on the Kedleston Road, which gave its name to the closes surrounding it – 'Whitecross Fields' – and a West End street. This may, however, be identical with the Friar Gate cross, for the relevant closes lay between Kedleston Road and Friar Gate rather than north of the former.

The Friar Gate cross shown by Speed is likely to be the present one, probably deprived of its head and shaft in the iconoclastic dog days of the civil war. It was certainly lacking both shaft and cross by the time the plague broke out, for Revd John Allin's letters tell us that during the Great Plague of London the traders of Derby at the beast fairs on Nuns' Green insisted that money was placed in the hollowed top of the cross, which was filled with vinegar as a disinfectant. Clearly it worked, for Derby's last known plague outbreak was 1637, and not, unlike Eyam, in 1665.

The Third Improvement Commission cleared away the cross in 1792, but its reappearance in the Arboretum 48 years later suggests that, in the interim, William Strutt had allowed his brother Joseph, who lived at Thorntree House by Gaol Bridge, to embellish his garden with it. When Joseph had the Arboretum constructed, much of his garden ornaments found their way there, including, without doubt, the Headless Cross. It was moved back to its present position in 1981.

Queen Mary's Endowment

The regrettable situation of two unendowed churches, two closed schools and a deal of land in the hands of speculators is one which took Queen Mary to put right. Although this monarch is often reviled for the ferocity with which she revived the Catholic faith in England, her influence in Derby was generally beneficial and pragmatic. By a charter dated 1555, and in return for a fine of £266 13s 4d (£266.67), the bailiffs and brethren of the borough were granted 55 pieces or groups of property, tithes, rents and so forth formerly belonging to All Saints', Darley Abbey, St Mary-by-Bridge and the Guild of the Holy Trinity. This gift included the advowsons of the parish churches of St Michael, St

Peter's and Heath (in the north east of the county) and the still-functioning free chapel of St James.

This gift was made in the realisation that the queen could not put the clock back but could at least make amends where possible. The intention was to provide income for the support of a vicar at St Alkmund's and two priests at All Saints' Churches with vicarages, to maintain their fabrics, and was framed to correct the extraordinary omission of the instrument of Dissolution whereby All Saints' College was wound up in 1548 without any spiritual provision whatever. By not actually restoring the college as a monastic foundation, she ensured that the arrangement would survive any subsequent regime, which might revert to the Protestant ethic. Further, the arrangement ensured a healthy surplus to the burgesses, thus ensuring that they would defend the arrangement against predatory governments in times to come.

Derby School

Mary further provided that the bailiffs and burgesses establish a free Grammar School to be staffed by a master and usher (or under-master) at a cost of £13 16s 8d (£13.83) per annum to be paid quarterly. It is by no means certain whether the school was immediately founded, granted the upheavals of the following few years, and, if so, whether the same fabric that survives today is the original. Strangely, Mary's 1555 charter was

Three carved oak wainscot panels from Babington Hall, where Mary, Queen of Scots, stayed in 1585. (Derbyshire Archaeological Society)

not enrolled until 1603, which may imply (as Glover plainly believed) that the entire matter did not become operative until that date. However, the procession of vicars at St Alkmund's and All Saints' during Elizabeth's reign suggests that it was and that the enrollment of 1603 was perhaps a confirmatory instrument.

Further, there seems no reason why Mary, with most of her reign before her, should not, having received the burgesses' fine, have caused it to be made immediately effective. Thus, in all probability, the school's foundation is datable to the mid-16th century. The surviving building in St Peter's Churchyard is, however, later, and an architectural assessment has established that it dates largely from the beginning of the 17th century. It served as the school house until 1861, more than three centuries.

Under masters like Anthony Blackwall (1674–1730) and Revd Thomas Manlove (1730–1802), the school's reputation soared and the scions of county families paid to attend, rubbing shoulders with the sons of burgesses and freemen, attending free of charge under the terms of the endowment. Unfortunately, a decline set in towards the end of the 18th century and in the early 19th.

This may partly be laid at the feet of the rise of the Public School, especially nearby ones like Repton, and partly the indifference of the burgesses, who allowed the post of usher to lapse in 1813 after headmaster Revd James Bligh had let the roll fall too low to justify the appointment. This continued, indeed, and by 1830 only William Hope, future vicar of St Peter's and father of the antiquary Sir W.H. St John Hope, remained a pupil. In the 41 years of Bligh's headmastership he only ever had 36 pupils!

Another factor was the desire among Derby's *elite*, stimulated by the advanced educational ideas of Erasmus Darwin, to give their children a scientific strand to their education, which a grammar school, with its traditional curriculum, could not provide. By the beginning of the 19th century there were numerous private academies, some very good, sending boys to Repton and other nearby schools. The passing of the Municipal Corporations Act in 1835 enabled the school to be wrested from the curmudgeonly grasp of the city fathers of the day and vested in trustees – but only for 70 years.

Joan Wast, Protestant 'martyr'

On the debit side, Mary's reign saw the execution, on grounds of religion, of Derby's celebrated 'martyr' Joan Wast, by burning. As this appears to have been the only instance of an adherent of the sort of Protestantism advocated under the reign of Edward VI being executed in Derby (unlike some other centres), her case has

become famous. Doubly so, insofar as Joan was handicapped by blindness.

She was the elder daughter of William Wast, the final '-e' of whose name was only of intermittent Elizabethan usage, although the name would perhaps more correctly modernise as 'West'. He was a barber and ropemaker of All Saints' and himself a younger brother of Thomas Wast, an opulent tradesman,

Joan was born blind in 1532 and, as so often with handicapped people, reached maturity and found in the church a 'very present help in time of trouble'. This introduction to the hope which the church can bring took place under Edward VI, reinforced by the vernacular Bible and prayer book. When Queen Mary caused the re-adoption of Catholic rites, Joan must have been hit hard, much in the same way as Church of England members have been affected in recent years by the unilateral imposition of new liturgies, by the rush to ordain female priests and by the calling into question of traditional beliefs.

She adopted a conservative and vocal stance, especially over the doctrine of the transubstantiation, and being blind was in some ways insensitive to the advantages of tact. Eventually, she was arrested on the orders of the Diocesan Bishop by the reluctant bailiffs Richard Moore and William Bainbrigge, being brought before the Bishop and her chief accuser, a hard-line Catholic, Dr Anthony Draycot, the Diocesan Chancellor. A stubbornness born out of a belief in her own rectitude, combined with the ruthless determination of Draycot not to allow his bishop to temporise with her, led to her condemnation and a writ of *De Haeretico Comburendo* was delivered. On 1 August 1555 the unfortunate girl was made to listen to a vituperative and unforgiving sermon from Draycot before being taken to Windmill Pit, on the north side of Mill Hill Lane, and burned. She is said to have died with considerable dignity.

Joan Wast is led to the place of her execution, Windmill Pit, in 1555. (Derby Local Studies Library)

RELIGIOUS TROUBLES

Despite all the fuss made about Joan's death, it made only fleeting impact. The accession of Elizabeth removed the dilemma for the Protestants but ultimately redirected the vengefulness of the government to the Catholic recusants.

At first, several local priests refused to sign the Acceptance of the Act of Uniformity and acknowledge the Queen as Head of the Church. One senior prelate was dispossessed, the vicar of St Peter's signed and the remainder fudged and stayed on. In the town itself, what recusancy there was quickly declined, although in parts of the county, grouped around the seats of loyal Catholic families – the Powtrells at West Hallam, the Beaumonts at Barrow, the Eyres at Hassop or the FitzHerberts at Norbury and Padley – it flourished. Indeed, John and Richard Fitzherbert were in Derby Gaol in August 1590 expecting to be 'sent up to London', although John died later of gaol fever. Their cousin Anthony, of Padley, was languishing there with 36 other Catholics the following May, asking for intercession from the Privy Council and dangling the prospect of recanting; in the event he too died of gaol fever. The returns in the 18th century consistently showed no Roman Catholics at all in Derby, yet some survived covertly, it is plain, for a congregation existed later and was allowed to flourish from the early years of the 19th century. It cannot have consisted entirely of Irish migrants and Italian weatherglass makers!

As a macabre counterpoise to the futility of Joan Wast's death, three men, one a member of a local gentry family, all Catholic priests, were executed for their faith at Derby. Nicholas Garlick, a Glossop man of good family, and Robert Ludlam were arrested hiding in a priests' hole in the FitzHerbert seat at Padley, now largely destroyed. Richard Simpson *alias* Gayle was apprehended elsewhere. They were held along with Edward Bagshawe of Wheston-in-Peak and two other priests, associates of Simpson. On 25 July 1588 Garlick, Ludlam and Simpson were hung, drawn and quartered, their remains being displayed on the town side of St Mary's Bridge – itself only just repaired after having been partly destroyed in a flood, along with the adjacent corn mills, the years before – as an awful warning and deterrent.

The savagery of their sentences and the ferocity with which they were pursued was a combination of hysteria stemming from the exposure of Babington's Plot which had the aim of replacing Queen Elizabeth with Mary, Queen of Scots, less than two years earlier. Anthony Babington, whose seat was at Dethick and whose town house stood on the north-west corner of Babington Lane and St Peter's Street, was decapitated only and was spared the other gory indignities – as was the less gruesome lot of a gentleman, even one convicted of treason. A contributory factor was also the jumpiness of Lord Shrewsbury – the Scottish queen's gaoler until her execution and Lieutenant for the county, of which he was at this time far and away the paramount landowner – and the unsettling reality of the Spanish Armada. Indeed, with reference to Babington, some of whose co-conspirators were local gentlemen, it is ironic to note that on 13 January 1585 Sir Ralph Sadlier was obliged to lodge Mary, Queen of Scots, in the future traitor's town house in Derby *en route* to Tutbury. The building, about which we know all too little, save that it was large and probably of late-15th century, was by that time sold by Babington to Henry Beaumont (d.1584), whose sister acted as the queen's hostess. The building was swept away in about 1811.

PUBLIC LIFE

The prison in which FitzHerbert and the others were held would have been the county one; that in which Joan Wast persuaded fellow convicts to read the Bible to her was that of the borough, beneath the Guildhall. The former lay by the Jail Brook *(sic)* adjacent to St Peter's Bridge and across the south end of Cornmarket. It was undoubtedly erected under legislation passed in 1531, prisoners convicted under the jurisdiction of the Sheriff having previously been lodged at Nottingham. This horrible establishment of brick and stone probably somewhat resembled Whitehall's Holbein Gate in London, with slim octagonal turrets and narrow mullioned windows. Because it formed a barrier across the end of Cornmarket, the Tudor arch giving access through it from St Peter's Bridge to Cornmarket acted as a sort of grand, if rather grim, gateway into the heart of the town.

In 1730 an extension was added to it to accommodate borough prisoners, due to the demolition of the old Guildhall, and it survived until 1756, when it was replaced. Hutton tells us that this gaol was so close to the Brook ('in' it, in his words) that the convicts were exposed to the sight of passers-by going under the gatehouse and over the bridge to St Peter's Street and that their health was threatened by damp and sewage from the brook, which itself, when in flood, might rise and threaten their very lives, as with three unfortunate felons in 1610. Hence the deaths of Anthony FitzHerbert and, another recusant, Humphrey Beresford of Newton Grange of gaol fever there in 1588 come as no surprise.

Executions were probably held in the gaol courtyard, but corpses were gibbeted – hung up to decay as a grim warning – in a boundary bank separating Derby from Litchurch called Gallows Baulk just south of Love Lane

Liversage Charity almhouses, London Road, 1998, designed by John Mason and built in 1836. (M. Craven)

(later Melbourne Street). It was levelled around 1880 to pitch Hartington Street. Another may have been on the Normanton boundary, where later lay Gallows Field, a close on which bookdealer John Lowe, heir of the Oakley family, pitched Vale Street and built three houses.

The town bell at the Guildhall was rung for curfew and at times of crisis to call forth the muster – emergency manpower summoned under an act called the Assize of Arms, the first in Derby being in 1539 – as at the time of the Armada in 1588 and also during 'a great Fray' between the supporters of 'Mr Vernon and Mr Longford's men' – another outbreak of upper-class sponsored yobbery between the partisans of uneasy neighbours, the squires of Sudbury and Longford. Nor was this an isolated incident, for the town annals refer to this bell being tolled at other times when squads of men led by members of the local gentry threatened to start fighting in the town, as on 1 March 1577 when Sir John Zouche of Codnor and Sir Thomas Stanhope of Elvaston (grandfather of the 1st Earl of Chesterfield) had to be restrained by the townsmen after a lengthy and unpleasant stand-off, and again in 1610 in a dispute over an election, the protagonists being Sir Philip Stanhope (son of the previous miscreant) and George Gresley of Drakelow, who was nevertheless elevated to a baronetcy within 12 months. What occasioned these petty local lawless outbursts led by men such as Stanhope, who had

been high sheriff of the county, were long-standing rivalries and resentments which almost always had an economic grievance behind them, often long running, although Stanhope was known as a law unto himself, as an attack on Sir Charles Cavendish by his men at Kirkby in Ashfield on 11 November 1599 rather emphasises.

Skirmishes in the town among Elizabethan Sloane Rangers were not the only misfortunes suffered by the townsfolk in this period. Two outbreaks of plague are recorded, a relatively minor outbreak in St Peter's Parish in 1586 and in 1593 a very serious visitation centred on All Saints' parish, which carried off nearly 250 souls. All Saints' was the parish wherein lived and functioned the majority of well-to-do tradesmen of the town, and this outbreak hardly left a family untouched; some like the Sowters – who lost husband, mother-in-law, wife and all three children – were destroyed.

PHILANTHROPY

The prosperity of the town in the Tudor age, however, continued to grow. There were dynasties of people following *elite* trades, like the Firebrace family from the Trent valley, who established themselves as pewterers, a younger branch establishing themselves in London, where later they earned a Baronetcy and one of them headed a plot to try and 'spring' Charles I from captivity in Carisbrooke Castle in 1648.

Most of the older histories of the town give exhaustive lists of local charities. Their chief value, however, is as a barometer of need and affluence. In the 16th century the population was such that provision of care for poor people and unsupported widows became a matter of urgency, especially as the monasteries upon which that role had previously fallen were by this time but a memory. At the same time, the increase in charitable legacies reflected the continuing increase in local affluence. Notable among these were two men of a new breed, Liversage and Crowshawe.

Robert Liversage was a wealthy dyer, a trade enjoying a 10-mile local monopoly since the charter of 1204 and one integral with the wool trade. He had been bailiff of the borough in 1515 and 1524 (and quite possibly earlier too, bearing in mind the thin record before 1513). Like many such donors, Liversage and his wife were childless, and in 1529 they left most of their considerable property in trust, including their residence, said to have stood on a site in the Corn Market – Albert Street corner where H. Samuel now stands; their original well is said to be still visible in the much earlier cellars. This trust was dedicated to the housing of 13 poor people of St Peter's parish. Liversage had also added a chantry to the church and appointed a priest. This, of course, was dissolved at the Reformation, like the other chantries within existing churches, as at St Peter's, St Werburgh's and All Saints'. An old supposition that the first almshouses stood in Walker Lane and consisted of five brick houses of a single storey and attics which declined into a lodging house by 1861 is contradicted by the evidence. If this was an almshouse at all, it may have been the last vestige of the undocumented Greycoat Hospital, recorded by all early historians of the town. This may, of course, be related to the contemporary legacy of sub-dean Johnson of All Saints' (whose wooden memorial image survives to this day in the church), who in his will of July 1526 left his house in the parish to be an almshouse 'for evermore'.

But Liversage's charity was extensive and was cannily added to over the years. Today, its trustees own more real estate in the town than anybody except the city council. A row of almshouses erected after Liversage's death in 1529 in St Peter's Churchyard to house all 13 beneficiaries of his trust lasted until 1722, when they were replaced. The annual income from the augmented Liversage estate was £590 8s 4d (£590.42) in 1833. We have, unfortunately, no illustration of either the first or second set of almshouses, but in 1836 Derby architect John Mason designed a new set of 21 almshouses with hospital and chapel on London Road on land purchased from the Castlefields Estate, which happily survive. New blocks of

Wilmot's 17th-century almshouses – the Black Hospital – in Bridge Gate, photographed in 1926. They were demolished in 1934 and replaced by municipal housing. Now all have vanished under the Inner Ring Road, St Alkmund's Way. (*Derby Evening Telegraph*)

housing have been developed by the Trustees, and the Trust has been an avatar of the local housing associations which have followed in their wake since the 1970s.

Richard Crowshawe (1561–1631) was, like Liversage, a self-made man, son of a blacksmith, a tenant of the Mundys at Markeaton. He became a citizen and goldsmith of London and provides an interesting contrast to William Shore. The latter was well-connected both in Derby and London and had at least three generations of prosperous tradesmen in Derby behind him. His rise to great wealth was, consequently, no great surprise. Yet Crowshawe's was exceptional. Although his monument at All Saints' displays a coat of arms, it seems that it was borne without authority; it is differenced by a crescent, suggesting (as he no doubt intended) that he was the second son of a gentleman. That he was a second son, however, we can accept. Of the details of his kin in his will it is plain that he had built up no powerful or extensive connections, despite the accumulation of considerable riches, yet his estate yielded nearly £5,000 at his death without issue. Much of this was left to benefit the poor of All Saints' to be paid out of an estate he had purchased from the Foljambes at the Rowditch.

A less curmudgeonly attitude was displayed by the members of the nobility and gentry who gave legacies to the Derby poor. Robert Wilmot of Chaddesden, who instituted the so-called Black Hospital on the north side of Bridge Gate in 1638, was by no means childless. The 10 poor people of St Alkmund's parish (six men, four women) wore the Wilmot livery of *sable*, trimmed *argent* (black trimmed white) which derived from Wilmot's newly-granted coat of arms, hence the colloquial name of the institution: the Black Hospital.

Bess of Hardwick's almshouses, as rebuilt by Joseph Pickford as the Devonshire Hospital in 1777. (Derby Museum)

Wilmot's grandfather was a rich Derby clothier who purchased some of the Abbey of Dale's estates in Spondon in 1539, and Robert acquired an estate at Chaddesden, building the first hall there, entering the ranks of the gentry. The buildings were swept away in 1934 and replaced by municipal housing, while the same donor's virtually identical almshouses in Chaddesden lasted until 1961.

Tomb in Derby Cathedral of Elizabeth, Countess of Shrewsbury (Bess of Hardwick), designed by her architect Robert Smythson and made, like her local benefaction, the Devonshire Hospital, prior to her death. (*Derby Evening Telegraph*)

A generation before, the flamboyant and aggressively upwardly mobile Elizabeth, Countess of Shrewsbury, had likewise instituted a hospital, or almshouses, in All Saints' parish in 1599 for eight men and four women. Like Wilmot, Bess of Hardwick's almshouses, actually erected in stone in the first decade of the next century, gave preponderance to men over women (a ratio of eight to four). She also made distributory provision to 50 other poor people of the parish, too. The original almshouses themselves survived until 1777, when they were replaced by the Duke of Devonshire to an elegant neo-Palladian design by the very capable Derby architect Joseph Pickford. The hospital was closed in 1893 and sold at auction in the September to the Corporation for £1,622 5s 0d to expand the borough's new electricity power station in 1894.

In 1716 Alderman Edward Large died, leaving money to build a pedimented row of very handsome almshouses for the widows of poor clergymen in Friar Gate, replaced by much more spacious – albeit far less architecturally accomplished – ones in 1880, now converted to offices.

Trade & Wealth

If the charitable foundations of the borough reflected an ever-increasing prosperity among its merchants, that prosperity represented a wider wealth. Yet a glance at the heralds' *Visitations of Derbyshire* of 1569, 1611, 1634 and 1662 indicates that the number of families of gentry status was rapidly growing. These held estates and traded their produce in the town, whether they were the Beards of Beard near New Mills, the Brownes down in Stretton-en-le-Field or living nearby, like the Wilmots, the Mundys or the Harpurs. Those seated further away now more and more maintained town houses to enable them to remain in Derby when necessary. These occasions included sitting on the magistrates' bench, years in which these men held the High Shrievalty and when supervising the disposal of their produce. In the 16th and 17th centuries no Derby gentleman despised trade (truth to tell, few did in private in any age) and many lesser families apprenticed younger sons in Derby. Further, increasing expectations, especially among their ladies, caused them to increase their standard of living and buy more luxury goods.

These gentry families were nearly all prosperous enough in this period to build new country seats. Some, like the Mundys' at Markeaton, (the estate purchased from the Touchets in 1516), or Harpurs' at Swarkestone, were very grand. Others like the Blounts' at Arleston, Milwards' at Eaton Dovedale or Alleynes' at Gresley were more modest. In either case they needed costly furnishings and fittings along with fine clothes, plate and utensils. All these needs were met in Derby by Derby tradesmen. The sheer range of trades in the town at that time amply reflects this, quite apart from those activities which had been staple to the town's economy since the 15th century and before, like the wool trade, the lead trade, dyeing, malting, brewing and glovemaking.

Simpler demands were met by those who sold foodstuffs, the butchers being among the most prosperous, especially those, like William Franceys, who in 1582 had some grazing land at Markeaton and rented a stall in the Shambles or Butchery at 8s (20p) for a 21-year lease. His descendant John was paying exactly the same rent in 1655 for a lease of 17 years and one of his sons (who had two other shops) renewed the lease, the buildings having been elegantly replaced, in 1708. John Franceys's fortune enabled him to build a grand house in the Market Place in the 1640s, and his descendants became rich and fashionable apothecaries, the first of whom, William, being able to afford to turn the family home into a veritable palace, in the latest architectural style in 1695, complete with frescoed ceilings. Here his son, Alderman Henry Franceys, is recorded as having thrown parties for his Whig friends at the high steward's expense.

A final, enigmatic, calling may have had a foothold in Derby: bell founding. An archaeological investigation of part of the site just east of the former church of St Alkmund, which survived as a sort of island amid the confusion of roads put in place as part of the Inner Ring Road works of 1966–68, uncovered a triangular building, the site of what may have been a crane or derrick, and a series of mysterious pits which the excavator considered might have constituted a bell foundry. The only problem is that no bell founder has ever been identified on the record in Derby, nor is any bell known to be from the borough – they were almost invariably 'signed' with a foundry mark, heraldic symbol or monogram. In fact, from the later mediaeval period to the later 17th century, Chesterfield was a nationally famous centre for bell founding, mainly under the Heathcote family who went on to become fabulously rich London merchants, being rewarded with honours, including the Earldom of Ancaster.

This would have left little room for a contemporary Derby bell founder anyway, although research is hampered by the lack of precise dating for the pits themselves. The answer may be that it was the works of a brazier who made large-sized bell-metal mortars (but not bells as such) for the local apothecary trade; Derby Museum, for instance, has two large late Tudor/early Stuart examples in its collections, both unmarked, but one provenanced to early 18th-century apothecary Alderman Henry Franceys himself.

Vestiges of Tudor Derby: the rear of 11 Friar Gate, showing earlier work. (M. Craven)

DERBY BUILDINGS

Indeed, the increasing prosperity and presence of the gentry in the town from this period may go some way to explain why they almost entirely supplanted the municipal trading families as representatives for the borough from the last decade of the 16th century. Thus, even the grandest of the Derbyshire nobles were building town houses. The opulent Leighs of Egginton had one on the east side of the Market Place, and by the 1630s the Cavendishes of Bolsover (as Earls and later Dukes of Newcastle) had a fine house on its north side. As this was demolished without a proper survey in 1971, it is difficult to be sure, but it may have had 16th-century origins, owing its existence perhaps to Bess of Hardwick's husband George, 5th Earl of Shrewsbury, who was quite often obliged to stay overnight in Derby. Her second son, Sir William Cavendish's family – those of Chatsworth – swiftly established themselves as high stewards of the borough, imposing on them an additional need to be in the town on occasion. We know they had a new house in Cornmarket from 1750 (only part of which evaded destruction in 1969), and an examination of the building shows it to have been a refronting of an earlier structure, which may date from this period.

The Friary, acquired by Abraham Crompton in 1712 and built by Samuel Crompton in 1731. (M. Craven)

Most houses in the town in the 16th century were built on the narrow burgage plots established at the time of the Saxon *burh* in the 10th century, and, as John Speed's map of the town (1610) so aptly shows, were built gable-end-on to the thoroughfare in order to conform to this ancient restriction. A classic example of a merchant's house of 15th-century date was unexpectedly revealed by the demolition in 1971 of Newcastle House, where it had probably been retained when the earl or one of his ancestors had purchased three adjacent burgage plots in order to present a show-front to the road as additional accommodation.

Indeed, a remarkably large number of Elizabethan and Jacobean buildings survive in Derby, although most were refronted in the 18th or 19th centuries. Many of these line both sides of Sadler Gate and others can be seen in the eastern part of Friar Gate; until fairly recently,

too, examples also lurked in Full Street, Market Place, St Peter's Street and East Street, but the majority have been swept away since the war. Anyone going around to the rear of shops in some of these streets, but most notably Sadler Gate – for instance via Old Blacksmith's Yard – will be able to see the narrow brick buildings with their steep straight gables and uneven roof lines.

Rich townsmen were also building grand houses, with show fronts extending over two or more burgage plots. A fine surviving example is that erected possibly in 1611 in the Wardwick and now called Jacobean House. It was later much rebuilt as a town house for the Gisbornes, former tenants of the Cavendishes, who rapidly took their place in the ranks of the gentry.

In 1626 Henry Mellor, later Derby's first mayor, erected an imposing mansion opposite Babington Hall on The Spot. This, incidentally, was a road junction, which was only created by the turnpiking of the new London Road in the earlier 18th century; its odd name is first recorded in August 1741 as 'The Spot in Derby', advertising Abraham Ward's chandlery there. In 1670 the hearth tax returns make clear that Mellor's was the biggest single residence in Derby, his successors paying tax on 18 hearths, making the house exactly comparable in size to Tissington or Norbury Hall. A 19th-century owner renamed it Babington House after the street which marked the northern edge of its modest park, but it was pulled down in 1897 to build shops, now Waterstone's.

A very large timber-framed house was built on the site of the Friary in about 1560 by William Bainbrigge, thrice bailiff of the town and twice MP for the borough; the hearth tax reveals it as half the size of Mellor's house, although it was probably nearly comparable in size but, being much earlier, had fewer heated rooms. This survived, divided as tenements, until 1760. Full Street, too, was becoming fashionable at this time, housing rich merchants like the Fletchers (glovers), the Mores (merchants), the Suttons (braziers) and the Allestreys at the college (where they were taxed on 13 hearths in 1670), where the canons of All Saints' had once lived. The Babingtons, Poles of Radbourne and the Sacheverells of Morley among the county gentry, also had houses there at this time. Thus the burgeoning opulence of the local gentry was increasingly being reflected in a grander style of building in the town, and the profits from meeting their needs was in turn being shown in the increasing opulence of the residences of the tradesmen who so readily responded to them.

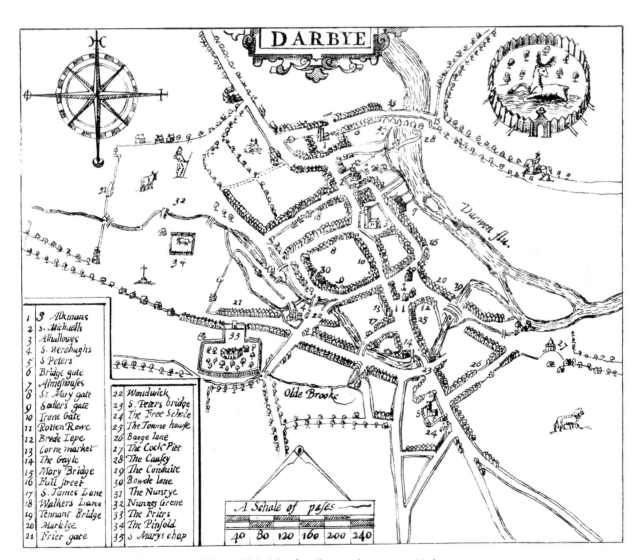

Speed's map of Derby, 1610. Recent research has established that Speed's town plans are surprisingly accurate.

St Werburgh's Church as rebuilt in 1694–99. The tower dates from 1610. A Richard Keene view from the 1870s. (M. Craven)

V

TROUBLED TIMES

GATHERING CLOUDS

The first year of the 17th century was marked by the sudden collapse of the 'steeple' of St Werburgh's Church, on 2 January 1601, an event which rather set a trend for the future. In Derby only the Church of St Peter retains mediaeval fabric, much renewed at that, and much of the need for replacement was generated by the willingness of the citizens of the town to allow such fabric to collapse. Even when, as with Dr Hutchinson at All Saints' in the 18th century, someone proposed remedial action, little or nothing was done. Consequently, St Werburgh's suffered collapses which accounted for all its mediaeval fabric in 1601 and again on 5 November 1698 when the remainder fell

down; similarly, St Michael's failed in a struggle against neglect after Sunday service on 17 August 1856.

As an event heralding a century in which another two plagues broke out, two destructive fires ravaged the town (in 1650 and 1675) and in which a civil war occurred – destructive of lives, trade and relationships – the collapse of St Werburgh's spire is supremely apt. The fact that the remainder of this church so tactlessly contrived to slide into the neighbouring brook within 18 months of the end of the same century, provides a telling coda to an era which, more than any, marked a watershed in the town's history.

Of course, the immediate cause of the fall of St Werburgh's tower was flooding of the Markeaton Brook, and it was not until works carried out in the aftermath of the flood of Sunday 22 May 1932 that this periodic

66

St Werburgh's Church. The Baroque interior shortly before demolition, photographed by Richard Keene in October 1892. (Derby Local Studies Library/Don Farnsworth)

scourge of the lower-lying parts of the borough was finally cured. A new tower, rather than a spire, which survives, is notable for the extreme conservatism of its still Gothic design; it was completed in 1608.

If the collapse of St Werburgh's spire foretold of disasters, they were not long in coming. The so-called 11 years' tyranny of Charles I saw the opening of the final act of the tragedy that was later Tudor and Stuart politics and, in 1635, Derby and Derbyshire were for the first time assessed for the unpopular levy known as Ship Money. Derbyshire, of course, was one of those places, far removed from any coast, where this imposition was, as a consequence, doubly unpopular. Derby was expected to contribute £175, the whole county £3,500. Even gathering the tax must have been unpopular, for it earned those in Derbyshire who bore this responsibility extravagant rewards: pensions, preferment and even including the odd baronetcy, among them the High Sheriffs and brothers-in-law Sir John Gell of Hopton and Sir John Curzon of Kedleston. Nevertheless, Curzon's churlish behaviour towards the widowed Lady Stanhope of Elvaston over this tax hardly suggests a lack of zeal on his part, although it might be argued that Sir John was suffering from operational frustration rather than a bout of fanaticism. The fact that the pair later married (on 25 December 1648) seems all the more unlikely given the acrimoniousness of their encounter over Ship Money.

A New Town Charter

The *burghers* of Derby, however, could perceive other advantages in the king's penuriousness. Their desire was to extend their own power and to increase the prosperity of their town. The king's desire was to accrue income from whatever quarter. They each seized an opportunity in 1636 when the king was staying in Derby, *en route* from treating with the Scots at Ripon, at the town house of the Earl of Newcastle, to dine with him. They ate in the first floor 'Great Room on the Market Place'. The Earl acted as host, but the burgesses footed the bill. The occasion led to the king granting the borough a new charter the following year in exchange for a fee: thus both parties were satisfied.

The most important provision of the new charter was that the two annually-elected bailiffs be abolished to be replaced by one mayor. That the burgesses could afford the fine payable in exchange for the new charter vouched for the opinion of Sir John Gell to the Ship Money Commissioners that 'there be many rich burgesses in that Town'. The first mayor under the new charter was Henry Mellor, of the fine Jacobean mansion on the corner of St Peter's Street and Babington Lane. He also achieved the distinction of being the first mayor to die in office. Unfortunately, we know nothing of his character and so cannot be sure whether 'Lines to Mr Henry Mellor for first Mayor of Derby' by locally-born poet Thomas Bancroft reflect that worthy's character or only whatever lustre reflected upon him by virtue of his pioneering office! For the record, the lines went:

'You see me the prime bough of an apple tree,
Whereon if faire expected fruits we see
Whilest others' fames with ranke approaches meete
As mel or manna shall your name be sweete.'

Nevertheless, the charter, only slightly modified by one granted 45 years later, provided the structure for the governance of the borough for the following two centuries. The mayor, who paid the Crown £70 per annum for the privilege of receiving tolls, was responsible to the high steward, the king's representative, – from 1611 to 1974 invariably the head of the Cavendish family – for the good ordering of the borough, supported by nine aldermen who chose the mayor from their number. The two most senior, the mayor himself and the most recent ex-mayor, were also *ex-officio* Justices of the Peace (JPs). Below them were 14 Brethren of the Corporation, from whose ranks the numbers of aldermen were replenished as vacancies arose. There were also 14 capital burgesses, who with four chamberlains – effectively acting treasurers – and six constables (the mayor's halberd-armed escorts), made up the common council, which was responsible for the recorder (legal officer), the town – or common clerk – the serjeant-at-mace and three liverymen of the mayor. The council could also bestow burgess-ships or disenfranchise wayward burgesses or freemen. There was also an open-ended number of ordinary burgesses who

White-painted Newcastle House, left centre, quite possibly originally built for Bess of Hardwick or her fourth husband Lord Shrewsbury, where the Earl of Newcastle entertained the king in 1636 at the expense of the Corporation. (*Derby Evening Telegraph*)

paid no tolls on goods and were free to ply their trades within the borough. Their number stood at 700 in 1712 but had doubled by 1782. Their sons and passed apprentices were also freemen enjoying similar privileges. Between 1611 and 1637 when there were two bailiffs, there were just 24 burgesses, a chamberlain, recorder and common clerk.

With the drift to civil war becoming daily the more apparent, the burgesses, alarmed at the prospect – especially insofar as it was likely to adversely affect their trade – petitioned king and Parliament to resolve their differences. The tone of these petitions suggest that the Derby burghers inclined to Parliament, although there is little corroborative evidence of this in the town's annals, events after the conflict showing the town leaning in favour of the Court, being thoroughly Tory at heart, right up until the start of the Industrial Revolution in the third quarter of the 18th century. Perhaps this was a reaction to the traumatic events of 1642–46.

CIVIL WAR

War having finally become unavoidable, the king passed through Derby on 12 August 1642 to raise his standard at Nottingham, being joined there by a paltry 20 Derbeians. *En route* back again, the king asked the burgesses for a loan to further his cause but obtained the

ungenerous sum of £300 plus some small arms before moving on. His departure left a vacuum in both town and county. Derby had no defences, so was of dubious value as a garrison, and the county gentry, in general a closely-knit group, were reluctant to throw in their hand with either side until pressed to do so. Only a few had declared themselves and, as a consequence, had been forced to leave their estates to follow the flag – or go into exile.

The vacuum was filled by Sir John Gell, recently elevated to his baronetcy, who entered Derby with a detachment of the Earl of Essex's troops on 31 October 1642. Gell appointed a committee to run the borough and to aid him, referred to by a contemporary as 'an incestuous bodye of men' because all except one were related to Gell: the odd one out was his hatchet-man, Derby Alderman Nathaniel Hallowes, a wealthy wool merchant. Gell also raised his own regiment of foot around the core of men Essex had given him, relying on his own tenants and those of his officers. Among the latter was Henry Mellor of Alton, a Derby mercer and a nephew of the town's recently deceased first mayor. He headed a company of Derby men.

With this regiment, Gell garrisoned the town for some four years, despite the fact that, for some of that time, Derby was a Parliamentary island in a Royalist sea. Sir John was declared governor and his administration at first replaced the normal functioning of the borough's officers and officials – some of whom, like the recorder, William Allestrey, were in any case active (and absent) Royalists – who were effectively at his beck and call. To cope with the administration of the town, the collection of taxes and the redeployment of the monies so acquired to the purpose of the payment and provisioning of his troops, Gell appointed a committee. This, too, was composed of his supporters and included not one townsman of Derby, undoubtedly a reflection of the uncertainty he felt about their loyalty. The burghers may well have been sympathetic to Parliament earlier in the year but by the end of 1642 may well have felt that being taken over by Gell and his rude soldiery was too high a price to pay.

While in Derby, Gell lived in the new family town house, 16 Friar Gate, with his brother, Thomas. Whether he built it then or had done so in the preceding decade when he was collecting Ship Money, is not clear, but it remained in his family until the 1860s, suffering little outward alteration. Today it is the most impressive and complete large Jacobean mansion in the city.

THE OCCUPIERS IN DISARRAY

Gell's committee was widely criticised, even by his supporters, for the arbitrary way it was used and by the lack of records kept of its proceedings, despite the considerable sums of money which passed through its hands, including, as the county increasingly fell into Gell's hands at the expense of the Royalist party, the incomes of seized Royalist estates. Furthermore, once the initial threat of Royalist counter-attack had receded, a party of opposition arose. Headed by the extremist and rabid republican Major Thomas Sanders of Caldwell Hall and Little Ireton, this faction included several wealthy burgesses (representatives of the thwarted townsmen), among whom were Robert Mellor (son of the first mayor), Robert Cotchett of Mickleover and the mercer Gervase Bennet. After a series of highly-acrimonious actions, the Earl of Essex, fearing for the stability and security of Derby as a lynchpin of his strategy in the Midlands, was forced to intervene and obliged Gell to include Bennet, Mellor and Sanders in

The Bull's Head Inn, Queen Street, allegedly founded by Alderman Henry Mellor, whose crest constituted its sign, c.1912. It was demolished in 1941. (Derby Museum)

his committee. Also, after about 1645 the committee was obliged by Parliament to regularise its proceedings, and it was also enlarged, thus securely clipping the irascible and unpredictable governor's wings. Gell, for his part, had declared that he would rather fight with Major Sanders than with 'any Cavalier in England' and that he would 'have his pennyworth out of him'.

Trouble also broke out with a portion of the Presbyterian Scots army quartered in Derbyshire, an anti-Gell faction cutting off supplies to the occupiers (despite their common cause against the king) and again firing Gell's wrath to such an extent that he sent the unfortunate ringleader of the trouble, Ralph Clarke (a Chesterfield lead merchant), into the Scots camp where he was very roughly handled indeed.

At this time, too, an election was called to replace the borough's representative in the Long Parliament, Royalist recorder William Allestrey MP, who had defected to the king at Oxford. The other MP elected to the Long Parliament in November 1640 was Nathaniel Hallowes, a political ally of Gell and a notorious persecutor of citizens in Derby suspected to be disloyal to his master's cause. That Gell was not able to nominate a supporter to replace Allestrey is an indication of the extent to which, by this time, he had allowed his influence to slip as a result of the factioneering against him. Had the vacancy been filled two years earlier, of course, this would have been possible, but the matter had had to be postponed until Parliament's position had

Sir John Gell of Hopton, bt. (Derby Local Studies Library)

been secured militarily. Gell's eventual nominee was his brother, Major Thomas Gell, but Sanders, with support from the townsmen, put up Robert Mellor. An extremely dirty and acrimonious election followed, gerrymandering being a word wholly inadequate to describe the tricks played by both sides. After an appeal to the Committee of Privileges of the House of Commons, Major Gell was, however, declared elected.

The strength of feeling in the town was indeed such that it was a miracle that the Royalists did not re-take it, but theirs was a saga of missed opportunities in the area. True, an attempt was mounted on 19 November 1643, but the occasion was premature and the burgesses had little taste for a change of allegiances and drove the men of their own hereditary high steward – William Cavendish, 1st Earl of Newcastle – from the town once and for all.

Generally speaking, Royalist inertia allowed Gell to pick off their strongpoints piecemeal. Nevertheless, he suffered several alarms during 1643, which culminated in another very serious threat from Lord Newcastle's forces at the end of the year. This latter crisis caused defences to be thrown up and a constant watch to be mounted from the tower of All Saints' Church. Men from the villages round about were conscripted to aid in the construction of these works, so extensive were they. Even Gell's regiment suffered desertions at this time, as did the borough generally, from under-committed personnel.

Derby's defences

Derby's Civil War earthworks were considerable and well planned, and it is not without interest to speculate where Edward Lyons, Gell's engineer, had them placed, apart from adding bastions to the east side of St Mary's Bridge and replacing one arch with a drawbridge.

Gell had 28 pieces of ordnance mounted on hornworks – crescent-shaped bunkers – around the town. All roads in and out of Derby were also protected by iron-reinforced gates connected to each other by earth bulwarks. A mouchette-shaped mound which appears on the 1883, 50:1 mile, OS map in the grounds of the infirmary near the Osmaston Road has been suggested as a remnant of the castle outworks, or as a tumulus (bearing in mind another such discovered in the area in the early-19th century); it is still traceable by the tennis courts of the Derbyshire Royal Infirmary and much resembles the truncated remains of one of these hornworks. The earthworks mentioned by 19th century Derby historians Hutton, Simpson and Glover, running north–south on what is now the alignment of Albion Street, might also be from this period, although their positioning would be difficult to explain in such a context: they might well indeed have pertained to the shadowy castle.

Today, determining the whereabouts of Lyon's remaining hornworks would seem an impossible task. Finds of ball and shot from this period in the town continue to be reported and these may afford some clues. The existence in 1691 of a disused gunpowder mill on the Derwent, east of St Michael's Church, may also be a legacy of these precautions, too. A bill exists for the saltpetre used in its manufacture dated 24 July 1645.

THE FALL OF GELL

Despite all these precautions, the Royalist threat never materialised. Further, as time went on, Gell committed sins of omission. By dallying, he avoided the Battle of Naseby (14 June 1645) and likewise later failed to apprehend the king as he fled from the battle towards Leicester. Cromwell was then reforming his forces into the New Model Army, and he took the opportunity to disband Gell's regiment. It is clear that, like several of the older generation of Parliamentary generals, Gell had no stomach for a fight to the bitter end. This, of course, left the field clear for the fanatics, who supported the tenor of Cromwell's reforms – men like Major Sanders and Robert Mellor – to consolidate their position in Derby. Gell lost his commission as Governor of Derby in September 1646 after nearly four years, and the control of the town reverted to the mayor and burgesses. It is significant that as Gell went to London to answer charges laid against him, many of them by his opponents in Derby, the garrison mutinied, due to lack of pay, another of the mercurial baronet's omissions and an echo of his gunners' plight: their pay had been cut earlier. Significantly, they were this time paid immediately.

Soon afterwards, the majority of armed men were withdrawn. Henceforth, Gell lived in London, increasingly shifting his position towards that of the Royalists, later serving three years in the Tower for his pains but being rewarded at the Restoration. Gell's superb multi-gabled brick house is the one tangible memorial to an intriguing and complex figure who loomed very large indeed in the life of Derby during the civil war.

THE COMMONWEALTH

The establishment of the Commonwealth gave the citizens of Derby an opportunity to return to a relatively normal life. Without periodic demands by the likes of

Gell for citizens' silver plate to melt down into coin to pay his garrison – £395.3.9d worth, for instance, had been collected by 10 November 1642 – or upheavals in the countryside wherein dwelt the bulk of the high-rolling custom of the Derby tradesmen, business began to return to normal. Gone now were the martial days when innocent people, like Catherine Gower, got caught in the crossfire of conflict: on 2 April 1644 this lady was 'killed with a pistoll bullett, shot through the head by a accedent'. True, draconian laws now existed against blasphemy, vulgar behaviour or such things as adultery: the incident in 1639 when 'William Yates farted as he passed by Mr Mayor and was imprisoned for it' was but a minor caution compared with the severe and unrelenting biblical approach to peoples' freedom after 1648.

This restriction also affected religion. The established church had been abolished along with its supreme head and the bishops and was replaced by a Presbyterian system, with individual ministers answerable to a panel of elected elders called a *classis*. In Derby at least one parish priest – Thomas Duxbury at St Michael's – adapted; the others were one by one ejected. Civil weddings superseded church ones in 1652 and tolerance diminished. It was, for instance, at this period that the founder of the Society of Friends, George Fox (1624–1691), came up before Maj. Sanders's radical *confrere*, the magistrate Gervase Bennet, 30 October 1650, charged with heterodox preaching:

'Justice Bennet of Derby', he wrote, 'was the first that called us Quakers, because I bid him *tremble at the word of the Lord…*'

A new Parliament was called and Gell's brother Thomas and the unsavoury Hallowes (also mayor in 1657) were replaced by two townsmen. One was none other than the ubiquitous Bennet; the other was John Dalton of The Friary (Mayor in 1646), later replaced by the obscure Robert Bainbrigge. Gell's son, John, and the uncompromising Major Thomas Sanders, sat for the county. However, the death of Cromwell and the accession to power of his amiable son, Richard, caused much unrest among those – undoubtedly the majority – who wanted to manipulate events in the direction of a restoration.

On 25 August 1659 one Colonel Charles White arrived in Derby from Nottingham and proclaimed the declaration of Sir George Booth, a Cheshire grandee opposed to the regime. This appears to have had an electrifying effect for 'all the town rose, shut up their shops, seased upon many of the militia horses with shouting'.

A local mercer, militia Captain Nathaniel Doughty, drew all these new zealots up on Nuns' Green and attempted to persuade Thomas Sanders to lead them. They should have known better, for the passage of time had left him no less dedicated to the cause Cromwell had made his own: he refused. They then committed a further serious error: they actually gave him a free conduct home to his estate at Little Ireton, by Kedleston. He, needless to say, once clear of the town, sent immediately to General Lambert (called in the relevant correspondence Lord Lambert on account of his elevation to Cromwell's Upper House the previous year) who dispatched a force towards Derby to deal with the uprising. However, they had got no nearer than Uttoxeter when word arrived from Sanders that Colonel Michel of Stubbing Edge had cowed the rebellious militia of Derby into submission. White was arrested and taken to London.

RESTORATION

The Restoration ushered in a new era of prosperity for Derby. Such was the era, indeed, that within 50 years prosperity had been instrumental in encouraging the first steps along the road to the industrialisation of the town. More immediate matters obtruded, however, and a period of adjustment ensued. Simple things which the burgesses had been unable to get done before had to be accomplished.

CIVIC REGALIA

So short, for instance, was the time between the institution of the first mayor under the 1637 charter and the suspension of civic business under Gell in 1642, that there were still two silver-gilt maces to carry before the former bailiffs on ceremonial occasions. Thus, in 1660, and therefore not in 1638 as the city council's publicity used to state, both were melted down and a single, somewhat grander one was fashioned from the metal, and this very important representative of the silversmith's art of the period is still carried before the city's mayor.

While the remainder of the city's civic regalia is more recent and mainly the gift of Sir Thomas William Evens, Bt, in 1870, the other major item is the mayor's chain of office. This is of conventional SS pattern which is first seen round the shoulders of knights on monuments dating from the 15th century. After the rise of the Tudors it came to be the preserve of the great officers of state and by the later 17th century was confined to the Chief Justice.

Derby's collar was reputedly made in 1798, thus for 1st Lord Kenyon, Chief Justice from 1788 to 1802. Like John Flamsteed's astronomical equipment in the Royal Observatory, it remained his property, not that of the

Sir John Gell's nemisis, the poisonous radical Col. Thomas Sanders of Cauldwell and Little Ireton. (M. Craven)

state, and seems to have passed successively to Lords Ellenborough, Tenterden and Denman, who followed him as Chief Justices of the Kings' Bench.

Thomas, 1st Lord Denman (1779–1854), was a local man who inherited the Stoney Middleton Hall estate. As the culmination of a distinguished parliamentary and legal career, he was appointed Chief Justice in 1832, and on his retirement in 1850 his successor, Lord Campbell, must have decided to commission a new chain, so Denman sold it to the Corporation who added a *repousse* gold pendant bearing the borough's badge. Since then it has always been worn by the mayor of Derby on a black velvet under-collar.

Further, the king was keen to honour those who had especially supported his and his late father's cause during the civil war and Commonwealth. His first idea was to institute an order of chivalry called the Order of the Royal Oak, named to commemorate the notable episode at Boscobel House in which the king narrowly escaped from capture after the Battle of Worcester in 1651. A list was drawn up of suitable candidates in each county. Meanwhile, people of grander status and of larger fortunes acquired baronetcies or peerages, the 'loyall' Earl of Newcastle, for instance, having been made a marquess in exile, was elevated to a dukedom for his colossal financial sacrifices in the royal cause, sufficient indeed to oblige him to let his large Derby town house on the north side of the Market Place, where the 1637 charter was bargained for to Sir John Shore.

The Royal Oak was to have been bestowed on

members of the lesser gentry, the Stuart dynasty being painfully aware that the award of great numbers of pensions for loyalty was beyond their pockets, while titles of honour cost them nothing and appealed more to men's vanity. Three Derby men (of eight for the whole county) were proposed as knights of the new order: Charles Agard of Mackworth, Nathaniel Bate of Little Chester and Simon Degge, the new recorder of the borough (replacing the Commonwealth appointee James Chadwick). In the end, however, the institution was laid aside on grounds of tact. Agard was later knighted, as was Degge, who amassed an enormous Derbyshire estate, fixing his town residence at Babington Hall.

The third adjustment was the ejection of ministers from the local churches who refused to conform to the restored Church of England and to the dignified, seemly, and clear Prayer Book which accompanied it (and which was so casually cast aside and turned out of the town's churches 320 years later). One often reads critical passages lamenting the cruel treatment meted out to these men, but it is important to remember that they themselves had mainly acquired their livings through the ejection of their Established Church – and Royalist – predecessors by the vengeful Commissioners of the Parliament. As so often in civil conflicts, what was sauce for the goose was sauce for the gander.

Of the five surviving parish churches, four of their ministers suffered ejection under the so-called Bartholomew's Act of 1662: Joseph Swettenham of All Saints', who had been rash enough to support Colonel White in 1659; Isaac Selden from St Michael's (although he clung on to St Alkmund's which he had held in plurality); Luke Canwell from St Peter's and Samuel Beresford from St Werburgh's. These gentlemen fade from the scene, yet ejection seems to have made the fortune of the families of four local ministers: John Crompton, Timothy Fox, John Bingham and John Hieron.

FOUR ENTREPRENEURS

John Crompton (1611–1669), a Lancastrian of gentle birth, was lecturer at All Saints' and installed in 1643 as rector of Brailsford to replace an ejected Anglican. A Royalist in many ways, he nevertheless refused to conform and was ejected in 1660 due to a local dispute and not as a result of the Act of Uniformity, then still 18 months off. His support of Colonel White did not help, either. He was then appointed vicar of Arnold, Nottinghamshire, from whence he was again ejected in 1662.

His son Abraham (d.1734) set up as a mercer in Derby, founding a banking business in the Market Place in 1685 to put his profits to good use. He purchased The Friary from the Daltons in 1712, which he replaced with the elegant surviving house, attributable to Richard Jackson of Armitage, Staffordshire, in 1730. His posterity went on to wealth, a grant of arms, considerable landed property and a baronetcy.

Timothy Fox (1628–1710) was rector of Drayton Basset in Staffordshire and, like Crompton, stemmed from the minor gentry, in his case, of Leicestershire and Warwickshire. Ejected in 1662, he became a farmer at Cauldwell, his fourth son, Samuel, being apprenticed to Gilbert Wagstaff of Derby, a woollen draper, whose daughter he later married and whose business and home (Thorntree House, St Peter's Street) he later inherited. The Fox family later branched out into soap boiling and also acquired a landed interest.

John Bingham (1607–1689) was Derby born, of a family of mercers. Despite losing a leg (which experience apparently turned his hair white), he took his degree, being appointed Master of Derby School in 1640 and, by the Earl of Devonshire, rector of Marston-on-Dove, where he decided to conform to the new order of things. Again, he was ejected in 1662, yet his son had become established as a mercer in Friar Gate, displacing the elder branch of his family who had practised that trade since at least the 16th century. Their descendants enjoyed prosperity and several mayoralties until moving from the town in the mid-19th century.

The final member of the quartet is Revd John Hieron (1608–1682), who was ejected from Breadsall, a village which lies only partly within the modern city of Derby, in 1662, at the same time as his nephew Samuel was ejected from the living of Shirley. John's descendants settled at Little Eaton in St Alkmund's parish, but outside the borough, as prosperous farmers and Derby tanners.

Branded Non-Conformists, the commercial success of this group of families stemmed from their being barred from access to official careers by newly-enacted penal legislation.

JOHN FLAMSTEED

One family badly incommoded by the vicissitudes of the civil war was the Flamsteeds of Little Hallam Hall. Minor gentry who came from Northamptonshire in the early 16th century, their estate was too small for them to eschew dirtying their hands with trade and, indeed, its chief asset was the coal beneath it. Stephen Flamsteed, a third son, settled in Derby, becoming a maltster, lead merchant and coal dealer. His wife, Mary Spateman, was the daughter of an alderman who fervidly supported Parliament in the civil war. As the Flamsteeds were

Revd John Flamsteed FRS (1646–1719), first Astronomer Royal.

the borough, but, in the event, better things beckoned. He met Sir Jonas Moore, Charles II's Master General of Ordnance, and Moore, much impressed by the young clergyman's talents, proposed him to the king as the first holder of the post of Astronomer Royal, created primarily to find a method to determine longitude. He was appointed on £100 per annum in 1675 and held the post, along with the sinecure of the living of Burstow, Surrey, until his death on the last day of 1719.

Flamsteed's great work was to map and publish an atlas of the heavens, which, despite an attempt by Sir Isaac Newton – whom he detested – to publish it prematurely, finally came out posthumously in 1735 as the *Atlas Coelestis*.

His wealthy father died in 1688, enabling him to spread his wings a little, and he found time, aided by an agent, to nurture the family coal and lead mines, and he stayed in the impressive Caroline-style house in Queen Street built by his father after the Restoration on his visits to Derby. This house was sold in 1745 by his nephew and heir and was later home to both John Whitehurst and the painter Joseph Wright, who died there in 1797.

Flamsteed was not only an important figure internationally, but he also presaged aspects of the work of John Whitehurst, and there is every reason to suspect that his legacy was kept alive locally by two *eleves* and transmitted via George Sorocold, whom we are soon to meet as the man who gave Derby a decent water supply and was, like Flamsteed, a competent surveyor and map maker.

otherwise related to several Royalist families, it was thought prudent, during the Gells' domination, to withdraw from Derby to a family property in Denby, a fine 16th-century house now called Crowtrees, and here John was born on 19 August 1646.

John's mother had died in 1649 and his father re-married Elizabeth, daughter of Royalist Nathaniel Bate of Little Chester, in 1652. Although a student of Derby School, ill health kept him at home, and he studied first astrology then astronomy, encouraged by two Derby-based friends of his father who were reasonably well versed in such things but, more important, were able to introduce him to Immanuel Halton of South Wingfield Manor, pioneer algebraist, sundial enthusiast and astronomer. John spent time devising and making precision instruments, like a 3ft quadrant, five barometers and an 'Improved sundial' developed from one made by Halton. He also published a set of solar tables and notes on *Some Eclipses of the Fixed Stars by the Moon* and compiled some equation of time tables which he published in 1673, by which time he had been able to gain a place at Jesus College, Cambridge, (receiving his degree and ordination in 1674) and an introduction to the Royal Society.

In 1673–74 Flamsteed also surveyed and took co-ordinates at Derby with a view to publishing a map of

The Hearth Tax

In order to replenish the depleted national fisc at the Restoration, a tax was imposed on the number of hearths in each house. Like all taxes, this was unpopular and similarly people tried to avoid paying it by bricking up hearths. Nevertheless, the Sheriff's returns during the first decade of the Restoration provide us with some interesting information.

Derby had 1,479 hearths taxable in 1662 (including a number exempt due to the poverty of those who inhabited the house in question), putting it on a par with Leicester, Northampton and Warwick in the 1,400–1,600 bracket. Thirty towns in England are revealed as larger than Derby, including Nottingham with 2,190 hearths. Derby had 615 households in 1670, 184 houses having only one hearth, 145 only two and 80 being exempt.

There were 22 houses with 10 hearths or more, of which several would have been inns, and it is a measure of the prosperity of the parish of All Saints' that 16 of these houses were in that parish, including the joint largest, Newcastle House with 18, the same as the Mellor family house in St Peter's, a parish with only four houses of this sort of size. St Werburgh's only had two houses with 10 hearths or more and St Michael's and St Alkmund's had but one apiece.

Some houses, though, were divided. We know, for instance, that the pioneer gynaecologist Dr Percival Willoughby, as the younger son of an aristocratic family, lived in a house larger than a medical calling would normally command, and that he had only part of the 15th-century timber-framed mansion called The Old Mayor's Parlour. He is listed as being taxed on seven hearths here, but the other half of the house was lived in by Richard Eaton, taxed on four, making the house another of those exceeding 10 hearths. Some prominent houses, too, were smaller than one might think, like the Burton family town house, Thorntree House (later 1 St Peter's Street), which was only taxed on nine hearths, the Jacobean House in the Wardwick on but seven (it was extended into the garden later) and the Friary on nine.

It is exceedingly hit-and-miss to try and derive an approximate population total from these statistics, but something in the region of 3,500 might be fairly close to the mark, with a margin or error of 400 each side.

TRADESMEN'S TOKENS

One of the difficulties with trade in the mid-17th century was an appalling shortage of small change. The silver 1d piece, current for nearly a millennium, had been reduced in size under the Tudors and Stuarts and was never plentiful. Nevertheless, a penny purchased a surprising amount of goods in the 1660s and change for shopkeepers and the less well-off was a serious problem. With the upheavals of the civil war and Commonwealth, there was a reluctance in government circles to produce a base-metal coinage of halfpennies and farthings, and it was not until 1672 that such coins were officially issued. Before the civil war the need had been met by private bronze issues, continental jettons and the local manufacture of unofficial and crude lead tokens, a trend which appears to have owed its inception to similar tokens issued by major monastic institutions before the Reformation.

Under the Commonwealth, however, local tradesmen all over England began to issue quite well-struck tokens, usually bearing their names, an allusion to their business, the denomination and the date. Some were manufactured to order in London, others were struck locally, as is confirmed by the discovery of a die for the tokens of the Wood family, apothecaries at Chesterfield.

A fine series of 48 different types exists for Derby, issued by 37 tradesmen between 1657 and 1671. These

The so-called Old Mayor's Parlour, Tenant Street, photographed by Richard Keene c.1862. This is where gynaecologist Percival Willoughby lived. (M. Craven)

Graveslab in St Peter's Church of Dr Percival Willoughby. (M. Craven)

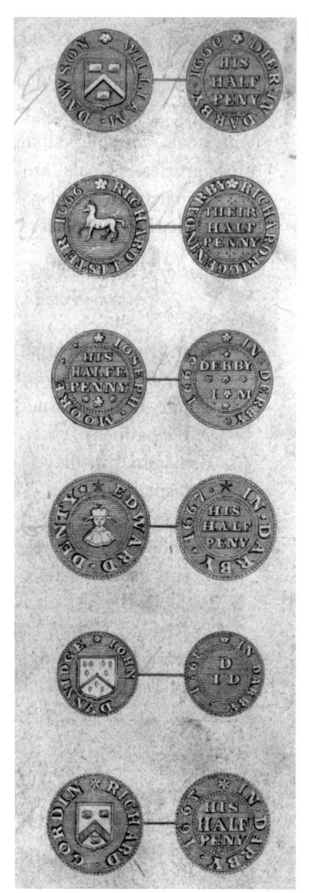

A page of engraved copies of 17th-century tokens from *The Reliquarry. (M. Craven)*

throw much light on the trades then flourishing in the borough, and the good preservation of parish records for the period enables us to piece together much information about the issuers' families. Nearly all the tokens were of halfpenny face value, but three types of farthing token are also known. Mercers were the most common issuers (5), followed by vintners and apothecaries (3), then carriers, bakers, innholders, shoe-makers and grocers (2 each) and one representative each of feltmakers, dyers, tallowchandlers, wool-packers, saddlers and pipemakers.

Two other trades represented on tokens are of especial interest. That of Luke Neyld, also notable for being octagonal, indicates that he was a coffee house proprietor at the sign of the *Murat's Head,* named after the bloodthirsty Turkish Sultan Murad IV (1623–1640), who died in a drink-crazed stupor after thinking he had killed his brother and ended the dynasty. In 1681 Hon. Anchitel Grey of Risley Manor House had his steward settle a bill for 1/- there. Yet the founding of a posh coffee house was a development which is a sure indication of the astonishing growth of social and intellectual life so soon after the civil war, aping the capital. Similarly, issuer William Newcombe was a bookseller, whose business doubtless owed its foundation to the huge upsurge in the publication of tracts, broadsheets and other politico-religious polemics of the age.

Several of the issuers were or had been mayors of the borough, the two John Dunnidges (in 1660 and 1684) being examples, and many families went on to greater prosperity in succeeding epochs, like the Bakewells, Bancrofts, Botts, Brookses, Holmeses and Sowters. The Cordens, vintners in the 1660s, ended with HM's Issuer of Stamps at Derby a century and a half later, the heiress marrying into the Roes, a family that obtained a peerage in the early 20th century, while the Strongs, pipemakers, kept at their profession until the end of the 19th century, their status declining with the standing of their trade. Their pipe kiln in Willow Row was discovered in the 1930s during slum clearance.

TRADE AND ITS REGULATION

Many of the token issuers – certainly all those who practised as either mercers, apothecaries, grocers, ironmongers, upholsterers or milliners – belonged, from its foundation on 28 July 1675, to the Derby Company of Mercers, the records of which miraculously survived the conflagration which destroyed the bulk of the town's records in 1841, mainly through having been retained at his home (Parkfields Cedars on Kedleston Road) by the retiring mayor of 1840, John Sanders, a descendant of the fearsome republican major from Little Ireton who featured so largely in the civil war at Derby.

The mediaeval tradesmen's gild has already been mentioned, as have the restrictive practices by which it excluded unwanted competition from outside. Derby's charter of 1637, reinforced by its last charter issued in 1682, also restricted new trading opportunities to protect the magic circle of the trading oligarchy that then ruled the borough. Only the son of a freeman or the passed apprentice of one could set up and trade within the town. Everyone else had to trade from a barrow, as it were, on market or fair days, as with the young John Whitehurst in 1736. There was also a Derby Drapers' and Tailors' Company extant by 1622. Much of the rights inherent in the burgess-ship reflected similar trends, yet the Mercers' Company and any other similar ones combined control of traders with a measure of self-regulation and welfare. Thus, although founded under an Act of Parliament dated as far back as 1436, it in some ways looked forward to the Friendly Society as well as to bodies such as the local Chamber of Trade.

The Derby Mercers' Company was controlled by an annually-elected steward and two wardens, although for many years it was run by a notable virago, the redoubtable Mrs Bloodworth. These officers and the 10 brethren of the company registered and regulated apprenticeships, had power to enter shops to test quality of goods, weights and measures (and fine offenders), tax members to cover expenses, distrain on the goods of members in breach of the rules, prosecute hawkers and pedlars and indemnify the Corporation of the borough against misdemeanours among its members. Out of the 50 original members, 15 were token-issuers from the previous decade. Of the total, 17 were mercers, 12 ironmongers, eight apothecaries, three each grocers and chandlers, two upholsterers and one each of milliner, salter, tobacconist, feltmaker and one uncertain. Whether the remaining trades of the town, apart from the drapers, had similar companies at this time is unclear, although as late as 1773 the framework knitters established one.

Many of the tradesmen of Derby held their premises by lease from the Corporation; indeed rental income from property, mostly amassed in the mediaeval period or through Queen Mary's grant of 1555, constituted the bulk of the Corporation's income. The Corporation, for instance, owned the whole of the butchery, otherwise known as The Shambles. This interesting edifice stood in the Market Place running north–south down the west side from Market Head (where Sadler Gate debouches) towards Cornmarket. The street thus created on its west was Rotten Row. A re-entrant on the north side contained the butchers' shops, and we have a very complete record

of the lettings, the earliest dating to 1540, the latest in 1750. All these were for 21 years each, and there would appear to have been three sizes of premises, for there were three rent scales extending over this period in 1582: 13s 4d (67p), 10s (50p) and 8s (40p). There would also appear to have been only two 8s shops, few at 10s and a considerable number at 13s 4d. As late as 1733, a shop was let at this rate – no increase for 151 years! In 1540 there had been 18 butchers' shops, 10 held in pairs with varying rents from a mark (6s 8d) down to 4d.

Prices, we may infer, were very static, although the reason may well be at least partly attributable to inertia on the part of the Corporation. When the butchery was knocked down (and a plan showing the shops drawn), photographs show it to have been a remarkably dignified brick building of two storeys, cross windows and a high-hipped roof carried on timber eaves, plainly of late-17th century date. Indeed, in 1708 we find cleared ground re-let (at the usual rate for a shop) to Philip Parr 'for rebuilding at the upper end'. Allowing for the architectural conservatism of Derby at the time, this date matches very well with the style of the building. Interestingly, Parr's first lease (1686) marks the continuation of a dynasty of local butchers of this name first recorded in the 1540s, whose shop in the Market Place finally closed in 1980, nearly three centuries later. The pair of giltwood pigs which latterly decorated the facia of their shop were rescued by the author and added to the museum's collections.

Another dynasty of butchers is represented by a lease of 1582 to William Franceys. He was a grazier from Mackworth, whose descendant John Franceys renewed this lease in 1708 along with those on two other adjoining shops. The senior branch of the family rebuilt their Rotten Row house in 1646 to produce a residence taxable at the Restoration on 11 hearths – no small thing. The next generation became apothecaries. Henry Franceys, the last apothecary of this family, married a Harpur of Twyford and was the only tradesman allowed into the Derby County Assembly in the earlier 18th century. This man, who also served as mayor of Derby in 1747 (like Henry Mellor, he died in office) and was a prominent member of the Mercers' Company, is commemorated by a large and splendid funeral hatchment executed by Francis Bassano, the eminent Derby herald painter, which still hangs in All Saints' Church (now the Cathedral). Franceys's father rebuilt their house again about 1696 in very palatial style with an eight-bay façade, four storeys high, with fine joinery and frescoed ceilings (by Bassano) within, not to mention ornamental pleasure grounds behind, with a small lake and summer house. This splendid building is still happily extant, and Franceys's apothecary business survived until it closed in 1971 as Messrs Cope and Taylor.

A Richard Keene view of The Piazzas and Shambles under demolition in 1871. The Piazzas, here still intact, were built by Samuel Crompton in 1708 as a form of proto-shopping mall, but failed to live up to expectations. (M. Craven)

The Piazzas

Abraham Crompton, son of the ejected minister and yet another prominent member of the Mercers' Company, had, as we have seen, became prosperous enough in his premises in Rotten Row to begin lending money professionally from about 1685, the date usually taken for the foundation of the bank which evolved from these at first relatively informal activities. Nevertheless, such was his success that in 1708 he felt able to erect an extension to the butchery. This took the form of a long, dignified, pedimented façade facing east across the Market Place, with shops on the ground floor set back under an overhang, itself supported on columns, forming a covered walk. The south side extended round into Rotten Row and was architecturally more satisfying, containing three or four larger shops. Unfortunately, no one knows who designed this innovative building, inspired by and named after Inigo Jones's Covent Garden prototype, The Piazzas, although it was effectively Derby's first purpose-built shopping precinct: would that those of today satisfy the eye as much!

Nevertheless, it did not really catch on, trouble being met in letting the shops, Woolley commenting at the time, '…it is supposed that Mr Crompton built this house intending to exchange it with the Corporation for their [guild]hall; at present it is only used by some button-makers that work therein.'

Nevertheless, the building, eventually fulfilling the role intended for it, lasted until 1871–77, when it was cleared to enlarge the Market Place.

A new Guildhall

This remark by Woolley certainly highlights a problem for the Corporation that, strapped for cash as they were, they were urgently in need of a new town hall. From 1610 until 1731 they made use of a large, brick-gabled Moot Hall set back on the east side of Iron Gate, originally intended to replace the mediaeval Guildhall. By 1700 this too was thought unsuitable, although it still survives, despite being completely hidden and made into an office block.

They obviously failed to take Crompton's bait, and, indeed, recent research has uncovered a design of 1713 by Francis Smith of Warwick for a new one with the market behind – just as we have now – on the south side of the Market Place instead of in the middle. That this was never built was because the owners of the property the Corporation wished to acquire saw them coming and asked too much. In the event, Francis Jackson of Armitage designed a free-standing building of immense elegance which was erected on the site of its predecessor in 1731, paid for by public subscription. All the finest craftsmen of the age cut their teeth on it, including Robert Bakewell. It lasted until 1828, when the buildings on the Market Place's south side finally became available, and it was replaced.

THE WATER SUPPLY

If private endeavour could provide the town with good and useful buildings, the mayor and burgesses were not to be outdone. They had living among them George Sorocold, born in 1668, his family from Ashton-in-Makerfield, Lancashire, with trading connections in London and an estate at Hargate in Egginton.

Sorocold was a pioneer hydraulic engineer and in 1684 had married a daughter of Franceys, the apothecary. In 1691 he offered to erect an engine to lift water from the Derwent and pipe it to various points in the town. Even so, the Corporation could not meet the cost despite the obvious need for the scheme. Water, up to this point, had been only available from wells, St Alkmund's and St Helen's to the north end of the borough, Friary Conduit Head, probably in Friar Gate and fed from the Odd Brook, Becket Well, west of Markeaton Brook near St James's Bridge (named, Professor Cameron assures us, not from St Thomas Becket as most people assume, but from a corruption of the old word, *bouget,* a bucket) and The Conduit in the Market Place, which emerged under a small gabled edifice in the north-east corner.

They therefore raised loans, for instance, one from the Mercers' Company of £41 16s 0d (£41.80) for three years at 0% interest, granted 1 March 1692; needless to say it was still outstanding 40 years later! Four days later, the mayor and burgesses granted a 99-year lease of 'the mill commonly called Gunpowder Mill near St Michael's Mills and two sluices adjoining and the Little Byflatt whereon the mill stands with free liberty to erect a water-house, a water-wheel and other engines, laying pipes for conveying water into the streets, lanes and passages within the borough… the said George to begin the work within three months next ensuing and to lay the pipes through the King's Streete, Irongate, Market Place,

The listed 17th-century head of Becket Well, seen shortly before removal in 1963 to build Duckworth Square. The well head was adapted as part of Sorocold's water supply system. (*Derby Evening Telegraph*)

Rotton Row and the Corne Market in Derby and soe to the Gaole Bridge … within three years then next following'.

Sorocold had liberty to assign the lease, providing all the works were in good repair, which he subsequently did to a board of trustees, who controlled the concern throughout the 18th century until closure in 1841. The trustees tended to let the operation to lessees in return for a revenue, as to Benjamin Granger in 1738 for 40 years at £23 6s 8d (£23.33) per annum.

William Woolley was able to describe the works in 1713:

'…and on the nearer side [of St Michael's Mills, south of Bridge Chapel] stands a water engine invented by Mr Sorocold with great art, which, at the same time with a

One of George Sorocold's elm water pipes being dug up in Queen Street during widening 1926. (M. Craven)

One of George Sorocold's water engines as installed at Derby. Drawn by Henry Beighton but with eight out of the 16 pumps omitted for clarity, from Transactions of the Royal Society. (M. Craven)

wheel, throws up water to a cistern joining to St Michael's Church, from thence conducted in pipes and supplies all parts of the town at an easy rate. And the same wheel also turns a malt mill and bores elm trees for pipes all at the same time and all managed by one man only. It pays to the land tax £50 17s 4d p.a.....'

In between boring the pipes for this and the 17 other schemes of a similar nature Sorocold built throughout Britain, the fall of the water also drove a wheel to grind flints, thus making it self-financing.

It is likely that Sorocold also improved Becket Well, reached from below an earlier 17th-century stone pyramid, and The Conduit, which later he rebuilt to make an ornament and centrepiece for the Market Place,

consisting, according to William Woolley, of a cupola supported on four Tuscan columns rising from a stone stepped base, as can still be seen at places like Beverley (Yorkshire), Bungay (Suffolk) and, more locally, at Mountsorrel (Leicester). Would that it still remained *in situ* today!

The Shire Hall

Improvements like Sorocold's represent a fundamental example of many more general improvements, which are apparent at this period. Surviving buildings, old photographs, records and the evidence of the Bucks' *East Prospect of Derby* enable us to identify nearly 20 major buildings erected in the mid to late-17th century. Of these, only one is, strictly speaking, a public building: the Shire Hall in St Mary's Gate, built 1659–1660 to a *bravura* artisan mannerist design by George Eaton of Etwall (1611–1681).

It is possible that the site was anciently one for juridical proceedings, although no clue exists to aid speculation. Nor was it dedicated initially solely to such functions for, suitably cleared, it also acted as concert hall, meeting room, assembly hall, ballroom and auction room. Both the Crown and Nisi Prius courts sat in the same open hall, segregated by timber balustrading, the unfortunate accused being brought up from an

Derby Shire Hall, built to a design by George Eaton of Etwall in 1659–60. Photographed in 1998, before rebuilding in 2002. (M. Craven)

Shire Hall: high sheriff's inauguration in 1931. Col. Godfrey Mosley's carriage, pikemen and trumpeters ready to take him back to his home, Calke Abbey. (Roger Pegg)

insalubrious subterranean chamber called, by Woolley, 'the Hole'. Grand and petty juries roosted between the two courts in the centre of the building under and on a galleried structure. Nevertheless, it was and is a first-rate building, of which Woolley said, 'If it had a little cost bestowed upon it, to adorn it within, it would be one of the best of that kind of buildings in England.'

In 1772 Joseph Pickford added a top balustrade and extended the building to increase the accommodation and provide a grand jury room; in 1828 Matthew Habershon built two impressive courts within Pickford's extension, adding further accommodation beyond. In 1798, following the creation of Jury Street, the King's Arms County Hotel was built to the south, being matched in 1809–11 by an extremely handsome Judges' Lodging on the other side, designed by John Welch (1759–1823), a screen of railings being provided between the two, punctuated by gates to form an impressive *cour d'honneur*. The whole grade I listed ensemble was probably the finest Classical legal set piece in the English Midlands but was long under threat after the new Crown Court was built in 1989.

However, 2003 marked its reopening, after 25 years of total neglect, as magistrates' courts, although almost a third of the 1828 extensions were sacrificed to accommodate a vast new extension behind, the design of which completely fails to match the quality or workmanship of the original. Furthermore, the Judges' Lodgings, until 30 years ago equipped with two complete suites of contemporary furniture, china, silver and flatware – now all vanished, mostly by sale – has been gutted to form office suites for bureaucrats. Modern security requirements for such premises regrettably now mean that ordinary visitors and tourists have no reasonable access to the place where the Pentrich Revolutionaries were condemned in 1819 or the silk mill strikers of 1833 acquitted of wilful murder, nor enjoy Sir

Francis Chantrey's superb bust of F.N.C. Mundy of Markeaton Hall, 40 years chairman of the bench in 1775–1815, set on its plinth beneath the fine cantilevered gallery provided by Habershon.

A GREAT REBUILDING

The Restoration marks the halfway point in the transition of Derby as a town of timber-framed and thatched buildings into an elegant one largely of brick buildings. Travellers in the decades following were beginning to remark on the elegance of its streets.

Two inns are also attributable to this era and could be described as architectonic: the Green Man, St Peter's Churchyard, a simple ornamental brick building with a pretty Dutch outer gable and originally dated 1671, and the George, Market Head. The former, with its timber cross windows and mellow brickwork, survived until gutted by fire in 1936; the panelled interior was lost and now only the rebuilt façade remains.

With the King's Head (once on the north-west corner of St James's Lane and Cornmarket), the George was one of the most important inns in the town, founded before the outbreak of the civil war. We can date the present handsome façade, with its ornamental architraves around the windows, to 1693, when its proprietor

Samuel Heathcote's George Inn façade of 1693, photographed in 2003. (M. Craven)

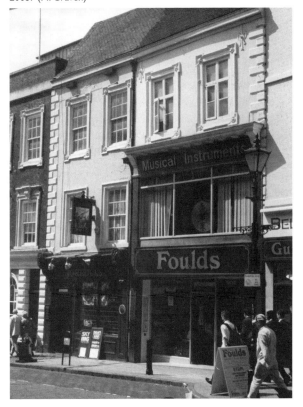

Samuel Heathcote arranged a restrospective 2,000-year lease from the Corporation of a sliver of frontage on Irongate on to which '…parte of the front of his [newly erected] house called the George' had obtruded. It later acquired a cockpit and a 100-foot ballroom, and parts of the interior of the present Foulds' Music Shop even predate the façade.

A very handsome burgher's house, immediately south of the George on the corner of Iron Gate and Sadler Gate, was erected within the next decade – undoubtedly by the same mason as the inn and perhaps to be identified as Roger Morledge's son George, describing himself in 1696 as 'architect', the first in the borough to do so. It was the HQ of Derby's first local paper, the *Derby Mercury*, from 1732 to 1824, after which it was the first base of the famous printing firm, Bemrose. Conversion to a bank led to the loss of its interiors, hipped roof and dormers in 1952.

The distinctive mouldings decorating the façades of these two fine buildings suggest that the same architect also designed Alderman Franceys's house of 1696 further down, the long-vanished house immediately to its north, probably built slightly earlier by the Meynells of Anslow

(Staffordshire), and the Mundy town house in The Wardwick of 1698. A number of other houses of this period survive, too – most notably the very up-to-the-minute Queen Anne house in The Wardwick built by Thomas Alsop in 1708 – suggesting that the burghers of the borough were reacting to increasing prosperity by building.

Two new places of worship were also built at this stage. One was the Unitarian Chapel in Friar Gate. Although essentially a brick box, this building was handsomely proportioned and well detailed. The galleried interior, with its four giant Doric columns, was very fine and apart from the addition of an awkward Tuscan portico in the late-19th century it remained unspoilt until its disastrous destruction to make way for a series of office blocks cheekily named Heritage Gate and built in 1972–73. The Puritans, later called the Presbyterians or Independents (of whom 101 were recorded in 1677), who refused to conform after 1662, had been given a licence to hold services in the Bridge Chapel at first, but under James II this arrangement swiftly came to an end and they used the Moot Hall courtyard in Iron Gate for a while before building their own chapel under the new dispensation.

A Richard Keene photograph of Storer's House, Market Place, c.1878, with part of Franceys's House (left) built in 1695–96. Built about 1692, its fine interiors survived until its demolition in 1936 to make way for a branch of Martin's Bank.

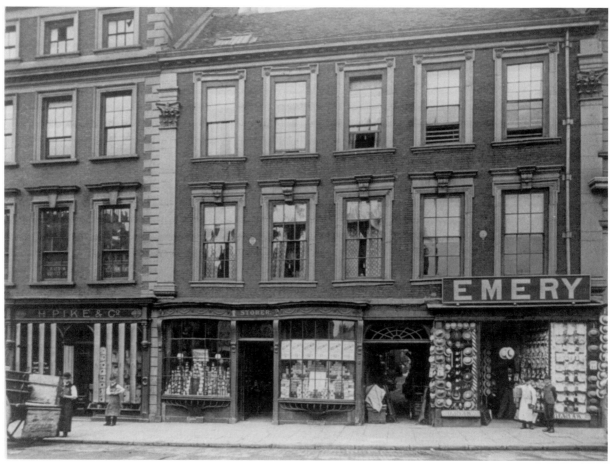

Friargate, Unitarian Chapel, built in 1694 and demolished in 1972. Photographed by Richard Keene in 1855. (Derby Museum)

Robert Bakewell's wrought iron in Derby Cathedral from 1725 was expanded by Edwin Haslam in 1873 and re-positioned in 1971. (Derby Cathedral)

It was from these surroundings that the Presbyterians' move was made, aided by the easier political climate engendered by the accession of William and Mary, to the new chapel in Friar Gate. 'Out of gratitude to King William, for giving them that liberty which they had a right to demand, they placed his arms over the pulpit,' Hutton commented; fortunately this artefact was saved when the Unitarians, who later took over the chapel in the 1780s, and more recently took themselves into a smaller space within the unlovely successor building.

Meanwhile, the Bridge Chapel was first divided as tenements and later sold as a workshop to a local tradesman who built, at its west end, a handsome gabled house, later the residence of the municipal Eatons, hosiers, which happily survives, albeit masked from the rest of the town by the concrete bulwarks of Causey Bridge, which looms within a yard or two of its upper windows.

A NEW CHURCH

The other place of worship forms the coda to the first incident in the 17th-century annals referred to above: the replacement of the nave of St Werburgh's parish church, the mediaeval fabric having collapsed in the flood of Guy Fawkes' night 1698. The resultant ashlar edifice (completed in 1699) was extremely fine, with segmentally-topped clear-glazed windows set between Tuscan pilasters, the interior lit by a low lead-covered dome, supported by Tuscan columns. All the more unfortunate then that we do not know the architect's name.

The reredos, however, was carved to the highest standard by the under-appreciated Henry Huss of Derby (1661–1716), who collaborated with George Sorocold on the design of the Liverpool Docks the same year, and it may be that the entire church was his design. In 1711 a fine brass font in the shape of a *pie pelicane* was fashioned to the order of Charles Benskin, an elaborate

wrought-iron cover being made by the celebrated ironsmith Robert Bakewell to descend upon it. Unfortunately, vicar Berry, in the 1870s, had the brass pelican remade into a lectern, thus utterly wrecking the whole unique ensemble. Subsequently, on the closure of the church in 1982, the Diocesan authorities gave it heedlessly away to a country parish, when they could have gained immense credit by reuniting it with its cover, which remains, rarely visited, in the now redundant church.

Of this splendid edifice only the chancel was left as a side chapel after Sir Arthur Blomfield had rebuilt the nave, on a north–south axis to minimise flooding, in 1894. It is full of monuments, by Sir Francis Chantrey, Richard Browne, George Moneypenny and others and bore witness to the unlikely marriage of Dr Johnson with Tetty Porter on 9 July 1735.

GRAND HOUSES

About a dozen domestic dwellings of architectural pretensions can be identified from this period of improvement to the town. From the prospects of the place three typical early-Restoration period houses can be seen, with high-hipped roofs, dormers, top balustrades and lanterns. One is Thorntree House, built by the Burtons of Aldercar Hall as a town house at the very bottom of St Peter's Street, right against the Brook. Bought early in the 18th century by Gilbert Wagstaff, it became home to the descendants of the ejected Timothy Fox but was rebuilt out of all recognition, almost certainly by Thomas Cooper of Derby for Joseph Strutt, and was where the latter kept his art collection, into which the public could go on Sunday afternoons in return for a small payment.

Woolley implies that a similar house at the bottom of Green Lane had been built by the Barnes's of Stanton-by-Newhall and a third, very similar to Thorntree

Robert Bakewell's wrought-iron balustrade on the perron at St Mary's Gate House. (The late D. Buckley)

House, was 27 Queen Street. This later rejoiced in early-18th-century additions including a Bakewell gate and a particularly fine oak-panelled dining room before being extensively refronted by Joseph Pickford for John Whitehurst FRS in 1764, the roof dormers being absorbed behind a Palladian parapet punctuated by Diocletian windows. It was later divided, one half becoming the Acorn Inn (demolished in 1908), the other half eventually being acquired by the Smiths, clockmakers, who occupied what remained until 1999. Unfortunately, Pickford's façade was removed to the depth of an entire room for street widening in 1928–29, but with the saving grace that the proprietor had it replaced to an agreeable design by newly-arrived borough architect Herbert Aslin. The unlisted house, in which Joseph Wright, ARA, died in 1797, is, at the time of writing, derelict.

A number of others have been identified and all attest to the prosperity of both town and country at this era. Only Exeter House stands out from the rest, however, in size and opulence, described in the 19th century as the biggest house in Derby. Rebuilt at the Restoration by MP John Bagnold, it later passed by inheritance from millionaire metal trader Thomas Chambers to the 8th Earl of Exeter, who refronted it, before it became Bonnie Prince Charlie's HQ in 1745. Even Jedediah Strutt lived there for a while, but it was demolished in early 1854.

It is strange to note that while Alderman Franceys was building his very stylish house in the Market Place, owing much to the school of Sir Christopher Wren, old-fashioned dwellings were still being erected: Cockpit Hill House, on the side of the mound near the east end of Bag Lane once called Cope Castle, latterly Cockpit Hill, was four-square, tall and very Flemish, with Dutch gables (rare in Derbyshire), roof lantern, close-set fenestration and good detailing. It was built in 1696, but

having been encroached upon by industry, it was demolished early on, in 1819, after a long period in the ownership of the Sacheverells and Sitwells. Even Alderman Gilbert Chesshyre's house, built as late as 1708, looked backward to the William-and-Mary style, while the contemporary Allsopp's House, Wardwick, seems to owe its superb parapetted façade to the effects of the London Building Acts – passed in 1707–08 in order to conserve timber by limiting the use of wood in building construction – and thereby seems well up-to-date for its age.

Nevertheless, the customary Derby habit at any age, prior to the wasteful 20th century, was to upgrade rather than build anew, which is what the aristocratic pioneer gynaecologist Dr Percival Willoughby (1596–1685) did with the river front of the Old Mayor's Parlour, half of which he had acquired as his residence in the 1630s.

ELITE CRAFTSMEN

These grander buildings represent the opening of a period in which much fine local craftsmanship blossomed. Unfortunately, few names are known until the opening of the 18th century: beyond Messrs Reeve and Morledge at County Hall, names are at a premium, and, although the annals of the town name many of those likely to be involved, few can be matched to identifiable work. Nor do we know for certain who executed the elaborate ceiling in Newcastle House, although it may have been one of the Needhams, a Derby family of plasterers, one of whom worked later for Francis Smith of Warwick; it is quite good enough indeed to have been the work of such as Edward Goudge or Edward Pearce; if, therefore, it was made locally, it says volumes for the competence of Derby's craftsmen in that age. Another Derby dynasty of *stuccadores* was that of Samuel Mansfield who worked at Sudbury Hall before Londoner Edward Goudge was brought in.

Robert Bakewell was of an old Derby family, his great Uncle Richard having issued a trader's token as a carrier in 1666, although his father, Sampson, was living in Uttoxeter at the time of his birth in 1682. The family must have been fairly well-connected, for in 1719 Robert's sister Mary married George Bage, the Darley paper-mill owner and father of the proto-novelist Robert Bage, a friend of Erasmus Darwin's. Bakewell served an apprenticeship with the superb French gatesmith Jean Tijou, who worked at Chatsworth and Hampton Court, which must have cost his father considerably more than an apprenticeship to a typical local smith. Training over, the young Robert Bakewell acquired a powerful patron in the courtier Thomas Coke of Melbourne Hall, for whom he made ironwork for the

Part of the ceiling of 'The Great Room on the Market Place' – the saloon of the Duke of Newcastle's town house, probably by Edward Pierce and put in during the 1670s. Much of it was retrieved on demolition in 1971 and installed in the foyer of the Darwin Suite, Assembly Rooms.

terrace, their London town house and his *piece de resistance* the delectable iron pergola made to stand in the grounds by the lake which was being simultaneously created by George Sorocold, who formed the pool to feed it, 1706–08.

He then worked from a small forge between the hall and the church, but in the second decade of the 18th century removed to part of Oakes' Yard, an enclave west of St Peter's Street in Derby. At Melbourne, he had contracted an irregular liaison, from which was born his son, Fisher Bakewell, but soon after he married and married well, his bride being the sister of Francis Cokayne, scion of a gentry family from Chaddesden. It was Mrs Bakewell's uncle who commissioned Francis Smith's design for a new Guildhall when mayor in 1713 and her three brothers were, respectively, Lord Mayor of London, a Colonel at Culloden on the government side and a vicar of Doveridge.

Hence Robert Bakewell was well-connected, not only locally but nationally, and in time his practice extended throughout middle England. He undertook at least 20 commissions even in Derby itself, most sensational of which must be the screen made for Gibbs' All Saints' Church in 1725–29, which happily survives. Another work in the town was the gates made for John Lombe and erected outside the Silk Mill about 1722. These were removed in 1935 to the Wardwick but replaced near their original position in 1982.

Bakewell worked with Sorocold, John Whitehurst and Francis Smith of Warwick. He later moved to premises behind Friar Gate, dying in 1752, being succeeded by his foreman, Benjamin Yates, son of a fellow apprentice with Tijou two generations before. Yates did the ironwork for Kedleston Hall and St Helen's House. He was succeeded by his son William, before the coming of foundries and architectural cast iron temporary put wrought ironwork into eclipse. There was then a gap of 50 or 60 years before the craft was revived by Alderman William Haslam, his son Edwin and finally continued by Messrs Taylor, Whiting and Taylor, who carried the tradition into the 1920s, before concentrating on electrical engineering.

VI

FURTHER TURBULENCE

POLITICAL UPHEAVALS

The junction between the 17th and 18th centuries was a period which saw renewed political turmoil nationally, and this had its effects locally, too. The accession of James II in 1685 had seen the beginning of trouble centred on the Catholic succession. In Derbyshire, opportunity was taken to strengthen the trained bands, the Earl of Scarsdale, as Lord Lieutenant, appointing several new officers in this year, like Sir Robert Coke of Longford Hall, appointed by him deputy lieutenant of the county and captain of the trained bands on 20 March 1685.

Great efforts, often highly fraudulent, had been made to exclude Charles II's brother from the succession, which had culminated in the Titus Oates affair and the Rye House Plot. Derby had not been free of these murky machinations. In 1678 a letter had been found at Thulston, on the Stanhopes' estate, hinting that 500 'Papists' would rendezvous on Nuns' Green on 2 December, although with what object was left unclear. Also, 1681 saw what amounted to a show trial, mounted in the Shire Hall, when a Grand Jury was empanelled to try George Busby, a Jesuit priest arrested at West Hallam Hall, the seat of the recusant Powtrell family. This was brought under legislation passed under Queen Elizabeth and, in the xenophobia of the times, revived. Busby was found guilty of treason by a grand jury of local gentry, sentenced to be hung, drawn and quartered, but, as was normal under the Stuarts, was reprieved.

In contrast, however, once safely on the throne James II, in 1687, began to place men sympathetic to his cause in public office. The only recorded consequence of this in Derby was the deposition, on 11 January 1687, of the Norfolk-born mayor, Leonard Sadd, a protégé of the Cokes of Holkham, who had acquired an apothecary's business from Thomas Gery, whose widow he had married and who had issued a token in the 1660s. Ralph Brough was the nominee installed in his stead by the Crown, but there is no record of any riots or voices raised in Sadd's defence; one can only surmise that such arbitrary interference in borough affairs must have provoked some adverse reaction. Probably Sadd appealed to the high steward of the borough, Lord Devonshire, the incident perhaps strengthening his resolve to stage the *coup d'etat* he eventually masterminded in 1688. Sadd retired to the Cokes' Derbyshire estate at Longford and died in 1697, leaving two nephews land in Norfolk and the Derby shop.

Thus on 21 November 1688 the Earl of Devonshire entered the town at the head of a body of men variously described as 'a small retinue' and as many as 500, fresh from his historic meeting on the 5th at the Cock and Pynot Inn, Whittington, with the Earl of Danby and Hon. John d'Arcy. He threw a lavish dinner – doubtless at his house in Cornmarket – 'openly declared his sentiments in favour of the Prince of Orange, who was then landed in England. He read to the mayor… and the Commonality, the declaration of the Prince' and delivered a manifesto of his own.

The following day, in the wake of a rising tide of indifference (for most of the citizens, temporarily including the government backed ruling *elite*, were unregenerate Tories), the earl left to try his luck in Nottingham. Not long afterwards, a group of officers of William III entered the town and the mayor, John Chesshyre – as Ralph Brough's immediate successor, sympathetic to James II – refused to billet them, although other burgesses, Whigs temporarily excluded from influence, managed to find them accommodation.

Thereafter, with William and Mary duly installed, the burgesses and freeholders were obliged to take the Oath of Supremacy; those who refused to take it constituted the 'non-jurors', a significant minority. Further, due to a 'Horrid and Detestable conspiracy formed and carried on by Papists and others for the assassination of the King and to encourage an invasion from France' – a Whig scare story put out to strengthen their position – a local association was formed, to which burgesses could attach themselves. This list of persons was eventually closed by the Corporation in 1701. Nevertheless, there is a distinct impression gained that Derby was either uncertain in its allegiance to the Protestant succession or else subscribed more than usually to the precepts of legitimate monarchy.

DR SACHEVERELL

With the accession of Queen Anne something closer to a Stuart restoration had been achieved, and the problems begun by the expulsion of James II went into abeyance until it was clear that Anne, too, was going to die without surviving issue. Thus the possibility for succession lay between George, the Elector of Hanover – a nephew of Prince Rupert, but a corpulent German whose

The man who started it all: Revd Dr Henry Sacheverell, who preached the Derby assize sermon on 15 August 1709. (M. Craven)

the upshot, he received an absurdly light sentence, which promptly brought about the fall of the Whig government, thus making all the drama thoroughly worthwhile from the good doctor's standpoint.

This result was greeted in Derby with wild enthusiasm.

'The bells of All Saints' clashed out a triumphant peal, which was shortly taken up by every steeple in the town, while huge bonfires were piled up and set on fire in the centre of the Market Place and on Nuns' Green' wrote a contemporary. The prevailing feeling was so strong that the Tory tide overrode the traditional Cavendish-inspired Whig gerrymandering and projected, at the following election, a pair of Tory MPs, Sir Richard Levinge of Parwich and Sir John Harpur of Calke, both baronets into Parliament. Later, however, Levinge was made Attorney General for Ireland (where indeed, he had an estate) and a by-election produced a Whig again, Edward Mundy of Shipley.

As for Dr Sacheverell – by birth a Wiltshire Cheverell of Cheverell Hall – when his local namesake the former high sheriff died, he married his widow and inherited his estates. What *chutzpah*!

THE FIFTEEN

A Tory *coup* to install the exiled Stuarts having been thwarted by the Duke of Shrewsbury and Anne's death occurring prematurely on 1 August 1714, before Tory countermeasures were fully in place, brought George I of Hanover to the throne.

Yet within the year a Jacobite rebellion had broken out in Scotland led by 'Bobbing John' Mar, echoed by riots in many places on behalf of the Stuart dynasty, not least in Derby. These highlighted the fact that the majority of the clergy favoured James, including three out of the five parish incumbents in town. Samuel Sturgess, of All Saints' for instance, is said to have prayed publicly for King James (III) but, after a pause, to have added 'I mean King George.' Simpson adds, 'The congregation grew tumultuous, the military gentlemen drew their swords and ordered him out of the pulpit, into which he never returned. He pleaded a *slip of the tongue*; but had he been so conversant in his New Testament as with politics, he might have pleaded as an excuse the commandment to *pray for our enemies*.' It should be noted, however, that he did not, in fact, resign. Harris of St Peter's was cautioned by the magistrates for Jacobitism, but was outdone by Revd Henry Cantrell of St Alkmund's who 'drank the Pretender's health upon his knees and the 30 January [1649: the martyrdom of Charles I] became the most holy day in the year'.

adulterous wife was declared mad and 20 years banged up in a distant *schloss* – or the distinctly odd James III, the 'Old Pretender' a native, legitimate, but over-devoutly Catholic successor. In general terms the Whigs were working for the former, the Tories for the latter.

But into this uncertain equation was catapulted the Tory firebrand Revd Dr Henry Sacheverell who, on 15 August 1709 (at the invitation of his admirer, the unrelated high sheriff for the year, George Sacheverell of Callow Hall), preached a thoroughly inflammatory assize sermon in All Saints', which, as a thinly-veiled attack on the so-called Glorious Revolution, was received very favourably by his congregation of county gentlemen and in the town. He went on to repeat his oratorical triumph in St Paul's Cathedral on the following 5 November, an act followed swiftly by impeachment before Parliament and a sensational trial. His defence was impregnable in legal terms, but once arraigned the Whigs could hardly allow his acquittal. In

TURBULENT POLITICS

It is difficult, however, beyond reporting such incidents, to assess how allegiances were split in the town. At elections, wherein only the 800 or so free burgesses (under the terms of the 1682 charter) could vote, the Whigs maintained their influence through the patronage of the Cavendish family now, by virtue of events in 1688, elevated to their second Dukedom, who had the *entree* to the administration of the borough through the high stewardship. The Tories were, in consequence, usually beaten at the hustings, although invariably by the slenderest of margins.

In 1701 John Harpur was actually elected in the Tory interest and was joined by a second Tory in 1702, as in 1710 as already described. In the first election of George I's reign (1715) the Tories were only most narrowly defeated 'after an orgy of bribery and intimidation…' Even as late as 1741 only manipulation and chicanery deprived the Tory candidate, the overtly Jacobite German Pole of Radburne Hall, of success against the Duke of Devonshire's son-in-law, Viscount Duncannon, and John Stanhope.

Title page of the Poll Book of the historic 1741 general election. (Derby Local Studies Library)

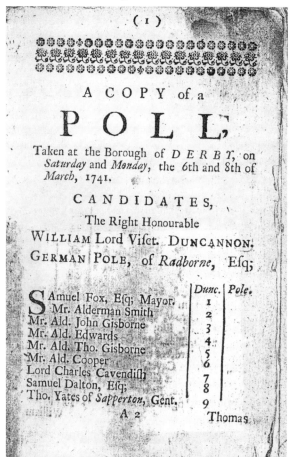

The main play on this occasion was the creation of large numbers of 'honorary burgesses' by the mayor in return for their voting for the Whig candidates. An analysis of these persons prepared by William Turner of Derby, German Pole's agent, revealed that several were ineligible to vote and indeed were receiving parish relief! This practice, of course, tended to erode the rights of the ordinary burgesses, whose position was owed to long apprenticeships and hard work as well as in many cases by being the offspring of other burgesses. The mayor, Samuel Fox of Thorntree House, also arbitrarily closed the polls after most of his 'honorary burgesses' had been through, to the exclusion of many of his opponents, most still refreshing themselves at local inns from the rigours of a journey from their villages! The Poll Books show that the backbone of the Tory vote, apart from the gentry, their kin and dependents, comprised the artisans, craftsmen and small shopkeepers of the town. The Whigs tended to draw their support from the greater shopkeepers, prosperous businessmen and merchants and including, of course, a large number of voters whose profession or calling is not shown and who constitute Turner's 'honorary burgesses'.

There is the example of Henry Franceys, the opulent apothecary, who on 15 November 1733 celebrated the marriage of George II's daughter with the Prince of Orange, 'gave a very elegant entertainment… at his own house'. After the meal, was 'brought in a salver of orange-coloured cockades which were distributed among the Company'. The Tories, if the example of Lichfield is anything to go by, employed (even then) blue cockades, with an additional white one worn by any who were not afraid to be additionally identified as Jacobites. A county election on 23 May 1734 resulted in a minor riot in the yard of the County Hall in which a man was killed.

The stratum of local society to which numbers of Tories belonged is further attested by the epitaph to Thomas Locker, 'a famous High Church Clog-maker', who died in Derby, 28 June 1735, aged 64.

'Under this stone here leith one,
Whom bribes could ne'er prevail upon,
From being for the Tories hearty,
In spite of all the Whiggish party:
He always cried up Church and King,
And scorned to do a Knavish thing:
Free from vain flattery and pride,
As such he lived, as such he died.'

As this verse implies, however, behaviour, especially on the losing side, was chivalric by and large. Faced with a threatened riot after the 1741 elections, German Pole successfully entreated with his supporters not to break the place up. Despite losing, he threw, a few days later, an outdoor feast at his home, Radburne Hall, then still being built, for some 500 of his supporters.

The statue of Bonnie Prince Charlie in Full Street by Anthony Stones, of 1995. Dr Johnson said of the 'Forty-Five:'It was a noble attempt'. (M. Craven)

BONNIE PRINCE CHARLIE

The gloves finally came off three years later, however, when Prince Charles Edward Stuart landed on the west coast of Scotland at Eriskay and raised his standard at Kinlochmoidart in 1745.

As far as the governing establishment was concerned, it was not until the fall of Carlisle in November that year that the danger was realised. Thereafter, increasing panic set in, culminating with George II sitting at St James', packed up and ready to go into exile, a barge loaded with treasure being moored in the Thames. At Derby things were little better, although a sensible beginning was made by the Duke of Devonshire who, as Lord Lieutenant, was charged with the defence of the county.

A circular letter arrived on 5 September imploring the authorities to act against likely enemies of the State. The good Duke summoned a meeting of the gentlemen and clergy of the county at the George in Iron Gate on the 28th to consider what steps should be taken to counter the threat of an invasion from Scotland. This inn was long associated with the Whig faction, as the King's Head was with the Tories. Yet it had been, as we have seen, rebuilt by Alderman Heathcote and ironically it was he and his son, another Samuel Heathcote, who were the leading Jacobites in the Corporation.

The meeting was well attended and it was agreed to raise money, £1,205 9s 9d per month being required towards forming a militia regiment of 10 companies from various points around the county, totalling 720 men. This was instead of calling out the regular militia, for the Whigs knew that it could not be relied upon. The new unit was first mustered on The Holmes at Derby on 3 December, when they 'went through their exercise to the great satisfaction of all present'.

But this satisfaction was to prove sadly misplaced, for it was within minutes of the determination of this review, with the Whig leaders brimful of confidence, that news came through of the Jacobite army vanguard's arrival in Ashbourne. The Derbyshire Regiment, as the Duke of Devonshire's hastily-levied shock-troops were styled, were recalled by 7pm, and at 10 they were 'marched off by torchlight to Nottingham, headed by His Grace the Duke of Devonshire' leaving Derby to look to its own defence, if it would. Lord Malmesbury wrote to Horace Walpole: 'The Duke of Devonshire wanted the inhabitants of Derby to defend their town, but not one man would stir.' This, from a Whig point of view, looks like a thin excuse, but may be yet another piece of telling evidence of the ambivalent attitude of the majority of the townsfolk to the Whig party. Not content, however, with remaining at Nottingham, the Duke then ordered his cohorts to Mansfield, where they remained for the duration of events in Derby, justifiably becoming the butt of an elaborate pseudo-biblical satire entitled *The Chronicle of the Derbyshire Regiment* and penned by the pseudonymous 'Nathan Ben Shaddai, a Priest of the Jews'. This document, of which several copies exist locally, is not only informative about several minor incidents and concerning motives, but also is exceedingly funny, as here, describing events at Mansfield, where the Blues were sent under the pretext of joining Wade at York. They sent out scouting parties to the south west, to reconnoitre:

'And they returned in the Night (having heard much talking and a great Noise, like unto the trampling of an Army) and they made their report unto D(evonshir)e, saying, "Now of a truth the Young Man approacheth, we are not deceived, for we have seen them with our Eyes and their Vanguard is about two thousand."
And when the men of Captain L(o)w(e) heard this, they cry'd out, saying, "Captain what shall we do to be sav'd?" And he answer'd them "RUN, LADS, RUN," and he turned his Back and fled and they followed him.
This was done that the words of the Captain might be fulfilled which he spoke unto Cope the Squire, saying, "My Men will follow me wherever I go."'

Verse 28 included a ponderous parody of the last supper; the expression 'the Young Man' is code for the Prince, elsewhere referred to as Issachar, and Captain Lowe was Edward Lowe of Hazlewood Hall.

Doubtless the people of Derby had a worrisome night on 3 December, their defenders having gone and the Scots in those days being an unknown quantity, believed to be violent, unruly, greedy and to a man molesters of women, if not worse. Many people hid their valuables, and dedicated Whigs, like the fashionable attorney John 'Equity' Wright, father of the painter, Joseph, removed their families from the town in haste and disorder, Wright himself going to Repton.

THE PRINCE IN DERBY

The first sign of Prince Charles Edward Stuart's army was manifested at 11am on the morning of 4 December, when two officers appeared at the George to enquire for the mayor, Robert Hague, who in fact had also fled to Nottingham. Being appraised of this they went to the newly-built Guildhall to demand billets for the accommodation of 9,000 and to commandeer a horse from Alderman Thomas Stamford, a rich glover. This solecism, be it said, was written up with awful venom in the *Derby Mercury's* rather biased account written after the event. The paper was Whig in 1745; by 1785 it had become unrepentantly Tory. The figure of 9,000 plainly represents the numbers which the Scots considered they

had, but it did not only include fighting men. Many of the senior Jacobites were travelling with their wives and other supernumeraries must have been included, too. The sources agree in the main on a figure of 7,587 men at arms, which squares well with the figure of 7,542 in Lord Ogilvie's Regimental Orderly Book. D.P. Davies gives a parish breakdown totalling 7,148, however.

Not long afterwards a party of between 30 and 60 cavalry appeared, took possession of the Market Place and at about three in the afternoon Lord Elcho appeared at the head of the Life Guards, with many of the Highland Chiefs, probably numbering about 150. These were the vanguard and were closely followed by the genial Duke of Perth with the main body of the army. They all must have approached down the old Ashbourne Road (now largely marked by hedgerows to the north of the later turnpike through Mackworth and Markeaton), Markeaton Lane, Friar Gate and thence via Sadler Gate Bridge and Sadler Gate to Market Head.

'Most of them,' reported the *Derby Mercury* broadsheet, 'are a parcel of shabby, lousy, pitiful-looking fellows, mix'd up with old men and boys; dress'd in dirty plaids and as dirty shirts, without breeches and wore their stockings made of plaid not much above halfway up their legs and some without shoes or next to none and numbers of them so fatigu'd with their long march, that they commanded our pity rather than our fear.'

Revd Henry Cantell (1685–1773), vicar of St Alkmund's for almost 50 years and a fervent Jacobite, who wrote a (lost) journal of events. (The late R.J. Hughes)

By mid-afternoon the Market Place was filled with troops expecting the arrival of the Prince. Revd Henry Cantrell, the Jacobite vicar of St Alkmund's, takes up the tale:

'Before he came into the town, Lord George Murray summon'd the Corporation to appear in their habits before the Town Hall. Alderman Cooper appeared in his furr gown; Smith, Bakewell and Franceys were without, pretending they were not near at hand; the Gisbornes (Alderman John and Thomas and your old friend John) had left the town as well as the mayor. Lord George (Murray) waiv'd the ceremony of the Habit and only insisted that they should by their Cryer proclaim James the Third, King of England, Scotland, France and Ireland, which was done by the cryer, the town clerk having likewise gone away.'

The proclamation having been made, Charles Edward duly arrived and Henry Cantrell described him: 'He is a fine person, six foot high, a very good complexion and presence majestic. He had a Scotch bonnet with a white silver rose…'

It is reasonable to ask how the Prince was received in Derby. The *Derby Mercury* broadsheet would have him ordering bells to be rung and bonfires lit, yet in nearly all eyewitness accounts, these events appear as spontaneous. Mrs Thompson's grandmother, then living in Derby, was busy making white cockades for people to wear and, like many others, was given a miniature portrait of himself by the prince. That he gave a diamond ring to Alderman Samuel Heathcote is also not in doubt, for it is kept in Derby Museum to this day. A letter posted in Derby on 5 December 1745 and recovered two days later from the Post Office (then in Queen Street), written by a Peter Auchterlony (one of the Highland Army) to his wife says, 'Wee arrived here last night amidst the acclamations of the people and publick rejoicings which wee have had in severall places…'

Another account adds 'Bonefires [*sic*] on the road, the Belles [!] ringing… it was really a fine sight to see the illuminations of the town' which sounds more like Blackpool 248 years later! In short, and given the political temper of Derby since the Restoration, the accounts are all perfectly believable.

Bonnie Prince Charlie took up quarters at Exeter House and clearly the billeting arrangements which had been sprung upon the townsmen at 11 o'clock that morning had borne fruit, for all were soon quartered, in telling contrast to the difficulties experienced by only a few of William III's men in 1688. Needless to say that Brownlow Cecil, 8th Earl of Exeter, was not at home in Exeter House, having no doubt deemed it prudent, with his Countess – the former Miss Hannah Sophia Chambers – to withdraw, despite his Tory sentiments, to Burleigh.

Bonnie Prince Charlie's Derby HQ, Exeter House, as rebuilt in the 18th century (*c*.1728–1740). Photographed by Richard Keene, in 1853.

That first night was not spent in idleness. An advance party went via Chellaston and seized Swarkestone Bridge, which intelligence reports gave the Jacobites to believe might be destroyed by Hanoverian elements. A picquet was posted at Stanton-by-Bridge, a party variously assessed at between 60 and 80. Most stayed in Derby, many houses being packed with soldiers, bearing in mind that the Highland Army represented nearly a doubling of the town's population. Many Derby people were terrified of the Scots, partly out of ignorance and partly through government propaganda.

The housekeeper of Lancelot Chambers of Cockpit Hill – possibly Cockpit Hill House – a cousin of Lady Exeter's and a Jacobite (although he had mysteriously left Derby), was in a terrible lather of fear and apologies when she received John Daniel, a Lancastrian follower of Prince Charles Edward. Another Derby woman is alleged to have presented herself in her own hallway to two surprised Scots officers surrounded by all the household plate and valuables. On being asked the reason for this odd behaviour by her startled Highland visitors, she is said to have tearfully cried out, 'Take me, take my valuables, Good Sirs, but do not let your soldiers take my child!' The officers assured her that, contrary to current malicious rumour, Scottish soldiers did not eat English babies, or pillage, and that their objective was to install on the throne their rightful sovereign. They added that their only immediate aim was a good meal and an early night. Apparently the atmosphere swiftly became cordial.

George English, a government spy 'visiting' friends in the town, went to the George and enjoyed a round or two of drinks with several Highland officers, including Captains McCarthy and Graham, General John Gordon also being present. He adds in a letter to John Danvers MP that he 'might have seen the Pretender had I stay'd Ann hour longer.'

91

5 DECEMBER

Derby County Assembly Rooms, built in Full Street in 1713 and the scene of Bonnie Prince Charlie's *levée* of 5 December 1745. Photographed prior to demolition in 1968. (Don Farnsworth)

The following morning, copies of James III's manifesto – a most liberal document for its age, promising freedom of religion, three yearly parliaments and Scots and Irish devolution among other innovations – were distributed. Samuel Heathcote got out a list of those who had subscribed money to the raising of the Derbyshire Regiment and everyone on it found to be still in the town was obliged to contribute a similar amount to the Jacobite cause. Those liable for excise payments who had not paid were dunned for their contributions, half a year's land tax was demanded and £100 commandeered from the Post Office. It appears that these measures raised nearly £3,000, which was good going indeed for a day's work. All available horses were also taken, but apparently paid for. None of the Whig-inspired stories – of cannon being pointed at the Guildhall to reinforce a demand for £20,000 for instance – are borne out by first-hand accounts.

The artillery, about 13 pieces, was indeed safely parked on Nuns' Green all the while; it is said that wheels from a piece of ordnance were later found by a house on the south side of Nuns' Green – by the widest end of Friar Gate where many of the fairs were then held – and are said to have inspired the name of an inn founded at about this time, the Wheel, since rebuilt and recently and

Bonnie Prince Charlie in the council chamber at Exeter House (reconstruction in Derby Museum). (Derby City Council)

pointlessly re-named the Garrick and subsequently the Thirsty Scholar. Needless to say, the Wheel was so called as early as 1732 – so much for local mythology!

A long passage in the *Mercury* broadsheet lays the charge against Prince Charles Edward's soldiery that on the 5 December they spent much of the time looting from shops, behaving high-handedly and generally mugging people of quality. Against this and bearing in mind that very many of the Highlanders could speak no English, is the statement from the hostile *London Gazette* that '…the Rebels behaved tolerably well in their march southwards'.

Lord Hartington, the Duke of Devonshire's son, wrote to the Duke of Newcastle that he 'was surpris'd to find they had done so little damage' and another report declared that 'The Rebels continued at Derby all that day and behav'd civilly to the Town's People'. One Derby gentleman had his house searched for arms, but not one of his valuables was touched. Further evidence of the favour, indeed, the Scotsmen encountered at Derby was evinced in 1763, when two Highland Regiments were being marched from Tilbury to Scotland. Supposing them erroneously to be Jacobites, the citizens of Derby received them exceptionally well, not charging them for accommodation and raising subscriptions for making gifts to the men: a stark contrast to the encounter between Ralph Clarke and the Scots at Derby in 1643!

One tradition places the inquisitive return to the town of the mayor, Robert Hague, on the morning of the 5th. Hague, a Whig maltster, decided to 'pay his respects' to Prince Charles Edward at Exeter House. On being asked his business there by a fearsome guard in Highland dress, he is said to have lost his composure and begged an audience with the 'Pretender'! The wretched alderman was promptly kicked down the fine oak staircase of Exeter House with the remark, doubtless delivered in the musical accents of the Highlander, darkened with ire: 'Rascal that ye are, if ye want to see a Pretender, get you to St James'!'

Recruiting was also pushed ahead at Derby on 5 December, but to no very great effect, apparently. Definite identified recruits from Derby appear to number only six, although there is reason to believe that the number may have in fact been nearer 40. Every move made on 5 December was observed by Hanoverian spies: George English, a Mr Orell, Eliezer Birch and at least two others, one of whom was a Dissenting Minister. Most reported back to the Duke of Cumberland at Stafford, albeit the inevitable delay rendering their intelligence of little real value. Birch, a resourceful man, got arrested on the evening of the 5th and did far more damage by giving disinformation to his interrogator at Exeter House, Colonel Hay. His false testimony was indeed used by the Jacobite faction wishing to return north to

Loughborough, reached by elements of Bonnie Prince Charlie's army, 4–5 December 1745. (M. Craven)

strengthen their case, insofar as he gave them to believe that a Hanoverian army was blocking the road south, whereas in fact the way to London was clear.

Indeed, a party of Prince Charles Edward's army had that day penetrated as far south as Loughborough without hearing of any impediment to an advance, as letters in the Royal Collection and material gathered by the Jacobite de L'isle family, then of Garendon Hall, by Loughborough, attest. The Leicestershire town at this time was 'a town full of Jacobites, who were known to have been pledging the young adventurer's health on their bare and bended knees'. Yet, paradoxically, it was Birch who was believed. Added to this, a roguish American soldier of fortune if impeccable ancestry called Captain Dudley Bradstreet rode into town and demanded an interview with the Jacobite commanders, telling them that their way south was threatened by Cumberland and 8,000 men at Lichfield,' which appeared to the Jacobite High Command to corroborate Birch's dubious news.

Prince Charles Edward himself seems to have ridden during the afternoon of the 5th with German Pole to Calke to see Sir Henry Harpur and to Foremark to see Sir Robert Burdett. A less likely story has it that he also visited 'Nether Hall near Burton' – perhaps the Nether Hall at Hartshorne – to see John Stanhope MP. Nonetheless, he was unable to obtain firm promises of

Rotten Row, photographed by Richard Keene in 1855.
(Curzon family)

help, despite their sympathy with his cause. The ultimate consequence was that after an acrimonious council meeting in Exeter House, in the famous dining room – panelling from which was rescued and now forms the backdrop to an excellent reconstruction of the occasion in the Museum – the decision was taken to retreat from Derby.

A story much repeated, often in respectable sources, is that a Catholic Mass was celebrated on that morning in All Saints' by a 'French Priest'. The truth, however, can be pieced together from contemporary accounts and circumstantial evidence, not least of which is the fact that Prince Charles Edward's Catholicism was fast in eclipse. He was indeed received, albeit incognito, into the Anglican Church in St Mary-le-Strand, London, in 1750. In fact the service that morning would appear to have been a High Church Holy Communion conducted by the Manchester priest Rt Revd Thomas Coppock, titular (Jacobite) Bishop of Carlisle.

Another event, on the evening of 5 December, was a *levée* or reception held in the Assembly Rooms – presumably those established for the County Assembly in Full Street in 1713 – attended by most of the Jacobite officers, the Prince and many townsmen. It is a testimony to the popularity of the Scots (or the insensate

curiosity of the citizens of the town) that such was the crush, that one of the Prince's standards, displayed before the dais, was knocked over and broken. It was taken as a bad omen by the very few people present who were privy to the momentous decision that a return to Scotland had just been decided upon for dawn the next day.

THE RETREAT BEGINS

Before first light on the 6th, just as panic was reaching its height in the capital, the vanguard of the Prince's army began its departure back towards Ashbourne, the darkness concealing from the men the direction of their march until dawn broke as they marched between Mackworth and Kirk Langley. Henry Cantrell wrote:

'On Friday morning at nine o'clock, their Prince, being well mounted, set out from my Lord Exeter's house, went over the Market Place, up the Rotten Row and down the Sadler's Gate on the way to Ashbourne.'

At the same time, however, a more bizarre departure was being made, albeit of less significance. The spy Eliezer Birch, at dawn, realising that his guards were distractedly coming and going, forced the window of the room at Exeter House in which he was confined, dropped 20ft without injury ('I was pretty much stunn'd with the fall but soon recovered myself'), and climbed a wall into the next door garden, Alderman Samuel Heathcote's, falling into the river in the process. He stripped off his wet clothes in the 'Garden House' – one of the pretty little garden pavilions at the water's edge, this particular one, like the house, later Dr Erasmus Darwin's – and then, despite the season, swam down to the weir, waded to the Derwent Navigation and then ran naked three miles downstream to Alvaston, where the startled wife of a farmer called Ridgeley took him in. After several more adventures, with Alderman Heathcote's men hunting him, he eventually escaped to Nottingham from Elvaston on a borrowed horse, to be told on arrival that the Jacobites were retreating.

'We were rid of them all', says the *Mercury* broadsheet, '(except a few stragglers) by 11 o'clock. Their Hussars were a parcel of fierce and desperate ruffians and were the last body that quitted the town.'

Not everyone was miserable, however. Dr Robert Mather wrote to Sir Nathaniel Curzon's son from Kedleston on 9 December,

'When they march'd out of Derby, Miss Glanville was seen dancing among them with a Highlander on her back.

"Oh!" cries He, "This will gollope, gollope, this will gollope!"'

Tales of final exactions of large sums of money at this juncture seem not to stand up to scrutiny. Eardley Simpson's judgement on the affair, still fairly convincing today despite his evident sympathy for the cause of the prince, is as follows: 'If the Army of the White Rose had marched over Swarkestone Bridge on the morning of 6 December 1745, within a week James III would have been proclaimed in London, while [the Dukes of] Newcastle and Bedford encouraged an enthusiastic populace to welcome Charles not only as Prince Regent of the Kingdom, but as the victorious leader who had restored the native House without the aid of a foreign bayonet.'

To the Jacobites themselves the day was ever after known as Black Friday.

Of the whole tragic tale, which ended so bloodily and discreditably at Culloden Moor, little of the aftermath in Derby obtrudes. The Whig Aldermen, who had so speedily decamped at the onset of the prince's army, came sloping back once the coast was clear. On 2 June 1746 the whole Common Hall – the Corporation – sent a Humble Address, full of weasel words, to George II professing their loyalty and offering congratulations on the 'late important success of your Majesty's forces' and signed by the self-same Robert Hague, as mayor, who had been so unceremoniously propelled down the great staircase at Exeter House by the Prince's Highland Guard on 5 December previous.

Eighteen months afterwards came the next election. As in 1741, German Pole, the Tory, challenged the Cavendish candidate Lord Duncannon, who was running in the interests of the Whig oligarchy, again with John Stanhope. Instead of nearly winning, as in 1741, Pole was trounced. Significantly, Simpson adds 'The number of voters at this Election was 646, being exactly the same number polled at the last contested Election for this town 8 May 1741.' In other words, chicanery of the same order was still operating, even though one might have thought that, in the reaction of the events of 1745–46, such unsavoury precautions were hardly necessary.

And indeed, the climate in Derby was slowly changing. The gradual advance of the Industrial Age into the town, the entrepreneurs and bankers who took up residence in its wake, all strengthened the radical and Whig element in the town, so that by the third quarter of the 18th century Derby's underlying High Church Toryism, a manifestation of its earlier position as a 'Town of Gentry, rather than Trade', as Daniel Defoe put it in his *Journey Through the Whole Island of Great Britain*, had succumbed to the political tenets of the new era.

VII
PROSPERITY RETURNS

aniel Defoe's oft-quoted remark stands in fact in counterpoint to some of the sights he saw when in the town in 1724.

'This is a fine, beautiful and pleasant town; it has more families of gentlemen in it than is usual in towns so remote, and therefore here is a great deal of good and some gay company.'

He goes on to say:

'Here is a curiosity in Trade worth observing, as being the only one of its kind in England, namely, a throwing or throwster's mill, which performs by a wheel turned by the water; and though it cannot perform the doubling part of a throwster's work, which can only be done by a handwheel, yet it turns the other work, and performs the labour of many hands. Whether it answers to the expense or not is none of my business.'

The date of publication was August 1726 (although misleadingly dated 1727) and the compilation was done in 1724–25, according to a recent editor. Yet there is apparently less first-hand material in this volume than in the previous ones. Nevertheless, Defoe's account of Derby is unlikely to have been in any way inaccurate in its essentials.

THE SILK MILLS

George Sorocold is a character who we have already encountered engineering Derby's first piped water supply. A few years previously he had also re-hung the impressive 10-bell peal in the tower of All Saints' and contrived a carillon to play seven tunes three times a day. He also built the first proper docks at Rotherhithe (London) and Liverpool and after two decades of delay had designed and built the Derwent Navigation, a semi-canalisation of the Derwent from Derby to the Trent.

In 1717–18 he had engineered and designed a large five-storey silk mill on the Derwent's edge for John and William Lombe, a pair of half-brothers from Norwich. The event was particularly memorable for Defoe, for, while visiting the mill, he claimed to have witnessed Sorocold in gesticulatory enthusiasm over his creation, overbalance and fall into the mill race. It was only through great good fortune that the eminent hydraulicist escaped with his life. Unfortunately, an account of a visit to Derby by the surveyor Thomas Surbey in May 1699 has Sorocold fall under his water wheel in the Derwent and survive thanks to '…one of

the lawyers braking [the wheel]', which sounds like the original source for Defoe's colourful tale!

Nevertheless, this mill is of importance as it is the first true factory to have been erected in England, containing within it all the processes of manufacture run from a single source of power, in this instance Sorocold's water wheel.

Silk throwing, that is the twisting of filaments of raw silk to form a usable thread, was a monopoly enjoyed by the Piedmontese in Northern Italy. In *c*.1698 Thomas Cotchett, junior, of Mickleover, the grandson of Major Thomas Sanders's Civil War *confrere*, had Sorocold build him a silk mill called 'The Old Shop', an engaging timber-framed building, slightly to the north of that seen by Defoe. Therein he, with the help of John Lombe who, as a younger son, was keen to seek his fortune independently, endeavoured for a decade to perfect a silk-throwing process. Yet, for all their efforts, a satisfactory thread could not be produced. Cotchett, as a result, reached the limit of his resources and sold out to Lombe who resolved to go to Italy, where he learnt Italian and obtained work in a silk mill at Livorno. Under the cloak of zeal he remained at his machine of a night, making detailed drawings. These he secreted in bales of finished material which, by happy chance, were shipped to England and agents of the Lombe family. On arrival, the drawings were sent to Derby, where associates had the machines made in the Moot Hall. Ironically, none of this effort need have been resorted to had Lombe realised that the details he required were in a 16th-century Italian publication in the Bodleian collection in Oxford, complete with detailed drawings, where it still resides.

Ultimately, Lombe had to beat a hasty retreat from Italy by sea, hotly pursued by the Piedmontese Navy, impelled by the awful prospect of losing their monopoly of silk. Safely arrived in England, however, Britain's first industrial spy proceeded to Derby and the two-unit mill was built, ultimately employing 300 people. It was successful, and he undercut the Italians with ease, this being helped in 1718 by the grant of a 14-year patent from the Crown.

Unfortunately, the enterprising young man did not live long to enjoy the fruits of his £30,000 undertaking, dying on 16 March 1722 of slow poisoning at the hands of a female Italian employee (who was acquitted of the crime through lack of evidence), sent at the instigation of those in Livorno who had had most cause to regret

Derby Silk Mill: the only known photograph (by Richard Keene, 1855) showing Sorocold's water wheel. On the left is Lombe's original house. (M. Craven)

his success. He was much mourned for his enterprise and pleasant character, and was buried on the Little Byflat island in the Derwent opposite his mill under an impressive marble monument set at the end of a line of yews, artfully trimmed to resemble obelisks.

His half-brother William succeeded to the business, but took his own life for no apparent reason other than 'a melancholy disposition', leaving everything in the control of his cousin Sir Thomas Lombe. He is alleged to have made profits of £80,000 and, on applying to Parliament to obtain the renewal of John's patent in 1732 (mendaciously failing to mention the extent of his profits), failed to achieve his object, although he received £14,000 by way of compensation. After Sir Thomas's death in 1739, the business was bought by Richard Wilson, and by 1826 it was in the hands of William Taylor.

Sorocold's main building stood five storeys beneath a parapet on arches raised over caissonned timber piling and was 110ft x 39ft, 'The Old Shop' remaining at its north end as additional accommodation until at least 1803 when Wilson's 79-year lease was renewed; it disappeared not long afterwards. To the south was built the doubling shop, which collapsed on 25 August 1890 from lack of maintenance and was demolished early in 1892. The waterwheel was 23ft in diameter. Sometime before 1730, a vast atmospheric engine was installed between the two buildings, probably built by Sorocold's friend Thomas Savory. Its purpose was to pump warm air round the building, not, as one might suppose, to improve the comfort of the workforce, but to ensure that the silk filaments did not snap, as they were prone to do when the temperature dropped much below 45°F.

The mill's later history was chequered. Joseph Pickford replaced the mill race bridge and improved the water flow beneath the wheel by raising the weir in 1776. The main mill burnt out in 1821 and was rebuilt with a hipped roof and an arcaded, octagonal tower carrying the bell that summoned the workforce. This rebuilding seems to have bankrupted Taylor, the owner, but it carried on, despite French competition through most of the 19th century. Silk throwing had, however, ceased there 15 years before when it burnt to the ground on 5 December 1910. It was subsequently rebuilt, but was only three rather than five storeys high. Only the carrying arches and bell-tower remained from the previous edifice. Since 1974 it has housed the Derby Industrial Museum.

Silk Mill Lane, photograph by Richard Keene c.1855, showing mill race bridge and Bakewell's gate, the overthrow embellished with the Lombe family's crossed lances crest and monogram in a rondel. (M. Craven)

The introduction of the silk industry expanded, at first to Macclesfield, Cheshire, as a result of John Lombe's enterprise and on the expiry of his cousin's patent in 1732. Yet Derby's role in the industry was by no means over. A letter of April 1774 from the banker Samuel Crompton to the prospective new owner of the Silk Mill, Richard Wilson, states '...there is twelve other silk mills in Derby besides the Great one (which makes that building not of the value it was) and they all complain that the trade is very bad.' This number included a later entrant into the field in the shape of cotton pioneer Jedediah Strutt, who in 1760 had a mill in The Morledge processing 'tram', an inferior quality silk which could be more easily made into a variety of trimmings. By 1789 there were 1,200 silk workers in Derby, although only seven actual mills are recorded by Farey in 1811. One of the best, Unsworth's of 1802 in Green Lane, lasted until the early 1980s before being demolished.

Despite French competition, by 1833 there seem to have been 11 such firms, with eight others making silk hose and three indulging in silk weaving. By the mid-19th century, silk throwing was a contracting trade in Derby, despite the award of a large bronze medal to Messrs Thomas Bridgett & Company at the Great Exhibition of 1851 for the excellence of their product,

John Lombe as portrayed by Morley Horder on the former Boot's building in St Peter's Street (1912). (M. Craven)

made in their impressively tall multi-storey fireproof steam-driven mill on Bridge Street, which in 2003 was upgraded to II* by English Heritage and converted into flats by a Nottingham developer in the wake of the failure of a destructive scheme by the University of Derby to convert the entire complex into students' lodgings.

COMMUNICATIONS – DERWENT NAVIGATION

This beginning of industry in Derby was in some measure due to its geographical position. The Trent was, as at the time of the Saxons and Vikings, a major artery of communication, enabling suitable craft to penetrate the heart of England. Yet the Derwent was by no means reliably navigable to Derby. As far back as 1673, a suggestion that the river be made navigable as far as the town had been mooted, and John Flamsteed's preliminary survey for a map, dated 1677 and consisting of several pages of co-ordinates connecting the centre of St Mary's Bridge with obscure datum-points like 'Mr Smith's summerhouse' and now in the National Maritime Museum's Collection at Greenwich, may have been connected with this. That some navigation had been feasible before is reinforced by the name of a 'yard or croft on the Derwent in Little Chester called the Boate Yard' which had been let to Nathaniel Bate in 1646. Indeed, the 1673 scheme had been based on a similar one planned in 1638 by Charles I and Sir Cornelius Vermuyden, the latter then being active in Derbyshire, pioneering soughs for lead mines.

Before 1703 the indefatigable George Sorocold had prepared another scheme called the Derwent Navigation consisting of a straight cut from the south end of the Siddalls to High Bank near Borrowash and another through Ambaston to the north end of Great Wilne and using no less than nine locks. The superb map drawn by Sorocold for the Parliamentary Bill in 1703 includes a map of Derby which is only the second new one after Speed's. Confusingly, though, it is oriented horizontally south–north.

After almost two decades of delays in Parliament, engineered by the burghers of Newark, whose trade might be threatened by its success, it was finally built on a much simpler plan using the canalised river and fewer engineering works, in 1719–21 acquiring legal status by an Act of Parliament of 7 April 1720. These works involved a cut through part of the west side of The Holmes – a series of water meadows much appreciated by local people for evening walks, bleaching cloth, musters, reviews and various other pastimes – crossed by a ferry and leading to wharves at the northern end, with a wharfinger's house and toll booth. The manager enjoyed a pleasant brick house at Great Wilne boasting an ice-house. This innovation much eased the position with regard to bulk trade to and from the town, although it was by no means a perfect solution. Trans-shipment of goods was made at Gainsborough. In 1828 heavy goods to London via this route (still open) cost £1 per ton.

ROADS

Transport by road, strangely, was not improved nearly so quickly. Local roads were always a problem and were the responsibility of the mayor and burgesses. A typical example was that now known as the Uttoxeter Road, for the repair and maintenance of which in 1660–62 the mayor and his colleagues raised forced subscriptions for the stretch 'extending from Foulbrooke Bushes [somewhere on the Bramble Brook] to Heynours [Rough Heanor, immediately east of Mickleover]'.

Nevertheless, material did go by road, and enough to make a profit for some at that. Richard Bakewell is recorded as a carrier in 1666, and two other names are known for the same period. In 1709 the Signpost Act ensured that at least the hapless traveller could find his way, and within the generation the first turnpikes were being established. On 3 April 1735 the Nottingham-Derby-London stage coach was inaugurated, running every three days from the George in Iron Gate via Swarkestone Bridge, the promoters of the service being Thomas Smith and John Needham.

The turnpike toll house of c.1820 at the junction of Radbourne Road and Markeaton Lane. Photographed by Richard Keene c.1880. Note the tariff board, top upper light, left of centre. (Derby Museum)

The coach road up the Derwent Valley from Derby was launched in 1739, following a meeting of would-be investors at the King's Head on 26 June previous. Following this, the Derby–Burton turnpike was opened in July 1754 using the Roman Rykneld Street, now mostly followed by the A38; a decade later the coach fare to Birmingham via this route was 10s (50p) inside and 5s (25p) outside. The Chesterfield Turnpike was opened in 1756 and the London Road turnpike two years later. The latter diverted traffic from the Osmaston Road–Chellaston–Swarkestone Bridge route, used since prehistory, on to a new one which left the old at the Spot, running via Alvaston and Shardlow to a particularly fine new bridge over the Trent by James Paine of 1758–61, funded by the Duke of Devonshire and known thereby as Cavendish Bridge which, unfortunately, collapsed in the flood of 1947. The 'Derby Fly' claimed to reach London by this route in a single day in the summer months, setting out from the *Bell* on a Sunday evening at 19.00 hours in the 1770s. The fare to London in 1761 was £1 8s 0d (£1.40p).

Despite the foregoing, Glover confidently asserts that the Shardlow–Derby–Brassington Turnpike was the first in the county, which left Derby northwards via the Kedleston Road, which was consequently improved. The toll house is a fine Gothic affair built in 1863, renovated by the Derbyshire Historic Buildings Trust in 1977. Numerous other turnpikes followed until the last road was improved in 1802.

At the entrance to the borough's boundaries, the turnpike trusts erected toll bars or gates controlled from a small purpose-built cottage, the toll house. Some 12 can be identified, of which survivors can by found at Botany Bay on the Ashbourne Road, Burton Road, Kedleston Road and London Road, Crewton – the last to sport a gate, removed in 1879.

Transport in the town, if not undertaken by private carriage or horse, was by fly or one-horse chaise, which at that time were largely available for hire from Mr Hoare (proprietor of the King's Head in Cornmarket), Mr Price at the White Lion on Ashbourne Road (now a shop), the coach-builder Charles Holmes – a useful diversification on his part, enabling hirers to sample the excellence of his manufacturers – and George Wallis. His New Inn, built c.1766 and demolished 1969 to accommodate the Inner Ring Road, was the last of the recognised posting inns. The others included the Talbot Iron Gate (before 1676–1876), Virgin's Inn, Market Place (before 1708–1767), King's Head, (c.1660–1872), the Bell, Sadler Gate (of c.1680–90), and the Tiger (1737, rebuilt by Joseph Pickford of Derby in 1764). Posting in its strictest sense was available at the Mail Office in Queen Street. This latter institution was moved in 1839 to the Royal Hotel complex.

Wallis himself, the son of a blacksmith in King Street, and brother-in-law of the painter Joseph Wright, built up a nationwide network of coaching routes of which the New Inn was the hub. He died in 1786, being succeeded in turn by his sons William and John, the latter also the founder of the Derby True Blue Club (owners of an important Derby china 'Rodney' jug). The third generation of the family transferred operations to the King's Head and expanded by acquiring the Green Man and Black's Head at Ashbourne, which they ran until the early 20th century. Fortunately, when the railway era arrived they had the foresight to diversify and adapt, becoming goods agents for the railway and running a pioneer omnibus service to the station.

COPPER & IRON

The consequences of the Derwent Navigation included the foundation of industries other than the Silk Mill. In 1734 Winster-born William Evans (1696–1773) founded 'slitting, rolling and battering mills' on the northernmost tip of The Holmes opposite The Morledge. The function of this works was to prepare iron and later (1737) copper sheathing for HM ships. The copper for this process apparently came from Wales, conceivably through connections of Evans's or Thomas Chambers of Exeter House, who had extensive interests in this metal.

The enterprise was inherited by second cousin Thomas Evans (1723–1814), who sold it on to John and Joseph Bingham in the 1780s, allowing him to concentrate on his bank and his new Darley Abbey mills. The firm moved in the 1840s to Chesterfield, and the site was later appropriated by the Corporation for their extensive new cattle market complex of 1861.

BANKING

We have already seen that Abraham Crompton founded the first bank in Derby in 1685 and his enterprise continued to flourish, his son and grandson putting up the money for several major enterprises, including the Rolling and Slitting Mills. It later became the Derby Old Bank of Crompton, Newton & Co. and in 1877 amalgamated with the bank founded by Thomas Evans as Crompton & Evans Union Bank, building a splendid new Italian Palazzo building in Iron Gate by J.A. Chadwick of Birmingham, now the Standing Order pub, having been closed by NatWest Bank in 1994. The Westminster Bank had taken Crompton & Evans over in 1914.

The third banker on the scene was Iron Gate based William Chase (1708–1784), whose family were frame-

Darley Abbey, Brick Row, built by the Evans family for their workers in two phases of six houses each between 1797 and 1800. The end house (right) functioned as the lodge for demolished Darley House where the Evans then lived. (M. Craven)

Copper magnate and millionare Thomas Chambers (1660–1726); portrait bust by Richard Ruysbrack from his monument in Derby Cathedral. (M. Craven)

The finest banking hall in the Midlands, Crompton & Evans's new building of 1880, now the Standing Order pub. (M. Craven)

Banker Samuel Crompton II, painted by Joseph Wright, 1778. (Derby Museum)

Thomas Evans, banker, cotton entrepreneur and merchant, d.1814. Portrait by James Rawlinson of Derby. (Bamfords Ltd)

Derby and Derbyshire Bank, Cornmarket, 1834, co-founded by William Baker. Building by Robert Wallace. (M. Craven)

work knitters but whose opportunity came through marriage into the wealthy Binghams. His concern was founded by the mid-1760s – when he sat for Joseph Wright – and eventually passed to his grandson William Baker, son of a stockiner turned hosier, whose homonymous grandson used it as the basis for the foundation of the Derby & Derbyshire Bank, a joint stock note-issuing company, in 1833, whose handsome premises designed a year or two later by Robert Wallace still grace the Corn Market. It too ended up as a branch of the Westminster Bank, being closed in the early 1970s.

Thomas Evans traded from 1771 in St Mary's Gate as the Derby Bank, merging with Crompton, Newton & Co. in 1877, removing briefly to their premises at Iron Gate House – a delightful early Georgian house with a ramped parapet, utterly wrecked by conversion into Yates's Wine Lodge in the 1990s. By 1879 their new premises on the site of the timber-framed Old Talbot Inn were ready.

Other banks which arose on the rising tide of trade and manufacture in the 18th century were Richardson's (before 1778), the breakaway Richardson & Mowbray (1778) which failed in 1815, Bellairs & Company (before 1783) – latterly in Dr Darwin's former house in Full Street where it failed in 1814 – King, Rodgers & Company's Derby Union Bank (before 1800), a branch of the note-issuing Nottingham joint stock bank, Smiths, in a Georgian House in Rotten Row in 1806, replaced in 1878 to a design by George R. Isborne (also

Rotten Row, premises of Smith's bank (centre) from 1806 to 1875, shown in Richard Keene's photograph of 1877 just prior to demolition and replacement.

now NatWest) and a latecomer, the Derby Commercial Bank founded in 1868, which concern commissioned John Somes Story to build an impressive new premises on the site of Joseph Strutt's old home, Thorntree House, in 1880. This joint stock bank merged with Parr's Bank (later the Midland, now HSBC) in 1914. Farrow's Bank had a branch in Derby from around 1899 but failed during World War One. Of these concerns, all but Richardson & Mowbray issued notes, but only the Heaths need detain us.

John Heath was a copyhold farmer at Makeney who died in 1765. He was almost certainly a descendant of a yeoman called Christopher Heath who was a tenant of the Corporation of Derby in a pasture immediately south of Darley Slade in 1652. John had five sons and five daughters. Of the latter, one became the mistress of Revd Francis Revell of Carnfield Hall and had his only two children. Another made a respectable match with Joshua Bradshaw, a scion of a local family of impoverished gentry. Three sons, John, Christopher and Isaac, sought their fortunes in Derby, acting as freelance

business entrepreneurs and fixers. John first comes to notice in 1730 when he acquired and let the freehold of Darley Hall from the bankrupt William Woolley, son of the county's first historian. He seems to have been acting as a banker as early as 1735 when he had illegally leased the estate to the Holden family – illegally, because it later emerged that he had previously mortgaged it to a London bank for £8,000. The likelihood is that the £8,000 was the start-up capital for the bank.

Crompton & Newton (Derby Old Bank) £1 banknote, early 19th century. (Derby Museum)

CERAMIC MANUFACTURE

In 1751 a partnership consisting of John Heath, Thomas Rivett MP and William Butts in a pot works at Cockpit Hill was in existence, with an implication that the concern had been going for a while at least. Butts was the potter – making earthenware and a miniscule amount of porcelain – the others merely investors, Rivett being the owner of the site. The works lay within the strangely-shaped close on Cockpit Hill, which may have been a vestige of the possible 12th-century castle. In June 1752 the Pot Works' proprietors had also leased for 21 years a water-driven flint mill at Darley Abbey from dyer Abraham Hurst, used to grind the minerals to make the colours for the pots.

Not content with this, we find Heath as tenant of another works, this time making wares in porcelain, on the Nottingham Road, close to St Mary's Bridge. This, it would appear, had been founded – undoubtedly with the benefit of Heath's money – about or just prior to 1750, the potter being a talented but un-businesslike man of Huguenot extraction called Andrew Planché, who had begun 'a foreigner in very poor circumstances' making 'small articles in china such as birds, cats, dogs, sheep and other small ornamental toys' at premises in Lodge Lane. Apparently he had at first used a supernumerary pipe kiln owned by the Strongs, whom we have already met as token-issuers.

But even before the notice of Heath's tenancy, we find a deed of agreement between Planché, Heath and one William Duesbury of Longton, Staffordshire, dated 1 January 1756, to manufacture porcelain on a site on Nottingham Road, yet we hear no more of Planché thereafter, giving rise to the suspicion that, having acquired the services of Duesbury – a man of considerable business flair as well as a potter of talent – Heath had elbowed the pliant Planché aside. Nevertheless, both potteries did well and were among Heath's wiser investments. Strangely, very few pieces of porcelain appear to have been made on Cockpit Hill, probably only experimentally. In the medium term it would appear that the success of Nottingham Road convinced Heath that the former should concentrate on what they were good at and leave porcelain manufacture to Duesbury.

It would appear that Duesbury was later able to buy the entire concern out and consequently his soft-paste porcelain factory – the products of which Dr Johnson in 1777 had said '…that it was too dear; for that (price) he could have vessels of silver, of the same size, as cheap as what were here made of porcelain' – escaped receivership when the Heaths went bankrupt in March 1779. The Cockpit Hill pot works, however, were sold to Thomas Evans and Walter Mather, the commissioners in bankruptcy, in March 1782, by which time the business

appears to have collapsed and the site was subsequently redeveloped as dwellings. John Heath, broken by the bankruptcy, died over Christmas 1780, although Christopher lived on in Duffield until July 1815, dying aged 96!

The Nottingham Road works kept expanding and altering as the demands of the business grew, and the reforming William Duesbury II (1751–1796) took over from his father in 1786. Sometime after 1761, a handsome house was erected on the site of a previous cottage, adjoining the north-west edge of the works, reflecting the social enhancement which Duesbury, originally a currier's son from Cannock, had undergone. The only sketch of the house and works as they were in the 18th century is one done in the century following by Moses Webster from childhood memory, so that such embellishments to the house as pedimented windows and doorcase which appear in his drawing may have never, in reality, existed. Nevertheless, the closeness of its plan to that of Long Eaton Hall (1778) suggests that it could have been designed by Duesbury's contemporary, the Warwickshire-born Derby architect Joseph Pickford. A beautiful drawing of a weighbridge office at the works in the collections of Derby Museum is undoubtedly from Pickford's office.

In 1773 the elder Duesbury received Letters Patent from the king to add the word 'Crown' to his factory's title. The firm, to which without doubt the Derwent Navigation must have been a boon, had reached its zenith with the regime of William Duesbury II, who was,

Silhouette of porcelain manufacturer William Duesbury (1725–86), probably by Edward Foster. (Derby Museum)

however, a man of fragile nerves, and what appear to have been repeated breakdowns led to a partnership with a talented but tactless Irishman, Michael Kean (d.1823), in 1795. Two years later, Duesbury died and Kean secured the business by marrying his widow, the daughter of an influential local attorney, cutting out, to a large extent, the true heir to the factory, the third William Duesbury.

Received history labels this talented man as disinclined to participate in the work of the factory and feckless, a reputation he may not wholly deserve, for he was a talented chemist, a gift that could have been of considerable value to the firm, had its proprietor been more forward-thinking. He is labelled as feckless because he got into financial difficulties in 1811–12, when he was the rates collector and secretary of the Third Improvement Commission, which got him in bad odium with the most influential men in the borough, as his embarrassment had meant that he had collected no rates for some time, leaving the Commission short on liquidity. It is not currently clear why Duesbury got into difficulties at this stage, but it may have been to do with his ingenious aptitude for chemistry. This talent, financially draining or not, led to the setting up of an enterprise at Bonsall to manufacture paint using a process he had invented without using toxic lead which was too far ahead of its time and failed, leaving him to go completely bankrupt in 1826, his assets taken over in lieu of the repayment of a loan by Robert Bloor. In 1830 he migrated to Lowell, Massachusetts, where he became a successful architect and chemist, experimenting with dyes for the cotton produced in that town, dying by his own hand in 1845. His posterity still live in America.

In 1811 the firm was sold for £5,000 to an employee, clerk and salesman Robert Bloor. Son of a Church Gresley farmer, Bloor and his brother Joseph (1783–1846) ran the firm through the first part of the 19th century, although the former, like the second Duesbury, suffered a nervous breakdown in 1828 and was declared insane at the beginning of 1846, dying in a private asylum in Hathern, Leicestershire, that March. It used to be said that the products of the company lacked the quality of those of the earlier period, but modern thinking tends to consider the best of Bloor's on a par with what went before, but to note that less was discarded and that the lesser products were, indeed, sometimes of inferior finish or quality.

With Bloor dying in 1846, closely followed by his brother, ownership of the works devolved onto Sarah, the only child of Bloor's daughter Harriet (d.1837) and her husband, the Liverpool merchant Edward Ramsbottom. Sarah was married to Alderman Thomas Clarke, whose malting and brewing empire adjoined the china factory on Nottingham Road, so it comes as no

Bloor Derby saucer, c.1815, with a very early view of Darley Abbey Mill. (Mellors and Kirk)

surprise to know that they sold it to Samuel Boyle of Stoke, who went bust almost immediately in 1848. They then sold part of the site for the erection of the flamboyantly Gothic but short-lived Convent of Mercy (attributed convincingly to Pugin) and expanded the Clarke maltings over what remained.

Nevertheless, a group of employees under W.G. Larcombe migrated to King Street, on part of the site of Old St Helen's House, and founded the 'Old Crown Derby China Factory' there. The most famous period of this well-regarded but never large firm was under Sampson Hancock. After his era, in the earlier 20th century, it passed into less determined hands and succumbed to the economic depression in 1935, being acquired by Royal Crown Derby, itself set up in the former Union Workhouse in Osmaston Road in 1877–78. Royal Crown Derby thereupon closed it down, although

King Street china works, interior, in the 1920s. (Private Collection)

The Royal Crown Derby factory, Osmaston Road, as adapted from John Mason's Union workhouse of 1839, in 1877–78. Photograph from 1880. (M. Craven)

most of the kilns and workshops survived until 1987. Thus, from 1935 the more modern firm has been able to claim an uninterrupted china manufacturing pedigree going back to 1750.

Royal Crown Derby itself had been in business continuously since its foundation by Edward Philips – whose family seems to have been somehow connected with selling the products of the old China Factory two generations or more beforehand – and William Litherland, with money from William Bemrose, the super-rich printing firm proprietor. It is famous, like its predecessor, for employing a number of world-class decorators, including the Gresleys, W.E.J. Dean and many others. It ended the 20th century as a flagging element in the Royal Doulton empire but was subject to a successful and widely welcomed management buy-out headed by Hon. Hugh Gibson, its managing director, and Roger Boissier, currently the chairman.

There were, in the late 18th century, a number of ex-Derby China employees who tried to set up rival porcelain factories in Derby. William John Coffee, later a successful sculptor in the US with the aged ex-President Jefferson as patron, had a go, and in December 1800 there is a fleeting reference to 'Mr Sheen's china manufactory in Derby' although, like a couple of others, it appears to have been under financed and thus very ephemeral – unless 'Sheen' is an error for 'Keen', in which case this particular example must be discarded!

DARLEY MILLS

The speed of the Derwent at Darley Abbey had made it an attractive place to build a mill from at least the Dissolution. There were three small ones there in the 1670s, and in the 1720s George Bage's paper mill joined them. In this context, another interest of the Heaths was in a water-driven flint-grinding mill there.

This was leased by Abraham Hurst to Heath, Rivett and Butts in June 1752 and later by William Duesbury. In the lease the mill's products are declared to be 'for ye Pott Works and other purposes'. John and Christopher Heath bought this lease out in 1770 and, after their bankruptcy in March 1779, the mill was purchased, with the pot works, for £170 in 1781 by none other than Thomas Evans (of banking and rolling mill fame), who just happened to be one of the Heaths' assignees in bankruptcy. Within a year, Evans had begun to build his Boar's Head Cotton Mill (named after his newly-granted heraldic crest) on the adjacent site at Darley Abbey, which was to ensure the prosperity of the family until its extinction, although the mill itself has survived, despite having burnt down as early as December 1788 and being rebuilt in that year as a consequence.

Walter Evans & Co., famous for its sewing thread, was sold on the death of Henry Evans in 1903, to John Peacock (1850–1930), the firm's long-standing manager, and his family ran it until a further buy-out post-war led to its closure in 1970. The complex miraculously survived, to be broken up into tenanted small business units and, belatedly, recognised as easily the best-preserved mill complex in the entire Derwent Valley – Arkwright's Mills at Cromford notwithstanding – re-graded I by English Heritage in 2003.

The Evans family began adapting existing housing in Darley Abbey as soon as the mill opened and soon began to acquire land, mainly from the Holden family and more from the estate of the bankrupt Heaths. Over the 50 years from *c.*1785, company housing to a very high standard by the standards of the day was built, the terraces and 'cluster houses' of four back-to-backs owing much to William Strutt, Thomas Evans's son-in-law, in their design. The Evans family built themselves a new mansion in the early 19th century called Darley House – also to William Strutt's design – although in 1835 they bought out the Holden family and acquired the Hall and park also.

In 1818 a church was built and seven years later an extremely handsome Classical school, both designed by Nottingham architect Moses Wood. All but Darley House (demolished in 1935) survive to make Darley Abbey, despite much infill post-war housing of indifferent design – an outstanding example of a Regency industrial hamlet, unsurpassed anywhere in England.

CLOCKMAKING & JOHN WHITEHURST

The necessity for accurate timing for kilns must have been of paramount importance to such as Duesbury, and there can be no doubt that he employed a local clockmaker to supply such items. The making of precision machinery was also a job for which clockmakers' skills were then valued as well. Sorocold, for instance, is said to have encouraged Lancastrian clockmakers to come to Derby to assist in constructing the silk-throwing machinery from Lombe's smuggled drawings for the Silk Mill. This seems likely as only two clockmakers are recorded in Derby in 1693, but some seven by 1725.

The Strutts were making similar overtures to journeymen clockmakers for their mills at Cromford in the 1770s. Doubtless most of these went on their way again, for in 1741 only three clockmakers voted in Derby. Nevertheless, one of these men was the celebrated John Whitehurst.

Whitehurst was the eldest son of a clockmaker, also named John, of Congleton, Cheshire, himself the scion of a family of wealthy yeomen long settled on an estate at Dilhorne in Staffordshire from which they had taken their name. The father was probably apprenticed in Liverpool and the son (and most of his seven siblings)

to his father. He then seems to have decided to seek his fortune elsewhere, spending time in both London and Dublin.

He eventually fixed on Derby as a place in need of his talents, yet, because of the closed circle created by the borough charter, he could not at first practise his trade except from a market stall, being neither the son of a Derby burgess nor the ex-apprentice of one. He earned this status in September 1737 by the simple strategem – probably suggested by his local mentor, James Woolley of Codnor – of making a turret clock and presenting it to the mayor and brethren to grace the pediment of the Guildhall, then newly completed on the site of its mediaeval predecessor to the designs of Richard Jackson. This offer accepted, he duly began in business, fixing his abode at 24 Iron Gate (recently listed grade II), which he equipped with a workshop at the rear (which survives) and a wind vane on the roof which, by way of bevels and rods, brought information concerning the direction and speed of the wind to dials either side of the chimneypiece in his parlour. Doubtless the vane itself was made by the ironsmith Robert Bakewell, who also worked with Whitehurst at Tissington Hall stables in 1738, and similar devices were

John Whitehurst's clockmakers' workshop in use by his firm from 1736 to 1830 and several times altered. Listed grade II in 2003. (M. Craven)

installed by him at Darley Hall and for the Bradshaws at Barton Blount – the latter, fortunately, surviving in a house designed by Joseph Pickford's pupil, Thomas Gardiner.

He further endeared himself by rebuilding the inadequate mechanism of the clock of All Saints' Church in 1745, which had been provided by one George Ashmore, who was later executed for counterfeiting and, once buried in the sod of his native Sutton-on-the-Hill, suffered the indignity of having his corpse stolen by body snatchers! Eighteen years later he also replaced Sorocold's carillon with one which played 10 tunes, by no means all sacred airs. Whitehurst made all kinds of clocks, not merely turret ones. He made long-case clocks, both simple 30-hour ones as well as very ornamental examples for the best houses, like that at Tissington. He also made bracket and turret clocks, specialist timepieces and nor were watches eschewed by him either: Derby Museum has a movement made by Whitehurst in retirement in London. He also made sundials and all types of barometer, his most celebrated being of the angled type using his own special 0–60 scale (instead of the much more difficult to read 28–31 inch scale) the evolution of which anticipated the millibar by a century and a half.

His clocks were always beautifully made, but in addition he used only the best materials and manufactured all parts in his workshop – staffed by family members and hand-picked apprentices and managed by his brother William – to the finest tolerances, thus improving the accuracy of his products while extending their life. He also standardised parts where he could, thus reducing costs. This desire to economise without losing quality led him to largely abandon the square dials of the period and adopt, from 1760, the round, silvered flat brass dial which could be easily read and dispensed with expensive cast brass spandrels, separate chapter rings and suchlike. In this he started a fashion in the region for round dial clocks, which those not in the know tend to consider Regency or later. He was also keen to improve and adopt new techniques, like bimetallic compensation of the pendulums of his turret clocks and so on. His effect on Midlands clockmaking was to raise standards all round and make Derby an important centre not only for clocks but other precision instruments, all of which were pioneered by him.

His firm survived his death and continued under his nephew and great nephew – both called John – until 1855; a firm started by John Smith, an ex-employee, in 1850 still flourishes in Derby, making turret clocks. Like Royal Crown Derby, John Smith & Son represents a continuation of Derby's 18th-century luxury industries through all the changes of the 19th century.

WHITEHURST & THE LUNAR SOCIETY

By the later 1750s, Whitehurst had made some interesting friends. One was the painter Joseph Wright (1734–1797), who set up in earnest in Derby in about 1760–61 and whose father, the fashionable lawyer John 'Equity' Wright, lived a few doors down from Whitehurst in Iron Gate, past the Cromptons and the Talbot. Another was Joseph Pickford the architect, an exact contemporary of Wright who, having worked for his uncle, a London contractor who had erected all the finest Palladian buildings of the day, had come to Derbyshire to build Foremark Hall for Sir Robert Burdett and then to work under his uncle's old patrons, the Cokes of Holkham in Norfolk, at Longford Hall, their Derbyshire estate. By 1763 he had been appointed the contractor for the building of the new Derby Assembly Rooms, designed by Washington Shirley, 5th Earl Ferrers, FRS, a leading freemason and amateur astronomer. Here he met Robert Adam, then building Kedleston for 1st Lord Scarsdale, a relationship that bore increasing fruit.

The year before, the instrument maker and astronomer, James Ferguson, FRS, (who, like Dr Johnson, lived at Bolt Court off Fleet Street in London) had come to Derby lecturing. He and Whitehurst subsequently corresponded enthusiastically, the latter's communications being peppered with finely-executed coloured drawings of mechanical devices, bearing out the assertion that his work was always 'beautifully made and closely fitted'. It was probably Whitehurst – or conceivably Ferguson – who is portrayed as the central figure in Wright's celebrated painting *A Philosopher Lecturing upon an Orrery* (1765, commissioned by Lord Ferrers two years previously), and the painting may well be a clue to Whitehurst's having made Orrerys – geared models of the Solar System – even though none by him have come to light. It certainly points to the ever-widening circle of his friends, talents and interests.

One man who is depicted in the painting is another friend, the cartographer Peter Perez Burdett, a talented but rather feckless mathematician who mapped both town and county to win a prize offered by the Society of Arts in 1767. He was also a protégé of Lord Ferrers, having lodged with him at Staunton Harold for four years to 1764, and Pickford built him a Gothick house in Full Street (demolished 1933) in 1765, partly paid for out of a loan from Ferrers disguised in the 200 guinea fee for the *Orrery*. Wright spent the next decade trying to extract 100 guineas out of Burdett, while still miraculously maintaining their friendship.

Whitehurst had an abiding interest in geology, too. When in Italy in 1774, Wright went to see Vesuvius, writing back 'Remember me to all my friends: when you see Whitehurst tell him I wished for his company on

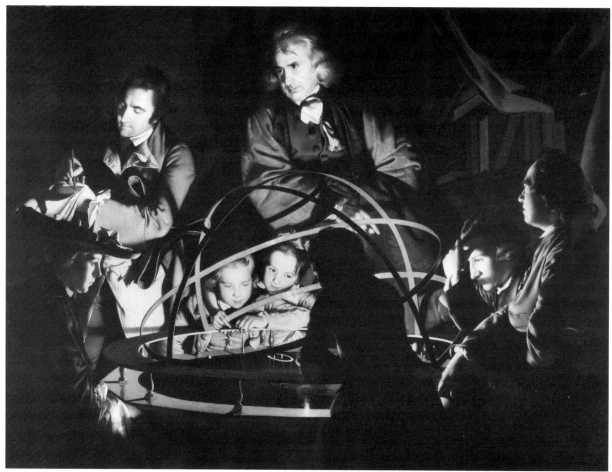

Joseph Wright: 'A Philosopher Lecturing upon an Orrery', 1765, commissioned by Earl Ferrers. The lecturer may well be the then 52-year-old Whitehurst; the man on the left is Burdett. (Derby Museum)

Mount Vesuvius; his thoughts would have centred in the bowels of the mountain, mine skimmed over the surface only. There was a considerable eruption at the time, of which I am going to make a picture.'

Whitehurst's study of minerals was put to good use, not least in his advice for his friend Josiah Wedgwood in selecting the right ones to grind to produce colours for his pottery made at his new Etruria Works at Stoke-on-Trent, designed by Pickford on his recommendation.

In 1765 he, the Birmingham entrepreneur Matthew Boulton and physician Erasmus Darwin, newly installed in practice at Lichfield, had formed a loose association in which they dined monthly together and shared the fruits of their fertile minds, also discussing all the latest in almost any field of science and endeavour to hand. They steadily gained more recruits from friends and acquaintances. By 1768 they had also drawn in engineer James Watt, chemical works proprietor James Keir, potter Josiah Wedgwood, the Birmingham doctor William Small (previously tutor of Thomas Jefferson at William and Mary College, Williamsburg, in Virginia) and the fertile-minded gentlemen of leisure Thomas Day and Richard Lovell Edgeworth. Their later recruit, the

chemical genius and dissenting minister Joseph Priestley, later named them the Lunar Society because they tended to meet at the time of the full moon – to render travel safer – although the inclusion of a minister of religion necessarily caused an alteration from Sunday to Monday nights for their influential deliberations, which were always informal and no doubt better for being unhampered by minute taking, although leaving posterity the poorer for it.

The Lunar Society was at the time perhaps one of the most influential intellectual coteries in Europe. They usually met at Boulton's house, Soho Hall, near Birmingham (perhaps built to a design by Pickford but much later rebuilt by James Wyatt). Most of them were radicals, too, unlike Whitehurst, who had voted for German Pole in 1741, and probably Wedgwood, who was a canny entrepreneur with a host of aristocratic and royal clients, as indeed had Boulton. Their *eminence grise* was the American scientist, philosopher, freemason and politician Benjamin Franklin, who stayed in Derby at Whitehurst's house three times and ordered clocks (two with 'tidal' dials) from him to be sent to America, including at least three 'three wheel' clocks made according to a materials-saving design by Franklin and James Ferguson in tandem.

Within a year, Whitehurst was selecting minerals to aid Wedgwood's glazes and was working on timing machines to improve the precision of the firing of his kilns. He may well have already had experience in doing this for William Duesbury as well, who cannot fail to have been acquainted with him. When, therefore, Wedgwood proposed to build a new works at Etruria, plus houses for both himself, his Scropton-born partner, Thomas Bentley, and much of the workforce, what would be more logical than to suggest his young friend Joseph Pickford as architect? Pickford's subsequent Etruria Works was a ground-breaking industrial building, much emulated in the area for some 50 years subsequently. All that has survived is a much-mauled Etruria Hall and a small 'beehive house' from the works.

Whitehurst's greatest achievement was the plumbing throughout of Clumber, then being built to the designs of Pickford's friend Stephen Wright, for the 2nd Duke of Newcastle, in Nottinghamshire. Probably the first large mansion to have been fitted with a successful waste management system, it also boasted, along with hot-air ducting, a back-boiler hot water system and a patent roaster, all devised by Whitehurst himself, who also made a sundial, two turret clocks and no doubt some domestic clocks as well. Unusually, patron and contractor got on splendidly, despite the yawning social divide, and Whitehurst spent Christmas 1774 with the Duke, being nominated by him Keeper of the Money Weights at the Royal Mint – a demanding post intended as a sinecure – which eventually freed him from the day-to-day running of his Derby works and led to his settling permanently in London (in his friend Ferguson's old quarters in Bolt Court) in 1780.

Here, elected FRS in 1776, he published one of the pioneering works of modern geology, *An Inquiry into the Original State and Formation of the Earth* (1778, 2nd edition 1782), devised a machine to measure 100th of a second and a unit of standard measure based on the travel of a pendulum which, had it been adopted, would have anticipated the metre – to which it related within a couple of millimetres – by a generation. Only his death, without surviving issue on 17 February 1788, prevented him from getting the Duke of Newcastle's momentum behind a campaign for its adoption.

His most felicitous piece of advice was in a letter of 1776 to Matthew Boulton, who had written to him (with diagrams) soliciting his opinion about the first manifestation of his and Watt's steam engine. Whitehurst deplores his ignorance of 'fire engines' but goes on to suggest a modification to bring exhaust steam back into the cylinder, including, in his turn, a

Joseph Wright ARA, self portrait, *c.*1772–1774 (Derby Museum)

diagram. In essence, he had invented the double acting steam engine which, after a further flurry of letters and visits, was patented by Boulton and Watt and a prototype built in 1782. One suspects that, all in all, Whitehurst was probably the most important figure ever to have come out of Derby, his reputation ever hampered by his own self-deprecating modesty and schoolboyish humour.

THE ARCHITECT JOSEPH PICKFORD

In 1764 Whitehurst's new house at 25–27 Queen Street was rebuilt in provincial Palladian mode, also by Pickford, consequently selling his old house at auction at the Tiger Inn on 5 June. It was undoubtedly through the influence of the Lunar Society, with added weight from Thomas Gisbourne – then the surgeon of the Birmingham General Hospital – that the Derby architect so painlessly won the competition to build the new St Mary's Church adjacent in Whittall Street there in 1772. In a Derby context, Pickford contributed much to the beautifying of the town. Apart from the very handsome Assembly Rooms, he built *inter alia* the Tiger Inn, Corn Market (1764), and added a twin courtyard hunting stables and orangery (including a kitchen packed with Whitehurst's patent ranges with back boilers) at Markeaton Hall for the Whig grandee Francis Noel Clarke Mundy (1772).

St Helen's House, c.1840, in a drawing by James Stephen Gresley and showing the original screen to the street. (M. Craven)

ST HELEN'S HOUSE

In 1766–67 Pickford erected a superb town house for the Whig grandee John Gisborne of Yoxall Lodge. This stone fronted mansion, St Helen's House (listed grade I), was in the Palladian style still favoured by Whig patrons like Gisborne, and was built to the villa plan as perfected by Sir Robert Taylor, entirely for entertaining but with sleeping accommodation limited only to family and to some staff, and survives as probably the finest Palladian town house in the English provinces. After over 30 years

The Pickford Children by Joseph Wright, from the copy in Pickford's House Museum. (Private Collection)

of neglect it was put on the English Heritage Buildings at-risk register in the 1990s, but was sold for restoration by the city council in 2007.

It was embellished within by a number of paintings by Wright and by the finest craftsmen available, all of whom also worked elsewhere for Pickford and whose work was well up to metropolitan standards. The wrought-iron screen and elaborate stair-rail, modelled on Robert Bakewell's balustrade at the Maister's House, Hull, was by Benjamin Yates; the superb chimneypieces in local and continental marble were carved by George Moneypenny, a London-born craftsman whom Pickford met when both were working under Adam at Kedleston, and there was abundant bravura plasterwork and stucco by Abraham Denstone, who had worked at the Assembly Rooms and whose homonymous father had undertaken the plasterwork in All Saints' and the new Guildhall.

St Helen's, like so many houses of this era in Derby, is a shining monument to the abundant talent of a whole host of local craftsmen and artisans and epitomises all that is best in the built environment of the city.

Gisborne's son, Thomas, a close friend of William Wilberforce, plotted the abolition of slavery here as well as at Yoxall, and in St Helen's park at Darley Grove the young Thomas Haden and Joseph Wright played the flute *al fresco* on summer evenings. Wright had painted Haden there as 'Edwin' from James Beattie's poem *The Minstrel* (1777) and taught young Gisborne to paint there and also at Yoxall. In 1807 the house and park, laid out by the Derby follower of Capability Brown, William Emes of Bowbridge, was purchased by William Strutt, much enlarged and became the focus for the continuing intellectual revolution in Derby.

Pickford, born in rural Warwickshire in 1734, died unexpectedly in his house on Nuns' Green in July 1782 leaving a wife and two sons. Like Whitehurst, his work and career had abruptly raised standards in and around Derby, in his case of architecture, building and decoration.

On Nuns' Green, Pickford took a further opportunity, abetted by the notorious John Heath.

THE FIRST IMPROVEMENT

COMMISSION

In 1768 an Act of Parliament was obtained to set up a commission to oversee the release land on Nuns' Green from Ford Street to the White Lion Inn on Brick Street for development, in order to raise money to improve the remainder of the green for public enjoyment. Since the dissolution of the convent of St Mary de Pratis, the estate had become a holding of the mayor and burgesses. Much of it was rented out as closes and tofts; more was enclosed in the 17th century. The remainder was common land. We have already seen that it supported a tilery and a brick works; there was also a bowling green. In its centre stood, we are told (but without much corroboration), the kennels of the borough's hounds, let in exchange for two dressed hares to be presented to each newly-installed mayor for his dinner on Michaelmas Day. It was also a place of public resort, quite literally Derby's first official park, although much abused before the Act by what may be called 'courting couples', the dumping of household rubbish, vandals and by criminal elements. It had also been used for militia musters, not to mention its use by the 1745 rebels as a place to park pieces of artillery.

Each of the plots sold by the Commissioners, who included two of the Heaths and most of their cronies, lay on the northern side of the road to Ashbourne, later to become Friar Gate, but called Nuns' Green into the 19th century. Each was 41ft 9ins wide and 165ft long. Examination of the deeds of many of the sites reveals that Pickford was involved in the purchase of at least five of them and acted as architect for three, possibly four. He was also at that time active with the building of Etruria Hall and Works, and it emerges from Wedgwood's correspondence that the relationship was not a smooth one and that Pickford was having trouble getting his money.

Thus, we know Pickford was short of cash, so how was he able to pick up so many plots on Nuns' Green? The answer, inevitably, lay in John Heath, who was not only a Trustee under the Act, but was also party to several of the deeds. At this time, too, advertisements appear in the *Derby Mercury* for houses for sale – usually the property of unfortunate souls upon whom the Heaths had foreclosed – the rubric ending 'apply to Mr Fallowes, attorney or to Mr Pickford's on Nuns Green'. Fallowes was a Cheshire solicitor related to the Gisbornes who acted for the Heaths. Pickford was plainly also 'fronting' for the brothers.

Each contract for a Nuns' Green plot was the same, stipulating that purchasers within five years were to:

'…erect, build or cause to be erected… one or more dwelling houses handsome in front towards the publick street not less than three storeys high decently sasht & shall convey water from the top…by pipes brought down by the house side and not by spouts hanging over the road…'

The documents go on to proscribe the building of a silk mill on any of the sites, and it is a measure of the cocksureness of the Heaths and their associates that a silk mill is exactly what *was* built on the site of what is now No.45 Friar Gate, the client being John Ward

Portrait by Joseph Wright of 1775, thought to be of Joseph Pickford (1735–1782). Note the drawing pen in his hand. (Private Collection)

(1728–1785). Pickford had an interest in the business, too, reserving a right of way for himself under the carriage arch to his builder's yard which lay behind this house and not the one he built for himself two doors down in 1769, later No. 41 and now an agreeable museum, bearing his name. The mill at No. 45 was sold after Ward died and was converted to a house in 1799, the architect H.I. Stevens, who had his offices there in the century following, adding a jolly Norman-style brick porch.

Nor were the houses always erected 'within five years', for although the site of No.27 changed hands four times (in 1772 it was sold for £148 to John Heath and William Duesbury, who made a £42 profit five years later selling it on) the house was not put up – to a design attributable to Pickford – until between 1777 and July 1780, when it was 'newly erected'.

The exterior of Pickford's own elegant house there is embellished with an impressive array of architectural devices to advertise his skills, his real genius being the fact that the façade neither looks awkward nor crowded in spite of it; his eye for proportion was flawless, unlike today's CAD wielding practitioners. The interior incorporated fine decorative stuccowork in the hall of the Muses by Abraham Denstone, at least one superb marble fireplace inlaid with Blue John carved by George Moneypenny and wrought-ironwork by William Yates, son of Bakewell's successor, Benjamin. From 1788 it also housed Wright's portrait of its builder, another of his

Pickford's elegantly Palladian Devonshire Hospital, Full Street, of 1777, photographed in February 1894, shortly before demolition. Note the new electroliers, installed the previous year. One survives at the top of Silk Mill Lane. (*Derby Evening Telegraph*)

children and there was doubtless a portrait of Mrs Pickford, too – the daughter of the Coke family's agent at Longford – now lost or separated from its identity.

The work of the Commission, while it seems to have been a vehicle for personal enrichment of some of its members and hangers-on, did result in Derby's most elegant street, most of which survives intact.

BEAUTIFYING THE BOROUGH:
PICKFORD'S LEGACY

In 1772 Pickford was employed – mainly through the good offices of the pompous F.N.C. ('French') Mundy, high sheriff that year – to extend the Shire Hall to provide more courts. Mundy and his wife, known as 'The Duchess', entertained lavishly a radical-chic circle of Whig friends, by no means exclusively drawn from the gentry, at their house at Markeaton, put up in 1755 by Mundy's father to the designs of James Denstone, brother to Pickford's *stuccadore*. Needless to say, Mundy was one of the subscribers to the building of the Assembly Rooms and nearly all of Pickford's patronage stemmed from among such men. He was also a member of a lodge of London freemasons. The same can be said of most of Wright's local sitters.

Of Pickford's other works in Derby itself, we find the

clammy hand of Heath in both. From the mid-1770s the architect was to work increasingly for the Duke of Devonshire at Chatsworth. One commission was to replace the almshouses on Full Street, erected under Bess of Hardwick's will in 1608. In 1777 Pickford designed new ones at right angles to the street and protected therefrom by a most elegant Palladian screen, based on his earlier design for the Moot Hall at Wirksworth (1771), forming an intimate series of dwellings around a central courtyard. William Hutton, however, stigmatised them:

Nuns' Green: Friar Gate's north side as built up from 1768. Left: William Fitzherbert's House; centre: Pickford's House. (M. Craven)

'…instead of that modest elegance, which ought to have dignified the front, we should suppose it a Publick-office, a receptacle of Magistracy, or a place to study the sciences. Who dresses a pauper in lace! We are treated with an ostentatious display of the Duke's arms and crest as leading objects… That charity which longs to publish itself, ceases to be Charity.'

Nevertheless, in his *History of Derby* (1791) he published an engraving of it by Pickford's old associate George Moneypenny, who also re-drew Burdett's map of the town at about the same time. To pay for this building, the Duke sent drafts to Heath.

A final commission undertaken by Pickford in Derby was in 1778 when he enlarged Darley Hall. By 1730 the house had changed hands once or twice and was then purchased by John Heath. In 1777, as the Holden's landlord, he prevailed upon them to employ Pickford to make alterations. He added new north and south ranges, which were typical of the economy of detail, quality of work and excellence of proportion associated with the architect in his later years. But when Heath went bankrupt less than a year later the Holdens found to their horror that they did not own the lease at all, but it had been assigned elsewhere. So, having paid Heath for their lease, Emes for new parkland and Pickford for improvements, they had little alternative but to acquire the freehold from Boldero at a valuation which, humiliatingly, included these improvements for which they had already paid! Surprisingly, little of the opprobrium rubbed off on Pickford by association, although he was almost continuously at Chatsworth from this time. He was certainly popular enough with the Duke to be elected to the Corporation in May 1778.

When Pickford died in July 1782. Moneypenny, his *elite* carver, was commissioned to sell his stock-in-trade and went on to display ever-widening talents including engraving and the design and carving of a series of stunning church monuments in the marble, alabaster and polished Derbyshire limestones. Moneypenny's son George (1768–1830) was also a budding architect. There is reason to believe that when Pickford died young George had just been articled to him. He probably then transferred to another Derby architect but from 1789 to 1793, when he went to London to work for Joseph Bonomi, he was probably in practice in Derby.

Not that Pickford's children were interested in succeeding him. One died as a young man, the younger, Joseph, after a miserable time at snobbish Oriel College, Oxford, became a parson. Thomas Mozley tells us that, hanging in his sitting room in 41 Friar Gate was a charming painting by Joseph Wright of the architect's children in a romantic landscape (page 112). Joseph, junior, had begun in the 1790s as a convivial fellow,

taking a full part in the rich social life of the town. Later he became misanthropic, let most of the family house after his mother's death in 1812 and eked out a baleful existence as perpetual curate of Little Eaton and Quarndon, dying in 1844.

'Joseph Pickford,' writes Mozley, 'had been an architect and builder and the intimate friend of Wright the painter and also of Whitehurst, a mechanician and author of *Theory of the Earth*. It was a coterie contemporaneous and on friendly terms with the Philosophical Society founded by Erasmus Darwin.'

ERASMUS DARWIN

In fact, the Derby Philosophical Society was not founded until 1783, a year after Pickford's death, yet Mozley's words may have reflected a truth in so far as the core of Darwin's members perhaps met informally from the moment he came to the area. This event happened in 1781–82 when the great polymath and co-founder of the Lunar Society left Lichfield for Radburne Hall on his marriage to his newly-widowed patient Mrs E.S. Pole on 6 March 1781.

For all his inventiveness, genius and creative thinking, Erasmus Darwin never ceased to practise as a doctor and

Bust in Chellaston alabaster of Erasmus Darwin by George Moneypenny, 1801. It was found in the attic of the Mechanics' Institute in 1993. (Christies)

Radburne was hardly a convenient place from which to set out on the 10,000 miles a year he is said to have driven in his carriage – with its patent steering and other refinements designed by its owner. He needed a town residence. Darwin already knew many people in Derby; some were probably his patients. Whitehurst had fitted Darwin's house in Lichfield with a fireplace-registering wind vane and anemometer as he had at his own house in Iron Gate and elsewhere. As early as 1770 Darwin had been painted for the first time by Wright, and it is certain that their relationship went back a few years before that.

The painter's clients (as Pickford's), his father's and Darwin's seen to have been the same people, drawn from the local gentry and professional men. Darwin also knew and corresponded with F.N.C. Mundy of Markeaton – whose poem *Needwood Forest* he had admired – Brooke Boothby of Ashbourne Hall, another gentleman poet, and, of course, the Poles. All were painted by Wright and all seem to have employed Pickford. It need not be doubted that all were clients of Wright *pere* and had patronised Whitehurst – Mundy and Pole certainly had. Consequently, we find the names of William Strutt, Jedediah Strutt, Brooke Boothby and Derby-born pioneer novelist Robert Bage among those who formed the early nucleus of the Derby Philosophical Society which had a *recorded* existence from January 1783. Bage, the author of *Hermsprong*, was uncle of Shrewsbury mill-owner Charles Bage, an intimate of William Strutt and builder of the first fire-proof mill. Interestingly, there had been a previous Philosophical Society in Derby, in existence 25 years before, which had included Whitehurst, the ingenious vicar of Mackworth, George Pickering – a sitter, like Whitehurst, Darwin, Pickford and others in this circle, to Joseph Wright – and other luminaries, which had flourished for an unknown period. Darwin occupied his house in Full Street (built for the Jacobite Alderman Heathcote in 1722) from early 1783 and may have commissioned Pickford to carry out alterations. In 1785 he dug the first ever artesian well in the garden and also built a hand-operated ferry across the Derwent so his daughters could reach their trans-riparian pleasure grounds without help.

Yet this coterie of local intellectuals, professionals and others in Derby ultimately went back to the first such grouping in the 1760s and Darwin's Philosophical Society was in reality a second-generation flowering of the potency of Derby talent, the effects of which were to reach deep into the 19th century. Yet the link to more practical achievements as represented by Whitehurst, Pickford and P.P. Burdett (who went on to invent the mezzotint, interest himself in Strict Observance freemasonry, act as a salesman for Matthew Boulton to the courts of Europe and map the Grand Duchy of Hesse) was lost except in the superabundance of talent displayed by Darwin himself and in his protégé William Strutt, elder son of the cotton pioneer Jedediah. The diverse interests of the latter, indeed, seem to owe so much to the innovations of Whitehurst that Strutt seems almost to embody the Lunar Society traditions into the 19th century – in Derby, at least.

Darwin, who was a radical, spent most of his Derby years on his scientific works, written throughout in heroic couplets and bolstered by stupendous quantities of prose footnotes: *The Botanic Garden* (1789–92), *Zoonomia or, The Laws of Organic Life* (1794–96), *Phytologia, or the Philosophy of Agriculture and Gardening* (1800) and *The Temple of Nature; or, the Origin of Society* published posthumously in 1803, Darwin having died at the house bought by his son Erasmus, junior, and left to him on his suicide, Breadsall Priory on 1 April 1802.

These writings contain too much of interest and importance to expatiate upon here. Suffice it to say that a passage from *Zoönomia* [I. 503] outraged orthodox Christian belief and provoked attacks on him, already apparent from his espousal of the American and French revolutions:

'The final cause of this contest among the males seems to be, that the strongest and most active animal should propagate the species, which should thence become improved.'

It also clearly sets out the agenda for Darwin's better known grandson Charles's theory of the Survival of the Fittest and underscores that of evolution. That such stuff should outrage Christian belief should come as no surprise; one of his visitors, Coleridge – *en route* to stay with Mrs Evans at Darley House in January 1796 – wrote to his friend Josiah Wade, 'Dr Darwin is everything but the Christian' but went on to say that he had '…a greater range of knowledge than any other man in Europe.'

One other writing of Darwin's from Derby days is of considerable importance. In 1797 the Derby publisher John Drewry brought out his *A Plan for the Conduct of Female Education in Boarding Schools*. It was a case of practising what he preached, as we shall see.

VIII

EIGHTEENTH-CENTURY LIFE

THE ASSEMBLIES

One way in which men of diverse talents could mingle with their patrons was to attend the Assemblies. Beau Nash had said of the Assembly at Tunbridge Wells:

'People of the greatest title, rank and dignity, people of every learned profession, of every Religion and Political persuasion; people of every degree, condition and occupation of life (if well dressed and well behaved) meet amicably here together.'

On the foundation stone of Lord Burlington's magnificent Assembly Rooms at York was engraved: '(A) place for public pastime where liberal arts should flourish and where new splendour should emulate the ancient glory of *Eburacum*'. The Assemblies' general philosophy was to inculcate the social graces, universalise the 'polite arts' and to bring all sorts and conditions of people together harmoniously.

Yet it had not always been so in Derby. From at least 1713 and probably earlier, perhaps even from the time of Luke Neild's fashionable coffee house in the 1660s and 1670s, there had evolved two separate Assemblies, one for the gentry and another for the burghers of the town and their ladies. The former was housed in a pleasant double-fronted and twin-gabled three-storey building of 1713, which survived as a china showroom on the corner of Full Street where that street once turned north to the Market Place (page 92). It was swept away, unrecognised, in 1971 to make room for the multi-storey car park which today serves the present Assembly Rooms.

The lesser Assembly was held in the old Moot Hall, on the east of Irongate. The rules of the former survive in Derby Museum and seem to date from the 1730s. These include such strictures as: 'No attorney's clerk shall be admitted' and 'No shopkeeper or any of his or her family shall be admitted except Mr Franceys.' The latter exception was not, certainly, because he was mayor (as Mark Girouard suggests – he was mayor in 1747), but either as a result of his supposed gentility of lineage (it was then understood that he was of a cadet branch of the Franceys family of Coxbench Hall) and his marriage to a lady of a junior branch of the Harpurs, or that, as the borough's leading apothecary, he was privy to too many of the medical secrets of the county gentry. Probably it was a combination of all three factors.

This Assembly was presided over by Mrs Barnes, called 'Blowzabella' by Lady Jane Coke, a daughter of the

Earl of Leicester whose nearby seat was Longford Hall. She was a lady of pretension but of no great family, whose husband was a 'Derbyshire Gentleman of small fortune', whose only claim to fame was that his grandfather, a rich Hartshorne agriculturalist, had married an heiress of the Darcy and Stanhope families. She held sway from 1741 to 1752, when she handed over to Countess Ferrers (wife of the 4th Earl, who was condemned for the murder of his steward in 1760), writing smugly on the back page of the Assembly account book: 'I told her that Trade never mix'd with Us Ladies.' Nevertheless, the two Assemblies plainly needed amalgamation. The precedent had been set that night in December 1745, when an Assembly, to which the whole town came, was held for Bonnie Prince Charlie and at which the Royal Standard was knocked over in the crush. Furthermore, Jane Coke wrote from London: 'Tis hard out of two Assemblies you have at Derby people can't agree to make one good one'. Apparently county ladies had become reduced to dancing with each other.

Eventually a committee of noblemen and gentlemen was set up under the chairmanship of the Duke of Devonshire, to raise subscriptions for and to supervise the erection of a new joint Assembly Room. The architect was one of their number, retired admiral Washington Shirley, 5th Earl Ferrers, doubtless through the good offices of his sister-in-law who, as we have seen, succeeded Lady Jane's 'Blowzabella' in 1752. The contractor for the job was the young Joseph Pickford, doubtless recommended by Wenman Coke of Longford

The Assembly Rooms (Earl Ferrers & Joseph Pickford, 1763–64) façade, photographed c.1950. (*Derby Evening Telegraph*)

A view in April 1939 of the western end of Full Street between the Assembly Rooms (left) and the 1713 County Assembly Room – the façade to the immediate left of the Horse & Trumpet, the inn which supplied the suppers. The pub's venerable façade was replaced a few weeks later. (*Derby Evening Telegraph*)

Hall, for whom Pickford had recently worked and the daughter of whose agent he had married. The resulting building was as elegant as any of its period in England, of brick with an elegant Palladian revival stone façade.

A further subscription was raised in 1770, eight years after building was started, to pay for finishing the interior, a scheme for which was drawn up by Robert

Derby Assembly Rooms: the interior of the main assembly room, decorated in 1774 by Abraham Denstone the Younger to designs by Robert and James Adam. (*Derby Evening Telegraph*)

Adam himself (through the influence of Lord Scarsdale no doubt) and executed by the gifted Derby plasterer Abraham Denstone, who worked elsewhere with Pickford. We do not, unfortunately, have the specification drawn up for the building of the Derby Assembly Rooms, but that for York sent to Lord Burlington on 4 May 1730 survives:

'What is wanted is a large Dancing Room, not less than 90 feet long, another large Room for Cards and play, another for Coffee and Refreshments and a kitchen or place to make tea in, with a Retiring place for the Ladies. And somewhere about the entrance, perhaps underground, a place with a chimney for footmen.'

Doubtless the requirement at Derby was very similar, although the arrangements were differently disposed in the execution.

The Assemblies themselves, held fortnightly, with additional occasions for race weeks and fairs, were 'A stated and general meeting of the polite persons of both sexes, for the sake of conversation, gallantry, news and play'. Normally they took place after dinner, a meal which was then taken in the late afternoon. Supper was served towards the end of the function. Occasionally the evening was declared a 'Derby rout' – a particularly informal type of ball. The artist Joseph Farington, in Derby to draw the town from Abbey Barns in 1808, relates just such an occasion:

'The Town was now all hurry and bustle, carriages and horses and foot people hastening to the Racecourse in every direction.

The Races begin about 6 o'clock. In the evening an Assembly to which William went – much company, but a much greater proportion of men than Women – The Marquis of Hartington was there being one of the Stewards of the Races. After, dancing till one o'clock when a supper is laid out for everybody – the price of admittance to Gentlemen seven shillings.'

Hartington, son and heir of the Duke of Devonshire and of the famous Spencer beauty, Georgiana, no doubt lodged that night (16 August 1808) and throughout the period of the meeting at Devonshire House in Corn Market. The fact that Farington and his companion were freely admitted underlines the much wider social spread arising from the inauguration of the new Assembly Rooms a generation earlier. One of the great advantages, therefore, of the Assembly, was that the men who formed the kernel of the burgeoning intellectual circle and also to some extent the better sort of tradesmen-craftsmen, like the Yates's (the wrought-ironsmiths), had access through them to their patrons. Here, introductions were made, and here Whitehurst lost his pocket-book in 1768, offering a guinea reward for its return. The Assembly was an element in the rising prosperity of the town, and it was the Assemblies that enabled client and professional man or tradesman to meet, with benefit to both.

RACING AND FAIRS

As is apparent from Farington's experience, Assemblies frequently coincided with race meetings. The origin of horseracing in Derby is quite obscure, although the first recorded meeting in England was at Smithfield, London, in 1174 and took place during a horse fair as still happens, for instance at Appleby, even today. That racing at Chester had begun by 1512, at the fair there, rather suggests that it began as a way of showing off their wares' talents by the horse traders. By the earlier 17th century, flat racing had become formalised at such places as Newmarket. Racing historian John Saville has uncovered a reference to the races at Derby in John Fletcher's play *Monsieur Thomas* published in 1639, and no doubt they were run at the appropriate fair time although the venue is unknown.

Until 1733–34, when several new ones were granted by Letters Patent, fairs had been on Friday in Easter week, 4 May, the Thursday before midsummer and 26

September, all extending over two days and, as a result of the 1682 charter, three more were added, the dates being slightly rearranged. Again, six of these ran for two days and horseracing was almost certainly an adjunct to those where horseflesh was an element of the wares on offer. Indeed, several Fair Books recording the sale of horses survive in the local MS collections covering the decades of the 1640s and 1650s – the very period when horseracing was, of course, proscribed by the Puritans.

The fairs were partly on the Morledge (continuing into fun-fairs into the early 20th century) and partly at the western extremity of Nuns' Green (Friar Gate), where the increasing width of the road remains to remind us of the fact that the latter was also a beast market.

Where races might have been run in the 17th century is unknown – Nuns' Green is a likely possibility – but by 1707 Sinfin Moor was the favoured location, if a reference to races on 'Sinfelmore' in that year is indeed a reference to this bleak tract of land to the south of the borough. By the occasion of the first known newspaper report of forthcoming races on 26 July 1733, the venue was undoubtedly there, just outside the town boundary.

These 18th-century meetings were highly formalised and drew a good part of the county gentry. In 1733 the Race Ball was held on Monday 20 August in the Assembly Rooms in Full Street and another after the meeting on the following day – doubtless attracting a wider clientele – took place at the Virgin's Inn, next to Newcastle House on the north side of the Market Place. Another meeting recorded was that commencing on 8 September 1737, on which occasion Mr Topham, a celebrated strong man, performed for the *après*-race punters' gathering at the Virgin's, as recorded so vividly by Hutton. If Mrs Barnes held sway at the evening Assemblies on these occasions, it was doubtless connected with the fact that her husband, Philip Barnes of Stanton Hall, was a prominent owner, whose entertainingly-named black mare, Moll Hackabout, raced Colonel Gery's grey, Cassandra, over an astonishing eight miles carrying 12 stone, for 200 guineas! On this occasion the lesser races seem to have been held at Foldbrook, 'within a mile of Derby'. Horses were entered for races at the town's inns, the appropriately-named Nag's Head in St Peter's Street, the George, the King's Head and the Old Ship, Full Street (where the patron, Mr Every, later inherited the family baronetcy from a remote cousin), all being used for this purpose.

Derby Races were considerably benefitted by the Act of Parliament of 27 March 1740, regulating horseracing. This led to the curtailing of racing at Alfreton, Bakewell, Wirksworth and Tideswell and, although more honoured in the breach, the Act effectively allowed the

A view of Cornmarket *c.*1897, showing the town house of the Duke of Devonshire, built in 1755 (centre). Here the Duke stayed when attending the races and assemblies until 1813, when the Bachelor Duke transferred to the Judges' Lodgings.

Derby Races to attract more custom. Thus, for instance, in August 1748, there was a 'great meeting of gentlemen and others each day and the diversion gave great satisfaction to the spectators, being conducted with great regularity and order'. Hire of spectators' booths cost a 5s (25p) fee, to be paid at the Royal Oak, Market Place. This meeting extended over three days, and entertainments at the Assembly Rooms included a concert by 'Mr Charles and his son from London… including several concertos and solos… on the French horns and other instruments never heard before'.

By 1770 the turnout was getting much more fashionable, with the future 5th Duke of Devonshire and his entire family present to celebrate his coming of age. Afterwards, quite apart from a glittering Assembly, the entire Cavendish clan, with the Polish Ambassador, gave 'lavish entertainments' at the George, King's Head and Greyhound inns to the 'nobility, gentlemen and tradesmen of the town and neighbourhood'.

Sinfin Moor, bleak and windswept, became the fixed venue for the races on 22–23 August 1748, but was no place for the fashionable, despite a prefabricated stand. Gambling booths were outlawed in 1756 and Sir Henry Harpur of Calke, a great owner of the day, set up a dedicated racing stables at Swarkestone Lows in 1774–77 with an exercise track that can still be traced on the ground, although the complex was adapted as a farm and agent's house after his death in 1789. Furthermore, the enclosure of the moor looked set to break up the integrity of the course in any case, and the races were transferred to The Holmes that year and a 'handsome and commodious' permanent grandstand was erected. This was not for the first time, however, for a meeting had been switched to this part of Derby for the Siddalls had been used in 1765, 1775 and 1799, due to Sinfin Moor becoming waterlogged. The new course's north-west turn lay at that point where the canal and Derwent parted south and south east respectively. Thus, with a new and fitting Assembly Room and a new and convenient racecourse nearby, the local county gentry were well set-up for their annual carnival, the new three-day meeting held in late July. Even the superb 1827 silver gilt Derby race cup survives, albeit in private hands. In the 1770s the Duke of Devonshire was also 'pleased to allow' the parishes of Derby £3 12s 6d to ring the changes at the time of the races, as a receipt of 18 August 1779 attests – probably a useful source of income for the five parish churches.

'Something of the races at Derby' – the races in full flight on the Siddalls, 1804. The building of the railway in 1838–39 caused the course to become unusable and in 1844 the races moved to Little Chester. (M. Craven)

Derby Racecourses: Derby Races in 1853, with Henry Duesbury's new grandstand. (M. Craven)

Unfortunately, the new locale only survived until 1844, when the steadily expanding railway establishment to the west of the canal made further meetings impractical. For two years the Derby Race Committee – Duke of Devonshire included – had a struggle to find a new venue. Eventually, some of the land in Little Chester, to the east of the canal, including Cowsley Fields, was lighted upon and the first meeting at the new racecourse was held in May 1848. It was graced with a very elegant new grandstand designed in 1852 by Henry Duesbury – grandson of the second William Duesbury – but was replaced by a larger but far less elegant building in 1911, itself closing after numerous rebuildings in 1998, being finally demolished in 2001. The last meeting was held on 9 August 1939; one of the last winners was ridden by the late Sir Gordon Richards. After the war the council decided a resumption of racing would 'bring the wrong sort of people into the town', and the racecourse became playing fields with the cricket ground at its southern extremity.

The present Duke of Devonshire, *de jure* high steward of the borough, as ex-Chairman of the Jockey Club and HM the Queen's representative at Ascot, happily continues the Cavendish link with racing. One day, perhaps, some entrepreneur will be allowed to reopen the racecourse and bring back some of the fun of race days before World War Two.

DERBY FOOTBALL

Another popular sport was that of Shrovetide football. It is unclear when this rumbustious pastime began; its origin was undoubtedly mediaeval, although it is not alluded to in any source before the 18th century. It was in no way dissimilar to that played even today at Ashbourne. The idea that it originated in a battle between the Saxons and the Danes with the head of one of the latter as the ball may safely be discarded. A junior version followed on Ash Wednesday.

The object was to get the ball through the town to goals situated on what were then the edges of the town. The contestants were nominally the inhabitants of the parishes of All Saints' and St Peter's. The goals were Nuns' Mill in the north west, defended by the former, and Gallows Baulk to the south, defended by the latter. The start ('tossup') was in the Market Place at noon on Shrove Tuesday. The usual St Peter's tactic was to get the ball into the Markeaton Brook at St Peter's Bridge and thus into the Derwent, up which it was crowded by as many as 1,000 people. A visiting Frenchman in Derby, in the days when this country was periodically at war with his own, remarked of Derby football: 'If Englishmen call this playing, it would be impossible to say what they would call fighting.'

There was even a badly scanning song, clearly derived from *Oranges and Lemons*. The last ball, as preserved in the museum, was a 13in diameter leather sphere stuffed hard with cork shavings.

Derby race cup, 1827, in silver gilt. (Christies)

On 27 February 1747, after a particularly physical Shrovetide event – perhaps the working-off of antagonisms arising from the '45 – an attempt was made by the mayor, the ultra-respectable Henry Franceys, to limit the game by banning participants from outside the borough on the unconvincing grounds that it might aid the spread of cattle disease. Needless to say, it was only with the total chaos arising from the enormous population growth of the town, combined with ease of travel, that a subsequent mayor of the town, William Eaton Mousley of Exeter House, managed, with a little help from the 5th Royal Irish Dragoons, effectively to ban it in 1846.

It was a dangerous game, too, for on 9 February 1796 one John Sneap was found drowned in the Derwent near The Holmes. The jurors at the inquest petitioning the bench subsequently concluded that:

'...the said John Sneap lost his life, an unfortunate victim to the custom of playing of football on Shrove Tuesdays; a custom which well has no better recommendation than its antiquity, for its further continuance, is disgraceful to humanity and civilization, subversive of good order and government, and destructive of the morals, properties and very lives of our inhabitants.'

Their recommendation for the game's immediate discontinuance was, however, in vain; a notice to that effect the following year was completely ignored, most of the magistrates being covert supporters of the game; it took a lawyer to ban it. A slightly later account underlines the hazards:

'The ball would be surrounded by hundreds of players, some pushing one way and some the opposite. Now they would get wedged in a corner, where they would sometimes remain fixed for hours together, a steam rising from the reeking mass of humanity as if from a large seething cauldron. Presently, some of the men, when thus heated, would plunge into the Derwent "hissing hot", as Falstaff has it, and swim down the river with the ball, the banks being lined with an excited crowd shouting and halooing.'

It might be noted in passing that the fact that the Full Street ground-floor frontage of Alderman Mousley's house was bricked up had little to do with Window Tax and everything to do with Derby football! Football-proof shutters may also still be seen on the ground floor windows of No.27 Friar Gate.

Sport in Georgian Derby

Other, less glittering, occasions to which the term sport might be applied, flourished in the 18th century. Sinfin Moor also saw the beginnings not only of horseracing but also of athletics. In July 1772 – concurrently with a race meeting we may be sure – a foot race was run there over 10 miles with a 10 guinea prize, although the venue was earlier used for rather less orthodox athletics. On the evening of 7 August 1735, almost certainly also as a side-show to horseracing:

'Six women ran, not incommoded with either clothes or modesty, three laps for a Holland smock and half a guinea and gave abundance of sport to a numerous company of spectators'.

Prize fighting as well as 'athletics' was much in vogue at race meetings. For instance; in *Cresswell's Nottingham Journal* it tells us that:

'On Wednesday 5 September, the second day of the Derby races, will be fought at Derby, between 10 and 12 o'clock in the Fore Noon, a match between Samuel Freeman of Birmingham and James Bromley of Pentridge, for 100 guineas; and also money taken at the door.'

Fishing has always been a popular sport with all classes, in Derby no less than elsewhere. Nevertheless, the *elite* ever attempted to reserve the best for themselves. In 1693 the fishing rights on the Derwent were reserved to the mayor, aldermen, brethren and common council to '...fish with ye rod in ye piscary or fishing' pertaining to St Michael's Mills and that the mayor and chamberlains 'May have a day of fishing yearely in the said River att a seasonable tyme in the yeare with nettes'. In fact, the mayor and council let these rights as a rule, the income going into the common fisc. As early as 1540 they were collecting 5s (25p) per year for fishing rents. Of course, even in the 18th century the Derwent was replete with fish, as was the Trent where in 1775 one of the Greaves family of Aston and Ingleby caught near Shardlow a sturgeon nearly 10 feet long, 6 feet in girth and weighing 200lbs. Only today (2006), after some two centuries of pollution, are fish returning to the Derwent.

We learn further (from his autobiography) that grumpy old William Hutton's grandfather, who lived near the Derwent in Bridge Gate 'Three or four days a week... attended with his rod to the detriment of his family. Not satisfied with the time allowed by the sun, he followed up his favourite amusement by the light of the moon and often found his way home with an empty stomach after midnight.' Hutton himself was playing fives with his friends in Derby in 1764, a pleasant sport no longer available nearer to the town than Repton School, although a pretty Gothic fives court, designed by the headmaster P.K. Tollitt himself, was built in front of St Helen's House in 1898 when it was host to Derby School. It vanished after World War Two.

Hutton tells us, too, that swimming was popular in his day but little else. He probably referred to swimming as a recreation rather than a sport and indeed the borough's first swimming baths was very early, being provided 'at the side of the river' by Walter, 2nd Lord Aston of Forfar (1609–1678), a Staffordshire grandee with a Scots peerage sometime before 1659. It was in that year that the young John Flamsteed – our only authority for these baths, which are not otherwise mentioned anywhere – and his friends were 'wont to bathe there after [Derby] school'. Exactly why Lord Aston – not a person obviously connected with Derby – provided them, precisely when, where they were situated and how long they flourished are all matters shrouded in utter mystery. Conceivably, the otherwise inexplicable name of Bath Street, pitched in 1819 just north of St Mary's Bridge, provides a clue. The next baths were in the proprietorship of Joseph Hall, the spar works proprietor between 1826 and 1828; either he or his predecessor Richard Brown seem to have provided them as a way of using clean waste water created by the firm's processes.

Coarser sports, now viewed with distaste, also flourished. Bear-baiting seems to have been practised only occasionally in Derby. Cock and dog fighting, on the other hand, were immensely popular, especially among country folk in town for the weekly market. We learn of a cockpit at Copecastle existing before 1607–08 and another being made on Nuns' Green in 1617, the rental for which was payable to the mayor and burgesses. By the 18th century several of the town's inns had cockpits. The Angel, Cornmarket, once the property of the College of All Saints', was the chief, another popular venue being the long vanished Crown, on Nuns' Green, probably utilising the cockpit built in 1617. The quality events coincided invariably with the races: 'A main of cocks to be fought at the Angel on Gaol Bridge on 30th and 31st May next betwixt the Gentlemen of Leicestershire and Derbyshire. 31 cocks a side; 2 guineas and 10 the main.'

And again, 'There will be fought a match of shakebags betwixt the Gentlemen of Staffordshire and those of Scarsdale… at The Angel. £10 a battle and £40 the odd battle.' Cockfighting had indeed been advertised 'each forenoon during the Derby Races at Robert Radford's at The Angel' 20 years before. For a lower-brow audience, matches were also advertised as an accompaniment to Derby Shrovetide football at the same pub.

With regard to cricket, the earliest mention of its popularity having seeped down to the humbler elements of the population is the story that 'Mr Fowke played bat and ball in the Derwent basin. The season so dry: no rain between 7 April and 30 November 1826. Severe winter previous' – shades of 1976! The formation of the Derbyshire County Cricket Club belongs, however, to a later age, although a match is recorded at Derby versus Castle Donington as early as 24 September 1792.

The Wardwick Brewery (Alton & Co.), 1891, which began behind Allsopp's house as Lowe's brewery. (M. Craven)

A NEGLECTED INDUSTRY

Derby at this time was famous for its pubs and over some centuries for its production of some of the beverages drunk therein, a factor noted by Blome in 1673. Woolley wrote, 'The principal trade is that of malting, with which many good estates have been raised.' As far back as 1691, when the English maltsters were alarmed at the resurgence in taste for French wines, a pamphlet was issued called 'A Dialogue betwixt Claret and Darby Ale,' in which the author recommended a pint or two of the latter to 'regale the senses and treat the palate'. Fuller, in the same era, wrote, 'Never was the wine of Falernum better known to the Romans than the Canary (Ale) of Derby to the English.' Even earlier, in 1619, we find William Frith 'bearbruer' leasing a house in Rotten Row with 'half a cellar.' In 1577 there had been 61 alehouses, two vintners and seven innkeepers in Derby, while it has been calculated that in Derby in 1762 there was one alehouse or an inn for every 92 inhabitants of the town, in which year there were about 108 of them. About 12 could claim to be proper inns and another 30 or so aspired to such dignity; in 1789 there were 42 maltings. Thomas Cox adds that the Derby malt was also sent to London and adds, 'This drink is made here in such perfection, that Wine must be very good to deserve a Preference' – all this before the pre-eminence of Burton-upon-Trent. He then quotes an engaging little rhyme (translated from his Latin):

> *'Of this strange Drink, so like the STYGIAN Lake,*
> *Men call it Ale, I known not what to make.*
> *They drink it thick and piss it wondrous thin:*
> *What store of dregs must needs remain within?'*

Which seems to say it all really, except that with modern keg beers, the position may well be viewed as reversed. It must be noted, however, that an ambitious poem of 15 stanzas appeared in the *Derby Mercury* in February 1775 in praise of Burton ale; the balance of excellence may have been even then tilting in favour of the Staffordshire town. Yet even as late as 1950 about 20 inns were still brewing their own beer, closing at intervals, leaving only The Friary where Tom Roome, previously 32 years with the King Street *Seven Stars*, brewed for Rowland Hadfield in 1962–68.

INNS & TAVERNS

In Derby as elsewhere, there were differences in these establishments. There had grown up a distinction between an inn and a tavern. The former was a house – later often a coaching house, too – where even a gentleman travelling, or not being able to run to a house in town, might put up for the night without qualms. To some extent they aped the lesser country house, wherein any traveller of means could demand, and legally expect, hospitality of a tolerably high order – even such as Prince Viktor Freidrich von Anhalt-Bernburg who spent two days at the George in 1763 (the same year as the Duke of York stayed) and the bizarre combination of the young Margrave Louis IX of Hesse-Darmstadt accompanied by the cross-dressing Chevalier d'Eon who were there in 1771 in an abortive effort to catch up with their fellow mystical freemason P. P. Burdett, who had left town pursued by creditors three years before.

Taverns and alehouses were a very much inferior kind of establishment. These places fulfilled many and diverse roles in 18th-century Derby. Their premises were let for a wide variety of purposes which, in later times, mostly graduated to specialist outlets. Certainly animals figure high on these, quite apart from Greek language-trained dogs. Vets practised by 'being in attendance' in hostelries: 'John Fowk the famous cow doctor from Kilburn is now removed from the Saracen's Head to the Bell *where his drinks* [author's Italics] are to be had at any time'. Heaven knows when his professional advice was to be had!

Game conservation was thought a fit subject for a session at the King's Head. In 1750 the High Sheriff, a grand jury and 'other gentlemen' met to discuss the preservation of game. Inns also acted as clearing houses

The King's Arms County Hotel, opened in 1798 to service the requirements of lawyers and plaintiffs using the Shire Hall. Photographed by Richard Keene, *c.*1876. (Michael J. Willis)

The yard of the George Inn seen from George Yard: the venue for cockfighting and other entertainment until the inn closed in 1814.

for lost property: horses, dogs, watches and wallets being the commonest. Animals were available to offer services themselves too: 'There is now at the Blue Boar on Nuns' Green a high bred Berkshire Boar (how appropriate) that will brim sows at reasonable rates' and 'Stallion available, a chestnut Yorkshire horse, Nimrod, to cover 12s 6d (62p) mare and 1s (5p) servant (!) at the Nag's Head 17 April 1772.'

It is notable that pubs are chosen with names associated with the animals offered, no doubt as a simple *aide-memoire* for slow-witted country yeomen. Advertising was pub-centred in other ways, too, being concentrated on such things as buying land, jobs, shows, assemblies, creditors' meetings and sales. Most of the pubs benefitted in being the venues for many of the events they advertised. Nor was art neglected: 'Auction in the great dining room of Brentnall's Wine Vaults (Market Place) a collection of prints and drawings belonging to Thomas Smith of Derby painter.'

Smith (d.1767) who lived in Bridge Gate with his wife and three sons – all named after famous Renaissance artists – was a landscape painter of some talent whose oil paintings are exceedingly rare, although his series of engravings of Peak scenery were very popular and both command high prices today. The George even took over temporarily as the venue of the post office from 1766, while that in Queen Street was being rebuilt.

Pubs undoubtedly benefitted from occasions like Mr Gillineaux's amazing tower-flying escapades of 1732, so graphically described by Hutton, and their unnatural sequel, the diverting but ultimately fatal passage of a donkey from the tower of All Saints' on a rope stretched much of the way down St Mary's Gate in August 1734. Such extraordinary entertainments were more often provided by the landlords themselves, ever on the lookout for a spur to the sale of ale. The Widow Raynor's Company of Rope Dancers performed at the end of July 1749 in a booth at the White Hart, a Bridge Gate inn which also advertised a dog with knowledge and understanding of Greek and Hebrew; Mr Furmston, the 'modern living Colossus', could be viewed at the Blackamoor's Head in the Market Place three years later, and the same hostelry advertised the viewing of 'a variety of delightful and magnificent grottos decorated with rockwork.' Misshapen or extraordinary people seem to have been far and away the most popular of these entertainments (if that is the word): 'Mr John Coon, the famous dwarf – weight 34lbs – will be at the Wheatsheaf Inn in the Market Place on 24 April 1754' is typical of the genre, just as the Wheatsheaf was the pub most associated with these freak shows.

Salesmen also set up in pubs, for instance, as the 'celebrated Italian artists' exhibiting 'a set of grand fireworks at the Ostrich Inn (Sadler Gate)' in 1772. The advertisement went on 'Rockets to begin at 5.30pm' (this was in January). The same year 'The artist Joseph Rose' – could this really be the man who did the plasterwork for Adam at Kedleston? – 'to teach gentlemen to make fireworks at the same place' – a practice which would be much frowned upon today, although fireworks were made until recently nearby at Great Wilne.

Pubs were certainly at the heart of politics. It has already been shown how the George and King's Head were prominent during the hectic days of the 'Forty-Five. In 1761 Sir Henry Harpur paid for drinks in nearly every pub in town in the hope of influencing the electors. Lord Scarsdale's son 'Entertained at the George and King's Head a great number of freeholders and several barrels of ale were given to the populace' as the price of being elected unopposed (as a Tory for the county) in 1775.

Theatre and concert tickets were invariably to be had at hostelries, too, and landlords were not slow to promote even cultural events. At the George in 1766, indeed, a concert of vernacular music was held in order to benefit a blind man called George Mullin, plainly an Irishman, tickets at 1s (5p). Before the theatre, large rooms in pubs were useful for theatrical performances. Several dancing-masters in town had rooms hireable for such purposes, too. Mr Putter's premises were the venue for Vanburgh's *The Provok'd Husband* in 1727 and Mr Turrell's rooms for Mr Herbert's company of comedians in 1733. There was also a group of Derby Comedians – not the gentlemen of the Corporation! – who were prepared to play, and Shakespeare plays were also performed in the ballroom of the George and in the County Hall.

THEATRE

In the 1760s Dublin-born James Augustus Whiteley (1724–1781) came to Derby with his theatre company, performing in the Shire Hall. In 1769 they returned and again petitioned the High Sheriff, then Sir Edward Every of Egginton, Bt., '…for permission to use the County Hall as a theatre'. The letter, still in the Every papers, goes on to emphasise what a thoroughly decent bunch they were but noting that the custodian of the building '…Mr Leach, will not give the key without a line from you, which will ever find your petitioner to pray it.'

Whiteley had already been running two salaried theatre companies, his troupe of actors receiving a share of the profits as well, an unheard of idea at the time; he himself was said to have been making £500 per annum, extremely good money. In the end, having encountered increasing difficulty securing the use of the County Hall, he acquired a malthouse in Bold Lane, supposed to have been built in 1712. It was in the proprietorship of

William Ratcliffe in 1755 and offered for sale in the press on 15 March 1772.

The building was purchased for £170 and some adjoining cottages for £50, and the former adapted very rapidly (inherent damp was never really eradicated) into what Whiteley called 'an elegant theatre' with a façade of recessed arcading and an ornate interior, almost certainly designed by the ubiquitous Pickford, to make Derby's first theatre, the Theatre Royal. It opened on 13 September 1773 – the beginning of race week – with a performance of Oliver Goldsmith's *She Stoops to Conquer*, the company presenting a different play every night each week. In 1777 tickets were available from the box office as well as from the George and King's Head, boxes being 2s 6d (12.5p) and the gallery 1s (5p). Mrs Jordan from Drury Lane appeared in 1790 in *The Belles Stratagem* being '…well received by overflowing houses'. In 1809 Francis Mundy of Markeaton played Richard III there to a fashionable audience who had been advised that 'Carriages must all approach down St Mary's Gate and leave by Sadler Gate' – surely the first one way system in any English town!

William Hodges (1744–1797), an important artist and a friend of Joseph Wright, was sailing with Captain Cooke's voyage to Australia at the opening, but from 1775–79 visited Derby frequently, being stepson of Whitehurst's niece. He worked as a scenery painter, making the association with Pickford the more plausible, especially as the work would have followed on from his known alterations at the Shire Hall. Performances were geared to getting in the gentry element and were especially timed to coincide with the races. A new inn, opposite (closed by temperance fanatics in 1903), was appositely called The Shakespeare, although the Ostrich in Sadler Gate was, before 1822, opportunistically renamed The Shakespeare as well, leading to the Bold Lane establishment to add 'The Old' to its name in retaliation!

In 1803 the executors of the founder leased the establishment to a company which included James Sheridan Knowles, an actor and playwright cousin of R.B. Sheridan; he also lectured when he came to Derby on elocution and oratory. This included Ellen Tree and her husband Charles, son of Edmund Kean. Other visiting actors included Edmund Kean himself, Sarah Siddons, Fanny Kemble, W.C. Macready and Madame Vestris. In the early 1820s it was one of the first Derby buildings to be 'brilliantly illuminated by gas'.

Non-conformists strongly disapproved of theatrical performances and, as this influence waxed as the town's industrialisation blossomed, later the attendances began to fall. Likewise the gentry began to desert the town once they could reach London in a few hours by rail from 1839. The Theatre closed at the end of the 1852–53 season and was advertised for sale in the *Mercury* on 22 June in the latter year, being purchased by Margaret Rose of Nottingham Road a month later for £830, but what her motivation was is unclear, although it appears to have been unfulfilled, for in 1864 the fundamentalist printer George Wilkins was able to acquire the premises and turn the building into a Gospel Hall. The boxes and the gallery were demolished, a floor was laid across the dress circle, the roof beams were exposed and the pit floor was lowered to make a ground floor hall. It reopened as an inter-denominational mission hall on 24 February 1865. Ironically, a descendant was one of the founders of the Little Theatre and its successor the Wilkins Memorial Hall, Becket Street, in 1947, from which small beginnings blossomed Derby Playhouse a few years later.

The Gospel Hall, used as a military billet in World War Two, was acquired by the county council in 1945, and the building, much gutted and mauled, was latterly a magistrates' court, which closed in 2003, since which time the building has laid derelict, although subject to a variety of schemes to revive Derby's first purpose-built theatre.

DERBY'S SPAS

One final relaxation needs to be considered: the events which almost led to Derby being able to add the accolade of 'Spa'. In 1733, we are told, William Chauncey 'discovered' a mineral spring at Abbey Barns, north west of the present Abbey Street. Chauncey was a local doctor, son of Charles Chauncey, an Ashbourne surgeon who died in 1707. Chauncey, whose connections with Derby seem to have gone back some way – two of his six children were baptized in the borough – decided to seize this opportunity to rival Buxton. His discovery was not quite so earth-shattering as might be thought, for this was the spring that had fed the Becket Well since mediaeval times and was well known to the canons of Darley.

The Scots physician Thomas Short, who wrote about the Spa in 1766, tells us 'He put down a basin into the spring of it, to come out fresh: he built a cover over the spring which discharges itself by a grate and keeps the place always dry. About 20 yards below the spa he made a handsome cold bath and two dressing rooms with a large room over the whole and pleasant walks… at considerable expense.'

However, Chauncey was merely exploiting something which was already known about. In 1611 the burgesses were receiving rent for 'A wateringe place at the nether end of Abbie Barne', which rather suggests that the spring had been known and exploited some 122 years

All that remains of Dr Chauncey's Spa is the main house, rebuilt as a residence in the late 18th century and adapted as an inn c.1830. It is seen here in the early 1970s, still with a row of artisans' cottages, built along the frontage with Abbey Street and demolished in 1978.
@ *Derby Evening Telegraph*

Dr Chancey's surviving 1733 Spa buildings now the Old Spa Inn, established a century later and seen here in 1976 before a recent facelift. (M. Craven)

Regency shop at 39 Corn Market, long the Kardomah and today a pizza outlet. This photograph was taken in the 1920s, when it was the town centre outlet for the *Derby Daily* and *Evening Telegraph*.

before. It might reasonably be suggested that the canons of Darley had known of it (for it was part of their Newlands) and used it. The matter thus becomes highly challenging and would make a splendid opportunity for an archaeological investigation; perhaps *Time Team* could be persuaded to step in.

Dr Chauncey, as it turned out, died in 1736, leaving his Melbourne-born widow to run it until she sold a lease of the spa in 1740 to Samuel Greatorex, who was still in possession in 1759. After having been recorded as a going concern by Dr Short in 1766, it rather seems to fade from record and, arguing from negative evidence, seems to have folded by 1784. Chauncey had erected a pretty, brick two-storey building, with two straight-coped gables to the road; the outbuilding to the north west once contained the spa's facilities. This edifice was extended and converted into a residence by William Boothby, who was still living there with three acres in 1821. In or shortly before 1832 it was adapted as the Spa public house, which, as The Old Spa Inn, it remains to this day. Elsewhere in the ancient sphere of influence of Derby was one other minor spa, at Quarndon, which flourished from the mid-17th century to the mid-19th, after which it entered a rapid decline.

NEWSPAPERS

All the components of Derby's citizenry's non-working lives are presented for us in the pages of the local papers, especially the *Derby Mercury;* would that there had been more than polemical tracts available to us from the previous century! However, the first Derby newspaper was only founded on 1 December 1717, called *The Derby Postman*, which was published by Samuel Hodgkinson at a penny halfpenny, which underwent a transformation as of 11 May 1726 into the *The British Spy* or *Derby Postman*. It continued until it was put out of business by its rather more professional successor, the *Derby Mercury*, much resorted to by researchers into the history of the city.

The *Mercury* was founded on 23 March 1732, the first issue being dated 2 March, by Samuel Drewry (d.1769) who came from Stafford and set up in the Market Place in a handsome and fairly new house on the corner of Iron Gate and Sadler Gate in the 1720s. At first it came out weekly, but towards the end of the 18th century it became daily. The family, succession in which over the first three generations was from uncle to nephew, continued as printers and proprietors of this organ (as well as the *Stafford Mercury*) into the fourth generation, when Alderman John Drewry (III), son of the like-named mayor of 1806 and 1823, married the heiress of Alderman Samuel Rowland, a country landowner of

Alderman Joshua Smith's house before its roof was rebuilt in 1951. For many years the office of the Drewrys, publishers of the *Derby Mercury*, and later William Bemrose's first home, but since Lloyd's bank. (M. Craven)

considerable fortune, whose sister had been Drewry's stepmother. He sold the business on 29 March 1839 and retired to Burton Priory, where (inevitably) his nephew succeeded him. The firm went to William Bemrose, tenant of the premises since 1824, who ran his fledgling printing empire from there, while the paper was sold on, its greatest editor thereafter being Alfred Wallis (1833–1918), a member of the coaching family.

Whereas the *Mercury* managed to put the *Postman* out of business fairly quickly, the former managed to see off its rivals until the *Derby Daily Express* put paid to it in 1930. As early as 22 June 1738 the *Derby Journal* began in opposition and limped along in a fairly anti-establishment vein, closing as *Harrison's Derby Journal* in 1776. It seems that the Miss Harrison who was the second John Drewry's second wife was connected directly with this venture. Marrying the opposition's heiress was then a common method of ensuring success in business, but is less practised nowadays.

From 1776 until 18 January 1823 the *Mercury*, which increasingly took a traditional, anti-radical viewpoint, had a free rein, but on the latter date the reformist *Derby and Chesterfield Reporter* was founded by brothers Walter and William Pike, booksellers and

printers in succession to their father, William. Walter Pike (1790–1859) was editor until 1843, succeeded by his nephew John Beard Pike (1829–1875), whose redoubtable widow Eliza Maria (1832–1905) kicked over the traces and founded a separate newspaper in 1879, the *Derby Daily Telegraph*, which she also edited from 39 Corn Market. After her death, under her daughter's ownership, the *Telegraph* went on to absorb almost all its rivals, including the *Derby Daily Express*, and in 1931 its founder's uncle's paper, the *Reporter*. Thereafter it changed from a daily to an evening paper and still continues today as the *Derby Evening Telegraph*, long part of the Northcliffe/Rothermere empire.

In 1846 the only other rival newspaper was founded. This was the *Derbyshire Advertiser*, always a weekly publication and the brainchild of John Hobson, an Ashbourne printer, and his son William (1825–1897), who edited it throughout his life, despite moving to Derby, becoming a councillor and serving as Mayor of Derby in 1883 and suffect Mayor in 1885. The *Advertiser* was also radical, and Hobson supported a number of causes, like the establishment of the Art School and the Museum. The paper remained in the proprietorship and editorship of three generations and four members of the family (which also produced zoologist Professor Alfred Hobson, mathematician Professor Ernest Hobson and journalist Sir Oscar Hobson), closing on the retirement of the last, E.G.B. Atkinson, in 1969.

One aspect of local life much favoured by the editor of the *Mercury* was the full and lurid reporting of crimes, tumults and their inevitable outcome. The *Reporter*, on the other hand, gloried in the more political aspects. It was indeed this aspect in the early 19th century that persuaded the government of the day to impose a stamp duty on newspapers in order to price them out of the reach of the small shopkeepers, the artisans and the better sort of workmen, in order to deny them access to radical opinion. In 1835 one Henry Robinson of Derby was fined £20 for selling a broadsheet without stamp duty – a common offence among radical sympathisers keen to maintain a hold on the awareness of their natural constituency. Robinson could not (or more likely, keen for the notoriety of martyrdom, would not) pay his fine and was consigned to gaol for six months, although he was granted an early release by a tactful Home Secretary, wisely unwilling to encourage such self-publicity. Nevertheless, the Press faithfully reported events in Derby and none with more zest than the inexorable course of the law upon wrongdoers, not to mention the fullest accounts of their crimes.

Derby Daily Telegraph advertising car in Exchange Street in 1929. (*Derby Evening Telegraph*)

CRIME & PUNISHMENT

The first great lawyer to be associated with Derby was undoubtedly Sir Simon Degge, appointed recorder of the town at the Restoration. His office, in some form or another, stretched back to 1446, but had been redefined by the charter of 1611, when Henry Duport had been the first in an unbroken line down to 1971 when the office was abolished. Under the old charter the recorder set times for the borough Sessions and superintended the borough Court of Requests – a sort of small claims court held at the Guildhall before the mayor every third Tuesday in the month – and presided over that of Record, the latter being held in the Moot Hall.

Degge seems to have had a strong streak of humanity in him, unlike many of his successors in the century and a half following, exemplified in the case of Noah Bullock.

NOAH BULLOCK – COUNTERFEITER

Bullock, in deference to his uncommon Christian name, betook himself and his family to live on a boat – an ark, as Hutton does not fail to style it – 'above St Mary's Bridge'. We are told he had three sons, whom he is said to have called, with crushing logic, Shem, Ham and Japhet. Hutton goes on, referring to Noah and his family becoming a standing joke in the town: 'If they publicly ridiculed him, he privately laughed at them: for it afterwards appeared he had more sense than honesty; and more craft than either; for this disguise and retreat were to be a security to coin money. He knew Justice could not easily overtake him; and if it should, the deep was ready to hide his crimes and utensils.'

How Bullock could operate a small furnace on his ark – essential to melt the metal required to cast counterfeit coin – is difficult to say. Perhaps such unwieldy apparatus was his undoing, for in 1676 he was sent for by Sir Simon Degge, whom 'he personally knew.' Degge said that he had heard that Bullock had taken up a new occupation and disingenuously asked to see a specimen of his work; both realised that the game was up. Against an assurance that he would be immune from prosecution if he should relinquish his trade, a capital offence in those days, Bullock produced a specimen, a sixpenny piece. As a result, Noah 'broke up his ark and escaped the halter'. The tale exhibits points of divergence with record, however.

Noah Bullock was born in May 1644, a son of William Bullock. Now it seems likely that this William is to be identified with Sir William Bullock of Darley Hall (1617–1666), an ardent Royalist in the civil war, nominated in 1660 as a member of the Order of the Royal Oak by Charles II and later knighted. The family

A memory of Noah Bullock on the Morledge: the Noah's Ark Inn, 1982. Underneath the faux Tudor exterior lurks a 18th-century building. (M. Craven)

A further difficulty is Hutton's placing of the ark's mooring as 'above St Mary's Bridge'. This would place the family in the parish of St Alkmund, which again fails to fit the facts, for all the children were baptized at St Peter's – well *below* the bridge. More likely the vessel was moored against the Morledge where, to this day, stands a public house named after Bullock's buoyant residence, the Noah's Ark.

Yet, despite this aberration, or example of constructive clemency, Degge set a high standard in justice in Derby and was long remembered for it. Gone were the days when citizens were burnt, like Joan Wast, in Windmill Pit for capital crimes: the last such had been a woman in 1602, convicted of poisoning her husband. Nevertheless, the citizens long recalled the barbarity of hangman John Crosland, who died in 1705 (three years after Degge), from whom the recorder had saved Noah Bullock. Crosland was doubly hated for having been a poacher turned gamekeeper. He had been appointed under the Commonwealth straight from the Assizes, at which he turned King's (or Cromwell's) evidence, at the expense of his own kin, who became his first official victims. It seems to make discordant counterpoint that this monster's career as hangman should have nearly coincided with that of so civilised a Recorder.

Noah Bullock's calling, however, did not die out. On 7 August 1740 George Ashmore, who installed the clock in the tower of All Saints', was found guilty of issuing counterfeit coin. Unlike his eccentric predecessor, he was sentenced to death, hanged and buried at Sutton-on-the-Hill. Nor was Ashmore the last to suffer for this offence, one Thomas Knowles being hanged for it at Derby on 5 September 1800.

We have seen that the County Gaol was in a Tudor building on St Peter's or Gaol Bridge and that, on the demolition of the old Guildhall in 1729, a lean-to extension was added to the County Gaol to house the borough's prisoners.

In 1753 proposals were put in hand for a new County Gaol, provoked by a happenstance symptomatic of the state of the old prison, which had been referred to as 'poor' even in the 1580s, in a letter from Sir John Manners to the Earl of Shrewsbury. On the night of 21 February 1752, four prisoners broke out of it by making a hole in the lower part of the wall, a testimony to the inadequacy of the Tudor fabric. Three escaped completely; one, Anthony Frost, for some reason known only to himself, returned to his cell the same way as he got out and was found there the next morning.

In due course a plot was acquired from the mayor and Corporation on Nuns' Green and William Hiorne of Warwick was appointed to design and build it. When completed in 1757, the pedimented Palladian street

were seated at Darley Hall from 1574 to 1682. Neither did (Sir) William marry until 1660 nor did he flee Puritan dominated Derby until 1643. Quite possibly, Noah's mother Joan brought him up alone and gave him and his brother Moses biblical names to boost their Puritan credentials, had their true parentage been suspected.

How else are we to explain both the leniency and the friendship of a grandee like Degge? For, despite the sheer impudence of Bullock's (capital) crime, had he been a man of any mean origin, surely Degge would have dealt harshly with him.

Furthermore, in 1667 Bullock married Anna, daughter of Isaac Clarke, a respectable tradesman, and there were eight offspring recorded. That he had a son called Japhet is not in doubt, albeit that the child was born five years *after* the incident recounted above. In 1676 there was but one son, Samuel. The other sons, Joseph and Benjamin, were born in 1677 and 1682 respectively. Benjamin married and his son Robert (d.1786) became a wealthy skinner.

W.M. and T. Cooper: houses on the site of the old gaol, Friar Gate, 1840–42. (Mrs A. Donnelly)

façade was seen to be in a monumental and severe Doric with muscular stone dressings. In plan, a central, domed hall had two corridors radiating from it, one to the façade block for felons and the other, on the same axis, to another block at the rear, for debtors and lesser offenders. The courtyard was 82 x 43ft, off which was a chapel with a two-room sick bay over. Small pavilions connected by high walls marked the angles, and beneath the structure were further cells on either side of a corridor parallel with the street. It was designed originally for 21 long-term prisoners, but by 1819 there were 69. There were also four cells set apart for women.

The small number of prisoners for which the edifice was originally designed reflects the smaller size of the town in 1756 and the generally low crime rate. Hutton, echoing this a generation later, says: 'Four prisons in so small a place as Derby might induce the stranger to suppose it a place of rascals!'

The ancient gaol in Cornmarket was demolished in 1757, apart from the former Gaoler's house, converted into a private residence.

A row of eight fine houses allegedly built for the turnkeys of the Friar Gate County Gaol, c.1805, seen here shortly before demolition in 1977. (Derby Evening Telegraph)

This new prison survived as County Gaol until 1828 when a new one was opened in Vernon Street a little distance away to the designs of Francis Goodwin in a robust Doric, along with governors' and turnkeys' houses, all laid out at the end of Vernon Street, set up as a sort of triumphal avenue from Friar Gate. A transverse street was also pitched as part of Goodwin's design, running across the grim Doric façade, called South Street, connecting Uttoxeter New and Old Roads. Vernon Street was lined with trees and elegant stuccoed villas, South Street with artisans' cottages. This prison's tall internal blocks were laid out radiating from a central octagon, with the automated hanging chamber, protected from public view, although public hangings lasted there until Richard Thorley was hanged for murder in May 1862, watched by – it is said – 20,000 people; thereafter four more hangings took place (discreetly), the last on 10 August 1888. For the curious, there have been 81 hangings in Derby between 1732 and 1888 for capital offences, including robbery, horse stealing, rape, forgery, counterfeiting, pick-pocketing, highway robbery and bestiality.

The County Gaol also took borough prisoners from 1840 and survived exactly a century before it was declared redundant and internally cleared in 1928, after which a dog racing track was set up within the tall brick perimeter walls. Racing ceased in the 1980s, although it was not until 1996 that a scheme got under way to build apartments and office blocks in a rather weak classical style and placed in a way which completely fails to take account of Goodwin's listed surviving centerpiece; the perimeter walls were sacrificed, however, despite the current striving for security: most odd.

Back in 1828, the old prison in Friar Gate was then sold as a going concern to the borough for £3,000 and was in use until the two amalgamated on the Vernon Street site in 1840. The building was then demolished and replaced by a very handsome, ashlar-faced and pedimented terrace of five spacious houses, designed and built by Thomas Cooper of Derby. The basement cells were preserved as the successor building's cellars and survive to this day, complete with original doors and graffiti. These, for some years part of what used to be called a 'dive bar', pertaining to the former Howard Hotel above, were taken over in 2000 by enthusiastic entrepreneur Richard Felix and turned into a rather ghoulish visitor attraction.

Between 1756 and 1828 the borough prison had been in Willow Row, almost as close to the ever-rising Markeaton Brook as had been its predecessor, although the building was replaced in April 1813. Even after that, it was small, consisting of a gaoler's house to the street with two small yards behind. The larger, in which were the cells of the male prisoners, was 30 x 18ft; the smaller,

The grim façade of the 1826 county gaol in Vernon Street as restored in 1999. Note the 'martello towers' or bastions added after the 1832 Reform riot. (M. Craven)

accommodating around it the females, measured 18ft x 15ft separated by a courtyard 33ft x 24ft. Debtors were held in three cells up a flight of stairs, but there was only one debtor held in 1801, three in 1802 and two the year after, each allowed three 'twelvepenny loaves' per week. Glover says 'There was no chaplain nor any divine service performed in the prison, nor rules for its government, nor employment of any kind.'

Minor offenders were lodged in the House of Correction, from 1730 part of the Guildhall, and after 1828 in a yard behind the new edifice (hence the late

Demolition of the prison buildings of the 1826 County Gaol, Vernon Street, in 1929, prior to conversion into a greyhound track. It had been one of the first in the country to have been built on the 'radial' plan. (*Derby Evening Telegraph*)

20th-century name for the old Tiger Yard connecting it with Corn Market: 'Lock-up Yard'), connected to the borough Magistrates' Court within by an underground passage. These offenders, up to the 18th century, were frequently sentenced to stand in the pillory in the Market Place.

A MURDEROUS VIRAGO

One person to stand in the pillory was the notorious Ellen Beare. The wife of the landlord of the Crown Inn, Nuns' Green (later Friar Gate), she was convicted of enticement, inducing abortion and destroying a foetus, none of which were then statutory crimes (although she was believed also to have committed infanticide, too, which most definitely was) and consequently her conviction rested on being found guilty only of 'misdemeanours', carrying a relatively light sentence. She had also shortly before been acquitted of a charge of the murder of the wife of a butcher called Hewitt, her lover, and an innocent party, Rosamond Ollerenshaw, detested by Mrs Beare, because she was hanged in her stead. As Hutton says, 'This wholesale dealer in human destruction was only sentenced to stand two market days in the pillory and to sustain three years imprisonment.

I saw her, 18 August 1732, with an easy air ascend the hated machine, which overlooked an enraged multitude. All the apples, eggs and turnips that could be bought, begged, or stolen, were directed at her…head. The stagnant kennels were robbed of their contents and became the cleanest part of the street. The pillory, being out of repair, was unable to hold a woman in her prime. She released herself; and jumping among the crowd, with a resolution and agility of an Amazon, ran down the Morledge, being pelted all the way: new Kennels produced new ammunition; and she appeared a moving heap of filth.'

Ultimately, she was put back and the Friday following she returned '…not as a young woman, but an old one, ill, swelled and decrepit; she seemed to have advanced 30 years in one week.'

Even so, her head coverings looking suspiciously bulky, they were removed to reveal no less than 12 layers of cloth and a pewter plate to serve as armour! She served her sentence, recovered health and beauty and lived to commit further offences for which she received three years. In 1735, now calling herself Merriman, and lately out of prison, she was again sent down for receiving. In 1740 she managed to get herself transported for seven years for ransacking two waggons on the Ashbourne Road on 10 July and provoking a riot. She is not thereafter heard of again. She also almost certainly murdered her 'cypher' of a husband, Ebenezer Beare.

So notorious was she that, once convicted, the inn's name was changed by her successor to the White Horse, a hostelry famed for its antiquity when demolished in 1876 to build the line of the Great Northern Railway (see page 181).

Whereas Ellen Beare got off lightly for her crimes, one could still be hanged for sheep stealing, as on 14 January 1801, a year in which was recorded the greatest-ever number of cases at the Assizes. Yet two men convicted of poaching, an offence which could carry the supreme penalty, were merely 'whipt round the Market Place' and on 5 December the same year farmer Thomas Bott of Langley was able to offer his wife for sale, also in the Market Place, for 1s 6d (7p)! The town annals add a long list of men hanged for capital crimes from 1621 until 1831; the list includes them because of their rarity apart from the prurient fascination of public hangings for spectators and chroniclers alike. There are only, at the most, five reported from the 17th century and barely more than a dozen in that following, of which only two were women. From 1754 no woman was hanged until 1819.

A more common punishment for serious crimes was transportation to the colonies, the fate that befell Mrs Beare. The West Indies and Virginia were used at first, and although Derby men must have been transported in the later 17th century, the first recorded instances were in 1732 and 1736. By the last decade of the century, however,

these cases were being transported to Australia rather than Virginia, closed to the export of undesirables by the American Revolution. Indeed, families living there today can trace their ancestry to Derby felons.

An example was Stephen Wain (1771–1827), charged with stealing 18 guineas and 7s (35p) in gold and silver coin from Joseph Webster of Chesterfield. He was sentenced on 14 August 1800 to seven years' transportation and left for Australia a month later on the *Glatton*. In Sydney in 1809 he married a half-caste girl, Elizabeth Mandeville (transported from London in 1808), and settled shortly afterwards at Castlereagh, New South Wales. Wain, who changed his surname to the more aristocratic Vane, ultimately settled at Kelso, New South Wales, and left descendants, the Beauchamps – many of whom still live in the area.

Far more disturbing, in the eyes of the burgesses, were occasions of riot, or worse, as Mrs Beare's hijacking of a convoy in 1740 and the events of 4–6 December 1745 showed. In August 1755 a sharp rise in the price of corn took place and a riot seemed imminent, especially in view of others at Atherstone, Birmingham, Tamworth and Nottingham. It was thwarted only by decisive action from the mayor, William Evans, who had intercepted an inflammatory note. Three years later there was much worry over 300 French prisoners of war paroled in the town for four years. Again, the Corporation, in consultation with the Lord Lieutenant, acted very level-headedly, setting them to work repairing the Derby–Nottingham Road and St Mary's Bridge, at that date in terminal decay. Their credit, notwithstanding their circumstances, was not at a premium; 'Their behaviour was at first impudent and insolent; at all times vain and effeminate; and their whole deportment light and unmanly… in any future war, this Nation has nothing to fear from them as an enemy.' Nevertheless, during their time in town they were reported as well-behaved and no criminal offences occurred among them.

Yet, occasional riots continued. In 1759 an account records a payment of £10 15s 0d (£10.75) for '27 dragoons and 16 deputy constables on account of the rioters on endeavouring to pull down the Corn Mills in this borough…' There is a theory which suggests that the urban crowd enjoyed a vital role in the fabric of 18th-century society. Somehow (and in mid-18th-century Derby there was by no means a large quantity of poor and unemployed men) there were always people who seemed to appear from nowhere to celebrate an election, to hail a new mayor, to hear a proclamation or cheer a demagogue. Indeed, leaving aside the Derby riots of 1740 (the 'flour riot' as instigated by Mrs Beare), 1756 (the 'millstone riot'), 1766 (the 'food riot') and incidents of football running out of control, the heyday of the mob was the Reform Riot of 8–12 October 1831.

IX

REGENCY DERBY

THE REFORM RIOT OF 1832

The Reform Bill, a Whig measure to democratise the House of Commons and extend the vote to all adult male owners of property over a certain value, was killed in the Lords by 199 to 158 votes on 8 October 1831, and the news reached Derby the same day at about 7pm.

Rioting began immediately, signalled by the ringing of a funeral peal on the bells of St Peter's and All Saints'. Windows of various prominent Tories were broken, starting in the Market Place with those of William Bemrose, whose printing business had been established in the Drewrys' old house in the Market Place. The next sufferers were Alderman Thomas Eaton at Bridge Chapel House (he escaped in disguise), the elder Henry Mozley of The Friary, another printer (like Bemrose, his father's former apprentice, from Gainsborough, Lincolnshire, and established in the town 14 years), Thomas Cox of 63 Friar Gate, lead merchant and Revd Charles Stead Hope. All suffered much damage to property, despite the entreaties of the Reformist banker, William Baker of 44 Friar Gate, who attempted to placate and restrain the crowd between their endeavours at The Friary and the west end of Nuns' Green. With bravery (or foolhardiness) he '…with much earnestness endeavoured to persuade them to desist from a course of destruction which would be of no benefit to the cause which they pretended to espouse. They cheered him and went on with other works of demolition.'

Arriving at the west end of Nuns' Green, they aspired to greater things and proceeded to Markeaton Hall, where the heirs of the Whiggish F.N.C. Mundy were less open-minded than 'French' himself, and where much superficial damage was done. They then went back via C.S. Hope's and Alderman Eaton's (in case any glass at the houses of those worthies had been left unsmashed), taking in Mr Harrison's on Bridge Gate in their destructive rampage, and finished up at Chaddesden Hall, where poor Sir Robert Wilmot 'suffered immense depredations'. Later, Bemrose collected a second assault and stragglers pulled in John Drewry, Mr Johnson (a surgeon in Full Street), Mr Abbot and William Whiston, an upwardly-mobile attorney.

The following morning a public meeting in the Guildhall, called by mayor Charles Lowe, was 'bounced' by a large number of the previous nights' rioters. The refusal of the chief magistrate to release a pair of arrested

rioters then caused a general surge to the newly-adapted borough Gaol in Friar Gate. Here the mob beat in the doors with an uprooted cast-iron lamp standard and released all 23 prisoners. They then turned their attention to Francis Goodwin's County Gaol in Vernon Street – recently finished – which was successfully defended with some vigour, four rioters being shot, one fatally. Three county magistrates of the Reformist persuasion then managed to persuade the mob to disperse. Unfortunately, in the afternoon, the make-up of the crowd subtly changed, many fanatical reformers unwilling to finally disperse being joined – as is so often the case, as in the rioting in the city in 1981 – by a largish number of miscreants and criminal elements bent on destruction of any kind. This was evidenced by a return to assaults on houses, but whereas on the first evening only the dwellings of opponents of Reform received their unwelcome attentions, on this occasion they smashed windows and looted fairly indiscriminately. Finally, the mob fatally mugged Henry, a son of the prominent physician Alderman Thomas Haden.

While this was happening, the mayor summoned a troop of the 15th Hussars from Nottingham, and when it was apparent that the nature of the mob and the aim of the rioting had changed, the Riot Act was read and the troops moved in to disperse the crowd, by this time desultorily breaking up empty market stalls in the Market Place, during which another innocent bystander was killed by a rioter while seeking refuge in the doorway of the Greyhound Inn; several members of the crowd were injured by the soldiers, however, who, to their credit, stuck to their sabres and sensibly eschewed the use of firearms. Nevertheless, order was soon restored and special constables were sworn in to help counter any further outbreaks. By the Tuesday morning, 12 October, order had been finally restored.

No one knew at this juncture how the political situation in the larger dimension would end, and thus precautions had to be taken. The arrested rioters were sent to be tried before the recorder, John Balguy of Duffield, but this was postponed to the spring (1832) assizes. On that occasion 11 young men (all but one were in their 20s) appeared before the future Chief Justice, Lord Wensleydale, who tactfully acquitted all but two, who were transported for looting. The mayor had the town gaol strengthened, and the County Magistrates ordered bastions – then called martello towers – be added to the curtain wall of the Vernon Street gaol in order to enfilade it with fire should the outrage be repeated, the architect being John Mason of Derby, the builder Thomas Cooper and the cost £1,540. The total number of prisoners in the County Gaol over 1831 had been 619, so, had the rioters succeeded in opening the prison, the results could have been alarming in the extreme. It might have been worse for the governor, for he was Richard Eaton, brother of the surgeon whose house the mob attacked on the first night of the riot.

This unsavoury episode was not repeated because of the fall of the Duke of Wellington's administration and the electoral success of Lord Grey's, which, in the year following, managed to ensure the passage of another Reform Bill through the Upper House.

THE PENTRICH REVOLUTION

Although a culmination of a tradition of urban unruliness going back to the conflicts in the 15th century, the riot had been matched as a threat to order only by the so-called Pentrich Revolution of 1817. This had started on 8 June that year, led by Jeremiah Brandreth, 'the Nottingham Captain', at an inn at Pentrich. It later turned out that his enterprise was initiated by a government *agent provocateur* and that he believed that by raising and leading a force to Nottingham he would be linking up with similar, likeminded, men leading irregular groups intent on overthrowing Lord Liverpool's unpopular government.

Brandreth's demagogy, linked to the results of the depressed times, attracted a largish mob (ultimately some 60), partly armed, and they set off south. They attacked but failed to take the Butterley works at Ripley, but Brandreth stamped his authority on his men by subsequently shooting a servant of the Wheatcrofts at Wingfield Park, a rash act that ensured his condemnation when caught. Having crossed the Erewash, they were met at Giltbrook (famous now only for a vast Ikea) and largely mopped up by the 15th Hussars from Nottingham under Lt. Col. Lord Waldegrave and by a detachment of Derbyshire Yeomanry under Thomas Hallowes, ironically a descendant of the republican fanatic who acted as Gell's Derby hatchet-man in the civil war. Others were later found lurking in the *bocage* by the civil authorities and mopped up. At Derby the Tory mayor Revd Charles Stead Hope had, with brewer Thomas Lowe and tanner-cum-amateur architect Richard Leaper, organised the defence of the town, using a company of infantry from the 95th (Derbyshire) Regiment, and ultimately five units of local yeomanry were mustered to secure the borough.

The insurgents were brought to Derby and tried in the Shire Hall before three judges and a grand jury; a future Chief Justice, locally-born Thomas Denman, appeared for the defence. The grand jury itself was stiff with landed gentlemen from the furthest reaches of the county, including two Baronets and three local peers' sons. Brandreth, with his lieutenants William Turner and Isaac Ludlam, were found guilty of High Treason, notwithstanding an inspired defence by young Denman on Ludlam's behalf, and executed at the Friar Gate Gaol publicly, *pour encourager les autres,* but were not quartered as the law technically required, this being 'justly omitted' in Glover's words. Nevertheless, once hanged they were beheaded, their heads being held up to the gaze of the crowd. These unfortunates were despatched on the 'new drop' in front of the County Gaol known to have been installed in lieu of the open gibbets on Gallows Baulk by 1812. The execution block was kept and is now in Derby Museum. In fact, the first criminal hanging undertaken at the New County Gaol did not take place until as late as April 1833 when one John Leedham was executed for the then capital offence of bestiality.

THE MILITARY

We have seen that by 1817 there was a military presence in the town. Although the yeomanry in its first guise (to 1827) was a collection of regional and proprietorial cavalry troops formed in or after 1796, it did not of its nature require a headquarters, although by 1818 it consisted of over 500 officers and men, divided into nine troops organised into two corps. The threat of a French invasion had been the catalyst for their formation, although they were available for riot control too. The lifting of the French threat from 1815 led to this unit's demobilisation from 1827; only a few landed proprietors kept the unit in theoretical existence through continued support for their independent troops – virtually miniature private armies – some of which proved invaluable in 1831.

Subsequently, the renewed French threat under Napoleon III (1852–1870) led to the yeomanry's revival in 1864 (reabsorbing the Independent Troops) and the regiment continued more or less uninterruptedly until 1956, serving abroad (in South Africa) for the first time at the turn of the century. In 1956 it merged with the Leicestershire Yeomanry and again, later, became a mere regimental troop in the later 20th century before re-securing a degree of independence.

The 95th Regiment had its origin in the militia raised in 1689 and revived in 1745 and 1757, although the 95th itself was raised in 1823 and adopted Derbyshire two years later. It was amalgamated with the 45th (Nottinghamshire) Regiment in 1881, forming the 2nd

Derbyshire Yeomanry barracks, Siddals Road, photographed in March 1957, not long before final closure and demolition. Flats were built on the site. (*Derby Evening Telegraph*)

Crimea veterans of the 95th (Derbyshire) Regiment. (Derby Museum)

The Drill Hall, Becket Street, designed and built by Robert Bridgart in 1868. (*Derby Evening Telegraph*)

Battalion of the new Sherwood Foresters' Regiment. The Foresters' finest hour was said to have been the bravery shown during the siege of Badajoz in 1812, in commemoration of which every 6 April a red jacket is flown from the flagpole of the current barracks and Derby Council House, as an echo of that flown over Badajoz to signal to those still outside the town's walls that the city had been taken, there being no Union flag to hand.

There were other volunteer units in the county, too. In 1796 further panic at government level led to another act allowing a mounted militia to be called the Provisional Cavalry. Lord Vernon (Sudbury Hall) was appointed Colonel in 1797, but the unit was probably never embodied. In 1859 a second volunteer movement led to the foundation of the Derbyshire Volunteer Rifle Corps, being preceded by four years by the 2nd Derbyshire Militia (Chatsworth Rifles). The North Midland Volunteers were established later with the Drill Hall, Becket Street, as their HQ.

The former had a compact barracks built at the Rowditch, designed by Derby architect George Thompson, consisting of gatehouses, drill hall, stores

and eight warrant officers' cottages. Miraculously, although decommissioned in 1881, it survived as a laundry, the drill square as a tennis club's courts and the cottages were suitably adapted to four reasonably spacious units instead of eight miniscule ones. The complex was eventually listed grade II in 1998 at the instigation of the Derby Civic Society.

Both these units were affiliated to the 95th Regiment in 1872, becoming the 3rd Battalion Sherwood Foresters from 1881. The earlier militia units had a nondescript barracks on the north side of the Uttoxeter Road beyond the brickworks. After the formation of the Sherwood Foresters, a large new barracks were built on Sinfin Lane in 1874–77.

The Derbyshire Yeomanry, on the other hand, had a barracks in Derby adapted *c*.1864 at 11 St Mary's Gate from the site of George Bridgart's builder's yard. This was required for the County Education Offices in 1897, and the regiment moved to the site of what had been Roe's timber yard, 91 Siddals Road, and it remained in use until 1960, latterly with two artillery and an RAMC unit sharing, being demolished in 1961 (page 137).

THE ORDNANCE DEPOT

Additionally, the French Revolutionary wars were the imperative for the Government erecting a colossal ordnance depot on the southern edge of the town, on Normanton Road, in 1803–05, to the designs of James Wyatt, consisting of a pedimented rectangle, 9 by 3 bays (75ft x 25ft) with stylistic overtones of Inigo Jones's St Paul's Covent Garden, set within a massive curved curtain wall punctuated by modest pavilions. It held 15,000 small arms on the ground floor, with lesser equipment stored above. There were also two magazines and accommodation for civil personnel with a detachment of the Royal Artillery. Oddly, as early as 1820 this building had become redundant and a new ordnance depot was erected in the newly laid out Cherry Street adjoining Lodge Lane, building contracts being invited in July 1820. It did not last long either, being itself declared redundant and sold off by auction in December 1832.

The previous building was sold off, had its curtain wall removed and was raised several storeys to make a huge silk mill, initially under the proprietorship of Messrs Ambrose Moore & Company of London (although Moore, related to the Strutts, was in origin from Twyford). Later still it became the warehouse of the Star Tea Company, and from 1884 it was used, much altered, as the brewery of Messrs Offiler, before being closed by Bass Charrington in 1965 and demolished.

DECLINE, POVERTY AND WELFARE

The rioting mobs were composed less of unemployed layabouts (who, even under the Reform Act, still had little chance of the vote) in the 18th century but rather small tradesman and artisans – several Pentrich revolutionists were framework knitters, for instance – and this group were being especially hard hit by up-to-date machinery and the increase in factory methods.

Stocking making was flourishing in Derby as early as 1712, if Woolley is to be believed, but the task was revolutionised in 1758 by the invention of Strutt's Derby rib machine. Independent framework knitters flourished thenceforth, in specially fenestrated upper rooms, especially in houses behind Queen Street, Cheapside, Burton Road – there are grade II listed surviving examples from 1800 behind the Bell & Castle here – and in Bold Lane, but they were in decline, many in serious financial straits by the 1820s and a good few were ideal material for demagogy and mob oratory, although in the event the trade lasted until the retirement of the last from Longden's mill, Agard Street, in 1967.

Another declining trade was that of wool combing (William Hutton's father was one), killed off by new machinery and the rise of the silk industry. There were,

Longden's narrow tapes mill founded on Nuns' Green (Agard Street) in 1804. Longden's were the employers of Derby's last framework knitter. The mill was replaced by a university hall of residence 1996. (*Derby Evening Telegraph*)

however, sufficient of them to play a leading role in the borough festivities for the Peace of Aix-la-Chapelle in 1749, yet by 1831 only one was left in business.

This was indeed an age in which poverty began to increase, along with the town's population. Whereas the boxes made in 1608 to hang about the girdles of the very few poor men of the town 'to beg withal' marked the approximate point in time when such people became the responsibility of each parish (officers of which were obliged to levy a rate to provide them relief) the construction of parish workhouses was not even considered necessary until the 1720s.

The evidence for more than a handful of paupers in the latter part of the previous century is very slight. The mason/architect William Trimmer built workhouses for All Saints' parish in Walker Lane in 1729 and a year later at the corner of Bridge Street and Nuns' Green (Friar Gate) for that of St Werburgh, latterly rebuilt in 1836 as an elegant house, which stand as monuments to change. Only St Alkmund's may have been built at an earlier period; in 1832 it was 'an ancient building… much out of repair,' although it housed 50. That at St Michael's may have been early as well, having to be enlarged and rebuilt by another local mason/architect, John Finney, in 1792. That of St Peter's was in the churchyard there and was later. Yet even in 1832 there were but 198 people housed between all of them.

For those in work, there were various vehicles for the relief of hardship and restrictive practices in the 18th century. In 1771 the 'hosiers of this town' met at the George 'To consider the petition of the framework knitters; it met with a favourable reception.' And in 1778 we hear of a 'meeting of the Society of Weavers in order to make a regulation of the said trade at the White Hart.' By this time the Men's Sick Club, one of the very first local friendly societies – wherein subscriptions were pooled to pay widows' relief and doctor's fees – had been founded 13 years, being preceded only by the Union Friendly Society, set up in 1764 by the Unitarian convert, poet and staymaker Samuel Pratt (1733–1808), whose father, William, also a staymaker, doubled as landlord of the Cross Keys in the Market Place. They were joined in 1777 by the Independent Friendly Society.

By 1816 there were 12 more, eight of them attached to pubs. There was a Female Friendly Society and two more for various groups of workers, the smiths (of 64 members) and iron-moulders. Further up the social scale, the Freemasons, founded locally after an earlier lodge failed to last by Dr John Hollis Pigot in 1784 (there were five Derby Lodges by 1895), then met at the Tiger, Cornmarket.

In 1815 a Ladies' Charity was set up for the relief of poor married women in child-bed at home, this being the forerunner of the Women's Hospital founded at the end of the 19th century in Bridge Street by ladies of the Mundy and Newton families. This excellent institution transferred to Friar Gate (Wilmot's town house) in 1926, was closed 60 years later and was largely demolished in 1988 to make way for a fearsomely lacklustre office block called St James's Court.

Dispensaries & Hospitals

Medical relief, for the less well-off especially, was sadly lacking in 18th-century Derby, a fact which the irrepressible Dr Erasmus Darwin was quick to spot. Shortly after arriving in the town, he founded a clinic and dispensary, financed through a philanthropical society formed for that end, membership being a guinea per annum. It was chiefly aimed at eradicating and treating smallpox. Darwin and a coterie of other willing doctors gave their advice free, while the local apothecaries got the benefit of making up the free prescriptions in strict rotation. Darwin hoped it 'may prove to be the foundation for a future infirmary'. In fact this dispensary, after a hiccup, continued into the 19th century, but was refounded in a house in Bridge Gate in August 1830, with 200 subscribers, which brought in £214 1s 0d (£214.05) in the first year, benefitting 2,212 people in the same period. Darwin himself took on ever less work in the 1790s.

The establishment of an infirmary was a logical development but no new idea. A meeting – significantly attended by Whitehurst who was to devise a heating and ventilation system for St Thomas' in London in 1776–78 – was called at the King's Head as early as 1771 to discuss the idea, but little happened as a result. Darwin constantly pushed for it, and had he been younger on coming to the town might have taken on the task of initiation himself.

Yet it was left to his philosophical and ideological protégé William Strutt to undertake the project.

This began in 1806, encouraged by a bequest from Isaac Hawkins, a Burton attorney whose daughter had unexpectedly married Sir Henry Harpur of Calke, and a powerful group of the local *elite*, led by the Duke of Devonshire, Revd Thomas Gisborne and F.N.C. Mundy. By 1809 £31,238 19s 0d had been collected. The cost of acquiring land from the borough and from the break-up of the borough family's Castlefield's estate in 1803 was £200 per acre; the cost for completing the project was £17,870 3s 4d. The promoters launched an architectural competition but none of the entries satisfied Strutt, who instead substituted a design of his own, as realised by Samuel Brown and with Whitehurst-type domestic contrivances for plumbing, heating and ventilation designed and installed by his friend Charles Sylvester, who wrote the whole project up in a book called *Domestic Economy* (1819).

The building was opened on its London Road site on 4 June 1810. The ashlared stone structure was of two storeys over a high basement, all under a hipped, wide-

Charles Sylvester, engineer of the Derbyshire General Infirmary; bust by Sir Francis Chantrey, c.1808, now in Derby Museum. (M. Craven)

Derbyshire General Infirmary, London Road, photographed by Richard Keene, before rebuilding in 1867. (Derby Museum)

eaved roof and a heavy cornice typical of Brown. The east and west fronts were of 11 bays, those to the north and south were each of nine and a separate building housed accommodation for infectious diseases. The whole was built of a 'beautiful hard and durable whitish stone'. The central entrance on the east front broke forward, with a tetrastyle Tuscan portico and tripartite window above. The whole building was heated by underfloor and wall ducts and ventilated by similar ingenious devices, the entire arrangement being strikingly reminiscent of that evolved by the quietly ingenious Whitehurst for St Thomas'. The whole was graced by a central dome surmounted by a terracotta statue of Aesculapius by William John Coffee.

Following on the heels of the infirmary came a private asylum on Green Lane, especially adapted from a house built for Archer Ward c.1800. Ward's son-in-law, Thomas Swinburne, had decided he wanted to live even higher up, and replaced it with Mill Hill House, built by Richard Leaper as a miniature version of Belsay in Northumberland on the prompting of Sir William Gell in 1814. The Asylum took a few subsidised patients from the poorer elements of society, but was superseded in 1849 by the County Asylum at Mickleover, which also accommodated some Derby patients. Thus, in 1850 it was divided as two villas, one occupied by William Stevenson, a retired Nottingham clockmaker. His son-in-law, George Wilkins of Gospel Hall fame, sold it in 1881, and it was demolished in 1913 to make way for the Hippodrome theatre, designed by Marshall & Tweedy.

DERBY SEEN BY OTHERS

Derby at the end of the 18th century was a delightful town in appearance and had yet to be spoiled by the little industry which had so far sprung up.

'Derby', wrote an anonymous gentleman of London in 1757, 'is large and has divers buildings especially about the Market Place, which is spacious and, it being market day, St James's fair, likewise the town appeared populous and lively'. It was commended more generally by Boswell, Celia Feinnes and even (grudgingly) by Lord Torrington. One of its earlier historians – and a most travelled man – William Woolley, said of it early in the 18th century:

'Derby... is at present a very large, populous and rich and well-frequented borough town – few inland towns in the Kingdom equalling it – yet has it a many very good houses, especially on all parts... of the town, mostly of brick... In it is many persons of good quality and a great number of coaches kept in it. It has a very handsome Market Place – a square with good buildings about it...'

The pleasantness of the environment was echoed by William Mavor, who chose also to allude to the diversions available:

'Derby, an elegant and pleasant town... in [it] are several churches and meeting-houses; and, considering its size, no small number of places of amusement.'

Likewise on the intellectual or cultural front, Sir Richard Phillips, at the beginning of the 19th century, was moved to comment on such things before remarking on the pleasantness of the environment: '...while no one can think about Derby without associating the names of Darwin in poetry and philosophy; of Wright, in painting; and of the Strutts, as patrons of all the useful and elegant arts. I entered Derby, therefore, with agreeable associations, and they have since been realised... I had never seen better shops in a county town – the streets were delightfully Macadamised – and great cleanliness indicated a good police...'

Until the coming of heavy industry so changed things, this kind of praise was lavished regularly upon Derby by outsiders. Only Pastor Moritz was unimpressed, but instead was struck by the politeness of all the inhabitants and the friendliness of his welcome. In this, at least, Derby has changed little. Even today one can see the substantial vestiges of the large numbers of high-quality, mainly brick, buildings. It still stands head and shoulders architecturally over similar towns, not only in the East Midlands, but even further afield.

IMPROVING THE BOROUGH

The civic amenities enjoyed at this period grew steadily throughout the century. In 1735 Margaret Chambers of Exeter House, widow of that Thomas who had been an enormously rich copper merchant, died, leaving a sum of money 'for the support and maintenance of 80 lamps or lights for the use of the borough.' This led to a pair of

Somewhat affected by the Reform Riot was John Gilbert Crompton,
FP, DL, banker, of Crompton & Evans Bank.

marble flambeaux to be added to Roubiliac's monument
to the family in All Saints' to commemorate the fact. In
1738 this amenity was 'franchised out' to Benjamin
Granger, who also took over the waterworks that year.
He and his successors were accountable to trustees for
the efficiency and viability of the service. A meeting of
the trustees for this purpose was recorded at the King's
Head in November 1774. As will emerge, the facility was
expanded two decades later – but at a price.

THE FIRE BRIGADE

In the 18th century insurance companies ran rudimentary
fire services, coming out exclusively to incidents only at
buildings bearing the usual jolly lead or brass plaque
belonging to the company in question. In Derby, though,
there was little of this, the main service being parish based,
sponsored by the burgesses and founded in the 1730s,
although some parishes kept an engine before that date, as
All Saints'. As was then usual, the service was franchised
out. On the night of 20 March 1741, fire engines 'from all
parts of the town' came to fight a serious blaze at the
Virgin's Inn on the north side of the Market Place. Yet this
service was felt to need buttressing, and in 1762
subscriptions were invited from interested parties to fund
a better service. These assembled at the George on 15
November 1762, and the improvements were instituted

successfully, for the sponsors again met 12 years later to
review developments.

One of the great aids to assist these early Derby firemen
was the water in the brook, the line of which snaked
through the town, and from which inexhaustible supplies
of water could be drawn; neither was it so prone to freeze
as were courtyard pumps leading to wells. Individual
parishes kept these manually-pumped engines which
survived into the late 19th century in parts of the town
not served by the municipality's consolidated service from
1883, that of Litchurch, based by St Andrew's Church,
remaining independent until 1878.

Dealing with serious conflagrations was also helped
by calling out of units of the militia (or later, the
Volunteers), for crowd control, clearing breaks and other
duties. In 1836 the St Werburgh's parish engine travelled
as far as Nottingham to assist at a fire. The watchmen
used rattles to raise the alarm, but by the 19th century
the scale of buildings like mills, or the 1828 Guildhall
(destroyed in a disastrous fire on the night of Trafalgar
Day 1841), made these engines less effective and poor
maintenance was a constant bane. Only the introduction
of pressured water mains somewhat later in the century
made any real improvement possible, followed by the
first steam-pumped fire engine, called *Vesuvius,* in
March 1888.

At this earlier period, of course, the only force for law
and order was the town watch. They patrolled the streets
at night, with their rattles, but often felons, when
apprehended, would be rescued by their friends. Early in
the 19th century, however, the indefatigable William Strutt
took the matter in hand. He armed them with staves,
positioned 19 watchmen's clocks at strategic points
around the town and thus regulated their patrols. These
valuable and innovative timepieces were evolved by Strutt
from an idea suggested to him by Darwin and almost
certainly stemming from work by John Whitehurst. The
first were made for him by Whitehurst's nephew and
successor, John Whitehurst II, from 1802. Also taken up by
the mill and country house owners (the first examples
went to Lord Exeter at Burleigh and Josiah Wedgwood at
Etruria), these watchmen's clocks were much imitated,
and one survived at Evans' mill at Darley until 1932.

THE DERBY CANAL

The greatest benefit, at least to the town's burgeoning
industry and to the prices of goods in shops, which had to
be brought in from elsewhere, was the building of the
Derby Canal. The Derwent Navigation had by the 1770s
been rendered less viable by the opening of the local
section of the Trent and Mersey Canal in 1777. What was
needed was a spur from this canal to Derby, and a body of

Derby Canal. The Long Bridge, north side, photographed by the late Roy Hughes, from Derwent Row, 1959.

local gentlemen and manufacturers came together and sought an Act of Parliament, which passed the Royal Seal on 7 May 1793.

Work, under the Alfreton-born engineer Benjamin Outram, began immediately, and the canal was opened entire in 1796, not only from the Trent near Shardlow to Derby, but also from Derby to the Erewash and north via the Derwent to Darley Abbey to serve Thomas Evans's Boar's Head Cotton Mill.

Within the borough, the 5½ mile route approached from the south, rising 12ft through two locks via the edge of The Siddalls, over an iron aqueduct, probably made by the newly-established Butterley Company. It then rose through another lock, just short of the old arm of the Derwent Navigation by Cockpit Hill, where a transhipment basin was constructed, which from 1820 boasted a particularly handsome grade II listed brick warehouse, demolished in 1977. The site now lies beneath the hideous Cockpit Hill multi-storey car park of 2001.

Here, too, was the boat-building yard of Alexander Street, who also was an early owner of the White Bear Inn, Derwent Row, across the Derwent (1819), where a lock brought the canal from its flat river crossing to a new level *en route* for Borrowash. The river received two new weirs, one approximately at the same latitude as the south-east corner of the Market Place and another immediately

north of the point where the Derwent Navigation debouched, to form a pond to facilitate the crossing where the towpath was raised on a timber causeway called the Long Bridge (see page 143).

The Erewash cut gave constant access to wharves and a way across the river whence it ran by Ford Lane to a junction on the south side of Nottingham Road. Here the arm that took boats for Darley Mill ran back to the Derwent debouching above the Silk Mill weir. In the other direction the canal snaked across the water meadows to make a junction with the Erewash Canal some 8½ miles east. The Darley arm cut off all the land between the canal and the river, a lozenge-shaped area then already known universally as Canary Island – whether through any arcane connection with the Derby Ale of the 17th century or not is hard to tell. This led to the town house gardens thereon, like the one Darwin had owned, being sold for the development of streets, like Erasmus Street, Exeter Street and Place, all in 1817–20.

This Long Bridge suffered the indignity of being washed away in a flood in 1795 before even the canal was fully open and had to be hurriedly replaced. The flood 'cut a new channel where the dead waters were formed. This gave 17 acres extra in Spondon parish'.

Within 30 years there were four basins on the Morledge, with coal wharves – others being on the

Narrowboats on the canal, crossing the Derwent, in the 1860s, with the second Exeter Bridge behind. A Richard Keene photograph. (M. Craven)

The Little Eaton Gangway; the exchange wharf showing the dismountable wagons, c.1908. (Derby Museum)

Nottingham Road. From 1828 a market boat complete with armchairs and a fireplace was run from Swarkestone on the appropriate days. Heavy goods to London by canal cost 50s (£2.50) or 70s (£3.50) per ton, the increase of cost over the sea route being fully justified by the increased reliability and vast decrease in time taken. Goods were transported on two types of boat: the lighter fly-boats, with a crew of four covering some 40 miles per day and carrying up to 10 tons, and the heavy 70-foot long barges, slower, covering 25 miles a day, with a crew of two and carrying an average of 20 tons. Big firms gradually eased out a majority of the smaller operators; Pickford and Company (still in the moving business and no relation to the architect) took over a wharf and warehouse on the canal at Derby in 1808. Needless to say, the canal company bought up the shares of the Derwent Navigation, swiftly closing the older concern down around 1835.

A further innovation relating to the canal was the plate-way serving the rising country to the north. From the Darley arm a further canal ran due north through the eastern part of Little Chester to Little Eaton. Here goods were trans-shipped onto wagons, which were horse-hauled up as far as Smithy Houses, Denby. The trucks ran on a flanged plate-way and carried equipment to the Drury-Lowe family mines and coal back down, not to mention, later, the salt-glazed stoneware products of the Denby Pottery. Built in 1795 and known as the Little Eaton Gangway, it was Outram's first plate-way. Tenders to make replacement rails were being advertised for it in July 1809. It operated continuously until the beginning of the 20th century, closing in 1908. The stone blocks which supported the rails are still *in situ* here and there, although most of its course has been obliterated by road widening.

NEW INDUSTRIES

By this time, several new Derby industries had begun, although by no means all rivalled Duesbury or Evans' enterprises in opulence. One unlikely one was Barber's carpet mill, employing 20 or so men and founded in 1777. Another centred around Robert Bage, the Derby novelist, who was a friend of Erasmus Darwin's and owed his fortune as a paper manufacturer at Darley Abbey and in Staffordshire to his father. His grandfather had purchased the mill there in 1713, which rather implies that the industry on that site at least was already established by that date. Indeed there were, apparently, three paper mills on the Ecclesbourne at Duffield by 1700 and the Peckwash Mill's proprietor, Thomas Tempest, in 1805 is said to have renewed a charter going back to 1425.

By the 1780s William Evans had the Darley mill, the Bages having sold out. The novelist's nephew, Charles, of Shrewsbury, an engineer and architect, erected a fireproof flax mill at Abbey Foregate, Shrewsbury, in 1796–97, employing brick and iron framing and eliminating combustible materials. Just as Robert Bage had been a friend of Darwin's, so William Strutt had become a friend – almost a protégé – of the doctor's once he had moved to Derby, not forgetting also that Bage was a nephew of Robert Bakewell, the gatesmith. To complete the circle, Strutt was also friendly with Charles Bage of Shrewsbury and it was from the former that the latter derived the technology of the fireproof mill for, inevitably, Strutt had already built one.

Strutt's father, the pioneering Jedediah – born of a well-to-do yeoman family of Newton-by-Blackwell – had, as we have seen, improved William Lee's 1589

Jedediah Strutt, engraving after Joseph Wright's painting. (M. Craven)

stocking-knitting frame to produce the 'Derby Rib' stocking frame in 1758. This coincided with the movement of the hosiery manufacturing industry to the Midlands from London, where prices of labour were high and the restrictive practices operated by the guilds of the capital were a bar to efficiency. In this context the hosiers bought the stocking frames and rented them to out-workers who worked from home, adapting or adding rooms with much horizontal fenestration to enable family members to join in and boost production and thus income.

By 1760, Strutt had set up in St Mary's Gate in Derby as a silk hosier, served in just this way by out-workers. In 1785 he had also set up a silk mill, south of the brook between St Peter's Bridge and Morledge – in other words, close to the site of his and his son's future fireproof mill – in order to prepare the raw silk he purchased in London. Soon afterwards he built another one around the corner in the Morledge itself. Further, he was in partnership with Samuel Need of Nottingham and Richard Arkwright, to whom Need had introduced Strutt earlier. Need died in 1781, whereupon the partnership fell apart and the two giants of the early Industrial Revolution went their own separate successful and, to a degree, complementary ways.

It was to increase the production of calicoes (begun in Derby in 1774, the year in which the excise duty on them was lifted) that William Strutt built the Derby fireproof mill. This immensely tall building was erected on Strutt-owned land, straddling the brook where Albert Street is now. It was not his first such structure – that had been erected at Belper in 1778 – but it was the first to be deliberately designed to be proof against combustion. Accidents with the myriad candles which illuminated such mills at night (and depicted with such relish by Joseph Wright in his night views of Arkwright's mills at Cromford) were commonplace. Evans's brand new cotton mill at Darley Abbey burnt down in December 1788, an event which must have made a deep impression on the under-insured Strutts.

In the new mill Baltic fir beams were encased in stucco, ceilings were vaulted in brick and honeycombed with earthenware pots, made at Smalley Common Pottery, to limit the spread of fire and lighten the structure. Such was the Derby mill of 1793, but Bage's mill at Shrewsbury went one better in replacing the encased beams of oak with iron: truly fireproof. Strutt's mill was, we know, 115 x 30ft and six storeys high. It was sold in 1815, when calico weaving ceased there and, ironically, was damaged by fire in 1852 and again, fatally, in 1876, after which it was sold in the February following to the Corporation for £4,750, being demolished to widen Albert Street and expand the Market Hall. Nevertheless, what with the fireproof mill and his

constant flow of innovations in the heating, ventilation and the general improvements in the places of work he provided, William Strutt's ingenuity appears to bear the dead hand of Whitehurst's restless genius, just as did his later achievements at the Derbyshire General Infirmary.

It is easy to see Whitehurst's posthumous genius inspiring Strutt, and it was transmitted via the open-handed, innovative generosity of Erasmus Darwin – the fruits of whose irrepressible genius he ever allowed others to claim. Darwin's lengthy correspondence with Benjamin Franklin – a visitor and correspondent of Whitehurst's too – had continued from about 1754, almost until his death. He was also in communication by 1792 with Wright's friend, William Hayley, a Sussex poet with a possible Derby ancestry, and prominent scientists, such as William Herschell, who is known to have called on him at Derby (in July 1792) and to whom Darwin stood in approximately the same relationship as, say, Patrick Moore might to the present Astronomer Royal.

There is a continuous line of scientific achievement directly associated with Derby stretching from John Flamsteed, the first Astronomer Royal, through Sorocold, Whitehurst and Darwin to Strutt, and this in its turn did as much to generate an industrial and entre-preneurial ambience in the town as the borough's geographical position, the presence of abundant water power or the access to raw materials. Further, Whitehurst's interest in geology did much to help his Lunar friend, Wedgwood's, appreciation of its possibilities, not to mention the interest evinced by Matthew Boulton, another founding father of that circle, and the aid it gave to those, like his friend Anthony Tissington FRS, a mining magnate on an epic scale, in locating minerals by using Whitehurst's codification of the geological strata.

Even while Darwin lived at Lichfield, the interplay of creativity between Franklin, Boulton, Bage, Whitehurst, Watt and Wedgwood was startling. The thread through Darwin and Richard Lovell Edgeworth to William Strutt laid a firm springboard for Derby developments in the 19th century, not to mention those across the Atlantic through Kirk Boott of Lowell and others whom we shall meet. Even James Brindley, the Derbyshire-born canal engineer, was drawn in, working on the Wedgwood-supported Grand Trunk until his early death.

Spar Manufacturing

Boulton, moreover, had branched out into the manufacture of *objets de virtu* including ormolu-mounted Blue John, that most elusive and attractive of fluorspars, obtainable exclusively from mines in the Castleton area. Darwin and Whitehurst were taken by the Swanwick-based Anthony Tissington and his brother to Castleton in 1767. It was just at the time that we find Boulton writing to Whitehurst urging him to find out if an interest could be obtained in such a mine, for the industrialist was at that time being asked to pay exorbitantly for his scarce raw material. He pleaded with his friend for secrecy, and it is reasonable to enquire why, in the Derby context, such secrecy should have been necessary.

The answer lies in the presence in the town of the Brown family. This prolific dynasty emerged in the post-Restoration period as masons, brickmakers and stonecutters. The senior line of the family transferred from St Peter's parish to the more fashionable All Saints' in the last decade of the 17th century, where Richard, son of Richard Brown, mason, was born in February 1700. Shortly after his second marriage in 1734, the following advertisement appeared in the *Derby Mercury*: 'Richard Brown, clerk of All Saints', performs monuments, gravestones and chimney pieces on reasonable terms' suggesting a transition from ordinary to ornamental masonry by this date. The further implication is that ornamental stones were in use, especially Ashford Black marble – perhaps obtained from Henry Watson of Bakewell, son of the Heanor sculptor Samuel and a leading supplier – and several such monuments in All Saints' bear the signature 'Brown Derby'. Being parish clerk, of course, was an astute move, placing him well to recommend his own services to relatives of recently-deceased municipal oligarchs and minor gentry.

Richard Brown, who had become a Freeman of the borough in 1737, died in 1756, being succeeded by his son, another Richard (1736–1816). He was a Freeman by 1761 and described himself in 1778 as a 'petrifactionist of Ashford-in-the-Water and Derby'. At this time he was running a spar works just around the corner from Darwin, in part of Lombe's Silk Mill. From thence, in 1802, he moved to Old St Helen's, vacated by Joseph Wright in 1793 and demolished in February 1800, the last substantial fragment of Derby's monastic heritage. Behind this proximity lies Boulton's plea to Whitehurst for secrecy concerning the Blue John mines. And, although Boulton achieved the greater fame, Brown became rich and successful, producing ormolu-mounted wares as good as any of Boulton's, and not giving up when the market went into decline in the 1770s. He and the younger William Duesbury linked up to show their wares in the capital jointly, although Brown later opened a showroom at 5 Tavistock Square. Brown was also aided by his partner and brother-in-law, the geologist John Mawe (1766–1829), whose daughter married the grandson of Anthony Tissington.

The new works at St Helen's along with Brown's house are still extant – although under extreme peril at the time of writing from a projected new road –

King Street marble works, Brown's house and Edwin Haslam's workshop, photographed in 1990. (M. Craven)

probably the only surviving purpose-built marble works in Northern Europe, albeit they underwent several changes between then and 1888 when the firm moved further down the street. When opened, Brown had installed a Boulton and Watt type double acting 6hp steam engine, built under licence at his Little Chester works by James Fox, a former footman of Thomas Gisborne's at St Helens' House, set up by his former employer there in 1783. Fox's was the first foundry in England to specialise in machine tools. This steam engine drove Brown's patent stone sawing machine and

Large Blue John Urn with Wedgewood plaque afer Wright's 'Maria and her dog Silrio' by Richard Brown, c.1780. (Christies)

Judges' Lodgings, Ashford black marble fireplace by Richard Brown; engraved plaque by Henry Moore, 1810. (M. Craven)

a variety of lathes, thus partly mechanising what was also an extremely refined art.

At the time of his death in 1816 the Derby end of the business passed to Joseph Hall (1789–1848), described in All Saints' parish register on his marriage to Ann Pitman, Brown's granddaughter, in 1816, as 'of London, mineralist'. He was one of the Castleton dynasty of Hall, who had considerable interests in Blue John extraction;

Richard Brown (1736-1816) Spar manufacturer of Derby, anonymous portrait of c.1800. (Mrs Ann Ibbs)

his mother, Hannah Brown, was a cousin of Brown's, his grandfather one of the carvers at Kedleston.

Like Brown, Hall was described as a spar manufacturer, lapidiary and petrifactioner. By 1816 there were also showrooms at Matlock, Buxton and Castleton with a 'museum' (showroom) at Derby. Although Blue John was the most expensive and exotic material, Brown and Hall also worked in alabaster from the Trent valley, Ashford Black Marble, a variety of polished Derbyshire limestones, like Grey from Ricklow Dale, light grey Hopton Wood and Duke's Red from near Hassop, and also in imported 'true' marbles. And whereas in the 1780s only Brown and Elias Hall were plying this trade in Derby, by 1831 there were a dozen 'petrifactioners', although some were merely back-parlour men producing a vastly inferior product.

Hall's wealth was sufficient for him to have erected 'swimming and other baths' attached to the works as a way of using waste warm water from his process. These were open to the public and probably lasted until the first public baths were opened in 1852. Hall's uncle by marriage was the eminent geologist John Mawe, a Derby man who had married another daughter of Richard Brown.

A by-product of the getting of alabaster for carving was the production of gypsum for flooring and render, the latter being brought to perfection as a weatherproof and inexpensive covering for houses of this Regency period in lieu of ashlared stone and made on the Morlege by John and Joseph Brookhouse as Brookhouse's Roman cement.

Lead processing

Brookhouse's plaster works was not the first industry to be established on the banks of the Derwent east of The Morledge. Some eight years before, in 1781, William Cox of Brailsford established a lead works there, seizing the opportunity to process some, at least, of the lead pigs exported in profusion from the White Peak through Derby via the Derwent Navigation.

Pipes and sheet lead were the chief products. Amazing is that, despite the noise pollution, the view of this area from the river as depicted by H.L. Pratt in the late 1840s is still relatively arboreal and pleasant. In 1809 the skyline was obstructed by the erection of a 149ft-high shot-tower with a crenellated top; this became a sufficiently celebrated Derby landmark to merit adverse criticism when it was finally demolished in order to clear the site for the building of the Council House in 1931. Nevertheless, the presence of these two works, combined with the rolling and slitting mills adjacent, underscores the necessity for the canal and its wharves hereabouts.

Morledge from the cattle market looking north west. Some of the row of five late 18th-century cottages are already boarded up prior to the area being cleared. Note the shot tower and Brookhouse's former plaster works (right), later a paint works and latterly a builders' merchants. (photograph by C.B. Keene, October 1931). (Derby Museum)

A second lead mill was built in 1792 on the Normanton Road near the corner of Mill Hill Lane. This was the works of Joshua Walker from Sheffield, which was in 1840 absorbed by the aggressive Cox family (the lead works proprietorship passed to a branch of the family settled at Spondon Hall) and survived until 1965 when the site was largely cleared and converted into a motor car emporium; it is now the site of a small shopping centre centred on a Lidl store. The works sported a windmill to grind the ore and the produce was white lead paint.

A third lead works, Depot Mill, was established further down Normanton Road, roughly where Cummings Street and Chestnut Avenue are now situated. It was started by prosperous farmers John and William Goodale of Normanton House between 1805 and 1818, but closed around 1850 and was being dismantled in 1855. The site was bought by National School headmaster Henry Cummings of adjacent Chestnut House, whose lawyer son developed it with streets 30 years later; the gardens thereabouts must be among the most polluted in England! This works windmill survived forlorn and alone until c.1880.

Another lead manufacturer was Charles Holbrook, of an old Repton family who ran the Derby Lead Works behind 49 St Peter's Street (roughly where the lower entrance to the Eagle Centre now is) and built himself a beautifully proportioned villa at Nunsfield in Alvaston in 1833. The younger William Duesbury also dabbled in lead by-products, chiefly for his china products' glazes.

MACHINE TOOLS

Joseph Wright's friend, the anti-slavery campaigner Thomas Gisborne of St Helen's House – son of the John for whom Pickford had built it – had a 'most ingenious and inventive' footman. With encouragement and help from Gisborne, James Fox – for such was his name – was set up in business on land that was part of the St Helen's House estate on City Road in Little Chester on the Derwent's bank in 1783.

Here, later in partnership with his son John, he made lathes, planing and gear-cutting machines, machinery for lace and hosiery manufacture and –

significantly perhaps – steam engines, under licence from Boulton & Watt, like that supplied, with numerous lathes and saws, to Richard Brown in 1802. Possibly Darwin's Lunar friend, James Watt, was also involved in the inception of this business. Fox also supplied the 2hp steam engine William Strutt installed in St Helen's House, too. These engines were obviously durable, since an advertisement in the *Derby Mercury* of 18 March 1810 announced:

'A steam engine of two horsepower to be sold by auction by Mr W. Smith at the Fox and Owl Inn, Bridge Gate, Derby, on Wednesday evening, 24 March, betwixt the hours of six and eight o'clock. The above named steam engine is in complete working condition and complete in every part, and may be seen at work on the day of sale by applying to Mr John Fox, engineer, Derby.'

Gisborne's presence as Fox's *eminence grise* returns us neatly to the Derby intellectual and radical elite who, by patronage, ideas and inspiration, seem to have been the sole powerhouse during the industrialisation of Derby and beyond. Fox's firm was supplying complex steam-driven lathes to Russia by 1806, later developing its Europe-wide client base; later it equipped railway works and lasted until 1870, when it was taken over by Sir Alfred Seale Haslam's Union Foundry, established alongside in 1868. Fox probably founded the first specialist precision tool-making factory in England.

The Growth of Non-conformism

Erasmus Darwin was positively evangelical in his agnosticism as became a thorough-going radical and man of science of that age, although he was obliged to keep a very low profile from 1791 after reaction to the excesses of the French Revolution provoked the destructive 'Church and King' riots which, although they seem to have passed Derby by, resulted in Priesley's house in Birmingham being fired, leading to his departure for America.

The Strutts, on the other hand, were convinced Unitarians, building a handsome stone Chapel in Belper and in 1779 acquiring control of the former Presbyterian one in Friar Gate, both of which are full of their monuments. Their first minister was James Simpson, who had been appointed the year before as assistant to the last Presbyterian minister, Mr White, and on his death seems to have engineered a take-over perhaps at the instigation of Jedediah Strutt. However, continued good relations – both social and financial – between the Strutts and the Presbyterian Cromptons (who lived next door to the chapel at The Friary at that time) suggests that the transition was done by prior agreement. Possibly

Simpson, if not a Unitarian fifth columnist, changed his allegiance to keep his job.

Darwin, on the other hand, is said by Coleridge (then also Unitarian) to have told him rather appositely that the sect was 'a featherbed to catch a falling Christian'. Later the Strutts inclined to the established church as they climbed towards their peerage. Yet their religious convictions had the beneficial effect of inclining them strongly towards the welfare of their workforce, reinforced by the obvious social and economic advantages of well cared for workers.

Nevertheless, while many philosophers inclined to agnosticism, many industrialists and their employees were turning, like the Strutts, to non-conformism. This was partly the result of the local ascendancy of the Cavendish-sponsored Whigs in borough affairs (bucking the national trend) and partly due to an increasing influx of families into the town, drawn in on the coat tails of industry.

The attempt in 1736 to obtain the repeal of the Test and Corporation Acts, passed in the wake of the Restoration, was symptomatic of the tendency to shield dissenters from the persecution still half-heartedly meted out to Roman Catholics. That attempt failed and technically all dissenters continued to be prevented from

King Street Methodist Chapel interior, c.1890, photographed by Richard Keene. Note the Spanish Mahogany pulpit and John Gray's fine organ. It was designed by James Simpson in 1844, and demolished in 1967. (Derby Museum)

The Friends' Meeting House, built in 1808 but by the end of 2007 to be enclosed by roads on three sides. (M. Craven)

holding municipal and other office. This tended to concentrate the energies of nonconforming families into commerce and hence one of the ingredients of their success.

The Methodists are said to have built their first chapel in St Michael's Lane, hard by a fellmonger's yard, in the same year as the failure to repeal the Test and Corporation Acts – 1736. John Wesley preached there on 20 March 1765 (which is in fact probably the true date of its opening, as his *Journal* attests), having failed to obtain a hearing in the Market Place a year previously, courtesy of the Derby mob. The stench of the fellmonger's yard and the internecine factionalism that followed, however, caused the abandonment of this chapel in favour of a new one in King Street in 1805, extensively and grandly rebuilt in a dignified Greek revival style by James Simpson of Leeds in 1841. The original chapel subsequently became a malthouse, and was much rebuilt, being demolished on 17 January 1973 after ending its useful life as an organ building works and then a lingerie factory.

An easier time by far was had by the Quaker evangelist Mrs Drummond in July 1739 who was chaired to the County Hall (perhaps inappropriately from the King's Head Inn) and preached to large congregations morning and evening. Another Quaker meeting was held in the Guildhall in 1774, also successful and, after

relying on meetings in private houses for many years, they too built a pretty little meeting house on St Helen's Street in 1804–08. It is said to incorporate some masonry of considerable antiquity from the old Hospital of St Helen. It would seem, nevertheless, that they must have enjoyed a discreet continuity in the town since the arraignment of George Fox before Gervase Bennet a century and a half before; a Mr Saywell's House was certainly used for meetings in 1740.

Other denominations begin to show in the last years of the 18th century in Derby. The Independents (Congregationalists) began in 1778, being established at a barn in Cross Lane (later Macklin Street) c.1781, later building a stylish brick chapel in Brookside shortly afterwards in 1782–83, in a plain neo-Palladian style, sponsored by the exceedingly wealthy Stenson-born merchant Thomas Wilson of Highbury, Middlesex (1732–1794), ancestor of World War Two commander Field Marshal 1st Lord Wilson of Libya and Stowlangtoft. He was uncle of Ambrose Moore, the silk throwster who adapted the Ordnance Depot on Normanton Road and great uncle of a Bishop of Calcutta – clearly not all the members of this distinguished local family were dissenters!

The Baptists began with an elegant chapel in Agard Street in 1794, which was paid for by Archer Ward of Green Hill House and may thus have been an early

St Mary's Gate House, the Osborne town house built to a design of James Gibbs c.1730 and converted into a Methodist Chapel for J.G.D. Pike by J. Fenton in 1841. It was demolished in 1938. Note the Robert Bakewell gates now outside the Cathedral.

design by his cousin, Richard Leaper, with a neat portico *in antis*. Unfortunately, the building of the Great Northern Railway line through Derby in 1876 led to its demise, leaving the congregation to share the Friends' Meeting House for a few years.

The first Baptist congregation in Derby is said to have first met in a house in Willow Row on 31 May 1789, but the movement subsequently split into three, each version erecting chapels: Agard Street being built for the Particular (Calvinistic) Baptists. The General Baptist congregation from Brook Street, hugely boosted by its charismatic second minister, Revd J.G.D. Pike, relocated in 1848 to specially adapted St Mary's Gate House, an important town house of 1730 built for the Osborne family to a design believed to have been by James Gibbs. Likewise, the Methodists spanned three factions: Primitive, New Connexion and Wesleyan, all building chapels. Later in the century, though, an *anschluss* was achieved, creating the United Methodists but leaving Derby with a superfluity of chapels.

The Roman Catholics in Derby managed to build a pretty Gothick chapel just off King Street behind the

Methodists' main chapel in King Street in 1813, the road to it later becoming Chapel Street. In 1839 this became an infants' school but had vanished by 1852. Interestingly, the baptismal records of this chapel go back to 1777 but there is no hint as to where the congregation met prior to 1813, unless the date of building has come down to us incorrectly.

As soon as the Catholic Emancipation Act of 1829 was passed, the Derby congregation – even at this early date much fortified by Irish migrants – began raising money, supplemented by a generous donation from the great Catholic patron John Talbot, 16th Earl of Shrewsbury, to build a new church. It was completed a decade later to the designs of A.W.N. Pugin, being extended in 1844 and embellished by, among others, the architect's son. The first incumbent was Revd John Synge, an aristocratic Irishman of a family originally from Staffordshire, ever a strongly Catholic county, remembered by the young Emily Mundy:

'Mr Sing *(sic)*, the Roman Catholic priest at Derby… a very pleasant man and not the least like a priest in any way… and quite refreshing to hear anyone talk of the

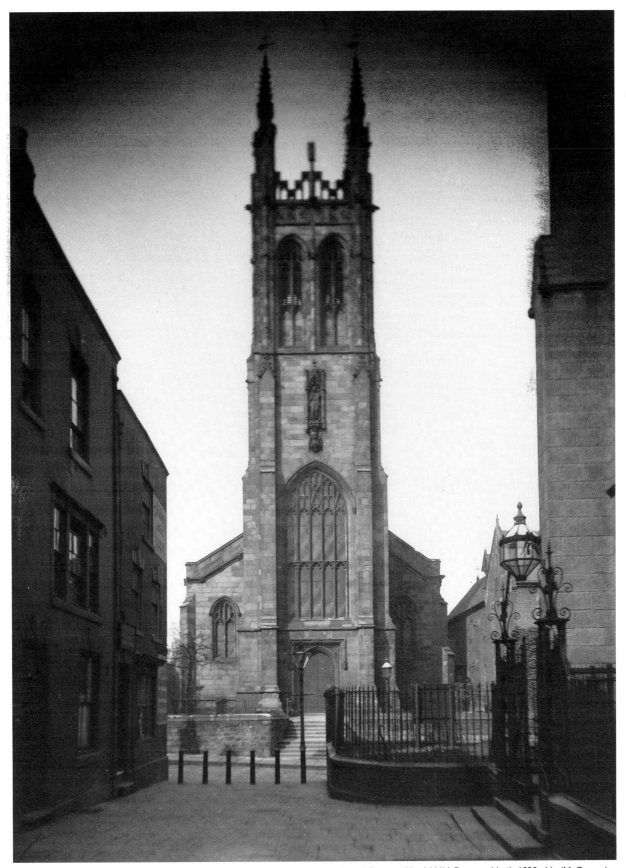

St Mary's Roman Catholic Church, Bridge Gate, seen from St Alkmund's Churchyard. Designed by A.W.N. Pugin and built 1839–44. (M. Craven)

Pope, Cardinals, St Ignatius Loyola, etc. etc., as if they were ordinary people.'

A convent of the Order of Mercy, partly funded by Mrs John Beaumont of Barrow Hall (born a Curzon), was built in 1848, although nowhere in the contemporary accounts is there any mention of the architect's name, that of Pugin only emerging later. The descriptions of it and the one engraving certainly point to the strong likelihood, and it is always known locally as 'Pugin's convent', yet proof positive has yet to emerge. It moved to Mrs Beaumont's town house next to the church in 1863, after the building turned out to have been impossibly damp and it was subsequently demolished. The order remains in the same building today, a house built for the Gisbornes in 1731 and rebuilt by Pickford – whose Neo-classical entrance aedicule survives on Bridge Gate and the Doric screen within – and much extended by Mrs Beaumont in 1840; even part of the delightful garden survives, embellished by a set of huge shaped cast-iron planters made by the Britannia foundry in nearby Duke Street.

The Swedenborgians, later called the New [Jerusalem] Church, were founded in the 18th century by the mystic and radical Swedish aristocrat Count Emmanuel von Swedenborg. Both their original Derby chapels were architecturally ambitious. The first was a Classical stuccoed one on London Road, with a pedimented Ionic portico, founded in 1818 by the Madeley family, silk throwsters. A second group started in an interesting octagonal stone one on King Street, built for them by a draper called James Robinson only two years later. The London Road congregation also moved to the King Street chapel in 1836 and both moved in 1863 to a former Primitive Methodist establishment in Babington Lane.

It is with this market town, beginning to expand in a new, industrial direction, pulling against the former dominance of the gentry and spawning mills, non-conformist chapels and all manner of unexpected strains on the fabric and organisation of the old borough, that

Horwood Avenue, New Jerusalem (Swedenborgian), chapel by Alexander Macpherson 1930. (M. Craven)

George Fox (1624–1691), the founder of the Society of Friends. (M. Craven)

the 19th century dawned. Some of the old influences remained unchanged into the new era, side by side with new institutions and modes. Others quickly faded.

The real importance of the whole 18th and early 19th centuries in Derby, however, lay with the ingenuity and intellectual dynamism of the three polymathic eminences: Whitehurst, Darwin and William Strutt, the creativeness of Wright, Pickford, Burdett, Brown and others and the entrepreneurial flair of men no less creative like Fox, Duesbury and Jedediah Strutt.

Yet, underlying all, and perhaps the unconscious inspiration of them all in combining a majority of the attributes enumerated above, is the increasingly significant figure of Whitehurst, for exactly two centuries chiefly remembered by most of his fellow townsmen as a mere clockmaker. Furthermore his intellectual and practical roots went back further to Sorocold and John Flamsteed as part of a continuous stream. Inspired, perhaps, by Darwin and the Lunar Society, he can now be seen as a figure of unexpected significance, as the ultimate fount of Derby's transformation. That transformation was to gain terrific momentum throughout the 19th century and into the 20th.

Yet the endearing element in Derby's history lies, however, in that despite this accelerating industrialisation, it never lost its bucolic roots: it retained its markets, close touch with its verdant hinterland, its leavening of gentry and the occupations which depended on their patronage. Further, an innate civic conservatism enabled the built environment created by those elements to retain its charm, largely unsullied by industry, into the middle of the 20th century.

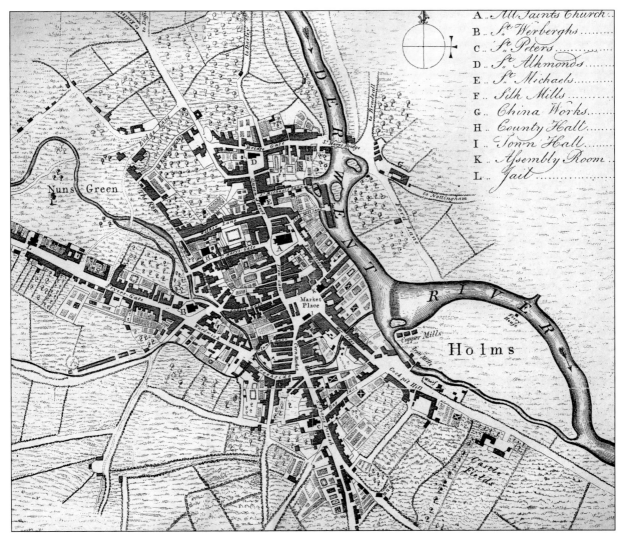

P.P. Burdett's map of Derby from 1767 (2nd edition of 1791), showing Derby just prior to the start of the third Improvement Commission.

X

TRANSFORMATION

The close of the Regency era saw the industrial base of Derby begin to change. Up to this time most of the important Derby industries were those that catered for the luxury end of the market: silk, clocks, porcelain, spar ornaments, wrought iron, carriages and *bijouterie*. Now, with the Victorian era about to begin, the preponderance was about to swing towards heavy industry and the manufacture of everyday objects: cast iron, railway components, stoves, grates, street furniture, refrigeration plants, and other specialised machinery. Yet throughout all this, some specialist luxury trades survived the immense changes, both industrial and demographic, to flourish into the 20th century and even beyond.

THE IMPROVEMENT COMMISSIONS

The year 1835 was of immense significance to Derby as well as to 177 other Boroughs in England and Wales, all affected by the changes in local government introduced by the Municipal Corporations Act of that year. The system of corporate control established in Derby by the charter of 1611 and honed by those of 1637 and 1682 has already been described and provided for a multi-tiered structure to the bottom level, from which newcomers were elected by those already in place. This led to a closed system in Derby, although some other Boroughs in England enjoyed a much more open one.

Strangely enough, however, the Commissioners sent round by Lord Grey's reforming Whig ministry in 1833 to enquire into the state of the boroughs – then in the midst of a severe cholera epidemic, which had begun in Sunderland two years before – found that on the whole the closed, oligarchal Boroughs were in general more efficient and far less corrupt than those which enjoyed a measure of what we might anachronistically term democracy. Mostly, however, the closed system gave semi-permanent control to cliques of Tory high Anglicans, resented by Whigs for their undemocratic nature and political kidney, by dissenters for their Anglicanism and religious antipathy and industrialists for their recidivism. Others, like Derby, on the other hand, were semi-permanently dominated by Whigs and subject to all the same criticisms, to which the dominant radicals did not, of course, object in the least!

Real power usually, as in Derby, lay in the hands of an *ad hoc* body of commissioners appointed as under the Nuns' Green Act of 1768; the qualification to participate in this first step towards modern local government being ownership of land to the value of £40 or possession of personal estate of £800 or over. A new set of commissioners took office, in tandem with the trustees of the Derby-Mansfield and Derby-Nottingham turnpikes – who had a vested interest in a new bridge, on 26 April 1788 when the power to raise a rate was granted in order to replace St Mary's Bridge and improve its approaches, which meant destroying quite a bit of property which had hitherto crowded close to the abutments of the old bridge. This was chaired by Jedediah Strutt's gifted son, William, and when a third such Act was sought in 1792 in order to exploit the resources of Nuns' Green, as we have seen, Strutt was again the instigator, and once the legislation was passed, again its chairman, the second Commission lapsing two years after the completion of the bridge in 1794.

The problem was that, unlike the two previous commissions, the 'mission statement' of the third aroused furious opposition. In order to keep the imposition of a rate at a low level, it was proposed to exploit Nuns' Green by sale and plough the money into improving infrastructure: new streets, paving old ones, lighting them – 172 new lamps were required on top of the 80 bequeathed to the borough by Mrs Chambers in 1738 – providing nameplates, drains and persuading householders to remove obstructions and fit downpipes. The Green, however, was effectively a public park, the site of the annual cheese fair, of the kennels of the town harriers, and the burgesses had the right to graze animals and collect furze there, not to mention extract clay for brickmaking, an enterprise

commemorated by Brick Street at the Green's west end, the pit adjacent, owned by the Roe family, being one in which the widow of the architect Joseph Pickford had a financial interest.

Much opposition was raised, mainly from the Tories. Some 40 different hand-bills, squibs, pamphlets, poems and songs not to mention anonymous letters, some of considerable erudition, are known to exist. There were also a number of petitions raised and the support gained of Derby's radical Tory MP Daniel Parker Coke (who later sat for Nottingham) and even its other MP, the up-county Edward Miller-Mundy of Shipley. Some of the songs and pamphlets were outrageously scurrilous, others libellous. The objectors, just as today, always knew they were onto a loser, as one poem clearly implies:

'Now Tyranny does put his Town in Fear,
Don't wonder why I drop this melting tear,
Tread on a worm, that Insect cannot bite,
But turns in Anguish to revenge its spite:
So let them know such Usage you'll not brook
While such a Man does live as PARKER COKE...'

Which, if nothing else, reminds us how the Cokes of Trusley pronounced their name! Most of the songs and poems go large on liberty:

'God prosper long fair DERBY Town
And may it still be free;
From Hellish Plots of Ev'ry kind
Against its Liberty.

A juncto [as *Junta*] formed of wicked Men
Though rich it's true they be,
They'd rob the poor of Common-right
That they may go shot-free.'

and so on. The bill gained Royal Assent on 15 June 1792, and the Commissioners met on 2 July, selected from people owning or occupying property worth more than £20 per annum. A rate was fixed at 1s 8d in the £1 for three years and 9d thereafter.

As the Commission was headed by Strutt, a radical reformist dissenter, it followed that the real power in the town – the Improvement Commission – was neither particularly Tory, nor Anglican, unlike the preponderance of the burgesses. Indeed, so successfully did this odd bilateral system work – relying, as it did, on self-appointed burgesses to come up through the system to the Aldermanic Bench and a semi-autonomous group of go-ahead commissioners – that the borough was in moderately enlightened hands by the first decades of the 19th century. Furthermore, as the Commission was able to levy a rate for which all the dwellings of the town had to be valued by their officers, it was not really in any way accountable, although this seems to have produced little resentment.

THE CREATION OF THE WEST END

The sale of Nuns' Green permitted under the 1792 Improvement Act, may have been envisaged by the burgesses as an opportunity to further beautify the town with residences akin in elegance to those built as a result of the 1768 Act. Strutt, Evans and Crompton undoubtedly knew better, however, as their opponents knew full well. Markeaton Brook was a valuable source of power and the plots released under their act nearly all went to manufacturers.

One of the first to acquire a plot was Francis Agard of Ockbrook (1760–1820). He already owned Cuckstool Mill, one of two ancient (probably *Domesday)* mills on the western reaches of the Markeaton Brook (the other was Nuns' Mill) and was a wealthy corn-merchant, ultimately descended from the Agards of Foston and Scropton, whom we have already met as relations of

William Shore in the 15th century. The Commissioners laid out a street from Ford Street to Bridge Street and named it after him in the 1790s along the north edge of the 1768 plots, the land between it and the brook being let for the erection of mills, like Messrs Longdon's (founded 1804) and houses like the exceptionally fine terrace of eight houses (designed to resemble four) nearby, to house the turnkeys of the County Gaol – regrettably cleared away in 1979 (see page 132).

At this early stage, however, only Brook Street (1799), Bridge Street (1793) and Green Street (May 1800) were pitched and Willow Row developed. Cole's Map (1806) shows that the heaviest development was confined to the area north east of Brook Street. Later, by the late 1830s, the area was very heavily built up, with mills and much very low-grade workers' housing infilled with courts containing dwellings of abysmal standard. Conditions were not of the best and the entire area became a byword for lawlessness, squalor and many of the least admirable side-effects of the Industrial Revolution. The irony is that Strutt, as chairman of this Commission, built excellent workers' housing, yet was rather taken off guard by the low standard of cottages built for their workers by many of his contemporaries.

Cole's map of Derby, 1806, showing the West End beginning to expand. (M. Craven)

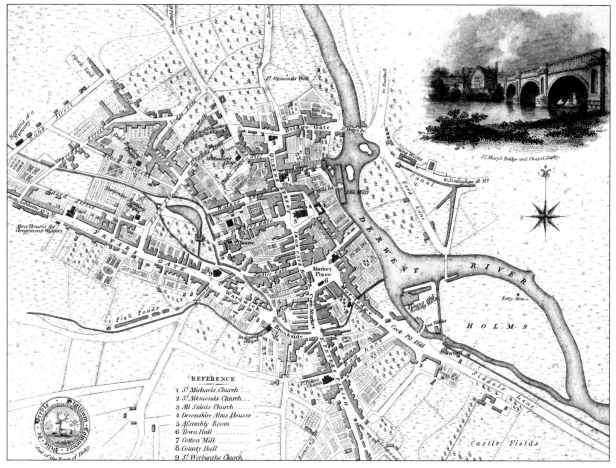

Derby's Commissioner's Church of St John the Baptist, Bridge Street, built in 1828 by Francis Goodwin. (M. Craven)

This area became the West End, which was progressively 'improved' and cleared between 1936 and 1977. Yet, despite its insalubriousness, it was an area which, in the 20th century at least, inspired a fierce loyalty among those who were born and bred there and has spawned at least three entertaining and informative booklets about life there in the period.

Of the promoters of the act, which led to the first real irruption of ugliness into the town, Strutt was doubtless thrilled by the progress of industry, while Crompton and Evans did very well financing the developments through their banking activities. All in all, the 1792 Act was a high price to pay for extending the scope of Mrs Chambers's lamps, Macadamising the streets, putting up nameplates or laying out new roads. On the positive side, on the other hand, there was the building in 1828 of the pretty Gothic Commissioners' Church of St John, Bridge Street – which provided for the cure of the souls of the teeming first-generation inhabitants of the West End – by Francis Goodwin in 1828, the contractor being Thomas Cooper.

In both cases Cooper and his brothers – Joseph the architect and William the plumber and glazier – did well, for they undoubtedly built the majority of the elegant villas on Vernon Street. Deeds in private hands also name the Coopers as the developers of South Street and their involvement in the pretty close opposite St John's,

across the brook, called St John's Terrace, from 1806 to 1832, is equally strongly suggested by the architecture of the finely-proportioned, stuccoed dwellings, somewhat superior to the run of houses thereabouts.

The church itself included much cast-iron (by Messrs Weatherhead, Glover & Company of Duke Street) and was intended as a miniature pastiche of the Chapel of King's College, Cambridge. Unfortunately the cupolas on pinnacles at the angles were found to be unsafe and were removed in 1903.

The Commissioners in 1820 set up the Gas, Light and Coke Company on land between the Markeaton Brook south of Bold Lane and George Street, off Friar Gate. By 1826 the site boasted two gasometers supplied by another Strutt protégé, William Wigston, who had a workshop in George Street and who also made some of Strutt's elegant epicyclic skeleton clocks.

In 1830–31 the Corporation spent £564 17s 2d on gas lighting their own buildings and the principal streets and, by July 1836, there were 210 gas lamps as against 110 oil lamps. Many industrial proprietors, however, did not consider the Gas Company's prices low enough and installed their own apparatus. This led to a swift reduction in tariffs on the part of the gas company – a glowing example of the beneficial effects of competition on a monopoly! The first recorded domestic customer

Joseph Strutt's former house, St Peter's House, 1 St Peter's Street, after its conversion in 1845 into George and George's shop. Note the original 'five lamps'. Albert Street is on the left. Photographed by Richard Keene from the Royal Hotel balcony, 1855. (M. Craven)

Derby's first gasworks, Bold Lane, in the early 1960s. (Don Farnsworth)

for gas – apart, inevitably, from William Strutt, who adapted St Helen's House for it in 1817 – was Archibald Douglas, father-in-law of Joseph Strutt, at his now-demolished town house in Osmaston Road. By 1840 the Gas Works were complete, lasting until the arrival of North Sea Gas in the 1960s, although supplemented from the 1860s by a much bigger works by the railway line at Etches's Park in the south of the borough.

In 1825 the borough managed to obtain a further act which set up the Fourth Improvement Commission (again chaired by Strutt, needless to say) which permitted the borrowing of £20,000 at a rate of 4% to extend the experimental gas-lighting, which had been inaugurated with a single lamp outside the old Guildhall on 19 February 1821 and to further improve, extend, name and pitch new streets. Compared to the role of the burgesses, which was mainly ceremonial and regulatory, the Commissioners – and the local Board of Health, brought into being, if only briefly, by an act of Parliament in response to the cholera epidemic – were the ones who exercised the real power, levied the rates and spent the ratepayers' money. A further, fifth, Commission was finally abolished in 1848 as a result of the Public Health Act of that year.

THE MAKE-UP OF THE CORPORATION

Most of the Derby Improvement Commissioners were, of course, members of the Corporation and, despite their relatively emancipated views, the borough remained under the control of a limited coterie. In the 100 years between 1735 and 1834 only 36 families had supplied mayors of Derby. Of these, 22 families had mayors who served more than once and 11 had more than one member elevated to the municipal chair. Multiple mayoralties were common: five men within the

period held office five times each: Robert Bakewell (not the ironsmith, but a cousin of the Dishley agronomist), Samuel and John Crompton, Revd Charles Stead Hope and the amateur architect and tanner Richard Leaper. Only 14 individuals in the century in question held only a single mayoralty.

The families of Crompton and Hope (dissenting Whigs and High Church Tories respectively) stand out as holding 11 mayoralties each in the period. After them came the Leapers – upwardly mobile bankers, tanners and squires – with eight and the brewing Lowes with seven. Some families, too, could trace their municipal office-holding in the direct male line back into the 17th century: the Bagnolds, Gisbornes, Franceys and the Hopes among them. The Smiths enjoyed the bailiffate as early as 1523 and the Newtons began as members for the borough as far back as 1471. They only severed their connection in 1908 when Charles Edmund Newton of Mickleover died in office as (honorary) borough treasurer. Most of these families enjoyed descents through the distaff from holders of mayoralties and bailiffates going back to the same era or even earlier.

The Gisbornes, originally from Hartington, but present in Derby from early in the 16th century, held their first mayoralty in 1659 and their last, long after becoming country gentlemen, in 1856. They, as so many other mayoral families, had a marriage link with the Allestrey family, the blood of which forms an unbroken thread through the life of the borough from their emergence from villeinage in *c*.1260 to the mayoralty of Alderman Alfred Moult in 1932, one of whose brothers, then the local coroner, had married a descendant. The Gisbornes also had in their veins the distinguished Norman blood of the Ashbourne Cokaynes, the Heathcotes and the Babingtons, and, as the 18th century gave way to the 19th, their connections ramified to include the Edwards, Bateman, Drewry, Evans, Bellairs and Bass families and, through the Poles of Radbourne, Erasmus Darwin and his circle. Through the Edwards they were also related to William Duesbury and through the Poles to the Binghams. This Whig family, the like-minded Cromptons and the Tory Hopes, bound together almost all of the office holders in Derby from 1735 to 1834. Those who appear to be ill-connected interlopers – Samuel Cooper (mayor [iii] 1744), Humphrey Booth (mayor [iii] 1752), Samuel Wilde (mayor [ii] 1766), Thomas Mather (mayor [ii] 1789), William Snowden (mayor [ii] 1803) and John Chatterton (mayor 1832) – probably would cease to be so were more research lavished on them, although Mather is known to have come from Wirksworth via Manchester with connections to iron founding in the county.

SOCIAL MOBILITY AND CONTINUITY

Yet, despite the almost incestuous connections of the oligarchs, they never lost touch with humbler folk. In a place the size of Derby only the grandest families could place hand on heart and aver that no members of their house toiled as an artisan or was on poor relief. Nevertheless, some of the lesser dynasties had poor relations a-plenty. Matthew Howe (1698–1763), who was mayor in 1748 and 1753, was landlord of the town's most prosperous inn, the George. That the hostelry was a major roosting place for the Whig faction – it had been patronised extensively by the Duke of Devonshire prior to the 'Forty-Five, for instance – is the reason why he did become mayor and his Tory-inclined opposite number at the King's Head did not. This was in spite of having a cousin, Edgar, who played a highly equivocal part in the 'Forty-Five. Yet Matthew, and his like-named son, also mayor in his time, were the only really well-found members of their family for several cousins were framework knitters and artisans, although through two female descendants Matthew was ancestor of the great 19th-century Bemrose clan, of which Sir Henry Bemrose was twice mayor. They were also related to the Brookes

family and from the latter sprang Joseph Wright's mother Hannah and the artist's daughter Anna Romana, from whom the Bemroses were also descended. Thus, again do we return to the pervasive ambit of Wright.

Another family who were, among other things, inn-keepers, connected with the same circle was the Denstone family. Not only did Abraham Denstone (1723–1779) own the Mitre, Amen Alley, at his death, but he also had a yard in St Mary's Gate, owned houses elsewhere and the lease of the brickworks at Rowditch Farm, in which he was succeeded by the Harpurs. From this it must not be assumed that he was in any way grand; after all in St Mary's Gate, the Bateman family's impressive mansion stood cheek by jowl with a notorious bordello. But Denstone was the second generation plaster worker of his family. Indeed, he worked for Pickford extensively and his craftsmanship can be admired at St Helen's House and 41 Friar Gate. He also did the ornamental plasterwork in the Assembly Rooms to Robert Adam's designs in 1773–74, which, had it survived, would have constituted as enduring a monument to the consummate skill of Derby craftsmen in the 18th century as anything in England. Yet, modest though his calling was, two of his uncles were attorneys.

Abraham junior died a reasonably wealthy man. His brother James (1724–1780) was a builder and architect. He was apprenticed mason and bricklayer to Solomon Brown, grandfather of Samuel, architect of the General Infirmary. A group of Mundy deeds show him employed by Wrightson Mundy of Markeaton Hall, including one which directly connects with the building of the new house in 1754. A plan and elevation exist of the new Hall – more or less as built – and the writing on a related survey of the old house matches Denstone's on the deeds. Clearly he was the architect for Markeaton Hall, completed in 1755; it also emerges that he built F.N.C. Mundy a town house in The Wardwick and succeeded Samuel Wyatt as clerk of works at Kedleston Hall, Pickford succeeding him in 1772.

On James's death in 1780 without issue, the combined brickmaking and building interests of the brothers devolved to Abraham's third son, Charles, who inherited the house in Walker Lane and established a builders' yard in Friar Gate beside the bowling green of the Wheel Inn. The building business passed to Abraham Denstone's grandson John Bridgart, son of his daughter Keziah and Seth Bridgart, a framework knitter. Seth Bridgart's uncle also married Keziah's sister Sarah and, significantly, one of their sons was a plasterer, another a builder.

Seth's son John carried on the business, buying the bowling green in March 1839 where the firm's headquarters were thereafter set. He was succeeded by his son Robert (1803–1860) and he by another Robert (1838–1881), the latter's brother George designing most of the buildings built by his firm, most notably the Drill Hall, erected for the Volunteers in 1869 in Newland Street, and the Probate Court in St Mary's Gate a decade earlier. The business eventually passed in 1887 to their manager, Joseph Parker. This firm continued on the site until the retirement of its last proprietor, Mr Howard Parker, in 1969, representing over two centuries of tradition of high-quality building and craftsmanship in direct succession from Pickford's *stuccadore*, Abraham Denstone and his architect brother: a quite remarkable survival from an era of massive achievement: the world of Wright, Pickford, Whitehurst, Darwin and the Strutts.

As families, both the Bridgarts and Denstones reveal astonishing extremes of social mobility, of wealth and poverty. The object lesson in the close examination of these families is that very many of the prominent dynasties of 18th-century Derby reflected exactly the same contrasts. Seth Bridgart, as we have seen, was a framework knitter, and while the eldest son became a prosperous builder, the third son, William, was also a framework knitter. His tragedy was to live in an era when the burgeoning new factories, with their ever more advanced machinery, were rendering his calling superfluous.

By 1840 there was 'great distress' among the surviving framework knitters – there were 640 frames at this time, still, mainly working in silk thread – and mayor John Sanders established a fund to provide relief for them. William Bridgart, however, did not live long enough to

The rear of Bridgart's builders' yard and works dated 1863, but built in stages from much earlier and finally enlarged after Robert Bridgart bought the bowling green of the Garrick Inn adjacent in 1872. Most recently – as here in 1987 – redeveloped by Derek Montague as Pymm's. (*Derby Evening Telegraph*)

benefit from Alderman Sanders's scheme, dying on parish relief in October 1822, aged 24, leaving a wife but no children. Likewise, in the previous generation, Joseph Denstone, a first cousin of Abraham, died a pauper, aged 63, in March 1789. He, however, left a like-named son, a staymaker; two of the latter's sons were tailors in a small way, showing the family recovering from what probably was the economic effects of decrepitude brought about by old age or serious illness.

In complete contrast, William Bridgart had not only a well-off brother, but also a rich uncle. This was Thomas Bridgart, who started, like William, as a framework knitter. Yet, by his own efforts he became first a hosier then a silk-throwster and a phenomenally successful one. His Brook Street mill was founded in 1807 and the pedimented eight-storey ribbon mill equalled Strutt's fireproof calico mill in size. He added a seven-storey throwing mill and a lower weaving mill. The ribbon mill was probably the first fireproof silk mill in Britain. The complex continued as a silk mill, with steam power added at an early date before being adapted in the 20th century as a narrow tapes mill which closed about 1995. Research by Peter Billson RIBA enabled English Heritage to re-list the whole complex II* in October 1998 and it was eventually restored as apartments.

Thus, while the ruling oligarchy of the borough was very closely-knit, opulent and manipulative, the realities of life for the majority were never so harsh as to seal them hermetically from their more fortunate kin. Typically, it was only after Government regulation in the shape of the Municipal Corporations Act in 1835 that any real cleavage became apparent.

LOCAL GOVERNMENT

By 1831 the population of the borough was 23,627 (of whom a paltry 1,500 were qualified to vote), but showed an alarming jump to 31,882 in 1833 especially when compared with 15,000 in 1811, 13,000 in 1801 and 8,563 in 1789. The coming of the railway put this figure up considerably more, and the old ruling elite, having had their wings clipped by the 1835 Act, was unable to maintain such close links as before.

From 1835 the Corporation consisted of an annually elected mayor, 12 aldermen and 36 councillors, the latter elected from six wards returning six councillors each. The mayor was elected from among the councillors or aldermen and the latter could be elected – triennially – from either the existing councillors or from among the free burgesses or men being 'possessed of £1,000 property or owning property with a rateable value of at least £30'. The 1835 Act obliged the Corporation to appoint a number of permanent officials: town clerk, treasurer, registrar of the court of records, coroner, clerk of the peace and overseers of the poor. The Crown appointed a recorder. It was not until 1890 that this latter appointment failed to go to a local man. Elections were held on 1 November each year and the mayoralty changed on the same occasion. Today the mayoralty changes hands in late May at a council annual general meeting, following elections early in the same month.

The qualifications in 1835 for ordinary (male) electors were that they must own or be in occupation of property in the borough of rateable value of £5 or more, that they must live in the borough or within seven miles of it, to have been enrolled as a burgess (a formality, all the other items being satisfactory) and to be fully paid-up in respect of rates. The officials of the borough, apart from those stipulated in the act, were normally: town clerk, chamberlain, high constable, sheriff's bailiff, two sergeants-at-mace, a superintendent of police, a town crier and 10 charity commissioners. the high stewardship continued, hereditarily, with the Dukes of Devonshire to 1974 when it became abeyant.

The first policeman, incidentally – long before Sir Robert Peel's reforms and more a glorified and officially sanctioned watchman – is said to have begun his patrol in 1792, an innovation of Wardwick maltster Alderman Thomas Lowe, mayor in that year. From 1839 to 1855 the watch committees set up by the Corporation ran a completely independent police force, but by 1856 all police forces were brought under Home Office control.

As time went by and the administration of the town became more complex, other officials were appointed, and they, in their turn, appointed assistants. In 1850, for instance, and after years of debate, a borough surveyor was first appointed: Samuel Harpur, later of Merthyr Tydfil, who left a journal of his two and a half years *en post* in Derby. He was a son of the Harpurs who owned the Rowditch brickworks in succession to Denstone and, amazingly, a descendant of the youngest son of the first Harpur baronet of Calke.

Harpur concerned himself with laying out new streets, like Burleigh Street on the site of Exeter House, demolished in spring 1854, trying to improve sanitation and housing conditions, improving drainage and commissioning the second Exeter Bridge, to be built to designs by James Trubshaw of Great Heywood, Staffordshire, in 1850. This replaced what Stephen Glover called a 'small bridge of wood', which crossed the river at this point, entered upon via Darby's Yard, the small enclave on the east side of the Market Place, just south of the Assembly Rooms, created by the demolition of the Every family town house. This bridge was a private enterprise venture, built early in 1810 by the Saxelbys, who owned a lead works in St Peter's Street, mainly for

their own convenience. The citizens of St Alkmund's parish saw it as a threat, likely to divert traffic and trade away from Bridge Gate, and that July petitioned the council to close it, but to no avail. Indeed, after the firm went into liquidation a decade or so later, it was purchased by the corporation who created Derwent Street to give better access to it, thus generating the extra traffic which obliged them to replace it in stone under Harpur's supervision. His – and Trubshaw's – bridge remained until replaced in 1928–31 by the present structure.

A CHANGING ELITE

From 1835 the background of the mayors hardly changed at first. As the franchise was wider than before 1835, it might be expected that many new men would penetrate this elite. As it had an economic base, the franchise was only able to be further extended through increased personal prosperity. And, indeed, this phenomenon is observable throughout the ensuing three or so generations. Yet it was not until almost 20 years after the 1835 act, in 1854, that a rank outsider, pawnbroker William Goodwin, managed to become mayor. He represented the return of the small tradesman to the mayoralty, free of powerful or influential connections and lies in contrast to the first four mayors elected under the Municipal Corporations Act: a Strutt, a Leaper-Newton, a Crompton and a Fox – all related and most on second mayoralties.

Indeed, in some respects, Goodwin's mayoralty was a turning point, for after his time multiple mayoralties became increasingly rare, it becoming more an honour reserved for men of exceptional effectiveness or distinction: William Thomas Cox MP (1859 and 1860); Sir Thomas 180 MP (later 1st Lord Roe; 1867, 1896 and 1910); Sir Henry Bemrose MP (1877 and 1909); Sir Abraham Woodiwiss (1880 and 1881) and his son (1888, 1901); Sir Edwin Ann (1898 and 1905), William Blews Robotham (1908 and 1918) and George Warburton (1947 and 1948).

Even so, the succession of gentlemen, attorneys, company directors and bankers largely resumed after Goodwin's mayoralty. Not one mayor between 1855 and 1921 was other than a man of independent means, a member of one of the traditional professions or self-employed. In 1921, however, Alderman William Robert Raynes became the first Labour mayor. He had been formerly an employed printer by trade and more pertinently a full-time trade union official; in other words, even he enjoyed a calling which allowed him the leisure to serve as mayor. The fact is that up until then no employed man could seriously hope to have a year's sabbatical from work and thus upstage his employer. The pressures were practical and social.

Despite the fact that the council ordinarily met but quarterly throughout much of the 19th century, few employed men even achieved the status of councillor at that period. Nevertheless, the traditional families who had dominated the town's affairs up to 1835 did begin to fade: the last Gisborne was mayor in 1856, the last Crompton mayor followed him in 1857. Of their kin and connections, the last flickers manifested themselves in the mayoralties of the newly ennobled Sir William Evans, Bt (1869), Samuel Cox (1870) and Hon. Frederick Strutt in 1902.

EXPANSION AND ITS LIMITS

With a 20,000 increase in Derby's population between 1800 and the Municipal Corporations Act, Derby was inevitably expanding faster than was good for it. In 1806 the areas of expansion were along Willow Row into Lodge Lane and from there into Green Street and down Bridge Street. There was scattered development along Agard and Brook Streets; to the south some new housing had appeared along Osmaston Street (now Osmaston Road) as far as Bradshaw Street. To assist, the Corporation was selling off their remaining commons. In 1806 Bradshaw Hay was sold to the trustees of the General Infirmary, and in 1833 those remaining were sold to the fifth Improvement Commission, although not all were used for housing, Cowsley Fields being purchased as the parkland of a neat Gothic villa.

For the while, the Osmaston Hall estate kept further southward expansion at bay, although this was not to last, as Herbert Spencer lamented in his autobiography when writing of his boyhood home, 8 (later 31) Wilmot Street:

'At that time [1827, when the philosopher was 7] its neighbourhood differed widely from that now existing. It was one of a newly built row, forming but a fragment of one side of Wilmot Street. Opposite was a large unoccupied space over which the town was seen; and behind stretched fields, instead of the streets and detached villas which now cover the surface. Not only the immediate surroundings are transformed, but also the region further away, where my boyish excursions were made, has had its rural beauty changed into the ugliness of a manufacturing suburb. Places where I gathered flowers and gazed with interest at the catkins of the hazel have now become places covered with iron works, where steam hammers make their perpetual thuds, and through which everywhere railway sidings ramify. Quiet lanes in which, during early boyhood, I went with a companion trying to catch minnows with a hand net in a clear little stream running by the hedge, have been transformed into straight roads between land allotments, with scattered houses built by artisans. And where I picked blackberries, factories now stand.'

In the south west, Dunkirk Close had been sold in the 1770s and a tiny suburb had grown up, with another called Kensington due north of it. By 1823 Kensington and Talbot Streets were partly built up by the Harpur family, brickmakers, underwritten by the Madeleys who built a silk mill here. New streets, mainly named after the family or its connections, were pitched across the Newlands by Revd Roseingrave Macklin, later appointed first vicar of the new Christ Church, Normanton Road, built by Matthew Habershon in 1839–40.

Abbey Street defined his land's north-west boundary from 1826, leaving its predecessor, Watery Lane, to continue beside the Littleover Brook as far as Spa Lane, which connected William Boothby's Spa House with Burton Road, on the rising ground above which a number of handsome villas were built from c.1810: Mill Hill House, Temple House, Prospect House and The Firs, all attributable to the prolific Alderman Leaper and all but the latter demolished in the 20th century.

37 Exeter Street, Canary Island. Herbert Spencer's birthplace in 1820. The family moved in the year before when the house was new. The photograph was taken by C.B. Sherwin in 1926 but unfortunately the building was demolished to make way for the Inner Ring Road in 1965. (Derby City Council)

Thus, Derby's expansion was still largely hobbled by a gilded girdle of great estates ringing the borough, most of which evolved through the 'booking out' of land from the old Northworthy estate by the later Saxon and Danish Kings to endow their thegns. The circle they formed round Derby was almost unbroken and any chinks therein had, by the 1820s, been filled by the creation of small suburban estates to replace town houses rapidly becoming insufferable as residences in the crowded town centre. These estates included those belonging to Allestree, Markeaton, Radburne Halls, Mickleover, Littleover Old Hall – an exotic Elizabethan house in the style of Robert Smythson, like a miniature Welbeck – a number of freehold farming estates in Normanton, Osmaston Hall, Elvaston Castle, Chaddesden Hall, Locko Park, Breadsall Hill Top and Darley Hall and House, the Evanses of the latter amalgamating their manufacturing base with an agricultural estate by acquiring the hall in 1835.

BREAKING THE GREEN GIRDLE

The first estate to crack was that of the Boroughs at Castlefields. The initial tract of land released was sold in 1803, the year the senior branch of the family removed to Chetwynd Park, Shropshire. The Infirmary had their share and the rest was later sold piecemeal, one extensive tract of parkland south of the house going to John Copeland of Lincoln for £22,000 on 13 April 1824. He laid out most of the streets west of Siddals Lane (later Siddals Road) and north of the station complex. An adjoining tract went to the Trustees of the Liversage Charity which, from 1845, pitched several streets – several bearing names associated with it. Castle, borough's Walk and Union Street along with streets off were pitched between 1825 and 1845, probably by Boden and Morley, adjacent lace manufacturers.

LACE MAKING: BODEN'S MILL

Castlefields Mill, later Boden's Mill, was a lace mill put up in 1825 and was operated by 56 steam-powered machines which were a development of the bobbin net machine perfected in 1808 by Duffield-born John Heathcoat, who had set up two mills in Loughborough to make lace. He was joined in this enterprise by John Boden, a Morley farmer's son, and by 1816 they had just about completed development of a steam-powered version when the Market Street mill at Loughborough was besieged by a considerable number of Luddites who broke in and destroyed 55 machines. Thereupon, Heathcoat, followed on foot by over 100 devoted – or desperate – workers,

decamped to Tiverton in Devon and re-established himself there. Recent research suggests that the move to Tiverton was already decided upon when the riot occurred on 28–29 June 1816 and that the Luddites had been bribed to make the attack by rival lace makers, facing a declining market without the technological benefit enjoyed by Heathcoat and Boden.

Heathcoat's firm and family went on to fame in Devon, but Boden, by 1824, had decided to set up in Derby. His mill was then the only lace mill in Derby, the industry being really centred in Nottingham. Boden was joined by Nottingham lace maker William Morley (of the family which ran Nottingham firm I. & R. Morley) in 1825. By that date John Leavers in Nottingham had improved the Heathcoat-Boden machines considerably. The Leavers machines weighed in at 20 tons and were 40ft long by 8ft wide and their length dictated the width of the huge shed-like multi-storey mills required to house them. Steam power was essential. The mill had to be immensely strong to withstand the lateral vibration then created, too. The mill was extended in 1839 and the firm made their own machinery until the outbreak of World War One.

Boden's son Henry and grandsons Walter and Henry Boden continued the firm, the second generation especially being extremely enlightened employers, and, having just prior to 1849 bought out William Morley, who took over Depot Mill, Normanton Road, went on to provide more advanced workers' housing, a working men's institute, chapel, concert room, almshouses, school and play space. In its heyday over 1,000 people were employed, and during World War One it turned out 22,000,000 square yards of mosquito netting. The firm eventually amalgamated with Black Brothers in 1955 and was closed down completely in 1958, although the family's long-standing mill at Chard – a spin-off from the post 1816 Heathcoat upheavals – continued.

The foundations of the mill were so strong that they had to be blown up in 1960 in the course of works to build Derby's first shopping precinct since 1708, the dreadful Main Centre – lacklustre and banal even by Derby standards – which itself only survived, along with a ghost (inherited no doubt from the Bodens) until 2004 when it was mercifully flattened to extend the Eagle Centre by Messrs Westfield Shoppingtowns.

By 1838 Castlefields itself having, after five tenancies, become unlettable due to the upheavals caused by the three railway companies on the adjacent Holmes, was pulled down and the gardens given over to building. Traffic Street was pitched along the length of a covert which had been planted from London Road to Cockpit Hill to screen house from town in 1824; Park Street from 1838 traversed thence in front of the site of the house on the alignment of the chief walk of the original garden to meet the new street planned from the new Trijunct Station to London Road.

Boden's Mill photographed about the time of its closure, 15 August 1958. The sheer size of the building is clearly apparent. The foundations had to be dynamited to get rid of them in the end – hardly necessary in 2004 when Westfield demolished its successor, Main Centre. (*Derby Evening Telegraph*)

Local residents boarding tramcar no. 24 in Osmaston Road, Litchurch, in 1906, just south of Grove Street. This area was built up from the 1820s to 1840s and, until mainly demolished to accommodate the expansion of the DRI, was a fine late Regency suburb, albeit latterly much run down. (*Derby Evening Telegraph*)

LITCHURCH AS A SEPARATE ENTITY

The main break in the straitjacket of estates was the sale of the Osmaston and Normanton estates by the Wilmots and the Pochins for development. This enabled the town to spread southwards on the axes of Normanton and Osmaston Roads, boosting the population of Litchurch from 30 in 1801 to 53,200 in 1866, when the ancient settlement was given its own separate local government, consisting of a local board of elected representatives under an executive chairman, a clerk, surveyor, rate collector and medical officer. It was thus for a while, almost as populous as Derby itself; a separate town contiguous to the ancient borough.

By 1877, when it was incorporated into the borough (along with New Normanton, Little Chester and portions of Littleover and Markeaton) the Litchurch population had continued to soar to 69,716. Oddly, the citizens of Litchurch – including what Sir Thomas Roe called 'The Mayor's Nest': Osmaston Road which, by 1899, had supplied 16 mayors since 1864, and thus had become a fashionable area – objected strenuously to being incorporated, and William Bemrose managed to attract a favourable rate for the area as the price of acquiescence. This extension was the first since the ancient borough's bounds were finally fixed by an act of Parliament of 1704.

THE ARBORETUM

The centrepiece of the Litchurch area was, of course, the Arboretum, given to the town in 1840 by Joseph Strutt of Thorntree House. It is arguably the earliest public park in England and was a vital lung for the swiftly-expanding suburb of Litchurch.

Sometime before 1822, Joseph Strutt had bought some land on or near the site in Litchurch to make a

The 'Mayor's Nest' area of Osmaston Road, Litchurch, with the corner of Bateman Street visible, right, in 1909. The surviving villas on the right are now much nearer the road as the thoroughfare was widened and dualled in the 1960s. The 'Mayor's Nest' area. (*Derby Evening Telegraph*)

Joseph Strutt, bust, possibly by W.J. Coffee. (Brian Mills)

headmaster of St Andrew's School and the architect's son-in-law. This led to a classical frontispiece by Henry Duesbury, a grandson of the younger William Duesbury of the china factory family. Two lodges elsewhere in the Arboretum, completed by the opening, were by E.B. Lamb. Their stylistic similarity to the rebuilding of Rose Hill Cottage strongly suggests that Strutt or Bingham was much taken with the idea of rebuilding the house to match. Although unlisted, it survives virtually unaltered opposite the south edge of the park.

Strutt's instructions to Loudon included the following passage:

> 'That two lodges with gates at the two extremities should be built; and that each lodge should have a room, to be considered as a *public room,* into which strangers might go and sit down taking their own refreshments with them, *without any charge* being made... unless some assistance such *as hot water, plates, knives and forks* etc. were required, in which case a small *voluntary* gratuity might be given. That there should be proper yards and conveniences at each lodge for the use of the public, apart from those to be exclusively used by the occupant of [each] lodge. That there should be *open spaces* in two or more parts of the Garden on which large tents might be pitched, a band of music placed, dancing carried on, etc. That certain vases and pedestals now in the flower garden [of Rose Hill Cottage], and also certain others in Mr Strutt's garden in Derby should be retained or introduced; and finally, that some directions should be left for the management of the garden.'

'summer rural retreat', where he planted trees. The centerpiece was probably Rose Hill Cottage, later rebuilt in a mildly Elizabethan mode, but retaining its original south-facing curved bay window, for James Bingham, who was in occupation by 1833.

The Arboretum was originally 11 acres in extent and was landscaped by the distinguished Regency architect and landscape gardener John Claudius Loudon. It was created with gently undulating hillocks, artfully contrived to between 6ft and 10ft, and among which meandered 6,070 feet of gravel walks, the major arteries 15ft wide, the lesser ones but 8ft. All this was set off with more than 1,000 trees, which were the true glory of the area and from which Strutt rightly christened it the Arboretum. Not only were the trees and shrubs grouped according to type and variety, but Loudon also had managed to achieve a pleasing effect despite this, which must have strait-jacketed him somewhat, the idea to group them being a consequence of Strutt's insatiable desire to educate.

The main entrance, not completed until 1853, was from a short avenue and square, known locally as 'Little Moscow', lined with decent villas, mainly of the 1860s, designed by Charles Humphreys, the Litchurch Local Board's surveyor, and built of white brick; one was his own, and next to it that of George Sutherland (1845–1899) – grandfather of the late Graham Sutherland –

The vases and pedestals were a mixture of terracotta sculpture by W.J. Coffee and cast-iron ornaments probably made by the Britannia Foundry of Messrs Weatherhead, Glover & Co. in Duke Street, founded in 1814. These mainly came from Joseph Strutt's garden at 1 St Peter's Street but were later joined by others, removed from the gardens of cheesefactor William Jeffery Etches of London Road, whose Italian wife managed to put up a shrine to Garibaldi by the road. Etches' parkland had been bought by the Midland Railway in 1866 to build their direct line to Nottingham and was also the site of the new gas works – hence the need for a new home for his (mainly Italian) statues. Also installed was a fine fountain from the Britannia Foundry, recently replaced by a replica.

Centrepiece of the whole ensemble was the full-scale terracotta reproduction by Coffee of the Florentine Boar

Derby Aboretum, W.J. Coffee's copy of the Florentine Boar in *situ* c.1900. (M. Craven)

on a gritstone plinth, also originally at Thorntree House and much loved by the public. Unfortunately, this was destroyed by flying wreckage when the later Victorian bandstand was hit by a bomb in 1941. The last pathetic vestiges were spotted in the bottom of a hedge near the bowls club in 1946.

The Arboretum opened on 16 September 1840, with a great procession, 6,000 people in the park itself, dancing to a band in an adjacent field, a ball at the Mechanics' Institute and a childrens' day on the 17th. The park was free on Sundays and Wednesdays during daylight hours but the small charge for entry on the other days was abolished in 1881.

Over the years this excellent park was extended and further embellished. In 1857 Lord Palmerston (then proprietor of Melbourne Hall) gave two Russian cannons captured at Sebastopol and it was physically extended south and west to Rose Hill Street in 1892. This extension was entered past the old Headless Cross and also contained a fine bandstand. By the 1880s an impressive iron and glass conservatory and a pretty aviary had also been built. The former, known universally as the Crystal Palace (hence the name of a beer house in nearby Rose Hill Street), was clearly inspired by Paxton's original, although not known to be by him. The frame may well have been cast by Andrew Handyside, but the designer is unknown and it was cleared away due to maintenance difficulties in the earlier part of the last century; even the timber aviary only just outlasted World War One.

By the 1980s the Arboretum was a poor thing indeed. The 'Dig for Victory' campaign of World War Two effectively diminished the landscaping, and industrial pollution killed off many trees. Vandalism and neglect did the rest. The Heritage Lottery grant aided a restoration, and in 2006 the last elements of the completely renewed Arboretum were in place to the

Arboretum Lodge (1853) from Arboretum Square, photographed when new by Richard Keene c.1855. (Derby Museum)

The replica pavilion built in 2005 to E.B. Lamb's original design by the city council. (M. Craven)

great credit of all involved. Lamb's lodges have been restored, a replacement new rustic seat built to his design and even the boar has been replaced, although instead of a correct terracotta replacement it was done in costly wrought bronze but looks reasonably convincing.

FURTHER EXPANSION

The next break in the girdle of great estates came in 1886–88 when the Midland Railway bought Osmaston Hall and the 3,706-acre estate. The house was turned into offices and the northern part of the park was rapidly covered with the new Carriage and Wagon works.

Part of the land, opposite the site of the hall, but between London Road and the canal south of Deadman's Lane, was sold off slightly earlier for housing and a new suburb was formed, mainly for railway employees, which was named Wilmorton, being a contraction of the former proprietor's surname, Wilmot-Horton. This acquired a board school in 1892 and a chapel – both of which have somehow survived – and has always been a close-knit community. In 1902 the vicar of St James's, the miniscule Osmaston parish church, commissioned a splendid new church just by the canal, along with a vicarage, almshouses and parish hall, all arranged round a quadrangle and designed by his brother, Percy Currey, FRIBA, the area's best Arts-and-Crafts architect. Artful planting around the edges of the enceinte make it today a well cared for showpiece.

From then onwards the estate was reduced in parcels for building, the core remaining as a golf course and occasional showground for the visits of the Royal Agricultural Show. The first of these on the site had been held in the estate's Indian summer, 1843; the following occasions (all accompanied by visits from Royal personages) being 15 July 1881, when the Railway Company provided a private siding to the site, 28 June 1906, when Edward VI also unveiled the statue to his mother at The Spot, 29 June 1921 and 3 July 1933. Thereafter World War Two prevented the 1944 show and

after it the imposing and ingeniously collapsible pavilion was disposed of (part allegedly forms the structure of a house in Mostyn Avenue, Littleover) and the site acquired by Messrs Ford and Weston, the remainder (86 acres) being purchased in 1947 and developed by the borough. This was to be a mixed residential and industrial estate, but the received wisdom in town planning in those days was against mixed development (which, thanks to the Prince of Wales's Poundbury, is now thought to be beneficial in the creation of a rounded community) decided otherwise, so the complex layout of streets named after racecourses, some partly laid out and all planned and named, was much simplified and proceeded as an industrial estate from the 1960s.

The house was demolished by the borough, which had acquired it, in 1938. A public park was retained to the south west, opening on 8 June 1922, with bowling and tennis. The ancient church and vicarage were cleared away post war.

Chaddesden Park was acquired from the other branch of the Wilmots, who had been decimated by World War One, in 1923, and the house demolished in 1926. In 1936 the park was leased by Quinton Estates of Birmingham to the parish council and 'developed', producing much soulless, if adequate, housing. Part was retained for recreation, however. This lease was transferred to the county borough for 99 years at £250 per annum in 1968 and 60 acres of freehold thereof was acquired by the city council for £11,000 in 1982. Thus, the second great expansion of the town, following Normanton, Litchurch and Osmaston, was the swamping of the delightful little hill village of Chaddesden.

Shortly after the demolition of Chaddesden Hall, the widow of Francis Mundy of Markeaton died, leaving

Osmaston Park, 1906: a view of the prefabricated pavilion designed for the Royal Agricultural Show. After 1938, the parkland was given over to an expansion of the housing near Rolls-Royce and after the war to the laying out of the Ascot Drive trading estate. (*Derby Evening Telegraph*)

Markeaton Hall, east front, in 1950, built in 1755 and improved by Pickford for F.N.C. Mundy. It was demolished in 1964. (M. Craven)

house and giving first option to the town to purchase the park. She and her husband had already released two considerable parcels of ground for public recreation. In 1895 Markeaton Recreation Ground was given on condition that the borough build a road across the site (then badly-needed) connecting Ashbourne Road with Kedleston Road. This, with its two bridges over Markeaton Brook and the (Nuns') Mill Race, was built and became Mackworth Road and, south of Markeaton Lane (itself once the town approach to the Hall), Merchant Street. Mrs Mundy opened a further section on 21 June 1905 and an open-air swimming pool for children was created in 1903 in this park by damming the brook south of Mackworth Road Bridge to form a miniature lake, the main flow being diverted to the west. The bank was paved and an amenity, much-enjoyed by the young of the West End, was created at minimal cost, but which today is long abandoned.

The house, however, and its 112 acres of park, landscaped by William Emes of nearby Bowbridge House, swiftly established themselves in the hearts of local residents. The modest lake was greatly enlarged for boating and was opened by Edward, Prince of Wales, on 4 July 1934. Yet the house never found a role. It and the park were vandalised by the military during the war and the house was destroyed after years of neglect in 1964, leaving only Pickford's orangery – much mutilated – and the numerous and hideous brick military buildings. Nevertheless, it is still much enjoyed and has for the last 15 or so years had a particularly fine steam-operated 15-inch gauge railway operating within it, a facility which richly deserves expansion.

It might be thought that the retention of the park at Markeaton for public enjoyment would continue to restrict the growth of the town in this direction. This was not quite true, for Humbleton Farm was purchased from Mrs Mundy's heirs, the Clark-Maxwells, and a developer laid out four streets before World War Two stopped work. The borough bought the land when peace

returned and planned an exceptionally ambitious estate of municipal housing.

Two years after Mrs Mundy's ill-used gift, the death of Mrs Evans – the last of her dynasty – caused Darley Hall, House and Park to drop like a ripe fruit into the lap of the borough. Again a pleasant riverside park was created and again the associated buildings were ill-used. Darley House was on lease as a school, and when it closed in 1935 the house came down, building of private housing on the site being delayed by the war. The greater treasure, Smith's and Pickford's superb grade II* listed Darley Hall, housed the Derby Central School through to 1958, but once this institution had been relocated the tale was the same as with Markeaton and this most interesting of all Derby's lost seats was bulldozed in 1962.

Nevertheless, until 1968 Darley Abbey itself was outside the ambit of the old borough council, and remained what by this time formed an effective barrier to development, thus preserving the Evans's unique Regency factory settlement. Subsequently, development has been on a modest scale and this historic industrial settlement has maintained its integrity, and it is now a conservation area and lies within the Derwent Valley Mills World Heritage site, designated in 2002.

The development of Littleover, Mickleover, Breadsall and Spondon has taken place almost wholly within the 20th century and was achieved by the piecemeal sale of parcels of land by the proprietors of the estates concerned. Thus, the breaching of the constricting belt of estates and parks was a vital element in the expansion of Derby and the beginning of the process early in the 19th century was most timely, not only to prevent the further proliferation of stinking, swarming courts and rookeries on the gardens of houses in the ancient town centre, but also because the land they released became available in the nick of time in respect of the next stage of the town's expansion. By the same token, the removal of pressure from the core of the town ensured the preservation of very many of the 17th and 18th century buildings there, at least until the mid-20th century.

Mickleover Manor, c.1864, garden front.
(Derby Local Studies Library)

TWO NEW GUILDHALLS

In August 1835 the route of the future North Midland Railway was surveyed between Derby and Leeds: the very year of the Municipal Reform Act. The coming of the railway – perhaps the most significant single event in Derby's history – was to test the adaptability of the town to the extreme. Moreover, between 1788 and 1835 much more had been achieved in improvements than had happened throughout the whole of the previous century, although the impetus as yet was not provided by the Corporation or even by the Improvement Commissioners. True, the burgesses had built a new Guildhall, but most other projects had been the result of private initiatives.

The matter of the Guildhall was primarily due to the sudden availability of the property on the south side of the Market Place, behind the old Guildhall. This presented the old Common Hall with the chance they had been denied when building the 1731 Guildhall, of placing the new edifice within the south side building line and thus making more room in the crowded Market Place. This was seized, and the London architect Matthew Habershon – a Strutt protégé – was recruited to design the replacement for Jackson's dignified building which, regrettably, had to be demolished. Whitehurst's turret clock of 1735–36 was probably moved to the pediment of the new building. The parapet urns of Jackson's building were rescued by Alderman Francis Jessopp and taken to beautify his attractive park behind the Jacobean House; others ended up in Alderman Haden's garden by St Michael's Churchyard.

Habershon's building was a very elegant Greek-revival essay in yellow brick faced in stone, with an Ionic tetrastyle portico carried on a rusticated base, containing an arched entrance into the court behind lined by stout Doric columns from the Phoenix foundry opposite the Silk Mill. Here was the police station (with its eight men in 1836) and cells. Beyond these lay a new market area with permanent stalls, shops, and a butter, egg and vegetable market, which took some of the pressure off the Market Place itself. There was an imposing eastern entrance towards the Morledge and a route to the west through Tiger Yard to the Cornmarket. Within was a Court of Session on the first floor behind the portico with, below, the magistrates' room and their retiring room on the one side of the carriage drive and the Court of Requests, watch office and Savings Bank the other side.

Unhappily, this building burned down on the night of 21 October 1841, destroying most of the borough's ancient records, and had to be replaced. Doubtless this catastrophe – which destroyed Whitehurst's 1736

clock – drove the Derby Savings Bank to extremely handsome Greek revival new premises in Friar Gate.

The present Town Hall was designed by Henry Duesbury, utilising the ground floor of its immediate predecessor. It boasts a 103ft 10in high tower topped by a lead cupola housing a clock by John Whitehurst III (which has not survived) and even today is a prominent landmark. The bas-reliefs at first-floor level, accompanied by an inscription in Latin recording the circumstances of its creation, were carved by London sculptor John Bell (1812–1896).

NEW BUILDINGS

The success of Habershon's new Town (or Guild) Hall seems to have led to a series of commissions for him locally. The High Sheriff for 1828, Sir George Sitwell of Renishaw Bt., employed him to modernise the Shire Hall. Within Pickford's walls, Habershon provided two delightful courts of 50ft x 30ft each with galleries on 'oriental columns' and much well-carved oak panelling and decoration. The ventilation system was to a design by George Benson Strutt, doubtless ultimately attributable to his talented brother William and thus harking back to Whitehurst's theories. Habershon also provided a spectacular gallery overlooking the interior of the hall and ancillary accommodation and cells were put in an annexe decked up to resemble a classical villa at the rear of the complex on Walker Lane. This was rounded off by Chantrey's bust of F.N.C. Mundy of Markeaton inside.

Even now, Habershon was still in demand. He designed the very chaste Gothic Christ Church at the junction of Normanton and Burton Roads almost opposite Little City. This was built in 1836–40 in memory of Bishop Ryder of Lichfield with money provided by the Oakeses and Macklins. Robert Bridgart was the contractor, the cost £3,250.

Finally, it must be noted that Habershon designed Trinity School, London Road, in 1829–30, adjacent to the newly rededicated Trinity Church, formerly St George's. This had been built speculatively in 1826 by architect Joseph Botham of Leeds. It turned out to have been rather cheaply built in brick and stucco for all its Gothic exuberance, and the patriotic Botham decided on the dedication and even decked the interior out in red, white and blue! This was intended to serve the burgeoning housing along London Road and on the Castlefields estate. Botham's church was eventually replaced in 1903–04 by the present Holy Trinity, a very plain Gothic edifice in machine-made brick.

CULTURAL LIFE AND EDUCATION

Mention of Habershon's designing a very minor school serves as a reminder that a town so influenced by radical thinkers as Darwin and the Strutts did not neglect its cultural well-being or the educational needs of its citizens. The Assembly Rooms were used for more than the idle pleasure of the better off, for from 1817 they were the venue for Choral Society concerts started that year, rising to 60 members in 1831 under William Gover, giving four annual concerts there.

The Philosophical Society went from strength to strength, meetings being switched from the King's Head to premises in St Helen's Street, and ultimately to the Athenæum Club, Victoria Street, in 1839, where it had a library of 1,500 books and a small museum. In August 1828 Joseph Strutt, his nephew Edward (later 1st Lord Belper) and Dr Douglas Fox founded the Mechanics' Institution to give 'improving lectures' free of charge, whereby artisans and men of limited education could broaden their knowledge. Membership in the first year was 274, rising to over 800

Dr Douglas Fox (1798–1885) terracotta bust, now in the museum, by George Cocker. A relation of Strutt, he was co-founder of the Mechanics' Institute where the sculpture was discovered in 1993. (M. Craven)

1925 centenary dinner at the Mechanics' Institute, the interior of the lecture hall after the 1882 rebuilding. The niches (right) used to hold busts of the founders – found in 1993 in the attic! (M. Craven)

in 1842, by which time there had been amassed a library of 6,000 books.

Premises had been acquired in 1832, beautified with a Greek revival lecture hall 75ft by 40ft, designed by William Mansfield Cooper and completed in October 1837. The School Board Act took much of the impetus out of the institute (which had to have a new façade in 1881–1883 to accommodate the widening of The Wardwick in which it lay) and it was in decline throughout the 20th century, forcing its ruling committee to put a shopping arcade through its lecture hall in 1951; and when closure came in 1997 the lecture hall was restored as a public house.

HERBERT SPENCER

An academy was set up at 4 Green Lane in 1789 by Matthew Spencer (1762–1827), a Wesleyan – the sixth generation of his family – born at Kirk Ireton in 1762. William George, his eldest son, carried this school on at his father's death in 1827. He then resided in a modest house in Exeter Street, wherein was born his eldest son, Herbert, in 1820. This house was most regrettably demolished by the council in the late 1960s.

W.G. Spencer was influenced strongly by the scientific experiments of Benjamin Franklin, Erasmus Darwin and Edward Delaval, the latter a friend of Revd John Wood – chaplain to the Duke of Devonshire and vicar of Edensor. Most central to the academy's philosophy was Darwin's *A Plan for the Conduct of Female Education in Boarding Schools* of 1797, based on the experiences of his natural daughters, the Misses Parker, running their school at Ashbourne. Suitably adapted to Spencer's requirements, the curriculum included demonstrations of 'philosophical machines', and a fine early Wimshurst machine inherited from him by Herbert is now in Derby Museum.

Herbert Spencer, photographed by John Watkins of Derby, c.1860.

Thomas Swanwick was the Spencer's only real rival in the education stakes. This is his monument in Derby Cathedral of 1814. He was succeeded by his son, who taught Richard Keene. (M. Craven)

THOMAS SWANWICK
Died on the 15th of March 1814
In the 59th year of his age.
Having fulfilled the important duties of
SCHOOL - MASTER
With credit and respect 32 years:
The Gratitude and Esteem of his Pupils
Have erected this tribute
To his Memory.

Sherwood.   Sculptor.

With such a solid, forward-looking liberal education on offer, Spencer attracted pupils from members of the Derby intelligensia, sympathetic to the Whiggish radicalism that then pervaded and doubtless mainly non-conformists. The pupils included Anthony Tissington's grandchildren, one of the sons of landscaper William Emes, Dr Haden's children (including the future Mrs Kirk Boott), Charles Hurt's son from Wirksworth Hall, two Duesbury children, three children of Richard Brown's partner John Mawe, the only child of Abraham Bennett, FRS, vicar of Fenny Bentley and inventor of the gold leaf electroscope, not to mention Joseph Wright's nephew George Wallis from the New Inn, John Davis the future barometer maker with two of his siblings, and John Whitehurst III, for whom his father paid an entrance fee of 2/6d. Although Erasmus Darwin thought Spencer's rival schoolmaster Thomas Swanwick 'a very ingenious philosopher' he nevertheless started the children of his own second marriage off with Spencer. Even the county gentry, specifically the Mundys, Gladwins and Sitwells, sent their offspring to Spencer prior to their going to Eton.

W.G. Spencer was co-proprietor from 1811, but it had closed by 1857, however, when we find Herbert Spencer's father settled at 8 Wilmot Street as a private tutor. This house, too, vanished in the iconoclastic 1960s. It would seem that in the Spencers' academy, the precepts of Darwin, Whitehurst and their friends were distilled and transmitted to new generations of Derby people, bearing fruit in the Victorian age, while Herbert, who died unmarried in 1903 – leaving kinsfolk still flourishing in Derby – built upon the same basic ideas to become one of the greatest philosophers of the Victorian era, espousing and supporting Charles Darwin's theories, wooing George Elliot and founding the discipline of sociology.

SPENCER AND THE GREAT FLOOD

Herbert, who had also acted as a pupil-teacher in his father's school, made one contribution to the benefit of his home town, albeit that it was not implemented until 29 years after his death. He was, however, as a 20 year old, much affected by the great flood of 1 April 1842, which inundated most of the borough. The cause was the Derwent backing up from the over-full Trent and preventing floodwater coming down the Markeaton Brook from draining into it. Hence, many previous floods, 12 being known since the first recorded in 1587 when the Bridge Chapel was damaged.

Spencer quickly realised that a barrier on the Derwent below Derby, equipped with a 'steam sluice', would effectively enable the backing up to be controlled

The Derwent barrier, installed in 1932, as suggested by Herbert Spencer in 1842. (M. Craven)

has been an unqualified success and is still doing its job. Spencer, on the other hand, left shortly afterwards to enjoy a loving friendship with Derbyshire-born Mary Ann Evans (George Elliot) and fame.

It was perhaps fortunate that among his wide circle of acquaintances William Strutt numbered Joseph Lancaster, founder of the Lancastrian system of primary education, who started a school in a Full Street mill (after giving an address in the town in 1812), which Joseph Strutt equipped. Two years later it moved to a building erected by Strutt's brother William for the purpose in Orchard Street, which flourished until closed in 1967 and was, sadly, demolished in 1968. In 1833 it had a master and 330 boys. Strutt also founded a Unitarian Sunday School attached to the chapel in Friar Gate about a decade before and nearly all the churches, the Catholics and dissenting chapels, too, were running associated Sunday schools by the time the railways came, which provided at least a rudimentary education for most of the borough's children.

and largely eliminate flooding. He accordingly put his ideas to paper and delivered them to the Corporation, which, in typical fashion when faced with a clever-clogs young upstart, thanked him off-handedly and shelved them. It was only after the next worst flood, on Saturday/Sunday, 21–22 May 1932 (there having been four lesser ones between that date and 1842), that professional consultants advised the council that Spencer's idea should be put into operation forthwith, substituting more modern technology, like electric sluice gates. Despite one subsequent serious flood, the barrier

Further and not to be outdone, Joseph Lancaster's coeval Dr Bell founded a school under Church of England auspices in Lodge Lane, also in 1812, for 230 children of both sexes. It was destroyed by fire in 1817 and moved to yet another mill, this time in Bold Lane,

The Wardwick: Derby Flood, Sunday 22 May 1932. (M. Craven)

An 1886 Richard Keene photograph of St Peter's Bridge – mainly intact beneath the hump in the road, foreground – Victoria Street and (right) Corn Market, with (centre) the Royal Hotel and Athenæum Club of 1838, centrepiece of the culverting scheme for Brookside, with the Derby & Derbyshire Bank to the right, of 1834, all by Robert Wallace. (*Derby Evening Telegraph*)

purchased for £700. A second National School (as Bell's schools were called) was founded in Traffic Street by Revd Robert Simpson (the Derby historian and first vicar of Botham's St George's Church) in 1829, with 256 pupils of both sexes. He also founded a school for infants in the outbuildings of Castlefields House in 1827, run on Wilderspin's system, and a further infants' and junior school was initiated by the incumbent of St John's, Bridge Street in excellent surviving buildings beside the church in Mill Street by 1830. When in 1839 the Catholics left their pretty little chapel of 1813, situated behind the King Street Methodist Church in Chapel Street, for the new Church of St Mary, the building was let to Bell for a British Girls' School for 112 pupils. This had been founded originally in the yard behind the former George Inn in 1831, 19 years after the inn had closed (see page 124). In addition, most of the churches and chapels at this date ran schools of varying quality.

VICTORIA STREET

The final improvement to the town at this stage, completion of which more or less coincided with the railway, was the redevelopment of Brookside. This thoroughfare was, until 1837, little more than a riverside path lined with fairly gracious residences. It stretched from Becket Well Lane, beside which still flowed the Odd Brook joining the Markeaton Brook at this point, on the corner of which stood the very imposing Greek revival Brookside chapel designed by W.M. Cooper in 1836, which replaced the one built in 1783 for the Independents, only to be replaced in its turn by Evans & Jolley's much larger Gothic creation of 1859.

A consortium of local businessmen then seized the opportunity to pursue a far more adventurous project, and in April 1836 resolved to culvert the Markeaton Brook from the mediaeval St James's Bridge, where the monks had once charged tolls, to that of St Peter. This was done between May and August 1837, producing a majestic sweep of broad thoroughfare, which remains impressive, even today.

The consortium then built a new post office, hotel and premises for a new gentlemen's club, the Athenæum. £10,000 was raised and a competition attracted 52 designs for the new complex. By a strange coincidence it was won by Robert Wallace, then still building the adjacent Derby & Derbyshire Bank. No doubt the homogeneity he was able to suggest with his own part-completed oeuvre appealed to the proprietors.

His building, 62ft of which fronted Cornmarket, returning along Brookside for 98, was of three storeys and again in chaste Neo-Grec style, with an imposing entrance on the angle graced with a giant Ionic order. All was in brick, faced with local millstone grit sandstone. The entrance, which boasted an hexagonal vestibule (now a jeweller's shop) and fine plaster ceilings, was graced with carved Royal Arms (now vanished)

proclaiming the hotel to be well and truly Royal. The post office was installed within the hotel's façade adjoining the bank in Cornmarket, where it remained until 1869. The Athenæum was on the south side and included a very impressive lecture hall-cum-ballroom which, after the closure of the hotel in 1951, was for 40 years given over to iron partitions and a Social Services office. It has since been restored and let most appropriately as a banqueting and conference suite. The Athenæum elevation, sparsely fenestrated, was originally intended to be graced by a frieze representing part of the Panathenaic Procession (to full size) by John Hemming, the elder of London (1771–1851), who had previously produced similar reliefs for the more famous Athenæum in London. Unfortunately, this does not appear to have been executed. The interior, which was lavishly finished with much fine plasterwork and good joinery, included the Town and County Museum, for which an entrance fee of 6d (2p) was charged and there was also a newsroom supported by 102 subscribers.

Creighton's map, c.1821, showing Regency Derby.

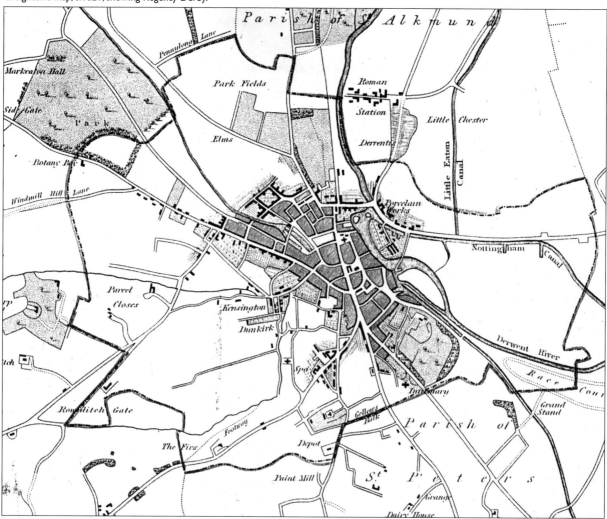

XI

RAILWAYS TO ROYCE'S

THE TRIJUNCT STATION

Derby nearly became part of one of the very earliest railways, had a scheme canvassed in the *Derby Mercury* for 29 December 1824 come into being. The advertisement read: 'London Northern Rail Road Company. To connect Birmingham, Derby, Nottingham, Hull and Manchester with each other and the parts adjacent and with the metropolis.' Nothing, however, appears to have come of this proposal, and it was not until the mid 1830s that anything similar was considered.

The survey of the future line of the North Midland Railway (NMR) was undertaken by George Stephenson in August 1835; the first sod was cut in February 1837. A little earlier, in August 1832, the idea of the Midland Counties' Railway (MCR) had been conceived at the Sun Inn in Eastwood, Nottinghamshire, the projected line being intended to link Derby, Leicester, Nottingham and Pinxton; the engineer was another pioneer, C.B. Vignoles. Their first sod was cut three months after the NMR's, in May 1837. At the same time, Stephenson was also surveying the line of the projected Birmingham and

Derby Junction Railway (BDJR) also first mooted as far back as 1824. Thus, three new railway companies were poised to converge on Derby and all intended to make Derby their headquarters.

A serious problem was where the three companies should have their stations. Darby's Yard, almost next to the Assembly Rooms on the east side of the Market Place, was suggested as one. Thomas Darby (d.1849) was a draper who occupied the 18th-century building which spanned the entrance to the ancient Every town house behind. The latter having been removed in the 1820s, the replacement buildings, immediately west of the Derwent, lay athwart a tempting alignment and were indeed purchased by the railway promoters, being subsequently occupied by the Midland Railway for very many years thereafter. Another site was on Nottingham Road and other suggestions abounded.

The burgesses, alarmed at the possibility of a multitude of sulphurous stations, called the interested parties together on 2 February 1836 and suggested a joint station; the place suggested, well clear of the historic town, was immediately south of the river and

Derby Railway Station – the 'Trijunct' station – designed by Francis Thompson and opened in 1839. It was finally destroyed in 1985. From a lithograph by Cole, c.1840. (M. Craven)

PERSPECTIVE VIEW OF THE GREAT CENTRAL RAILWAY STATION, DERBY.
Drawn & Engraved for the British Gazetteer

Midland Place on 8 February 1988, shortly after the restoration of Francis Thompson's railway cottages, built for the North Midland Railway in 1841–42. (*Derby Evening Telegraph*)

canal between The Holmes and The Siddalls with a triangle north thereof where the NMR met the MCR on the Old Meadows. By a near miracle, the three companies agreed to these enlightened proposals; Williams, the MR historian, adds that they agreed on nothing else.

The initial area set aside was over 30 acres, the NMR erecting the station, a hotel adjoining and three streets of workers' cottages – the first by a railway company in the country – all designed in a 'stripped down' classical style of most elegant proportions by Francis Thompson (1808–1895), the company's architect. The train shed, of glass and cast iron, was triple-roofed and covering nine tracks, lasting until hit by a German bomb in January 1941. All three companies shared one platform, a colossal 1,050ft long.

All three companies also had separate workshops, Thompson providing the NMR with a polygonal (of 16 sides) engine house, 130ft across, with an intricate roof structure and a central turntable. Locomotives entered it via an engine-shaped aedicule in the integral administration building, beneath a stone tower containing a Whitehurst clock. To the east were the MCR repair workshops and locomotive shed in two most handsome buildings with a blind arcade, probably designed by William Parsons of Leicester. The whole complex fell redundant in the early 1980s and were only saved from likely destruction by a last-minute relisting to

II* by English Heritage, 'leant on' by a senior railway sympathiser in the then Conservative Government. Subsequently it has been in terminal decay, endless schemes have been aborted either through financial problems, local indifference or lack of vision. Only in 2006 did it emerge that Derby College, formerly the FE College at Wilmorton, were prepared, with huge grant aid, to convert and use the buildings.

The BDJR's buildings were designed by Joseph and Thomas Cooper, and were more conventional, but like all of the buildings, much cast iron was used. Regrettably, we are not told which foundry supplied it. However, the Coopers invariably worked closely with Weatherhead, Glover & Company of Duke Street, and we may tentatively suggest that this company supplied the BDJR at least.

The entire complex was lit by gas and the 747 lamps and 1,000 yards of four-inch piping were installed by Thomas Crump of Derby. Thomas Crump the elder's many talents embraced the patenting of a flush WC only months after the pioneering patent of Thomas Crapper of London; had Crump managed to get his application in first it might have changed a whole aspect of English slang!

The three railway companies wasted no time in opening their lines. The Midland Counties were first, opening theirs on 30 May 1839, beginning official services five days later, with the Leicester extension opening in May 1840. Three months later, on 15 July, Robert Stevenson, George's son, drove the first BDJR train into Derby, although services proper did not commence until 5 August, but endured two rather shaky years before the effects of the opening of the North Midland Railway on 11 May 1840 worked through and traffic picked up all round.

The North Midland's opening had been delayed by the formidable engineering problems posed by the terrain between Derby and Sheffield, but, once ready, celebrations could be got under way. A train of 34 carriages packed with 500 people and pulled by two locomotives left Leeds for Derby, which it reached in five hours. A lavish buffet lunch awaited the passengers of this first train on the Derby station platform. Within a year the company had more traffic than they could easily handle. This led to a need for increased investment at a time when profits had yet to match the potential volume of traffic. The NMR made an additional share offer early in 1841 and began to make swingeing economies. Even Robert Stephenson, the son of the line's engineer and its locomotive superintendent, offered to take a £400 per annum reduction on his £1,000 salary, and Francis Thompson, the firm's talented architect, was made redundant.

Nevertheless, this was the year in which Thompson's very fine Midland Hotel was finished at Derby, although it was run by an independent company and did not come into full railway company ownership until 1860. This sort of uncertainty, aggravated by irate shareholders complaining that the company should be paying dividends of more than three percent instead of intensively reinvesting their net revenues, was a symptom of these early years on all three lines, and suggestions that they should amalgamate and pool resources began to look increasingly persuasive.

Midland Railway, Midland Hotel, built in 1841 by Francis Thompson with modern portico. (Peter Billson)

THE MIDLAND RAILWAY

A price-cutting campaign had been initiated by the MCR, and when the other two companies responded – having little choice in the matter in reality – things began to look bleak. The long single platform at Derby station further exacerbated the situation by encouraging gerrymandering wherein the train of one company, ready to depart, would be obstructed and prevented from leaving by the inert presence, fouling the points, of that of another. Worse, the shareholders of all three lines were chafing at dividends which never passed three percent, whereas the entrepreneur George Hudson – Hudson of York, the 'Railway King' – was offering them five percent plus on the back of savings of £25,000 if they amalgamated. This pressure proved irresistible, even to the reluctant management of the MCR and, eventually, terms were agreed. The three companies merged to form the Midland Railway (MR), with Derby as its base, in September 1843. The first shareholders' meeting of the new company took place in the town on 16 July 1844, chaired by Hudson, whose reputation has been much rehabilitated by Robert Beaumont's recent biography. Royal assent to the Parliamentary bill was required to confirm, this being obtained shortly afterwards.

Hudson is often denigrated because his fall revealed a commercial life replete with fast practices and double-dealing, yet he served the Midland well, vigorously defending its interests against competitive schemes during the 'Railway Mania' period, which immediately followed the amalgamation. He even secured £2,500,000 within the year to expand the network in order to beat off a threat from Edmund Denison MP to promote a direct London–York line – eventually the Great Northern Railway. When Denison and Hudson happened to meet on the platform at Derby in January 1845, the latter accused the former of pursuing his ends by unfair methods, to which Denison retorted loudly, 'Have a care, Hudson. I have warned you before now to restrain your language. You are a blackguard and I have done with you. Go, go away!' All of which merely spurred Hudson on.

Yet in April 1849, with shareholders beside themselves with worry that the company was financially overstretched and aware that Hudson had fingers in other pies, they accepted this remarkable man's resignation, and he soon afterwards began his spectacular slide into oblivion. Williams, however, adds to his account with great fairness in the writing of events less than 30 years before, 'We may add, that some of those who were best acquainted with the activities in which Mr Hudson was at that period engaged, are of the opinion that scant justice was done to his work and to the motives by which he was actuated in the performance of it.'

Sir James Allport (1811–1892), 'creator' of the Midland Railway. (M. Craven)

Nevertheless, the Midland Railway thrived and went on from strength to strength. In 1851 the first 'in house' locomotives were built in the workshops at Derby, to designs by the company's first locomotive engineer, Matthew Kirtley (1813–1873). Eventually, the workshops in which the Midland made nearly all the equipment they required covered 128 acres. In 1876 the largest building – the Carriage and Wagon works of 120,000sq ft – was erected and another for making signalling equipment where today the *Derby Evening Telegraph's* offices stand, reflecting a pioneering use of large-scale buildings. Another major building is the monumental but superb brick office building on Nelson Street designed by company architect John Holloway Sanders (1826–1884) – who was, by no special co-incidence, son of Joseph R. Sanders, the line's general manager – restored with panache in the early 1990s.

The General Manager after Sanders was James Allport, appointed in 1853 and who held office almost continuously for 27 years, being knighted and given a directorship for his pains. He continued to increase its network both within the Derby area and further afield. His greatest achievement was to construct the line from Leicester to London (St Pancras) in 1863–68 to improve services to the capital, which had begun in 1857 but with the disadvantage of having to share the Great Northern Railway (GNR) route south of Hitchin. He also opened

the route to Manchester (1867), Swansea (1874) and Scotland via the Settle and Carlisle line a year later. He was later described as the 'Bismark of railway politics'.

In 1852 the North Staffordshire Railway (NSR) ran trains to Derby from Stoke-on-Trent, courtesy of running powers over the Midland from near Willington. In 1876–78 the Great Northern Railway (GNR) – rival of the Midland from the earliest times – constructed a line from the Erewash Valley just north east of Ilkeston to Egginton Junction, where their trains were also to gain access to the Potteries over NSR metals. In January 1847 communication with London by electric telegraph began, too.

THE GREAT NORTHERN LINE

The GNR made a considerable difference to the Derby townscape. It entered from the north east, cutting through Little Chester on a high embankment over unlovely iron bridges spanning Old Chester Road and City Road, now both mercifully removed. Indeed, the closure of this line to all traffic in 1967 enabled this embankment to be levelled and the opportunity taken to excavate a section of the Roman defences beneath it. It crossed the Derwent just south of the township on a fine bowstring girder bridge made by Andrew Handyside & Company at their Britannia Foundry in Duke Street.

From thence the four-track line, which opened in 1878, clipped the end of Bath Street and dived beneath North Parade, North Street, Arthur Street, Edward Street and King Street in a cutting. It threw off a headshunt north along Darley Grove to serve a siding leading to Handyside's Foundry – one wonders if Andrew Handyside did a deal over this in return for supplying two bridges at a reduced cost. It destroyed Cherry Street utterly, crossed Willow Row on a bridge leading to a long

West End: a Richard Keene photograph captioned 'Ford Street Yard' (1876), taken during the building of the Great Northern Railway's line. (M. Craven)

A view of Friar Gate Station taken from the roof of the Bonded Warehouse just four months into nationalisation, in April 1948, looking east.

line of brick arches nearly parallel with Ford Street, crossing Brook Street, Brook Walk and Agard Street, before gobbling up Short Street and crossing Friar Gate on another cast-iron confection by Messrs Handyside, this time graced with filigree spandrels containing the borough's Buck-in-the-Park symbol, mainly as a result of an outcry by the well-heeled residents of Friar Gate. To allow the road to pass comfortably beneath this structure (which, in carrying four lines of track at this point, is effectively two identical bridges on a slightly splayed alignment) it was dipped, creating a flood-trap, just as Nottingham Road had been dipped 40 years before in order to carry traffic beneath the NMR. Both dips were made greater c.1904 to clear electric tramwires, and the one under the Friar Gate Bridge was again deepened in 2003.

South of Friar Gate was the massively constructed GNR Derby (Friar Gate) Station, replete with subterranean passages and stairs to the elevated platforms. A large area here was cleared, mainly gardens and fields belonging to Large's Charity, and a great deal of spoil was brought in to raise a large goods yard to the height of the main line. This was then finished off with a colossal bonded warehouse in shiny red brick designed by the company's architect, looming over the neighbourhood like a nightmarish Escorial but today gutted and extremely derelict.

In crossing Friar Gate, the line caused the demolition of the mediaeval Old White Horse Inn (Mrs Beare's Crown) and Eyre's town house, which caused an outcry

The old White Horse Inn, a mediaeval market pub which became a much lamented casualty of the building of the GNR. Richard Keene photograph from c.1875. (M. Craven)

Friar Gate, Handyside & Co's GNR bridge of 1877, seen in 1967. (M. Craven)

at the time (not to mention what today we would call environmental damage to Derby's finest thoroughfare) in ironic contrast to the equally loud cries of anguish when the bridge came under threat of destruction in 1971. It is exceptionally fine, but Friar Gate itself is finer. In an ideal world, the perfect solution would be to move the bridge to a preserved line and rehabilitate the street, especially as a plan to run the projected Derby Inner Ring Road extension over it on a concrete raft was abandoned on cost grounds and the structure is currently entirely cosmetic.

Suburban stations

In 1890 the Midland opened a station at Peartree and Normanton to serve the burgeoning housing south of the town. It was an act of self-interest, for here lived the majority of the company's employees, and it was to the MR's advantage to enable them to get to work simply and cheaply. This station closed in 1968, defeated by competition from the Corporation's buses, but was reopened in 1976 when a service was developed from Matlock to Sinfin Central via Derby and Peartree to serve the needs of Messrs Rolls-Royce's employees. Sinfin Central (and another station, Sinfin North) were also

1976 creations for the benefit of Rolls-Royce using the line of the former branch to Melbourne. This line had closed to passengers in 1930, but in 1974 the stub-end was left as far as the Rolls-Royce works. The branch once also served a station at Chellaston and Swarkestone (now in the city), from 1868 to September 1930.

Otherwise, of the suburbs of the modern city, only Spondon (opened 1839) and Mickleover for Radbourne (opened 1878) had stations, the latter on the GNR, which closed to passengers in 1939 and to goods in 1964. It was converted a decade or so ago into a pleasant family home by Barry Sims, the last Head of Music at the old Bishop Lonsdale College. There was also a GNR station serving the Racecourse from 1885 until 1939.

As the Midland Railway grew, so did its ability to attract new industry and bolster the old. In 1844 it was very much a provincial system, but by the time it had reached Glasgow in 1875 it had acquired a nationwide reach. These achievements, supported by ruthless marketing which, for instance, led to the addition of upgraded third-class accommodation to all expresses around 1874, the consequent and pioneering abolition of second class from 1 January 1875 and the introduction of American-style Pullman cars on services to London, can be largely laid at the feet of Allport.

Victoria Street looking south east in September 1904, with a line of three of the new electric trams sidling up behind one of the horse trams they were eventually to replace, this one, no. 22, bound for Ashbourne Road, the last route to be electrified in June 1907. (*Derby Evening Telegraph*)

Victoria Street again, this time showing the transition from trams to trolleybuses, in this view which must date from 1934, for trolley route 22 down Ashbourne Road began 31 December previous. Derby tram, no. 78, foreground, was delivered in 1927 and scrapped in this very year. Why its indicator reads Osmaston Road at this date and in this location is a mystery. (*Derby Evening Telegraph*)

STREET TRANSPORT

This expansion sounded the death-knell of the stage coaches and the redundancy of the turnpikes, which were finally wound up under Acts of Parliament of 1888 and 1894. The London–Manchester coach Diligence (hence, colloquially, the Derby Dilly) which ran via the Bell, in Sadler Gate, under the proprietorship of W.W. Wallis, had long since shed its southern portion when it left for Manchester for the last time on 3 November 1855. The service had lasted just 120 years. Wallis, however, had plenty of irons in the fire. He was already the MR consigning agent, and he had turned his hand to running an omnibus service from Derby Station to the town centre (for which purpose he had bought the *Bell*) as far back as about 1840, although he ran one from 1834 to Leicester from Ashbourne via the Bell following the passage of the Road Carriage Act in 1832. He was not to be without competition, though, for in August 1833 John Mitchell and J. Shepherd started an omnibus service between the Saracen's Head, Derby, and the George at Leicester once a day in each direction. The coming of the MCR, though, put both out of business.

The Derby omnibus service was replaced by the first horse-drawn tram from 6 March 1880, inaugurating the Derby Tramway Company's system, which was laid to the less-than-usual gauge of 4ft. This innovation had been preceded by a network of horse bus services started by F.J. Horsley three years earlier and the two greatly facilitated people's ability to get to work feeling reasonably fresh and gave impetus to the expansion of the borough. The trams gradually took over from the horse buses, except in the first instance, on the Uttoxeter and Kedleston Roads.

The development of the tramways met with much protest from the 'better sort of householder' and especially in 1881 when Sunday services began. The flat fare was at first 2d (1p), later reduced to ld (½p). By 1885 the horse buses had ceased to run and under powers vested in them under the 1878 Tramways Act, the Corporation, sensing the continual financial confusion of the tramway undertaking, took the entire concern over as of 1 November 1899.

Back in 1880 the stables and sheds were on Station Street (later Midland Road) but within about five years had migrated to a cobbled yard on the west side of the

GNR's viaduct off Friar Gate, the horses being stabled beneath the arches. The rails still remain in their original setts to this day, 102 years after the tramways were electrified on 20 July 1904 and 99 years after the last horse tram ran – along Friar Gate – on 28 November 1907. The splendid Arts-and-Crafts new offices for the undertaking were completed in Victoria Street at the same time to designs by John Ward, the borough surveyor; since 2001 they have been in use as the Post Office.

THE SURVIVAL OF SILK

The manufacturing base of the town by 1835 was remarkably wide, and the railway revolution gave it the final fillip it needed. The oldest industry was silk throwing, but a century later it was showing no sign of flagging since the end of Lombe's patents in 1732. Indeed, the railways bestowed on the silk throwsters an Indian summer. Allusion has already also been made to Taylor, Lombe's ultimate successor, Ambrose Moore, who took over the Depot on Normanton Road and also to Thomas Bridgett.

Alderman Madeley's company at Little City was another, and other firms at the dawn of the Railway Age included Thomas and Samuel Job Wright of Friar Gate Mill, which had strong trading links with Russia and was backed by their brother-in-law, banker William Baker. Robert Ward, the heir of the last proprietor of the mill erected by Pickford at 45 Friar Gate, had a mill on Full Street, later a tannery there. G.B. Unsworth had an establishment on Devonshire Street and in 1827 took over the large 18th-century Green Lane Mill from Sarah Davenport, widow of Thomas, and it flourished until 1927, the mill itself being destroyed as recently as 1980. The Davenports also took over Strutt's calico mill on Albert Street. There were several other firms active up to the 1820s, too.

Additionally there were firms weaving the silk thrown by their neighbours. Bridgett's did both, as did Ambrose Moore and many others, including the three brothers Peet (1823), later amalgamated with Ralph Frost. Samuel Fox and the Peets also made a lot of silk hose, and in 1802 Robert Longdon founded his manufactory in Agard Street – the fine mill replaced by university halls of residence in 1997 was a little later – and also pioneered elastic fabric manufacture.

A future Mayor running a silk throwing business was William Higginbottom, who built the Alexandra Mills on Dog Kennel Lane in 1863, standing until destroyed to create a 'brownfield site' on which have been erected some woeful looking apartments; the mill would have converted admirably. Charles Dould and Son were real latecomers, building the Spa Lane Mills in 1874,

switching to artificial silk in 1916, the year that Ernest Turner optimistically founded a mill in the old Phoenix Foundry. His son, Alan Turner KSG, a keen Catholic, took over in 1939 and bought out the Spa Lane Mills in 1943, adding a Catholic Chapel in which Mass was celebrated during the annual works 'feast'. With his wife Barbara, he was an enthusiastic supporter of amateur theatre and opera. He retired in 1961, after which the firm eventually was taken over and closed. Also in 1916 Courtaulds were setting up in Spondon the massive works that were later to blossom into British Celanese and which eventually came to dominate the artificial silk and fabric market. This concern is now called Accordis.

Alderman Albert Green, a kinsman of Turner, served as Tory MP for Derby in 1918–1922, having previously been mayor. He was a silk fabric and trimming manufacturer on Pear Tree Road in succession to his father, Joseph. Later, in 1910, he also acquired a narrow tapes mill on Agard Street, which he converted to silk fabric manufacture, but this burnt out on 26 April 1925 and effectively ended this business for the Greens; they reverted to narrow tapes. The Agard Street mill miraculously survived until 2006. Yet the calamity was timely in many ways, for the industry in Derby was fast retreating in the face of French competition and the expansion of Courtauld's at Spondon making *ersatz* fabrics; the writing had been on the wall for the Derby silk trade for some time by the 1920s.

FABRIC MANUFACTURING

A worsted mill near St Werburgh's had been long in operation by 1828 and other fabric firms appeared, notably the serge cloth manufacturers like James Smith of Drewry Lane, founded in 1856 and closed in 1987. Smiths were in the event most famous as clothing manufacturers, especially uniforms, kitting out the personnel of the MR, the police and armed forces for generations. They also had several other factories over the years and only closed in the 1980s, when most of their factory was, indeed, converted into houses and apartments by a developer more enlightened than most.

The chief fabric industry in Derby, however, was that of narrow tapes, fabrics and webbing, an industry which, indeed, still lingers on. The first firm in the borough would appear to have been that of Messrs Riley, Madeley, Hackett & Company, founded in 1806, in their mill between Kensington and Talbot Streets, but, like Bridgett and the Peets, it made silk-based narrow fabrics. Often silk manufacturers switched from silk fabrics to narrow tapes, using the same premises; indeed, the Peet's, Bridgett's and Longdon's were examples. On Siddals Road a large narrow tapes mill was erected in 1854, alongside a large cheese warehouse right on the edge of the Derby Canal, by T. Mitchell & Company. This ended its time in 1983, grimed in furious yellow hues, having been for many years an ICI-owned dye works making paint for use on the roads to restrict parking.

Narrow tapes manufacturer Joseph Bonas was also one of the coterie established along the leafy thoroughfare of the Uttoxeter New Road. His family were in the fabric trade in Fazely, Staffordshire, but became insolvent, the young Joseph deciding to start afresh in Derby. By 1883 he had become prosperous through his mill on Lynton Street in the St Luke's district. A firm later interlinked with Bonas's was that of the Lilleys, who later fragmented into three separate concerns, operating from mills in Agard Street, Boyer Street, Parliament Street and Olive Street, the latter being helpfully dated 1900. The Bath Street mill – still a very impressive building – was founded earlier than some, in 1848, as a silk mill by Alderman George Holme (1813–1896) and extended considerably to a total of 32 bays in 1868 supported by two engine houses and extensive weaving sheds. By 1857 he was making elastic web, and gussets, a diversification which saved the business when the Cobden-Chevalier Treaty of 1860 removed the protective tariffs on silk, throwing the industry into sharp decline. The firm survived until after World War One by rapid diversification. The mill survives, firmly within the World Heritage site, which may protect it.

The Markeaton Mills, again on the brook, were the headquarters of G.H. Wheatcroft & Company. George Hanson Wheatcroft was unusual in having no other connections with Derby, being the head of an upwardly mobile Wirksworth family who had the Haarlem Mill in that town and several sons too. This site was cheek-by-jowl with one of the later firms, Moore, Eady & Murcott Goode, who built the stylish Britannia Mills on Markeaton Street on the site of the ancient Nuns' Mill, in 1912, to make fine knitwear, something for which Derby had not previously been particularly famous. The firm lasted until the 1970s before inexpensive imports rendered it unviable. Happily, the mill building itself has been adapted for academic use by the university, the only loss being the epically-proportioned statue of Britannia which used to grace the top of the domed entrance portico, last seen in the company's yard at Leicester in the 1980s.

THE SILK TRADES' LOCK-OUT

It was in the fabric industry, specifically the silk trade, that one of the most notable events in the rise of the trade unions took place in Derby. This was the Silk Trades' Lock-out of 1833. In fact, it seems not to have been the first strike in the Derby silk mills, as one James Boultbee was arraigned before the assizes for organising what was called the 'Silk Gate Strike' at Derby in 1812, but its causes and course are quite obscure.

The context for this lamentable confrontation was partly the repeal in 1825 of the Combination Acts, which forbade the formation of trade unions, and partly an economic recession, which encouraged the less enlightened employers to freeze or more often reduce the remuneration of their employees. In a sense, the coming of the railways a few years later was doubly beneficial, for it had the immediate effect of pulling Derby sharply out of recession and encouraging new investment, as it turned out, on a vast scale. In 1833 and under the influence of one or two rather mischievous demagogues, it was a widely held belief among the silk workers of Derby that to combine into a trade union would have the immediate effect of browbeating the employers into granting an increase in wages. In November 1833 some 800 such men were supposed to have joined, when Ralph Frost, of Peet and Frost, Bridge Street, silk-hose manufacturer, fined a workman for bad workmanship, a reasonable practice in its day, introduced to maintain quality.

> 'Whereupon,' writes Walthall, 'the whole of his hands ceased working and declared they would work no more till this man was employed again by Mr Frost. The reason they gave for this proceeding was that the man Mr Frost discharged made good work and that the true reason was his having joined the Union.'

Less reasonable, but no doubt understandable from Frost's point of view, if not that of his men.

Thereafter, some 20 proprietors met and decided to stop the rot at the outset and lock out their men after a certain date if they did not foreswear the union. The workforce declined the offer or just stayed away and a lengthy and antagonistic confrontation ensued with workers brought in from elsewhere in some numbers – called 'black sheep' rather than the later blacklegs – leading to violent clashes, including a trial for murder in which John Whitehurst's young great-nephew Charles Howard Whitehurst (1796–1879) appeared successfully for the defence.

Although workmen from other mills joined in and members of various other trades to some extent too, the strike was by no means universal, although accounts like Davison's suggest it was. Nor is there any evidence directly connecting Taylor's workforce at the Old Silk Mill with the lock-out. Moreover, Taylor was not a signatory of Ralph Frost's Declaration of Twenty, which started the trouble. The curious annual ceremony, still kept in the city but lately turned into something of a political circus, of laying a wreath on the pier of Bakewell's gates to Lombe's Silk Mill, is thus a little misplaced and should strictly speaking be laid at the entrance to the former Brook Street mill (Peet & Frost's having long vanished) because at least Thomas Bridgett was a signatory of the Declaration.

The strike, in fact, collapsed on 21 April 1834, when a large number of the strikers were reinstated, although, nearly 600 were left, bereft of employment.

Strangely, little of this unrest permeated to the more *elite* workforce of the foundries, the colour works or the tanneries. Indeed, this might occasion surprise in view of the fact that Ralph Frost of lock-out fame also owned a plaster mill, the only rival of Brookhouse's on the Morledge.

PAINT & VARNISH MAKING

The paint-making or colour-grinding industry was started before 1800 by Joseph Mason at the old mill on Markeaton Brook. The firm greatly expanded under his son Edmund Cartwright Mason (1817–1881), in face of competition from Benjamin Challinor (1819), Ratcliffe and Nutt (1827), Robert Jones (1830), Robert Pegg (1835) and William Ellam. In 1869 Mason's opened a works on Burton Road marked by a Moorish chimney designed by Edwin Thompson (1801–1883) called Mount Carmel Tower, a delightful conceit that was demolished in 1962 to make way for a motor garage.

Robert Pegg was based beside Brookhouse's cement works in the Morledge, going into partnership with an uncle of borough surveyor Samuel Harpur, eventually becoming Pegg and Ellam Jones. Pegg, who also produced gypsum and plaster, initially on Uttoxeter Old Road, served as mayor in 1855. He is another striking example of social mobility, having been born in Melbourne of a poor family in 1801, fourth son of John Pegg of that town. The latter's great-grandfather had gone there from Yeldersley *c.*1700, being a descendant of Humphrey Pegge (*sic*) of a gentry family with an estate at Osmaston. Humphrey's ancestor in 1520, however, was just a simple yeoman farmer at Shirley – a positive switch-back of changing circumstances.

Pegg was a generous supporter of the Baptists, the faith of his immediate forebears in Melbourne – and was the chief subscriber to T.C. Hine's new chapel on Osmaston Road, built in 1862 but demolished in 1969. Hine also built Pegg's house, almost alongside, at the same time. Appropriately named Melbourne House, it is one of the best and most pleasing of the high Gothic domestic buildings in Derby; the interior contains much ornamental work in local alabaster from Hall's

workshop in King Street. It was later home to Richard Mountford Deeley, later the Locomotive Superintendent of the MR and perfector of the fine 'Midland Compounds'.

The most ambitious paint firm in Derby was that of Alderman Charles Leech, mayor in 1885, which, by the 20th century, had a very large works in Spondon called Leech, Neal & Company.

CARRIAGE BUILDING

Other long-established industries related to the traditional Gentry-and-Trade aspect of the town which, it must be remembered, still maintained itself, despite the ever-growing industrialisation of the borough. Derby was the home, for instance, of a nationally-renowned firm of coachbuilders. This was Messrs Holmes, later Sanderson and Holmes, who enjoyed Queen Victoria's Royal Warrant and on which company's Derby works the sovereign herself bestowed a visit in September 1852.

The firm was set up in 1795 by Charles Holmes (b.1735), a Lichfield man, on London Road. By the time of the Queen's visit in 1852 the works, set around a courtyard, were closed off from the road by a stylish screen. At Calke Abbey a full set of high-quality vehicles made by the firm still exist, and when the house was being restored all the bills from Holmes were discovered. Interestingly, Arthur E. Holmes, grandson of the founder, was a leading campaigner against the Derby tramways in 1877, doubtless seeing it as a threat to the profusion of private transport to the detriment of his business. His brother, Herbert Mountford Holmes (d.1893), ran their London showrooms.

In the 20th century, Holmes's firm took to building

The equipage of Dr R.W. Innes-Smith of Don House, Sheffield; the vehicle was supplied by Holmes & Co. of Derby *c.*1898. (Robert Innes-Smith)

The later London Road premises of Holmes & Co., carriage builders to Her Majesty, seen here in 1908. The pedimented portion survives as an amusement arcade. (M. Craven)

car bodies and merged with F.G. Sanderson & Sons of Midland Road. They were taken over by Mann Egerton in the 1970s, becoming little more than prestige automobile concessionaires until vanishing from the scene completely. Yet the tradition, represented by 13 firms or individual craftsmen in 1898, still lives on in the shape of the specialist car body builders and restorers I. Wilkinson and Sons Ltd of Stafford Street.

TANNING AND FLOUR MILLING

If specialist coachbuilding is a reminder of the heyday of Derby as a town of gentry, so such flourishing industries as tanning – which continued (latterly on Sinfin Lane) with the very old firm of Richardson – and corn milling are reminders that Derby is yet a market town.

William Richardson (1803–1871) set up in St Peter's Street, Derby, in 1824, being later joined by his brother John (1805–1873), but the family had been tanners and curriers in Chaddesden from 1749 and Horsley Woodhouse from the 1770s. The Derby branch produced W.H. Richardson, the last owner of Abbott's Hill, the Baroque mansion on Babington Lane built c.1710 by Simon Degge, who saved much panelling from that fine house and a chimney piece from Babington Hall and installed them in The Leylands in 1926. One of

his sons, the late Arthur Richardson, was an eminent cricketer, captaining Derbyshire to their County Championship title in 1936; another was a memorable Archdeacon of Derby from 1952 to 1973.

Of the corn millers, the Sowters were pre-eminent in the early 19th century, living in Friar Gate and building an elegant Regency stuccoed mill and warehouse in Curzon Street by 1819, with three courts of workers' cottages behind called Sowter Square. The cottages were cleared as unfit in 1935, but the mill, with its York sashes, was demolished in 1990 at the behest of a Government agency despite a spirited defence by the then Chairman of Planning Cllr Robin Wood (also secretary of the Civic Society).

MALTING AND BREWING

The Sowters were originally bakers and went on to be corn millers and also maltsters. Malting and brewing – another traditional industry – then still flourishing in the town, doing so decreasingly right up until 1965 when Offiler's, the last such firm, was taken over by Bass: the last triumph of the *arriviste* brewing industry of Burton-upon-Trent over the long-established trade in Derby. The Wheeldon family, like the Sowters, made the same leap in 1820 when Joseph Wheeldon, son of a Derby canal promoter, purchased the Alvaston Hall estate. His elder son, Parker, was famous only as an owner at Derby races, the grandson, S.P. Wheeldon, achieving fame as a notable author on angling. The latter's cousins, three brothers (and nephews of William Billingsley's kinsman, Thomas, the china factory co-owner) were respectively corn miller, corn factor and maltster; the latter was Alderman George Wheeldon, mayor in 1873.

The link in this industry from the 18th to the 20th century lay in the Lowe family, who founded the Wardwick brewery in 1788. Several members served as mayor of Derby, Revd Henry Lowe (mayor in 1812, 1821) being, with Revd Charles Stead Hope (mayor a staggering five times, in 1797, 1805, 1816, 1825 and 1830), one of only two men to be both mayor and parson. Charles, the Revd Henry's brother, was also mayor (in 1831) and sold the firm, long based in Allsopp's town house in the Wardwick, where he built a large brewery in what had been the garden, to Moreton Charles Wedge in 1837. William Alton took it over in 1869 and expanded rapidly in 1874, enlarging the brewery (see page 123) . Early in the 1920s this firm sold out to Stretton's Manchester Brewery – in fact a long-standing Derby firm founded in 1835 by Mancunian John Porter – which had built maltings on a grand scale just off Ashbourne Road in Surrey Street in 1869–70 – and the entire outfit was taken over in 1931 by the Burton firm of Ind Coope and Allsopp. There were several other firms in the first half of the 19th century, including that of Alderman Clarke (who shut down the China factory) of the Derby Brewery and the Wheeldons. Several were gathered along the Ashbourne Road. Most were taken over by Stretton's.

In the 1800s a newcomer on the scene was Robert Foreman, a scion of an old Chellaston yeoman family. He founded a malting on Curzon Street – renamed from Dayson Lane on turnpiking in 1825 – which survives, as does the line of once pleasing workers' cottages opposite, built in the 1880s but now marred by inappropriate uPVC fenestration. It must be confessed that the Offiler family were hardly in the same league in the 19th century, George Offiler (1837–1899) coming from Nottingham to start as landlord of the Vine, Whitaker Street, in 1875, selling the surplus from his brewery behind the pub from 1877; by 1881 he employed all of three men. Yet his success then was remarkable, for in 1884 he bought the old Ordnance Depot on Normanton Road from the Star Tea Company and rebuilt it to the designs of William Bradford into a brewery on the tower system, which produced 509,000 gallons of ale by 1890 when Offiler's owned 40 pubs in the region. The firm was the last of a very long line in the borough when taken over in 1965.

INSTRUMENT MAKING

Whitehurst had expressed an aspect of his particular genius in his series of angle barometers bearing his unique scale. He also perfected a very fine type of wheel barometer bearing it. On his death in February 1788, his successors continued to make these, but in the case of the former, without the 0–60 scale and in the case of the latter in a more conventional form. Furthermore, his former apprentice, John Stenson, an eccentric and apparently loveable character, made similar instruments, but also much less expensive examples including a very simple stick barometer with a paper scale.

In 1806 a north Italian migrant, Samuele Bregazzi (1782–1841), settled in Derby as a carver and gilder, usually – and in his case invariable – a formal description for a barometer maker. His first instruments closely resembled Stenson's cheaper items, but he proved to be the first in an extensive dynasty at Derby and elsewhere, making instruments of the first quality and occasionally collaborating with the Whitehursts.

Also in the tradition of the experimental genius of the first John Whitehurst is the important firm of John Davis and Company. After a modest start in Iron Gate, they moved to the east end of Amen Alley; later, the firm moved to the fringes of the city. Historically, they made mining implements like dials, anemometers, microscopes, barometers and similar instruments for both domestic and industrial use – even simple tools like spirit levels. In 1913 the family funded the adaptation of the Ruskinian Gothic villa (built on Burton Road by the artist and designer Thomas Simmonds ARCA in 1879) called Ravenshoe into Derby's first synagogue for some 656 years, with help from Selig Bressloff and the Levy family. The Davis firm, much taken over, still flourishes in Derby.

IRON FOUNDING

The railway benefitted these traditional industries; moreover, by beginning to make the most of its own equipment in Derby, it gave a powerful incentive to new industries, especially those supplying components. Yet the Midland Railway, as we have seen, was by no means the first organisation to establish foundries. When the Midland set up their first one, Derby already had 11. Heavy industry had begun with Evans' rolling, slitting and battering mills with machinery driven by the flow of the Derwent, but that was an exception.

Before 1800 there was a single iron foundry, that of Thomas Wheeldon (1760–1829) in St Peter's Street. This concern moved to the Derwent Iron Works, by the river, in March 1810, but Wheeldon himself was made bankrupt over an unrelated matter in May 1817, and the foundry was rescued by his son-in-law, a former nailor called William Gibson, who was still running it in 1833.

Another important early foundry was that set up in Bridge Gate by John Harrison, whose initial announcement that he was manufacturing 'steam engines, steam kitchen and every other description of wrought-iron boilers… brewing and bleaching pans, press plates and other vessels or utensils…' appeared in the *Mercury* on 6 March 1822. The reference to steam kitchens is an allusion to Harrison's collaboration with William Strutt in his domestic improvements, and he went on to pioneer ranges, grates, stoves, heating systems and the like, developing an extensive country house practice. Harrison built Chester House, an elegant small Regency villa later subsumed within Daniel's chemical works at Little Chester and destroyed by a developer in 2002. His firm later passed to the Whalleys.

ANDREW HANDYSIDE

The architectural founders, Weatherhead, Glover & Company of Duke Street, had begun as ironmongers in Iron Gate in 1734. Present day Bennetts represent the continuity of the retail side of the business, Robert Bennett having married the sister of Samuel Weatherhead. They were on the scene by 1815 as founders, their Britannia Foundry set up by 1817 and released by William Strutt to aid the town's expansion. Samuel Weatherhead used capital from William Baker of the Derby & Derbyshire Bank (grandson of banker William Chase) to fund his operation, but a downturn in trade around 1830 forced a takeover by Barber & Marshall of Walsall, and by 1842 it was owned by Baker's brother-in-law Thomas John Wright.

Wright, primarily a silk throwster with a base at St Petersburg, recruited a young Scot there, Andrew Handyside (1805–1887). He was working with two of his brothers in his uncle's Charles Baird's foundry. He came to Derby with his Russian wife and bought the Britannia foundry in spring 1847, probably capitalised by Baker and Wright. Handyside, first of several Scots foundrymen in Derby, was later an alderman.

Handyside also made, from 1853, a notable series of pillar boxes for the GPO, starting with an octagonal one costing 11s (55p) and cylindrical ones from 1878 to 1904 (although the firm continued to make oval double aperture boxes for London after that date) and from 1930. Many survive, including in far-flung former colonies, although the only Derby examples are a Victorian one in Hartington Street and a small early Edward VII example in Bishop's Drive, Oakwood –

Handyside & Co. 'rustic' seat, originally commissioned for Midland Railway Stations and domestic use, available in single or double form. This one has been restored by the Great Central Railway, Loughborough, photographed in 2004. (M. Craven)

oddly a 1980s thoroughfare! They also made garden urns, municipal fountains and soon branched out into bridges and railway engineering as well. The quality of his work is epitomised by the GNR bridge over Friar Gate, and the same railway's bridge over the Derwent is a fine example of the firm's more workaday engineering, both dating from 1876 and both now listed buildings. They also made Royce's works at Manchester, the Rolls-Royce factory at Derby (1907–11) and the station roofs at Manchester Central (1880) Nottingham Midland (1903) and Charing Cross (1905). The firm also had a close relationship with the Butterley Company through its existence.

On Handyside's death, Alexander Buchanan (1829–1912), his nephew, took over, but after his retirement in 1910 the firm became insolvent no less than three times, finally going under in 1932, despite the GPO contract for wall letter boxes. It limped on until 1934 as Derby Castings Ltd., when a variant of the wall post box was developed with an attached stamp vending

1852 advertisement for Handyside's Britannia foundry – before their move to heavy engineering.

BRITANNIA FOUNDRY,

DERBY.

ANDREW HANDYSIDE,

ENGINEER AND IRON FOUNDER,

RAILWAY WORK OF EVERY DESCRIPTION.

WATER CRANES,

WHEELS, COAL TRUCKS, &c.

CASTINGS, PLAIN AND ORNAMENTAL.

An extensive assortment of Patterns in

WINDOWS, COLUMNS, GIRDERS, PALISADING, &c.

machine. The famous Britannia Works was replaced in 1934 by two modest rows of municipal housing: Handyside and Buchanan Streets.

The 1820s also saw the emergence of some more, smaller foundries. In 1834 James Haywood, of another long-established firm of ironmongers, started the Phoenix Foundry on Stuart Street. Like Handyside, he made bridges, but is perhaps better known for stoves, grates and ranges, which were sold through the ironmongery shop of J. and G. Haywood, Iron Gate. Haywood himself became mayor in 1849 and among his descendants was Captain Henry Mansfield Haywood, the borough's Chief Constable from 1898 to 1926. Although the foundry made the spectacular roof of the 1864 Market Hall, it was the shop, in the event, that outlived the foundry, which closed before the end of the 19th century. Haywoods's shop front was notable for having a full-height, cast-iron façade, made by themselves at a cost of £900, but to the design of distinguished London architect Owen Jones (1809–1874). It most unfortunately failed to survive the demolition of the premises in 1924.

Brass founding on a small scale had been a flourishing Derby trade since the 17th century. In 1844 large-scale brass founding, mainly associated with the railway, was established by George Smith at an address in Nuns' Street, moving under the tutelage of the son, John, to King Street in 1862. Much later the firm moved to Cotton Lane where it could better serve the railway.

In 1849 John Jobson (1819–1889) established an iron foundry in Litchurch Lane, again conveniently near the railway. His was a Sheffield grate manufacturer and kinsmen were coal-owners with interests in South Yorkshire and East Derbyshire. He, too, moved on to Cotton Lane, cheek-by-jowl with Sir John ('Brassy') Smith, and at first specialised in domestic grates. His takeover of the Derwent Foundry therefore was logical in terms of product compatibility, and in 1929 Jobson's moved to Victory Road (pitched, as one might expect,

Jobson's Qualcast foundry, glimpsed from between two council houses, in 1950. (M. Craven)

in 1918–19) expanding further along the railway line. The firm was more recently famous as Qualcast, specialising, from between the wars, in lawnmowers and the like, as well as motor-car engine castings. Qualcast later became part of a much larger conglomerate, BirmidQualcast. Their change of direction (diversification it would be called today) was almost certainly under the influence of the casting requirements of nearby Rolls-Royce in their earlier phase. They ended up as QDF and went into liquidation in 2005.

If Handyside was an early industrialist come to Derby from Scotland, then he was soon joined by others. In 1851 the Glasgow-born Robert Russell (1819–1901) came to Derby from Falkirk and joined local man Henry Fowke in setting up a foundry on Meadow Road bearing the name of Prime Minister Sir Robert Peel. Again, ranges and suchlike were the staple products and Russell rose to be Derby's first Scottish-born mayor, serving in 1882. The family (Russell had six sons) were later allied to the lace-making Fletchers and the Whitakers, accountants, and the firm survived through three generations.

The next foundry set up was that of Eastwood and Frost in 1852, less than a year after the Midland Railway had begun to make their own locomotives at Derby. The site chosen was 25–27 The Morledge, a street already crowded with Roman Cement, colour-grinding, copper and silk works, an uncomfortable situation which encouraged a swift move to Cotton Lane, rapidly becoming 'Foundries' Row'. James ('Handsome Jim') Eastwood (1808–1874) was of a Wirksworth family but had previously run a founding operation in Toxteth, Liverpool. Thomas Frost, however, was a second-generation Little Chester millwright and founder, but within 18 months had died, leaving Eastwood entirely dominant, despite leaving two sons. Thereupon, Eastwood re-established the firm in Osmaston Road as the Railway Iron Works, his main product being railway wheels. His son Levi's refusal to halt 24-hour production, combined with the noise of his steam hammers, drove Samuel Fox from his tenancy of nearby Osmaston Hall in 1886.

Meanwhile Frost's son John William (1832–1893), cast adrift by Eastwood, joined Leicester man Thomas Swingler (1819–1873) to make axles for railway wheels. Again, Frost does not appear for long, for Swingler set up the Victoria Foundry close to Eastwood's new emporium within a year or so, making specialist permanent-way equipment. This foundry closed in 1925 and was later (1932) adapted as a trolley-bus garage and still stands. Inevitably, by 1864 the two concerns had amalgamated as Eastwood & Swingler, James Eastwood's daughter Sarah marrying Swingler's son Henry. Eastwood's younger son, Rueben, at about

Ley's Foundry, Colombo Street, seen in the 1970s, not long before closure. (*Derby Evening Telegraph*)

the same time married a sister of Sir Thomas (later Lord) Roe, thus cementing an interesting and complex series of alliances. Four generations of both families remained associated with Eastwood & Swingler until it went into liquidation in 1925, Rolls-Royce taking over the foundry.

This was a great period for the establishment of foundries, for contemporary with the separate foundation of Eastwood's and Swingler's was that of William Abell, a member of an old Derby family, whose father had settled in Duffield. The firm, established in Brook Street and which closed in 1961, specialised in castings for silk manufacturing machinery, but is best remembered for their handsome cast-iron bollards topped by strapwork globes. Examples survive along City Road by Chester Green, at the top of Silk Mill Lane, in Friar Gate and in one or two other locations. The family were doubly allied by marriage with silk manufacturer William Higginbottom.

In 1860 George Fletcher came from 22 years of small-scale ironfounding in Southwark, and established the Masson Foundry, Litchurch Lane. This firm, whose founder had been an apprentice of George Stephenson, the railway pioneer, and had travelled in the Americas, produced, inevitably, steam engines and, as a contrast, sugar-refining machinery. One of their 'Grasshopper' steam engines survives in Derby Industrial Museum. In

1956 the firm was purchased by Booker McConnel and eight years later merged with Stewart's of Glasgow (another Booker McConnel firm), becoming Fletcher and Stewart. The original foundry was subject to a management buy-out in 1983, continuing as Atlas Works (Derby) Limited for another decade or so.

Less than a year after George Fletcher's arrival, Henry Fowkes (1818–1885), having broken away from Robert Russell, founded the Wellington Foundry on Osmaston Road in 1861, also making stoves. He, like Russell, served as mayor of Derby in 1884–85, dying in office in August the year following, allowing the *Derbyshire Advertiser* founder William Hobson a second, suffect, term of office; his eldest son succeeded to the firm, but it was gone by 1926.

Of the several smaller firms, in 1868 George Henry and Alfred Brown started the Nelson foundry in Stockbrook Street, making a variety of domestic and architectural castings, including the inevitable stoves and ranges. It is worth bearing in mind that with so rapid an expansion of the population of Derby, as with many other towns, the insatiable demand for such items left room for plenty of competition without too many casualties. Brown's closed two years before Abell's in 1959. A similar firm was that of Parker (also producing castings in steel) established on Siddals Road and latterly at Little Chester until its closure in the 1980s.

The surviving element of Ley's enterprises, Ewant Chain Belt Factory, Shaftesbury Street, 2005. (M. Craven)

Finally, in 1874, Francis Ley established his malleable castings foundry on Osmaston Road beside the old B&DJR main line. The Leys, in contrast to most foundry dynasties, were an old family from Mayfield, Staffordshire, going back to the 16th century. Francis Ley himself, born at Winshill in 1846, eschewed living cheek-by-jowl with his works in Derby or any part of civic life and settled at Epperstone Manor, Nottinghamshire. His change of calling from minor gentry to foundryman occurred at 15, when he decided to train as a draughtsman with Andrew Handyside, leaving at 28 to set up on his own.

The firm was registered in 1883 and became a private limited company in February 1897. Ley himself had been sufficiently attuned to future trends to follow Fletcher in visiting the US and eventually obtained the rights to the manufacture under licence of the Ewart Chain Belt. By his second marriage, to a daughter of John Jobson (who had settled in Spondon), he cemented an alliance between two of the foundry families whose concerns were to be in the long term the most enduring. Uniquely, among this coterie, Francis Ley was elevated to a baronetcy in 1905, which honour his posterity still enjoy. Ley's, too, like Qualcast, and also with the incentive of Rolls-Royce, expanded into supplying the motor-car industry. The main foundry closed after a takeover in 1986 and has since been demolished for factory units; Ewart's survives, however.

HASLAM'S

More refined products of forge and foundry emerged as more than just castings. The requirement for a finished product which included castings led to the establishment of more *elite* companies, supplying a variety of products. In a sense the manufacture of locomotives by the Midland Railway epitomised this, but they did not supply a product for anything other than their own use,

except for use on various joint lines in which they had an interest, like the Somerset and Dorset, the Midland and Great Northern and in Ireland. The firm of John and James Fox, already mentioned, had been the first such, with a distinguished history stretching back to 1783. It was ultimately taken over by Haslam's in 1870.

Haslam's Union Foundry, in City Road, Little Chester, started life by the founder receiving a letter from his father on 19 May 1868 pointing out that Fox's firm was on the market and that it '...would be a good opening for anyone who thoroughly understands the business.' With his father as partner, Alfred Haslam (1844–1927) started in business as Haslam & Co., with extra finance from a relative, Joseph Smith of Lullington. All loans had been paid off by 1871, and in 1876 the firm was registered as the Haslam Foundry & Engineering Company with a nominal capital of £100,000.

Haslam was not so much an innovator as a gifted exploiter of others' innovations added to commercial acumen of a high order. It was about the time of incorporation that he suddenly changed from heavy engineering and boiler making to participate in a race to develop the first commercial dry-air refrigeration plant to be put into ships to enable the importation of frozen meat from the Empire or South America, although this development was seen by the equally newly-fledged canning industry as a direct threat. He collaborated with two London firms and took both over, and by 1881 he had installed his first plant in the SS *Cuzco* of the Orient Line on the Australia run, beating French rivals by a whisker. *Cuzco* was able to bring 17,000 lamb carcases back and the firm enjoyed a virtual monopoly until 1894. Haslams also supplied many land-based institutions with refrigeration plants, like docks, asylums, hospitals, barracks and hotels. The works, which were continually expanding into the Edwardian era, were powered by three steam engines and in 1891 employed 650 hands, nearly all of whom were housed in Little Chester, which Haslam transformed into a company fiefdom. The works themselves were shielded from City Road by a blind arcaded wall, which eventually ran to 44 bays.

Haslam himself, unlike Ley, did not eschew municipal involvement; rather, he revelled in it. Alfred Haslam, the firm's founder, was fourth son of William, a whitesmith and bell hanger of St Peter's Street, who sprang from a line of Duffield farmers. William was a long-serving Derby councillor, as were three of his sons, including Alfred. William Gilbert Haslam, the fifth son, was associated with yet another foundry, Peach's Union Foundry, also on City Road and, like Fox's, soon to be gobbled up by Alfred's firm. The third brother, Edwin Haslam, succeeded to his father's business, and it is worth remembering that Haslam *pere* had revived the

Sir Alfred Haslam is knighted by Queen Victoria on platform one of Derby station at the conclusion of her state visit to Derby, 21 May 1891.

craft of ornamental wrought-ironwork in Derby, more or less extinct since the death of Benjamin and William Yates. Edwin continued the trade in the workshop in St Helen's Street, right next door to the Marble Works, using a shop in Iron Gate as a showroom.

Alfred served as MP for Derby, mayor in 1890–91 and as mayor of Newcastle-under-Lyme in 1901–04. His Derby mayoralty coincided with Queen Victoria's state visit to lay the foundation stone of the Derbyshire Royal Infirmary in 1891, and he spent lavishly out of his own pocket to make a virtual festival of the visit, during which he had the great gratification to be knighted on platform one of Derby Station by his Sovereign. The foundry was taken over on Sir Alfred's death in 1927 by

Edwin Haslam posing by an example of his work at his forge in St Helen's Street. (The late Mrs P. Haslam)

Newton Brothers, then from 1939 by E.W. Bliss (UK) Ltd., a US firm, which specialised in the manufacture of the very tin cans which Haslam's inventiveness hoped to eliminate! They also made hydraulic presses, but the works, as Aida Bliss, and now in the World Heritage Site, closed in 2004.

LATER ENGINEERING FIRMS

The firm which took Haslam's over in 1928 was among the earliest electrical engineering firms in Derby, having been founded in 1899, and changed its name to Newton Brothers (Derby) Limited in 1935. They started by making such things as presses but graduated to generating equipment and eventually to specialised lightweight equipment such as that used in aviation.

Another early electrical engineering firm was that of Crompton, founded in London in 1892 by Colonel R.E.B. Crompton CB, FRS, a descendant of Derby banker Samuel Crompton II, with collaboration from his second cousin, George Crompton of Stanton-by-Dale Hall, then proprietor of Stanton Ironworks. They became Crompton-Parkinson in 1927 with a works on Mansfield Road not far from Newton Brothers. George Crompton's house, Stanton Hall, was the first country house to be lit by electricity in the county, from 1892.

Two important engineering firms were brought to the town in 1907 by virtue of a committee set up by the Derby Chamber of Commerce (founded in 1864). One was Aiton's, a specialist pipe works founded in Willesden in 1900 by Scotsman Sir John Arthur Aiton CBE (1864–1950), son of a civil engineer whose career had flourished in India. They came to Derby in 1907 and latterly made water distillation plants, steel pipes and the like and flourished until the late 20th century, when taken over and closed down by a rival. Their rather stylish *Moderne* HQ on Stores Road was designed by Sir John's daughter, Norah, with Betty Scott and was listed Grade II quite recently. Between the wars the firm pioneered such forward-looking developments as workers' welfare schemes, sick pay, company pensions, works committees, social and sporting facilities, the physical welfare aspects being inspired by the Bodens at their lace mill.

ROLLS-ROYCE

The other company represents the last manifestation of the sort of luxury industry upon which Derby's 18th-century prosperity was founded. It dealt at first with an exclusive product made with considerable crafts-manship. Over 32 years that element changed and

A Rolls-Royce Silver Ghost, 1920s, at a Rally at Calke Abbey in 2001. (M. Cravern)

vanished, but what it left behind was to be of immense historic, international and economic importance. The firm was Rolls-Royce, and the luxury product was motor cars – the best in the world.

The firm also started as electrical engineers under Henry Royce in Manchester and had been making motor cars for only three years when it was decided to move somewhere with room for expansion, in order to mount production of the new 40/50hp car, later known as the Silver Ghost. Royce was an engineering perfectionist, working, like Whitehurst before him, to much finer tolerances than his contemporaries. Factors which decided them included relatively cheap land (formerly

part of Osmaston Park), wages up to 3s per week lower than Manchester, the proximity of raw materials and the plethora of established companies – foundries in particular – able to supply components.

Despite the lower local wages, once established Rolls-Royce (known universally in Derby as 'Royce's') paid at Manchester rates in order to attract labour from elsewhere. They were, in 1907, looking to make a modest 200 cars a year, and Henry Royce commissioned Handysides to build the factory to his own design. The 1.5 acres of buildings were complete by September 1907, and the works opened on 9 July 1908. A new street, Nightingale Road, was pitched from Osmaston Road past the works, which are still in use but scheduled for closure in 2007. The fate of the more historic elements on the unlisted site – No. 1 shop of 1907 and the administration block of 1910–12 – are very much in doubt at the time of writing.

Hon. Charles Rolls, a son of Monmouthshire peer Lord Llangattock, was the marketing genius of the firm, a pioneer aviator and, indeed, believed fervently that Royce should actively consider the production of an aero-engine, then a very imperfect tool. When his young partner died in an aviation accident at Bournemouth in July 1910, however, this idea was firmly put on the back burner by Royce, especially as he had then some local competition.

Rolls-Royce works, Nightingale Road, built by Handysides in 1911–12, centre section, 1938. © Peter Billson

Rolls-Royce works, Nightingale Road, No. 1 shop, c.1911. Silver Ghosts under construction. (Olga Fraser)

This was from the Alvaston Motor Company of 1044 London Road which, by the time Charles Rolls had been killed at Bournemouth in the July, was offering 30hp petrol 2 opposed-cylinder engines, later also offering 20hp (£65) and 40hp (£120) models. Indeed, in an advertisement in *Flight* of April that year the firm was confidently calling itself 'Alvaston Flight Motors' [AFM] and was thus Derby's first aero-engine manufacturer, whatever they may say down at Royce's! They were also agents for the Aeroplane Supply Company of Piccadilly, London – telephone number, Alvaston 1. In 1910–11 no less than five experimental aircraft flew fitted with Alvaston engines. The Littleover aerial works, also advertised in *Flight* at this period, is, however, an enigma. AFM soon reverted to being general motor engineers and as such survived until the Depression.

On the outbreak of World War One, however, Royce's genius for perfection was again turned to the problem and the production of his first fruits, the *Eagle*, soon took priority over cars, and was followed by the Kestrel and Falcon. Nevertheless, well controlled expansion into the Sinfin area of the town from the 1920s, in succession to the maximum that could be achieved around Nightingale Road – somewhat hemmed in by associated municipal housing – enabled the ever more powerful series of aero-engines to be produced alongside the continuing perfection of the cars.

The end of the Silver Ghost series in 1925 was followed by three successive developments of its successor, the superb Phantom, along with the smaller 20/25 and 25/30hp models. Even before World War One the Rolls (never a 'Roller' – far too Arthur Daley) was being acknowledged as one of the best cars in the world. Post-war, with fewer rivals, the accolade was rarely disputed. Furthermore, in 1931 the company took over their old rivals, Bentley, and developed the Rolls-Bentley 3½ and 4¼ litre 'silent sports cars'.

The aero-engine facility benefitted from continuing inspired development, especially over the very advanced 'R' engine, which powered the 1931 Supermarine SB6 floatplane, which won the Schneider Trophy outright for Britain. This was the basis for the Merlin engine, which is generally agreed to have been a vital ingredient in Britain's air superiority in World War Two, powering such immortal aircraft as the Supermarine Spitfire (itself developed from the S6B), Hawker Hurricane, Avro Lancaster and De Havilland Mosquito. Further, the more powerful Griffon was developed from the *Merlin* during the war and development of the governmentally ill-treated Sir Frank Whittle's pioneering jet engines was taken under the wing of Sir Ernest (later 1st Lord) Hives, Royce's successor, and his team.

Royce himself only briefly lived near the town – at Quarndon – having suffered a major health breakdown

Hon. Charles Rolls – statue unveiling at Monmouth, 1911. (M. Craven)

in 1912 from which he never really recovered. He died a baronet but without an heir to his title in 1933, being commemorated by a somewhat bland statue by F. Derwent Wood RA, since 1988 outside the Sinfin headquarters building of Rolls-Royce.

With the incentive of war, leading to a rapidity of development which would have been quite inconceivable in peacetime, it became clear that if car production was to be resumed after 1945, it would have to be based elsewhere and a factory in Crewe – previously a Merlin making outstation – was set up for

Second position: Sir Henry Royce Bt, as portrayed by F. Derwent Wood RA, standing in the River Gardens, 1977. (Derby Evening Telegraph)

just that purpose, where the cars were made until very recently; they are now made in Sussex and German owned, something of an irony bearing in mind the firm's wartime importance!

The adage attributed to a past chairman of the company, E.E. Smith, 'Your Company never admits that there is any finality in perfection,' probably encapsulates the trouble surrounding the evolution of the RB211 fanjet, the development of which forced the company into bankruptcy in 1971. Nevertheless, its success under the aegis of the successor company, Rolls-Royce (1971) Limited, at first a nationalised industry but successfully sold off to shareholders in the 1980s, surely justifies the truth behind the saying.

The bankruptcy, it might be added, did not affect two separate companies bearing the illustrious name. One was the Crewe-based motor car firm, the other was Messrs Rolls-Royce and Associates, set up on Raynesway in 1959 to manage the design, development, procurement and continuing support of the nuclear engines and systems for HM submarines. The firms behind this company are Rolls-Royce (1971) Limited, Babcock Power Limited, Foster Wheeler Limited and Vickers plc. In 1986 there were 1,200 employees, over half of whom were graduates. When the eccentric leadership of the Derbyshire County Council optimistically decided in 1983 to declare the county a 'nuclear free zone,' they overlooked Rolls-Royce & Associates completely!

THE McEVOY

Oddly, Royce's were not the only manufacturer of prestige motor vehicles in the 1920s. One of their engineers, Michael A. McEvoy, by no means unusual among Rolls-Royce expert employees in those days in being an Etonian, produced a prototype racing motorcycle at his home in Duffield in 1924. The following year he went into limited production of high-quality machines, exhibiting at the motor show for the first time. The same year he resigned from Rolls-Royce and devoted himself full time to making what were essentially finely-tuned racing bikes, using such muscular power as 1000 cc Anzani and 500 cc JAP V-twin engines.

1926 saw a move to dedicated premises in Leaper Street, Derby, where he employed one Balderson and the Watkiss brothers, aided by financial backing from C.A.C. (Archie) Birkin, younger brother of Sir Henry (Tim) Birkin, 3rd Bt., Nottingham lace-making millionaire and one of the famous 'Bentley Boys'. With works rider George Patchett, the marque soon managed some impressive victories at Brooklands. Although some of the machines exhibited were prototypes, which were never likely to reach production, those that did were extremely good, although expensive: the aim was to provide machines for the wealthy enthusiast.

All that changed, however, when in June 1927 Archie Birkin was killed aged 22. Without his backing, the firm's position – still in need of 'start-up' capital – became perilous. McEvoy made some lighter, more popular machines, including a 175cc bike, along with a 1928 4-cylinder model, but to no avail: production stopped in 1929. Today the surviving models are exceedingly rare and valuable, a 980cc JAP engined example being sold at auction in 2005 for £59,000.

Although the McEvoy motorbike was never to rise from the ashes – the Great Depression saw to that – McEvoy himself turned to fine tuning motor engines, becoming M.A. McEvoy (London) Ltd., 'super charge specialist', by 1935, but the firm closed with the outbreak of war. That said, the McEvoy, like the Rolls, was a manifestation of the luxury trades that made Derby great in the 18th century.

The expansion of the foundries, the evolution of engineering and the rise of industries supplying raw materials and components are the legacy of the coming of the railways to Derby. That event in a sense marked the consummation of the first phase of the Industrial Revolution in Derby, itself arising from the very potent intellectual one inspired by the Lunar Society, their patrons and associates. The second, more workaday phase, found its apogee in the establishment of Rolls-Royce in 1907, which brought developments back full circle to the luxury market. The third phase lies securely in the 20th century.

XII

VICTORIAN IMPROVEMENTS

The population explosion in the wake of the rapid advance of industrialisation and the consequent vast increase in the built up area of the town soon began to place strains on facilities which the City Fathers had thought modern and advanced at the dawn of the Railway Age. It has already been shown that, with the Midland Railway expanding rapidly over borough's Fields and a whole bevy of foundries, with attendant housing along Cotton Lane and nearby in Litchurch, the latter, long separated from the borough proper, had had to be constituted as a mini-town with its own local government and officers to cope.

WATER SUPPLY & SEWAGE

Many streets in the mediaeval heart of the town were inadequate for the traffic which traversed them and such things as sanitation and water supply were woefully inadequate. For instance, it was not until the new waterworks at Little Eaton was built in 1848–53 that Sorocold's water supply could be phased out of use, although most people relied on wells by this time; however, many were polluted with raw sewage. Some of these wells survived a time for local and occasional use, but by the end of the 19th century almost every house or court had at least a standpipe from the mains. It is also unclear whether the pretty conduit head in the Market Place was taken down at this time or in Autumn 1872

The Victorian brick lined culvert and buried remains of the bridge at Sadler Gate, as exposed during re-lining works in The Strand in 1968. Culverting the Markeaton Brook was a late acknowledgement that it had gone from late 18th-century inland waterway to full blown sewer in a very short time. (M. Craven)

when the Market Place was cobbled over and the 'market pump' removed, to be replaced – or so the council hoped – by a 'lamp, fountain and statue'. The latter may indeed have been its successor, but was never built – at least not until 1990. The lamp was certainly erected and for a statue, that of Bass had to suffice, installed in 1884.

The waterworks, designed by H.I. Stevens, came on stream in stages from 1850 and was run by a private undertaking until 1880, when it was purchased by the borough. In 1881 water was being supplied to 15,187 homes, leaving a mere 1,001 still unconnected, a good record for that time. By the beginning of the 20th century even the Little Eaton operation was proving inadequate and a new, much larger scheme was initiated in the upper Derwent Valley to ensure a better supply. Derby and Sheffield had a 25 percent share each, Leicester 35.72 percent and Nottingham had 14.28 percent. The first phase opened on 5 September 1912 and the second on 19 September 1929, at which date Sir Henry Bemrose was the first chairman of the newly-

Derby's sewer revealed: a steam road roller falls into the culverted Markeaton Brook, August 1935. (*Derby Evening Telegraph*)

198

The Full Street power station seen from the Derwent, 12 November 1948.

constituted Derwent Valley Water Board and under which Derby received 5,000,000 gallons per day from a total of 20,000,000 pumped.

Prior to 1876, however, little or nothing had been done in the direction of sanitary reform, despite an extremely critical report of 1848. Sewage fell untreated into the river, and the Markeaton Brook, at least from St James's Bridge, was itself a sewer and indeed still is, although upgraded 40 years ago. By 1879 the borough engineer had prepared no less than five schemes of varying expense to meet the statutory requirements of the Rivers Pollution Prevention Act.

The Corporation's inertia led to an injunction being served upon them, which was in strange contrast to the Litchurch Local Board. This more responsible body had actually erected a sewage filtration plant, although even in the 1880s it was considered inadequate. In the event, despite the abolition of cesspools in the 1880s, the sewage scheme which the Corporation eventually adopted was not complete until 1910.

PUBLIC UTILITIES

The gas works in Bold Lane was joined by a second, larger one at Etches Park (now Pride Park) in the 1860s.

Handsome offices were built in Friar Gate in 1889 for the company, designed with a steel frame (the first in the town) by Messrs J.R. Naylor and G.H. Sale. These two installations continued to supply the town, under national ownership from the late 1940s, until natural gas was introduced in the mid-1960s.

In 1863 a great wonder was shown to the citizens of Derby, a mere 43 years after the first gas lights. An electric light was displayed on the tower of All Saints' to celebrate the marriage of Edward, Prince of Wales. It was, by all accounts, rather feeble, but it was in its way a landmark. The next demonstration of the efficacy of electrical illumination was displayed outside the Drill Hall in Becket Street on 18 November 1878. Only 14 years later, electricity generation began beside the silk mill on Full Street, and in 1893 the first electric lighting was inaugurated.

This had been extended throughout most of the core of the town by 1906, but the generation facility was already inadequate, partly due to the electrification of the tramways. A new power station was begun on an adjacent site, the first phase of which, with two turbines of 1,000hp each, was opened in 1908. However, the chosen site was far too central, the once elegant and sequestered Full Street leaving little room for expansion for such an important facility, its east side being then still

The Derby Corporation Electricity Supply Station in all its awfulness, seen from the Derwent Street roundabout in 1966. Note the truncation of Stevens's elegant St Alkmund's spire – removed a few years before in an early example of Health and Safety obsessions! (*Derby Evening Telegraph*)

lined with dignified Georgian and earlier houses, including an eclectic group opposite the cathedral including Gothick of P.P. Burdett's house, the handsome Full Street Baths, and Pickford's Devonshire Hospital. The writing was on the wall for the entire group. In 1894 the Devonshire Hospital was sold to the borough for £1,622 with the intention that it should be torn down in order to enlarge the baths. In the event, nothing was done and the finest piece of small-scale Palladianism in the town mouldered, unused until the beginning of World War One, when, in one of the first of Derby's periodic acts of official iconoclasm, this dignified and unique structure was cleared to make way for the second phase of the power station, opened in 1922.

In townscape terms it was an unmitigated disaster, being separated only by the width of a mediaeval street from one of England's most chaste and satisfying Baroque churches. The late Dr Heath-Gracie, organist of All Saints', caustically commented on his impressions of this phenomenon when he took up his post in 1934, recording that his *bete noir*, Provost Ham, had to plan services with infinite care in order to avoid any part of the sermon overlapping with one of these fossiliferous libations, reserving that pleasure to the efforts of Heath-Gracie's choir, nurtured to excellence against appalling odds, of which the power station constituted one of the least aggravating. He wrote in his unpublished memoirs:

'The windows of Derby Cathedral were forced to show the sordid spectacle of a filthy electricity power station, also letting in the clanking of machinery, the hissing of superfluous steam while endless tons of finely-powdered ash, the end product of the whole enterprise, were being carted away in open trucks to be dumped on hitherto green and pleasant English farmland, minus the appreciable quantity sprinkled on the streets and passersby.'

Final extensions, showrooms and offices were made to the power station complex on Sowter Road in the 1930s.

One of the last and most gratifying acts of the old borough council before its demise in 1974 was to remove this monstrosity completely – although with much prodding from the then Provost, Ronald Beddoes, the president of the Civic Society and others – leaving the site grassed over, providing a stunning vista both to All Saints' from the Derwent and from it to the Silk Mill. This uncluttered green has been embellished since 1995 by a particularly fine equestrian statue of Bonnie Prince Charlie by Anthony Stones, presented to a rather reluctant council by free newspaper pioneer Lionel Pickering (1931–2006) (picture, page 89).

STREET WIDENING

The improvements to the streets themselves, once the Victoria Street scheme had been completed in 1839, were at first slow in coming. It was nearly 30 years later when Alderman Thomas Roe senior successfully managed to persuade his peers on the council to consider improvements. An exception must be made for the period in office of the first borough engineer, Samuel Harpur, who made numerous minor improvements.

When it is considered that the main streets of the town were the width of Sadler Gate today and that of the lesser streets, like St James's, were but that of Amen Alley, the appalling problems posed by the vast increase in traffic can readily be imagined. In 1866, however, it was projected to demolish the Piazzas, Rotten Row and the Shambles in order to extend the effective area of the Market Place and widen Iron Gate.

A start was made in the same year on Iron Gate. The east side was selected for demolition and as both sides had their fair share of distinguished buildings, the choice was as good as any. The Corporation had to raise loans and subscriptions in order to find the money to buy the freeholds, the hope being that the sale of plots on the

Iron Gate prior to widening. Richard Keene's studio, shop and gallery, 24 Iron Gate, c.1864, taken by himself. (M. Craven)

The Market Place pictured soon after the removal of The Piazzas and Shambles. The date is 1885 and people are still reading the inscription on the plinth of Sir Joseph Boehm's statue of M.T. Bass MP, then newly erected. Within a few years, pressure of traffic had forced its removal to the museum. (*Derby Evening Telegraph*)

widened streets would provide sufficient return to balance the books. In the event both processes were slow. The lower part of Iron Gate was widened by 1869, the upper part by 1871; yet it took another 15 years to sell all the plots and to see buildings erected thereon. Nevertheless, the slowness of the scheme ensured a collection of very varied buildings, erected in styles ranging from Ruskinian Gothic to Italianate.

Rotten Row and the Piazzas were similarly problematic: the leases had to be bought out. Half, including the butchers in the Shambles, were acquired in the first stage enabling the northern end of Rotten Row to be demolished in 1869. The same year saw the widening of St James's Lane to make St James's Street under the aegis of a private agency, the Derby Hotel and Improvement Company. As with the Royal Hotel, this proved a far more efficient way of effecting the development than those just described, the company having sufficient capital to see the scheme through fairly quickly. Their profits were to come from the construction of the St James's Hotel (on the north side) and the building and letting of shops and offices. At the Victoria Street end, the opportunity was taken to demolish a large house on Curzon-owned land to erect a new post office in 1869, an extraordinarily handsome ashlar-fronted building. St James's Street was complete by 1871; Cornmarket was widened in 1877. This same year, too, St Peter's Street was widened, again the east side being part demolished, the decision being dictated by the presence of St Peter's Church and churchyard on the west, although the latter was trimmed back with the loss of a 15th-century building on the south-west corner in 1882.

A series of plots south of Bag Lane (renamed East Street in 1883) were acquired by Edwin Ann, of a Bristol family, to establish Derby's first department store. He had started in older property in St Peter's Street a year or

two earlier and began building on the cleared site in 1887, his Midland Drapery store being completed on four plots in 1892. Ann was mayor of Derby in 1898–99 and 1905–06, receiving a knighthood by virtue of presiding munificently over the Royal visit in the latter year, when Edward VII unveiled Charles Bell Birch's statue to his mother (donated by Sir Alfred Haslam) *en route* to the Royal Show on Osmaston Park. The store closed in 1970, the site being redeveloped as smaller shops with a rear arcade called the Audley Centre, in lacklustre style and of no great height.

Beyond East Street, widening was delayed until 1898, enabling a new and exceedingly decorative Boot's store to be opened on this corner site in a pretty arts-and-crafts style with pargetting and niched statues of local worthies, executed by P.R. Morley Horder, in 1912. Further extensions were made in 1936 in matching style. Essentially, however, it was only the lower part of the street that was really narrow. The demolition of Henry Mellor's once fine house, latterly called Babington House, in 1897 also enabled the part of St Peter's Street by The Spot to be set back when Babington Buildings (now Waterstone's) were erected in 1899 for Cllr.

St James's Street *c*.1909, widened in 1867–71. (*Derby Evening Telegraph*)

Street widening: St Peter's Street/St Peter's Churchyard with mediaeval buildings boarded up ready for demolition, 1881. Richard Keene photograph. (M. Craven)

Franklin for his Public Benefit Boot & Shoe Co., to designs by the Methodist chapel architect John Wills. St Peter's Churchyard was widened in 1883.

While development was taking place in St Peter's Street, Sir Abraham Woodiwiss was buying up land on either side of the Markeaton Brook from the mediaeval St James's Bridge to Sadler Gate Bridge. He pitched a serpentine street over the culverted brook with a uniform line of buildings on the north side and a large corner block into Victoria Street. Named after the London model, The Strand, it opened in 1878. An arcade, aping the Burlington Arcade in London, was added in 1880 connecting The Strand with Sadler Gate, the architect being John Story. Further widenings had to wait until the 20th century.

St Peter's Street, looking north from Babington Buildings, January 1898. Imposing, stone-faced Holbrook House (centre), built in the 1820s for lead entrepreneur Charles Holbrook, has become a shop and the entire street was widened by 1890. (*Derby Evening Telegraph*)

NEW STREETS

By 1882 the continued expansion of the borough had resulted in 362 streets in Derby with a length totalling 60 miles. This included the extension of Rose Hill Street, Upper Boundary Road and City Road at Little Chester. This latter scheme envisaged the provision of an open space of 14 acres bounded on either side by roads and was eventually achieved despite opposition of those holding rights of common in Little Chester. The money was raised by selling land to the Great Northern Railway for their line in 1877. Chester Green and its attendant roads, Chester Green Road and St Paul's Road, opened in 1886. Immediately east of Little Chester, a new road linking Nottingham Road with the Alfreton Road was built beside the canal two years before: Stores Road. In 1882 a private road, impressively gated at either end, had been built between Normanton and Osmaston Roads: Hartington Street. The terraced housing was available for freehold purchase at £50 and the footpaths were planted with limes; this too was done on the initiative of Alderman Sir Abraham Woodiwiss, whose unauthorised armorials decorate the gables of the houses. The gates went in World War Two, however, and it is now a very run down area, most of the houses divided as bedsits.

The plans evolved in the 1860s to widen the streets were thus by no means complete by the turn of the century, although much had been done. Between then and 1925, when the first Derby Town Planning Scheme was proposed, a few more improvements were made, although

The Strand and Strand Arcade, 1880-81. (M. Craven)

The short section of thoroughfare joining the bottom of Sadler Gate with Bold Lane is called Sadler Gate Bridge, because one of the bridges across the Markeaton Brook, giving access to Cheapside, stood there before being incorporated in the culvert in 1878. The once handsome row of shops, seen left in this summer 1925 photograph, was demolished just before the war. (*Derby Evening Telegraph*)

at a heavier cost in historic buildings. In 1911 The Spot was widened and, after World War One, part of Nottingham Road. The Market Place having been cobbled, traffic swiftly began jostling for position with the market stalls, which had been there since the 12th century. This was aggravated by trams and later by buses. The statue by Sir Joseph Boehm, Bt., of M.T. Bass MP, limited widening of Market Head to Corn Market, and in 1925 it was removed to Derby Museum. The final widening of The Wardwick, begun in 1882, was completed in 1913, from opposite Becket Street to Cheapside. In Queen Street the west side was also being widened from St Mary's Gate (1922, when the vestiges of the mediaeval St Mary's Church appeared) to King Street (1928–29).

The north end of Full Street, anciently Alderman Hill or Nanny Tag's Lane, was also widened to allow access for the lorries which fuelled the ghastly power station, which thereupon left via the recently pitched Sowter Road to St Mary's Bridge, causing the demolition of the early Jacobean Bull's Head Inn, Queen Street, in 1944–45, the vernacular early-18th century wrought-iron sign being saved for Derby Museum.

The serpentine course of The Strand, created in 1878–80 at the sole expense of super-rich railway contractor and serial mayor Alderman Sir Abraham Woodiwiss by the simple expedient of culverting the brook between Sadler Gate and St James's Bridges. The sweep of buildings were designed by Giles & Brookhouse. (*Derby Evening Telegraph*)

New cattle market, by H. Stevens and Edwin Thompson, 1861. Right, Stevens' Corporation Hotel. All cleared to make way for the Inner Ring Road in 1967. (Derby Museum)

NEW MARKETS

In 1860 two projects were being initiated. One was the cattle market on The Holmes, replacing ancient markets on The Morledge and Friar Gate. This development included the Cattle Market Hotel, all by Stevens, designed to free up the west end of Friar Gate. After 106 years, however, the entire complex was swept away by the coming of the Inner Ring Road, and a new market was built on the east of the Derwent, on Chequers Road, to which the wholesale market had already been banished in 1924.

To relieve the congestion and *ad hoc* market trading in corn and related commodities in the area between the Regency bow-fronted Cross Keys Inn, later the *Derbyshire Advertiser*, and to facilitate the flow of traffic in Corn Market, a new Corn Exchange was opened in 1861 in Albert Street. This imposing building, with its drum-shaped grand entrance and copper dome, was designed by Benjamin Wilson. Its great hall, at one time used as a music hall, became a Palais-de-Danse in 1921 with a bravura period interior by Grey Wornum, but this was lost when the *Derby Daily Telegraph* took it over in 1928.

The covered area of stalls built by Habershon behind the Guildhall had also, by this date, become inadequate and a decision was taken to clear it and build anew. An impressive covered hall with an iron roof made at the Phoenix Foundry covered an area of 220ft x 110ft. The roof span is 86ft 6ins, with an apex at 64ft. The architect

Benjamin Wilson's rather grandiose Corn Exchange of 1861, seen here after its conversion into the printing works and offices of the *Derby Daily Telegraph*, in 1928. The building is seen here decked out to celebrate the Coronation of HM Queen Elizabeth II in 1953.

Tenant Street Market Hall of 1864–66. Photograph by Richard Keene, 1866. (M. Craven)

was the borough engineer T.C. Thorburn, but he departed for a new post in 1865 and his successor George Thompson was forced to make expensive modifications to alleviate a serious design flaw in the structure. The exterior is of brick and rusticated ashlar with a pedimented façade to the south, facing Albert Street. A large turret clock by Edward Johnson of Victoria Street was removed in 1988 to Crich Tramway museum when the building was completely refurbished and extended eastwards.

Market Hall interior in the 1950s. (Derby Museum)

A Great Rebuilding

After 1888, when the control of the whole county was embodied in a new corporate entity, a headquarters had to be found. J.S. Story was appointed the county architect, and he erected a remarkably fine brick building on the south side of St Mary's Gate, completed in 1894 and later twice extended. An annexe was constructed by Story in 1910 and, in spite of using much the same detailing, he produced a building of a distinctly different character. Both are decorated with ornamental wrought ironwork by Messrs Taylor, Whiting and Taylor. Meanwhile, the various departments of the municipality were scattered widely, in the Guildhall, The Old Mayor's Parlour and in a dreary but newly-built office block on Babington Lane on the corner with Gower Street, a thoroughfare adapted from ancient Blood Lane in 1852.

Gower Street, too, was the site of a new Masonic Hall erected in 1873 and designed by G.H. Sheffield. It was demolished in 1972 to make way for an over-sized office block which looks all the worse for being in an elevated position. Previously, prior to their permanent establishment locally in 1784, the Masons had met at the Tiger, Cornmarket. A century ago, apart from the first Derby lodge, the Tyrian (No. 253), there were four other lodges, too. Today they have adapted Littleover Grange, rebuilt after a fire in 1990, but having previously added a concrete windowless 'chapel'.

Derby's second Union Workhouse by Giles and Brookhouse,
1874–77, later Manor Hospital, was demolished in 1991. (M. Craven)

In 1877 the rear of No.10 Friar Gate was opened as a
Turkish Bath with all the usual Moorish arches and the
sort of facilities the paying customers might require, the
front becoming a fashionable coffee house as 'The Friar
Gate', later a Temperance Hotel. The complex failed to
survive the provision of superior facilities of this type at
Reginald Street in 1904. It has long been the site of a
notable motor engineering firm, light still falling across
the burnished flanks of the finest products of Munich,
Frankfurt and Coventry from the incongruous Moorish
arches.

Also in 1877 the Union Workhouse was ready for
occupation in Uttoxeter Road, almost on the Mickleover
parish boundary, leaving the 1839 building on Osmaston
Road ('the Bastille' to locals) empty. It was taken over,
however, by the newly-founded Derby Porcelain
company (accorded the prefix of 'Royal Crown' by
Queen Victoria in 1890), which added a pilastered, full
height portico and a dome bearing a rather eclectic-
looking crown. The dome, replaced in 1988, was
extremely interesting, being supported by a structure of
cast aluminium, a very early use of this material indeed.
The main block was further rebuilt in the 1950s to no
very good effect externally.

To oversee the administration of the new workhouse,
Giles and Brookhouse also built an imposing ashlar-
fronted building in French style in Becket Street for the
Board of Poor Law Guardians in 1861–68, extended 30
years later. A much prettier building opposite, of 1872,
housed the Derby School Board. Both have been recently
restored, the former as a 'fun pub', above the bar of which
towers a stained-glass window awash with insipid alle-
gorical figures bearing the now incongruous motto
'Blessed is he who careth for the poor'.

MICHAEL THOMAS BASS MP

The second major park in Derby was given by another
great local philanthropist, Michael Thomas Bass (1799–
1884), one of Derby's two MPs from 1848 to 1883. He
was a man not only generous in an age of good works
but also one with a sense of humour in an earnest one.
As public opinion over the last 30 or so years has been
roused against smoking, so in the 19th century a major
preoccupation of the middle-classes was for temperance.

So when Bass was asked, at a public meeting, by a
leading light of the temperance 'do-gooders', what
contribution he was making to their crusade, he
answered wryly that he ensured that his beers were 'Allus
well-wattered, Madam.' It is worth noticing in passing
that such was the dissenter-fuelled strength of this
movement in Derby, that sufficient cash was available
for a large, rather opulent, Temperance Hall to be built
in the classical idiom to the designs of H.I. Stevens on
Curzon Street in 1852, later the Churchill Hall and until
2007 a Pentecostal Church.

In 1867 Bass gave land at the north end of the Siddalls
for a recreation ground at a cost of £3,850 for purchase
and preparation. Soon afterwards work began in creating
open-air swimming baths on the site. Although destroyed
after the last war, each of the two was 100ft x 50ft with 129
dressing boxes between them. The architect was George
Thompson and the cost, again borne by Bass, was £2,500.
They opened in 1873. He made pretty free use of his
entirely unauthorised coat-of-arms, too; it appears on
several buildings associated with him. His benefactions
were such that within six month of his death a statue by
Sir Joseph Boehm, Bt., had been erected in the Market
Place, unveiled on 17 October 1884.

Michael Thomas Bass MP, Derby's leading Victorian benefactor.
(M. Craven)

LIBRARY, MUSEUM & ART GALLERY

Also in 1873 Bass purchased the Baroque panelling from the saloon at Exeter House – the room in which Bonnie Prince Charlie's famous council meeting had been held – from Hardcastle Mousley of Etwall Lodge, son of Exeter House's last owner. His intention was to build it into a specially designed room in the museum he was determined to persuade the reluctant City Fathers to accept from him. In 1878 he had his way, and R. Knill Freeman of Bolton-le-Moors won a competition to design the new free library and museum to be built on the site of Lockett's town house in The Wardwick, which building up to this time had housed the facilities after they had outgrown the Mechanics' Institute. The new building was opened on 28 June 1879 amid much celebration and junketings, which was in stark contrast to 1868 when the Corporation had refused their MP's previous offer. By the time John Story's neo-Rennaissance Art Gallery extension on The Strand had been opened on land given by Woodiwiss with more Bass money in 1882, the three elements of library, museum and art gallery were at last under one roof.

A Jacobean extension to the museum designed by T.H. Thorpe was completed in 1915. The original arts-and-crafts style curator's house had to be sacrificed for this, although its smaller twin, to the south east of the original building and provided initially for the custodian, survives, although obscured by a clumsily-designed access ramp.

A further extension was planned as a result of pressure on Art Gallery space and through the incentive of a legacy from A.E. Goodey (d.1945), who wished it to house the collection of over 500 local topographical views he had acquired or commissioned. Work finally began in 1963 on a dreary modernist box designed by borough architect T.W. East (1906–1997), opened in 1964. On The Wardwick side a small garden left over from the 1913 demolition of Francis Fox's house had accommodated Bass's statue – except for a few weeks in 1942 when it had been inadvertently sent by the curator to a scrapyard in Kensington Street to help with the war effort (it was purchased back at cost by the council). The garden was fashioned into a neat square in 1964 – called Museum Square – of which a re-sited Bass made a central feature, which was further re-landscaped in 1992.

FURTHER PARKS

Another park was created out of part of the grounds of Derwent Bank, formerly Darley Grove, the house built for Thomas Bridgett in 1811. This linked with the grounds of St Helen's, a dog-end of which (Strutt's Park)

remained at the end of Darley Grove after the development of North, Arthur, Margaret and Otter Streets and Belper Road, starting in 1889. In 1929 Darley Park was developed out of the park of Darley Hall and, all three being contiguous, form a pleasant area of parkland on the west bank of the Derwent. Taken with Parker's Piece, adjoining Stone House Prebend along City Road and stretching to the line of the Great Northern Railway and Darley Playing Fields – the portion of the Darley Hall estate on the east bank of the Derwent – virtually the whole northern part of the Derwent within the present city is green.

In 1889 a recreation ground was created between Uttoxeter Old Road and the barracks and graced with a large cast-iron drinking fountain made in Kilmarnock. This was followed by a 24-acre park created between New and Old Normanton in 1908 and graced by a pretty Arts-and-Crafts pavilion with a large cupola or lantern between its two chalet-style gables sporting a Smith turret clock, opened 6 September 1909.

The next piece of green to open was a small area of land between St Werburgh's Church, the nave of which had been rebuilt by Sir Arthur Blomfield in 1889–94, and the gas works and offices, into the new showrooms of which the old dome of the church had been incorporated in 1895. This had been at the instigation of a director, Capt. Basil Mallender, a great rescuer of dismantled bits of

A wrought-iron gate made by Taylor, Whiting & Taylor to embellish Boden's Pleasance, Bold Lane, in 1910, pictured in the 1950s. (*Derby Evening Telegraph*)

Derby; the Bakewell railings at the front of the Gas offices are also there thanks to him. This green was given in memory of her late husband, Henry Boden of The Friary, the lace magnate (d.1908), by his widow, a keen temperance enthusiast, 'for the perpetual enjoyment of the citizens of the town' and opened 7 July 1910. It was graced with pretty railings and gates in wrought-iron with the Boden's crest on top by Taylor, Whiting and Taylor, the area behind being asphalted and equipped with swings and so on for children. In the early 1970s it was given over to a colossal multi-storey car park, its concrete horizontal emphasis being broken up by a series of dark-brown verticals strongly reminiscent of Cadbury's Flakes fashioned in fibreglass. This was privatised to Belper firm Parksafe in 1997 and upgraded with mild steel scenic panels and sophisticated security devices, becoming the 'safest car park in England'. Meanwhile, Mrs Boden's gate stands alone, rotting, its crest mutilated, on a miniscule patch of grass nearby. A 30-acre recreation ground on London Road at Alvaston, ultimately complete with a miniature lake (added 1923), was opened in August 1913 with a Carnegie Library opened adjacent in May 1916, but which was cruelly demolished in 1977. Rykneld Recreation Ground was added to the borough portfolio in 1923, created from the pleasure grounds of a Burton Road Regency villa called The Firs.

GOLF COURSES

The Cotton's farm estate – *Domesday's* Codinton – was acquired by the borough in 1920 and a municipal golf course of 6,150 yards laid out on part of it (the rest going for municipal housing) opening in torrents of rain on 4 July 1923. The Sinfin Golf Course was not the first in Derby. The Markeaton Golf Club was founded in 1908 and lasted 50 years. There was also a course on Huffin Heath at Mickleover which suffered a deleterious redesign as a result of the A38 link road being built from 1970. Even Littleover had a course for a while, on the crest of the Burton Road to the east side, sacrificed to housing in the early 1930s.

In 1948 the Allestree Hall estate was acquired by the borough, although it then lay wholly outside the town's boundaries. This included the Derbyshire Golf Club, established in 1935, having transferred from Humbleton Farm at Markeaton estate, the original course having been founded in 1892. At Allestree, the clubhouse was the James Wyatt-designed hall itself, built in 1802–06, the former dining room becoming the bar, a felicitous arrangement which persisted until they were moved into the service wing to make way for a projected natural history museum in 1989. It is leased from the council on condition that it is open for all to play on it.

A rather short-lived nine-hole golf course was established by Rolls-Royce on part of the former Osmaston Hall estate, part of the hall, demolished in 1938, serving once again serving as a clubhouse; it lasted until the war.

MUNICIPAL SPORTS GROUND & BATHS

In 1922 a public park on the south-western portion of the former Osmaston Park was opened and the Corporation spent considerable sums equipping it with crown bowling greens, tennis courts and so on. Adjacent was the Municipal Sports Ground which included a banked concrete track opened in 1925 intended by the council for motorcycling events but which proved to be too small and was given over to cycling events and athletics (see page 235). It covers 25 acres, and cricket, bowls, boxing, soccer, rugger, hockey and lacrosse were envisaged as being catered for.

Recreation grounds and baths frequently went together, as at the Mundy Pleasure Grounds in Markeaton Street in 1903. In a sense, the handsome new indoor baths at Reginald Street, opened in 1903, marched with the Arboretum. John Ward's design, which made the proposed extension of the Full Street baths redundant, was dignified, sported a bracketed

The Moorish arch in the slipper baths of Reginald Street Baths, taken not long before gutting and conversion into flats. (*Derby Evening Telegraph*)

An Aslin whimsy: the ironwork ordinary bicycle worked into the side gate of the Queen Street Baths in Cathedral Road near the site of a demolished bike shop. (M. Craven)

turret clock and had fine *Art Nouveau* detailing. Because it included slipper baths and other facilities of great value to local residents without fitted bathrooms in their houses, the building had an important social role to play, too, and put the Turkish Baths in Friar Gate out of business with remarkable rapidity. Yet they closed about 1980, but the façade at least was kept, and the building converted into housing association flats. The loss of this facility was keenly felt in the Arboretum area.

In 1930 a new site was partly created by Walker Lane slum clearance on which the borough architect Herbert

Queen Street Baths, Herbert Aslins entrance, as opened up with new glass doors in the 1990s. (M. Craven)

Aslin designed a handsome complex with a delightfully contrived Greek revival portico set amid a slightly later row of neo-Georgian shops facing Queen Street. They were opened on 30 July 1932 and boasted jokey details like the cast-iron side gate decorated with a simple representation of an ordinary bicycle to commemorate the site of a former cycle shop and a ground glass scene with poultry to mark the adjacent site of the Old Hen & Chickens pub. In the 1960s a children's pool was added in a style quite out of keeping with the remainder, but in 1988–91 the whole complex was rebuilt with a new elevation to Walker Lane side by Keith Hamilton RIBA, which pulls it together in a satisfying and convincing way.

Finally a new pool was built by the council on Moorways Lane close to the Municipal Sports Ground in the 1960s, a piece of atrocious brutalism (and one which needed a complete rebuild in the 1980s) with a gymnasium, restaurant and other adjuncts. Nevertheless, it was regarded as an important sporting venue, with an Olympic pool, rather then merely a recreational facility.

THE TRAINING OF TEACHERS

The middle of the century saw further developments in education. In 1849 a Ragged School was established for the children of the very poor and H.I. Stevens built two attractive church schools, in Curzon Street in 1839 and in Vernon Street two years later. National Schools continued to be opened right up to 1870 when the School Board Act was passed.

To staff these schools more teachers were urgently required, and in 1850 the Bishop of Lichfield, John Lonsdale, initiated moves to open a college for training female teachers in Derby. The site chosen was in Uttoxeter New Road and Stevens was again the architect, producing an impressively massed and lively Tudorbethan building, bearing the legend 'For the Training of School Mistresses' above the entrance. The project excited much local enthusiasm – especially as it was the first institution for higher education in the town. It acquired extensions from as early as 1858 and ultimately these included further accommodation with a chapel over (1899–1900), a practising school (1906) and gymnasium (1914), all by Percy Currey, and they made an impressive ensemble, being set in two acres of delightful grounds. An Infants' practising school was also added, achieved by the conversion of F.J. Robinson's St Luke's Vicarage, Bedford Street, now flats.

Regrettably, all were to some extent blighted by the Uttoxeter New Road dualling scheme of the 1960s, and it was only the spot-listing Grade II of the main building

The college practising school, built in 1906 for the training college and designed by Percy Currey, demolished in 1996 to make way for a housing development. (*Derby Evening Telegraph*)

by the Derby Civic Society and of the gymnasium by the city council that prevented summary demolition, although the grounds were sold for housing development by the newly-founded university in 1992 and the practising school, refused the listed protection granted to its adjacent twin, the Gymnasium (now flats), was demolished for more housing in 1998. The college itself was adapted to become a small-business centre.

The college itself, after exile at Elvaston Castle during World War Two, was renamed the Bishop Lonsdale College of Education in the early 1950s and expanded to an additional site at Mickleover in 1964, having taken its first male students four years before. In 1974 it amalgamated with the Higher Education College on Kedleston Road and subsequently the Matlock Teacher Training College (housed in Parker & Unwin's spectacular former Rockside Hydro) was added, and the entire institution was re-christened the Derbyshire

H.I. Stevens's 1851 Derby Training College, Uttoxeter Road, with Percy Currey's 1898 extensions nearest the camera. Although the photograph was taken in 1960, 15 years after the end of World War Two, the blackout stripes still grace the trolleybus poles. Spot-listed and saved from demolition in the 1980s, it is now a business centre. (*Derby Evening Telegraph*)

College of Higher Education in the mid 1980s. In its long heyday it achieved a wide reputation under such inspired leadership as that of Canon A.B. Bater (1898–1927), Miss H.K. Hawkins OBE (1927–1952) and Miss A.E.G. Sephton (1952–1970). The late Russell Harty was a lecturer at the college during 1966–67.

The college had a distinct effect on the Uttoxeter New Road, for it began buying adjacent villas from c.1903, to house students as the numbers began to exceed the capacity of the college building. Later it added Sir Henry Bemrose's former home, Lonsdale Hill, Lonsdale Place, converted into a 90-person residence for females in colossal additions connecting it to a second villa in 1951, almost all sold and demolished for housing by the university in the 1990s.

DERBY SCHOOL & ST HELEN'S HOUSE

In 1860 the governors of the reviving Derby School were offered St Helens House by Edward Strutt, 1st Lord Belper, son and heir of William. After many financial difficulties, they moved from temporary accommodation in the headmaster's house in Friar Gate in September 1861, becoming sole owners in 1873.

When the GNR line was mooted, it was to go through part of the school's grounds, destroying the grand stable courtyard, then used for teaching; generous compensation was offered to the school. The council was also offering compensation to widen King Street in front of the house, too, and both were accepted. The governors decided to capitalise on these fortunate events by a bit of astute property development of their own. They pitched a street down the east side of the school's grounds, to be called Arthur Street, but which would, though, have the effect of destroying most of the large extension of 1807. The street was laid out in 1877 and plots on the east side sold, which enabled the school to compensate for the two losses by building a large annexe on the north front of St Helen's, completed in 1878, which did the original house absolutely no favours aesthetically but more than doubled accommodation.

A chapel designed by Percy Currey was added in 1891, replacing a nine-year-old 'tin tabernacle', and extended in 1894. He added a fine headmaster's house and science labs a few years later. A scheme to rebuild completely in 1934 was prevented by the outbreak of war (when the school relocated to Overton Hall, Ashover), undoubtedly saving Pickford's impressive mansion.

Derby School went comprehensive in 1965 and the following year removed to a new site in Littleover. The Portland stone obelisk by Sir Reginald Blomfield erected

Derby School, c.1906. St Helen's House, right, the Pearson Building, set back behind, and chapel (by P.H. Currey). Left, the street has been widened and the classical screen was replaced by a low wall in 1873.

as a war memorial after World War One went too. Regrettably, Derby School was peremptorily closed in August 1989. A entirely new school began using the same buildings, although in November 1992 the war memorial was returned to the forecourt of St Helen's, the move paid for by the Old Derbeians Society.

View of Derby School of Art seen from T.C. Hine's Stuart Terrace house (1851) in a view from 1924–25. (M. Craven)

EDUCATIONAL REFORM

In 1870 the Kay-Shuttleworth Act led to the foundation of the Derby School Board. Typical early schools built under its terms were those at Gerard Street (from 1873), Traffic Street (1879), Ashbourne Road (1880, extended 1895) and Wilmorton (1892). Of these the first two have been demolished. The Catholic school on Gordon Road was built by James Hart of Corby in 1897, alongside his Church of St Joseph, now the Polish community's St Maksymilian Kolbe.

In 1879 Dr William Robert Roe, of a Heanor family, founded the Derby Deaf and Dumb Institution, in which he pioneered education for those with these handicaps. He early realised that if he could board his pupils he could achieve more and, on completion of a daunting piece of fundraising, commissioned R. Ernest Ryley to design a purpose-built school just west of the Great Northern Railway bridge in Friar Gate. This enormous edifice was opened on 18 October 1894 and was being run by Roe's son, William Carey Roe, in 1934. In 1973 the school, by now the Royal School for the Deaf, moved to a new site further up Ashbourne Road in banal modern buildings, and the old building was unfortunately demolished, to be replaced by a series of dreary flats (see page 43).

Another important institution of this kind, built nearby to the French chateau design of A.A. Langley and Edward Fryer, was the Railway Servants' Orphanage, Ashbourne Road, in 1887. It replaced a Regency villa on the site – 67 Ashbourne Road – in which the institution had been founded in 1875. Although entirely charitable in nature, it seems to have been a grim old place for a child deprived, usually suddenly, of its parents, and it only really gained a humane face with the appointment of the late Miss Marjorie Seaver MBE in 1948. The fine listed Grade II building itself was replaced in 1978 by a dreary modern building, but the institution finally closed in 1982, becoming an old folks' home for 11 years before it, too, closed, to be sold to the university and bulldozed, to make way for a lumpish barracks of a hall of residence for the students.

Higher education had made another step forward in 1878 when the distinguished-looking Derby School of Art was opened in Green Lane, having been designed by T.H. Huxley's son-in-law Frederick Waller of Gloucester (1846–1933), a distinguished architect who just happened to have been a student of the newly-appointed head of the college, Thomas Simmonds, at Cheltenham Art College. Indeed, Simmonds (d.1912) was, with the Derby artist Augustus Oakley Deacon (1819–1899), the virtual founder of the institution, which the latter had first set up on a voluntary basis in 1857 in St Peter's Street.

Green Lane: Derby Art College, by F.W. Waller, 1878, from a postcard. (M. Craven)

After the passing of the Technical Education Act of 1891, wherein grants were available from beer and spirit duties for technical education, the money was used locally to take over the Art School and enlarge it in 1893, and it reopened fully in 1899.

In 1903, after yet another Education Act, the School Boards were dissolved and educational responsibility transferred to the local authority, which had become a county borough in 1888. The first school erected under the act by the borough was Ashbourne Road Wesleyan. Thereafter schools opened at regular intervals: 1906, Kedleston Road School (later Markeaton Primary) and Clarence Road Elementary (later Dale Primary, in a fine building by Maurice Hunter of Belper); 15 April 1913, Reginald Street Schools – infant and primary, now St James's and pleasantly housed in an Arts-and-Crafts style building by Percy Currey,

In 1917 Parkfields Cedars, a mansion built by c.1820 on Kedleston Road, was adapted and opened as the Derby Girls' Municipal Secondary School, with extensions by F. Antliff of Draycott and C.B. Sherwin. The council had bought the fine stuccoed house with 5.5 acres from the executors of the redoubtable Mrs Pike of the *Derby Daily Telegraph* in 1905 for £5,800; the school itself had been founded as a Higher Grade Board School in Abbey Street in 1887. It became the borough's only

Girls' Grammar school shortly afterwards and remained so until 1938 when Homelands School at Normanton opened. The council had been planning a replacement for Parkfields Cedars behind Humbleton Farm on the Markeaton estate, but the war ensured that this did not go ahead until 1966, a year after the original premises had burnt down leaving the school with temporary accommodation which included an ex-LMS first class, all-steel railway carriage. It was opened in 1969 by Alderman Jeffery Tillett and Cllr W.N.K. (Jim) Rowley but only lasted until merged as a new comprehensive in 1975.

In 1928 Sir Henry Bemrose laid the foundation stone of a new boys' grammar school to be built on Uttoxeter Road. The site, Elm Tree House, had been acquired for £8,360 and the new school, to a design of considerable presence by Alexander MacPherson, opened on 11 July 1930. It enjoyed an enviable reputation until merged and made comprehensive. Grossly unsympathetic additions to the buildings were made in 2002.

Thereafter school provision continued steadily, Derby running 186 primary and 24 secondary schools in 1935. Ironically, the borough's last school to be built before the county took over for 22 years under the terms of the 1973 Local Government Reform Act, Sinfin Community School (1974–76), was destroyed in a serious fire in spring 2006. Derby had been one of the first authorities to introduce nursery schools, too, with two built in 1937–38: Nuns' Street and Central.

In 1996 Derby, which had become a district council under the 1973 act, regained its autonomy after a campaign began by the Conservative council of 1988–94, but which came to fruition only under their successors. From 1 April 1997 education once again became the preserve of the city council. There was much catching up to do, and it was only in September 2006 that several schools, which had been re-inherited in terminal decay, were finally replaced.

HIGHER EDUCATION

After World War One it became apparent that the art college in Green Lane was inadequate and plans were drawn up for an extension not far away in Normanton Road, opened in October 1925. After the war the decision was taken with the county council to move the entire college – art and higher education having combined to form the Derby Technical College – to Kedleston Road. The new campus centred around a pair of huge glass stumps built in 1956–73 in three phases by the Building Design Partnership. In this prominent position it was ever a visual intrusion into a gently undulating landscape except at night, when lit, when it

Wilmorton Road School, 1892, built by the Alvaston Local Board. (M. Craven)

Royal School for the Deaf, Friar Gate, seen on 21 February 1973, just prior to demolition. (*Derby Evening Telegraph*)

still resembles the superstructure of an Edwardian battle-cruiser and assumes a beauty which is all its own. These buildings now form the nucleus of the University of Derby.

A college of further education was established at Wilmorton in the 1960s and expanded in stages from 1974 to 1997, of course under the aegis of the county council. Since 1997 it has gathered up various peripheral institutions, sold the old site for housing – an enlightened move – and built the Joseph Wright Sixth Form College on Goodwin Street in 2005. The college's next move is to be into the former NMR/MCR works complex, centred on Francis Thompson's pioneering grade II* listed locomotive roundhouse of 1839.

The successors of the Midland Railway also set up a training establishment, the London Midland Scottish Railway's School of Transport, London Road, Wilmorton, built to a striking Neo-Classical design by W.H. Hamlyn in 1938, being a pioneering gesture in several respects, training signallers and other railway operatives in residential surroundings close to the line itself. The *Moderne* interior is embellished with a pair of murals by Norman Wilkinson, CBE (1878–1971), who also embellished the staterooms of RMS *Titanic* and *Queen Elizabeth,* as did – in the case of the latter – David Dunlop, who carved some reliefs on the exterior. The dining room also sports a 28ft 6in mural of transport through the ages by Hamlyn. The building was spot-listed in 2005 when on the verge of being sold for demolition and redevelopment, and as a result is still in its original use.

MEDICAL INSTITUTIONS – THE DRI

The Derby General Infirmary was not the last addition to the medical provisions in the town either. It was ahead of its time when built and was extended twice subsequently, on each occasion (1849 and 1869) by H.I. Stevens in restrained, matching style. The second extension was named the Florence Nightingale Wing by its initiator, Dr William Ogle, who had consulted with Florence over the perceived shortcomings of the building. One addition included an operating theatre, artfully contrived by the architect in a very powerful style, ashlared with battered walls almost like a redoubt. The original block was also rebuilt, the ground around it being excavated so that the basement could be opened up as another storey, the original portico being lowered to match. Yet the advance of its original design proved its undoing, for the ventilation ducts contrived by Strutt and Sylvester were found to have been constructed without any means of cleaning them, and in the 1880s it was realised that, far from keeping the building

Statue of Florence Nightingale, Derby, by Countess Theodora V. Gleichen (pseudonym of HRH Princess Ferdora v Hohenlöhe-Langenburg), erected in 1911. Photographed in 1950. (M. Craven)

healthy, they were materially aiding the spread of disease.

A decision was taken to replace it with a new building designed by Keith D. Young and Henry Hall of London in neo-Jacobean style and on the then newly evolved 'pavilion' pattern, where the major components of the hospital were all separated from one another. The foundation stone was laid by Queen Victoria on 21 May 1891, on which occasion she graciously allowed the new institution to be called the Derbyshire Royal Infirmary (DRI). It was opened on 7 July 1894 by the Duke of Devonshire. The original nurses' home, completed shortly afterwards, was replaced by another opened in 1929 and a third – Derby's only real tower block and

Royal Infirmary, Derby, as built in 1892–96, photographed in 1951.

Derby borough Lunatic Asylum, by Benjamin Jacobs of Hull, from 1888, closed in 2007. (M. Craven)

doubly an eyesore because of its high site, was contrived by Morrison and Partners of Derby along with a new A&E block in 1970–74. In 1899 a rather jolly-looking half-timbered convalescent home was put up in part of the park of Holbrook Hall at the expense of the Alderman Hon. Frederick Strutt and to the design of Maurice Hunter of Belper, as an element of the infirmary's after-care.

Funds for the original hospital were aided by fundraising days. The first Infirmary Saturday was held during 1874 on the inspiration of the mayor, the manufacturer George Holme, and raised £544. These occasions were put on a more ambitious footing through the initiative of Alderman Eggleston on 4 September 1920 when a carnival, gala and large-scale parades took place in the town centre and at the Arboretum. The £5,000 target was attained easily. If you had already given money during these junketings, or were a member of staff or similar, you were given a small gilt and enamel exemption badge to wear. These occasions were suspended during World War Two but the coming of the National Health Service in 1948 ended them.

MENTAL HEALTH PROVISION

The scandal caused by the murder by one inmate of another at the Green Hill House lunatic asylum on 2 December 1848 led to the closure of this institution after 30 years, a move also due to the work in progress on a new asylum, intended to serve the whole county, with numerous towers and pinnacles to the designs of Henry Duesbury in Mickleover, which opened in 1851. Designed to accommodate 300 patients, it was later extended to take 700. As the new building was a county establishment, the borough felt obliged to follow. A competition was then held in 1886, won by Benjamin Jacobs of Hull, who designed a colossal asylum of brick built around four courtyards. The patients' rooms faced east, south or west and the main façade was a whopping 49 bays wide. It opened in November 1888 and was extended five times to 1915.

An adjacent Regency villa, Thornhill, had been sold to the Mosleys of Hulland Hall but in 1924 was acquired as an annexe to house children and an innovative new building, Kingsway House, was designed in *Moderne* style by Herbert Aslin in 1934. Half the site was sold to English Partnerships, a Quango, who demolished Thornhill in August 2006; meanwhile, the future of the original building is under review. The site may end up as a vast housing estate.

CHILDREN'S HOSPITAL

Victorian Derby had no provision for children under seven and only 12 DRI beds for those above that age. Surgeon Frederick Wright formed a trust under the chairmanship of his namesake FitzHerbert Wright, a son of the Butterley plutocrat Francis, of Osmaston, who underwrote most of the changes to the General Infirmary. In 1877 premises were rented at 4 Duffield Road to set up the Derbyshire Hospital for Sick Children.

Derby Children's Hospital, North Street, pictured in 1996, just prior to closure. Designed by Alexander MacPherson and opened in 1883, it was unlisted and was replaced by a housing condominium. (*Derby Evening Telegraph*)

Within 18 months the ever generous Michael Bass had donated £1,000 to the building fund, which never looked back, and a new children's hospital was built on North Street, off Duffield Road, to the designs of Alexander MacPherson, which opened in October 1883. This enjoyed 119 years of valuable service before the NHS decided to build a new 'facility' attached to the City Hospital, which opened in October 1996, whereupon the old hospital closed, the writer's two-month old daughter being one of the very last patients. The fine building was thereupon destroyed, but the 1930s nurses' home was converted to flats.

ISOLATION HOSPITALS

On land also lying in The Rowditch, roughly between the present Kingsway, Albany and Uttoxeter Roads, a temporary isolation hospital was 'erected in haste during an epidemic of small pox' in 1872. Lord Belper paid the lion's share of the cost as well as having given the land. As a result it was resolved to build a proper isolation hospital. On 1 May 1890 the first phase of the Derby Hospital for Infectious Diseases (from 1948 the Derwent Hospital) was opened, situated on the ridge overlooking Little Chester, at a cost of £7,000, and was later twice extended. This allowed the timber hospital on The Rowditch to be burned to the ground (to eradicate latent infection) in May 1890 'at 5.15 pm, by order of the Sanitary Committee'. Several of the huts, however, escaped the inferno and, irrespective of potential for infection, were offered to three districts to make mission churches, later becoming church halls.

In 1910 a sanatorium for 230 patients was built adjacent to Derwent Hospital and it too was extended in 1913. In 1949 the hospital was being used solely for cases of Tuberculosis and infectious diseases, but by 1977 the complex had been turned into an acute hospital. From 1981 it was wound down and closed on 28 September 1986. The remaining patients were transferred to the DRI and the City Hospital, and the site was given over to new housing.

WOMEN'S HOSPITAL

About 1893 Emily Newton – who lived in The Leylands – Mrs Mundy of Markeaton and Mrs Evans of Darley founded the Derby Hospital for Women in Bridge Street. This consisted of one of a pair of Georgian Houses originally built by Charles Finney for the third Improvement Commission in 1794–95. It was quickly extended around into Agard Street and enlarged again a little later on.

This moved in 1928 to the former Wilmot town house at 77 Friar Gate, which was drastically rebuilt and extended with modern facilities and provided with a modern wing furnished with up-to-the-minute equipment. It closed in 1986 and the additions to the 18th-century house were demolished for yet another anodyne neo-Georgian office block.

THE CITY HOSPITAL

Derby City Hospital, on Uttoxeter Road, was the first major inter-war medical project, although conceived in 1914. Built of brick and stone in a muscular and rather stripped down provincial baroque by T.H. Thorpe, it used the 'pavilion' layout, like the original DRI, evolved by post-Nightingale medical theory.

It was built under the aegis of the Derby Board of Guardians, facing the 1877 Union Workhouse. Work began on the 28-acre site in 1926 and it opened in November 1929. It was bounded on the west by Owler's Lane, Littleover, marking the line of Roman Rykneld Street, beyond the end of which the clearly defined *agger* was utterly destroyed in the 1980s by the building of the new portions of the hospital to accommodate those decanted first from Derwent Hospital and then from the Womens' Hospital starting in 1979. From 1989 to 1996 the children's wing of the hospital and the maternity unit were added. A rather good, Lutyens-esque, nurses home was built to the west in 1934 by C.H. Aslin but destroyed in 2003.

The Guardians were abolished in 1932 and the borough council took over, converting the workhouse into a geriatric hospital called Manor Hospital. Never popular among its patients for its associations, it was closed and demolished in 1990, despite an attempt to buy it to start a boys' grammar school.

Derby City Hospital, summer 2004, just prior to demolition. (M. Craven)

In 2000 it was announced that a medical school would be added to the City Hospital site, sponsored by the University of Nottingham, and shortly after that it was decided that it would become an economically efficient 'super-hospital', with the aim of ultimately replacing the DRI. To this end all the old structures were replaced by the end of 2006. Why Thorpe's rather good central block could not be retained for the administrative staff – popularly believed to far outnumber front line staff – is not clear; its retention would have been a decent gesture and might have mitigated the sheer awfulness of the structure being built to supplant it.

BIRTH, DEATH AND RETIREMENT

Other, more limited, medical facilities existed. In 1927 a thumping great new wing was added to Parkfield, a delightful Regency villa on Duffield, latterly the much enlarged home of Sir John ('Brassy') Smith. This was the Queen Mary Maternity Hospital, which closed in 1992. Despite being in a newly-designated conservation area, Parkfields and the hospital were summarily demolished and replaced by a close of what might be termed 'executive homes'.

Nightingale Nursing Home, 1903, originally built in 1821 to house the agent for Castlefields estate; it still has its cast-iron sliding jalousies. (M. Craven)

For the terminally ill, a particularly fine house on Osmaston Road, Douglas House, was converted in 1901 to the Queen Victoria Memorial Home of Rest, which institution moved in the 1930s to Alderman Sir Edwin Ann's old house off Wheeldon Avenue. Since then its role has merged with the MacMillan Continuing Care unit of the DRI in Trinity Street, housed in Chetwynd House, yet another fine Regency villa of c.1820, built by the borough family for their agent in charge of disposing of the Castlefields estate. Both the previous homes of this valuable institution have been demolished.

Even the building of almshouses did not die out in the later 19th and 20th centuries. In 1903–04, Elizabeth, sister and heir of Alderman John Turner (mayor in 1875), left money for some eight houses to be erected on the south side of Ashbourne Road near Markeaton Park. They are in a debased arts-and-crafts style and could easily be mistaken for private housing. The Liversage Charity erected more on Nottingham Road in 1896–1902, along with three streets of 'low cost' rentable housing, all fronted by an ornate range of shops and a pub – the Liversage Arms – on Nottingham Road and all designed by Alexander MacPherson. The whole complex is now a conservation area, despite the new Inner Ring Road having been built some 10 yards from the first-floor windows of the Nottingham Road section (including the pub) in 1969. The Licensed Victuallers also built almshouses on Nottingham Road in 1872 on land donated by the Cox family. This was a gabled brick building with stone dressings, for five couples, but in 1908 only three units were in use, the others being let off separately.

XIII
VICTORIAN HOUSING & FAMILIES

VICTORIAN HOUSING

All this time, of course, the backbone of the town – the ultimate centre of the life of its people and the bulk of its environment – was its housing. Mention has already been made of the homes of the *elite*, the surprisingly numerous houses in Derby owned as town residences by landed county families, chief among the such palatial mansions as St Helen's, St Mary's Gate, Mellor's, Gell's, Jacobean, Newcastle and Devonshire Houses. Nor did the wealthiest burghers reside in houses that were much less ambitious. Joseph Pickford and those who followed him were assiduous in providing houses for the municipal aristocracy that were every bit as refined as the town houses and were erected to the highest standards of architecture and comfort. Friar Gate is a monument to the prosperity of Derby in the later 18th century.

The only difference in the following age was that the better off and especially the county gentlemen began to build away from the core of the borough, which was starting to become overcrowded, noisome and polluted. Hence the ring of elegant Regency villas built on the higher ground which ringed the town, followed by ever increasing numbers of large Victorian houses usually set in less ambitious grounds. At the same time, however, the old town houses in the town centre were being divided up as rooming houses and rookeries, and reeking courts of extremely poor housing built over their gardens, although this pattern was by no means consistent.

In 1849 the Cresy Report counted 352 'courts', although careful inspection of the 1852 Board of Health Map inclines one to wonder exactly how this figure was actually arrived at; could there have been a mendacious element of rhetoric in this weighty official report? That Derby was far from the worst of similar towns was owed to some extent to radical philanthropist employers like the Strutts, who early on set a standard which many of the industrialists who came after tried to emulate. Although few Strutt-type 'ideal' workers' houses survive in Derby, they can still be seen in Darley Abbey, Belper and Cromford, where they have become delightful and sought-after residences.

The reason why some of the earliest Derby terraced housing had become rather awful in the 20th century, like that in Castlefields, along Willow Row or Walker

Sale Street, c.1900. (Don Gwinnett)

Lane, was that it was among the oldest and consequently the most neglected. An example of fine old buildings degenerating into rookeries of poor tenements even in the elegant Wardwick about 1825, comes from Thomas Mozley's *Memoirs:* 'We had large blocks of tenement houses on both sides and one nearly in front of us. That on our right was very ancient. A low passage led through it to a deep court behind. The whole had been occupied time out of mind by a numerous Irish colony. It was a nuisance and worse. It separated us from the handsome residence of Mr W.J. Lockett, Copley's friend...'

Plainly this stood on the site later occupied by the Mechanics' Institute. Nevertheless, some housing in these areas was sufficiently roomy and well built to have been upgraded and rehabilitated rather than pulled down, but Central Government legislation on sanitation and slum clearance from the 1930s until recently was framed in such a way as to make clearance inevitable. Refurbishment would simply not have attracted the necessary central funds. Some early housing, especially the courts behind older property in the central area, some around the Cavendish Street area, the West End and the Little City estate was, however, very seedy by the 1930s.

Some early schemes were really very good. One scheme was the ambitious building containing 30 artisans' dwellings intended to be built on Ford Street in 1842 to the designs of William Wigginton. It was eventually built to a slightly watered down formula in Bridge Street and called Cavendish Buildings: Derby's first flats and well ahead of their time, but being largely unplumbed and poorly heated, only 12 units were

Summerhill Yard, a court leading off Becketwell Lane behind Victoria Street, seen in the 1940s. The spire is that of Hine & Evans's Brookside Chapel, Victoria Street. The area was cleared in the 1960s and is currently a car park. (*Derby Evening Telegraph*)

Cleared slum properties near Union Place, Castlefields, 1951. (Derby City Council)

occupied by 1935 and it was demolished in 1958, ironically, as unfit. Elsie Goodhead wrote of them being known as 'Mulligan's Mansions' in her childhood, from the number of Irish families housed there.

The railway cottages, built in 1839–42 for the North Midland Railway opposite the station and designed in three different sizes by Francis Thompson, were not only a pioneering development of their type, but were spacious and well built. A criticism from a local politician after the Derby Civic Society and the Derbyshire Historic Buildings Trust had won the battle to conserve them was, divested of spurious rhetoric,

Privies, Goodwin Street, c.1900 – a view in one of the courts cleared in 1939.

centred on their lack of sanitation. But then, in 1840, even the grandest houses in town lacked such facilities. Rehabilitated, these properties are today commanding remarkably high prices; better, they make a positive contribution to the environment, form the core of the Railway Conservation Area and would make an even more spectacular one had the city council not been browbeaten into allowing the station itself to be demolished in 1985.

SLUMS AND SLUM CLEARANCE

The point about good, if ancient, buildings in Derby becoming dilapidated through change of use to mass housing was made by the pseudonymous author ('Sand') in an article in the *British Architect* in 1882:

> 'Among the many old buildings are to be found some delightful specimens of old work, and here and there crops up the quaint Queen Anne redbrick gable among the dilapidated cottage property of which *there is much more than there should be*. And in this latter particular we may again trace the vacillating and dilatory action which seems to characterize municipal progress in Derby.'

The area referred to – that to the west of St Mary's Gate and east of Ford Street – had long been recognised as containing some of the most decayed property and overcrowding in Derby. In 1850 Thomas Orme, owner of some of the town's worst slum property, was threatened with prosecution for renting out the roof space above some communal privies in No.2 Court, off St Helen's Street, as 'sleeping rooms'. There were already 12 very mean dwellings in the court.

In Willow Row stood Court No. 1, a particularly grim block otherwise called Turpin's Yard; each of the 24 dwellings in which consisted of a kitchen and bedroom measuring 8ft x 8ft, the bedroom being without a fireplace; the whole court contained 102 people in the damning Cresy report into housing and sanitation in Derby of 1848. A further Privy Council report of 1865 describes Turpin's as still containing a proportion of cottages considered 'totally uninhabitable' even by the raw standards of those days. In one lived a couple and their four children, who were charged 1s 8d (8p) per week for the privilege. The same report describes how a Mr Bailey, the borough's Inspector of Nuisances, turned out of a dozen cottages in one yard 163 persons who were sitting around fires at three in the morning.

Sink estates are nothing new, either. Parcel Terrace and Pegg's Row, Rowditch, were particularly bad, inhabited by the workers from the brickyards and ropeworks on the floor of the valley of the Odd Brook. One disapproving dissenting minister wrote of it that the area was: 'Frequently the scene of the wildest riot and disorder especially on the Sabbath Day – dog and hedgehog fighting, immorality and every species of wickedness being a constant occurrence… many of the cottages there being vacant owing to the disorderly character of the neighbourhood, it having gained the unenviable soubriquet of "Little Sodom".'

Even before the Corporation was allowed to designate slum clearance areas, it had powers to close houses considered unfit for human habitation. These they executed only rarely and only in the worst possible cases. The closure of housing in the two courts off St Helen's Street in 1865 was one of the few recorded cases. Council officials did not, however, shirk their duties, but usually preferred litigation and persuasion to more drastic measures. The unpublished *Journal* of Samuel Harpur reveals how active he was in inspecting lodging houses and slum property, though his definition of what constituted a slum would be far more limited than our own.

Nor was the concern of the Privy Council in 1865 the first formal expression of official horror at conditions in Derby. The 1848 Public Health Act Report by Edward Cresy said of Walker Lane:

'(It) may be termed the St Giles of Derby… although called a Lane it is a street of some length, and has several courts opening into it.

The houses are of the most inferior description and the inhabitants of a piece with their houses; to crown all, there are lodging houses, which are the principal headquarters of vagrants, and of those comers and goers who for reasons best known to themselves prefer darkness to light. Fever (typhus) prevailed here to a great extent between 15 June and 14 September 1847, there being 75 cases, besides several others, which were sent to the Infirmary. The total number of houses in Walker Lane and its courts are 166, of which 66 are in the Lane and the remainder in the courts.'

In Court No.4: 'In the lodging house kept by Mr Molloy, an Irishman, is a room 14 feet by 13 feet containing four beds, where lay for some time a young woman affected with typhus fever, while in the remaining beds nine or ten slept every night.'

Bold Lane, Court 5: '…is remarkable for cases of cholera… the dwellings' condition, the court imperfectly paved, a privy without a seat and the surface of the yard covered with oozings from the overcharged cesspool… there was smallpox prevailing at the time of my visit in one of the houses near the Theatre…'

Ram Yard, Bridge Street, Court No.2: 'The court is 17 feet wide and not paved. There are 12 houses on each side, each having one room below and another above. Here is another instance of constructing a chamber over a privy or rather over three. Out of 60 inhabitants, forty to fifty are children.'

In Court No.1 a single room abutting as privy was let out to Edward Eyre, his wife and two children at 1s 6d

A notorious court off Bradshaw Street, Spring Gardens, c.1825, photographed in 1947 and cleared in 1959. (Derby Museum)

(7.5p) per week. Further details from this report are too loathsome to detail here.

In fact, in 1878–79 a clearance plan was drawn up which envisaged the demolition of the courts off Walker Lane and nearby streets, but nothing was done. Yet a serious start to slum clearance only began between 1892 and 1900 in Willow Row and Walker Lane. At first, the inhabitants of these houses tended to be pitched out unceremoniously into the street in the name of progress, until the Chief Medical Officer of Health suggested that the Corporation arrange provision for the accommodation for these unfortunates before clearing a street. Otherwise most ended up in speculative tenements or the workhouse, as did as many as 700 in 1911. In some cases, back-to-back houses were thrown into one house, which was a sensible and economical idea.

Yet we have the testimony of many, most recently of Elsie Goodhead, that nearly every house in the West End was kept absolutely spotless, as indeed we would expect. Despite grinding social conditions in such areas, a recent community researcher, R. Davies, was surprised by attitudes, of West Enders especially. 'Their interests were living from day to day, getting enough money, getting enough food and just to survive until the next week. In a perfectly happy manner, that is how life was. There is a very low level of resentment. The only strong resentment that I have come across, even though they say it [life] was hard, is that the place was pulled down and the community split up.'

He added with evident surprise that, despite the conditions, politics were neither prominent nor especially oriented to the Labour Party. The latter is interesting for in the early 1790s, the Strutts, Samuel Fox and others had founded the ultra-reformist Derby Society for Political Information, under the inspiration of the French Revolution. Although *elite* middle class in inception, it was designed – even down to the low level of the subscription – to appeal to artisans and workers. Yet it, as well as others up and down the country, failed most singularly to attract such people. Moreover, when Strutt distributed copies of Paine's *Rights of Man* to his Belper workforce, they called a meeting and resolved that they 'wanted for nothing and were determined to live under the present constitution' and burnt Paine's pamphlet.

The old housing of the West End was finally razed in the 1970s, yet the replacement housing, consisting of cheaply built maisonettes into which little thought appeared to have gone, was neither beautiful, comfortable nor socially manageable. In 1985 a start had to be made on rebuilding several three and four-storey blocks of flats as two-storey houses, although only the worst were replaced or rebuilt. Only then could the various agencies agree that the clearance had been a success.

Demolition of sub-standard housing in Whitecross Street, West End, 24 April 1974. Although this street was pitched and built up in 1847–48, the cottages' design has not changed from the style of 40 years before; this is also a very late date for 12 and 16 pane sashes. (*Derby Evening Telegraph*)

Little remains of the old West End, in all conscience. St Anne's, Whitecross Street, built at the expense of the Poles of Radbourne Hall to the designs of F.W. Hunt of London in 1872–73 to evangelise these poor folk, stands out very starkly without its surrounding terraces; some mills poke darkly against the sky, others (mercifully) restored along Lodge Lane have found new uses; a handful of the pubs remain, fairly unspoilt, and the wrought-iron pawnbroker's sign from Wellington Pickering's shop in Brook Street is now in Derby Museum.

Land Societies

Improvements in housing, perhaps on the back of William Strutt's example, did come fairly quickly. One avenue was through land societies or building clubs, a sort of poor man's housing association, being a cross between building society and speculative developer. Originating in the mid-18th century, most were self-help organisations, buying up largish areas of urban land and dividing them up into building plots. These were sold or leased to members at cost, for the member to build his own house thereon. As time went on, it was more common for the society to build the houses – usually terraces and more or less uniform – to sell to members at cost or on a weekly basis, a sort of hire-purchase.

Along Osmaston Road, the earliest, the Birmingham-based Grove Street Club, built houses in Grove and Leonard Streets as early as 1807, at a cost of £40 each. Many of these houses were occupied by silk workers, few of whom could hope to own their own homes. In reality most houses built by such clubs in Derby were bought speculatively as investments by small business men and then let.

The land society movement got a considerable fillip from the Reform Act of 1832, whereby the owner of a freehold estate of an annual value of not less than 40s

(£2) was entitled to a Parliamentary vote. Both Whigs and Tories saw this as an opportunity to increase their vote and, through encouraging land societies, were able to go a considerable way to achieving their aim. Indeed, it may not be going too far to suggest that in this incentive lies the reason why the UK has the highest home ownership per head compared with the rest of Europe, where renting one's home bears no particular stigma.

A further reform was proposed in February 1852, to extend the vote to those paying rates of £5 or more per annum in the Boroughs or tax of £2. This raised the expectations of small property owners which, in the event, were frustrated when the relevant bill was defeated in the House. The Freehold Land Society's first estate in Derby, west of Uttoxeter New Road, reacted by naming three of their new streets Franchise, Parliament and Freehold, along with the erection of a fine pub, named the Gisborne Arms after the local landowner who had supported the bill and bankrolled the Land Society itself. This estate was mainly demolished in 1977 in a redevelopment scheme which took in most of St Luke's parish and in which most of the replacement accommodation is for rent only, and built smaller in square footage terms than the houses replaced. Further, the demolished houses were built as freeholds, whereas

their successors largely were not. Franchise Street itself – and the pub – were finally cleared in 2005.

Some charities also built housing on the land society scheme. The Liversage Charity built several streets immediately east of London Road opposite the Infirmary in the 1840s (demolished as unfit in the 1970s). Ponsonby Terrace, off South Street, is another building club development example dating from the 1840s, preceded by Litchurch Street, developed in 1825 by the Litchurch Street Building Club, one house equalling one share in the club. Others included much of New Zealand (the area between Slack Lane and Ashbourne Road), the second estate bought by the Freehold Land Society, built upon from 1851, and Strutt's Park, originally a tract of land between Darley Grove and the Derwent, east of St Helen's House, made available by William Strutt. Thus River, Duke and Bath Streets were built up from 1818 by a club, and even rather grand North Parade, higher up, designed as two terraces of eight very spacious Neo-Greek houses by William Smith and erected in 1819–22, was sponsored by a building club as the surviving deeds attest. Many such societies long continued to function, in order to collect instalments from purchasers; the Litchurch Street Club was not disbanded until 1841, when it still had 30 houses on its books.

Superior Building Club housing: 10–16 North Parade, built in 1819–21, to designs by William Smith (photographed in 2004). (Peter Billson)

Normanton Road, developed during the four decades from the 1830s, seen here from near the corner of Lyndhurst Street (right) looking towards the Normanton Hotel with Rose Hill Street entering on the left some way down, photographed in 1928. From the coming of the tram lines in the 1880s, the street was widened and the respectable villas on the right lost their front gardens and were turned into shops.

SUBURBAN DEVELOPMENT

Because of the relative ease by which Derby was able to expand in the second half of the 19th century, very few 'terraces' in the strictest sense of the term were built. Derby builders preferred to build individually designed houses butted on to one another to form the appearance of a terraced group rather than design and build a unified terrace, so as the century progressed fewer and fewer of the latter were built.

From the 1850s onwards, the publishers of architectural pattern-books had issued volumes of designs for suburban houses, often supported by working drawings, specifications and bills of quantities. It was not until 1877 that small builders and superior artisans had their own magazine to match the more upmarket *Builder*. This was the *Illustrated Carpenter and Builder*, the front cover of which was embellished with perspectives of buildings, plans of which, together with specifications and details of cost, were supplied to enquirers. In addition, it contained a 'Notes and Queries'

column. A prospective developer or private builder who required plans would write to the journal stating his needs and asking for suggestions and a few weeks later a reply would be published, illustrated by a small-scale elevation and plan.

In the early 19th century, the most important changes to take place in the design of speculative middle-class suburban housing on the other hand did not take place in the house itself, but in its setting. The introduction of avenue planting and of the front garden, stemming to some extent from the romantic socialism of William Morris, ensured that by the 1880s all the outdoor ingredients used later in the century by speculative builders were in existence.

Front gardens had been introduced earlier, but mainly were miniscule green margins. Today such houses are called 'palisaded villas' by estate agents. Those opening directly on to the road tend to lack a hallway and are, strictly speaking, 'cottages'.

The planting of trees to form an avenue was not a feature of the urban British street until the 1860s. One of the first recorded examples in England being Margaretta Terrace, Chelsea, of 1851, when the eccentric explorer-turned-architect, Dr John Phene, included such an avenue in this speculative development. The project caught the attention of the Prince Consort and so he and the Queen went to visit it. The Prince's congratulations encouraged other developers who began to plant avenues to keep abreast of fashion. In Derby, Hartington Street, Charnwood Street, Leopold Street and Swinburne Street are early examples. Unfortunately, as the trees grew they cut out light from the houses whose appearance they had been designed to enhance. The trees had to be pollarded, becoming ugly stumps with stubby branches ending in callouses of bark from which grew a bunch of long straggly stems.

Nevertheless, the vast majority of the population in the late 19th century lived in 'terraced' housing, groups of streets forming the basis of close-knit communities, served by shops, pubs and so forth, usually placed prominently at corners or intersections. In the main, the houses were of reasonable quality, although only from the earlier 20th century did most have lavatories built within their fabric and then usually not interconnected within the house. The author's 1902 house in Carlton Road, although deceptively spacious, had no bathroom as built, and the person for whom it was built, the chief cashier of a bank, just had a lavatory adjacent to the scullery and only accessible from the yard.

With the installation of modern plumbing, the surviving houses have entered upon a second lease of life, but those which were unplumbed and unimproved were largely cleared in the 20 years between 1964 and 1984. Although very many terraced houses remain, the original close-knit communities have been largely broken up, as the descendants of the original inhabitants moved out into municipal housing in the 20th century or improved their standing generally, being replaced at first by new generations of Derbeians as the town expanded or, since World War Two, by migrants – from eastern Europe, the new colonies and the sub-continent and today from Eastern Europe again, the Balkans and Pakistan – and themselves usually keen to move on to better accommodation.

SOCIAL MOBILITY – 1: THE SELVEYS

Joseph Selvey was the son of a Belper nailer, being born there in December 1844. Ultimately the slightly mutated family name suggests a mediaeval connection with Selby in Yorkshire, but Belper had harboured them for many generations. Joseph came to Derby to obtain work in a West End mill and settled in what must have been a very crowded and decaying accommodation at 12 Willow

Row, a 17th-century building. He married in June 1864 at St John's, Bridge Street – the first West End church – to Ruth, daughter of John Redfern. This John later migrated to Australia in 1869. Between them they had six sons and seven daughters, of whom six married and produced issue.

A cousin also settled in Derby, becoming a tailor in Abbey Street. In fact, most of the progeny were at some time or another small shopkeepers or married small shopkeepers. Meanwhile, Joseph and Ruth had, by the time the former died in January 1894, become fish shop proprietors in Willow Row, and Ruth carried on as such as a widow until she remarried John Thomas, a former soldier in the 95th Regiment who was a barber with premises at 3 Queen Street. At the same time Elizabeth, Ruth's second daughter, had married George Coxon, a proprietor of a sweet shop almost next door to her family at 17 Willow Row.

The Selvey's connections by friendship, business alliance or kinship with over a third of the residents of Shaftesbury Crescent and neighbouring streets a century ago, where they worked at Ley's foundry, are truly instructive. Among connections and acquaintances was Alice Parnell, who then kept a fish shop on the corner of Harrington and Holcombe Streets nearby. One of her sons was Reg Parnell (1911–1964), well known in the 1950s as a successful Formula One racing driver. The father William later ran the Royal Standard, Exeter Place and then an Alfreton Road garage.

The Selvey family shop in Osmaston Road was, in the Edwardian period, fitted by another Shaftesbury Crescent neighbour, Sydney Royce Turner, who also fitted out Boot's in St Peter's Street in 1912. His daughter, Norah (1905–1983), later became unforgettable as the wife of the late Sir Bernard Docker. The sheer diversity of the Selveys' circle and those of their peers in the

Once in the shadow of the Baseball Ground and centre of a rich series of inter-relationships, but flattened ready for the developer: Shaftesbury Crescent. (M. Craven)

socially lively micro-communities which were the 'drab terraces of Derby' is rivetting and deserves further study before all memory is lost.

Joseph Selvey's third son, Arthur Henry of Loudon Street, latterly an insurance agent, had married Martha Elizabeth in 1889. She was daughter of John Lowe, of Colyear Street (later also of Loudon Street, by the Arboretum), a bookdealer, himself descended from two generations of Bramcote lacemakers. Martha's brother, William Henry, was a fruiterer, living at 71 Vale Street. This was one of the three houses, noted much earlier, built by his father on land left to him by Deborah Roe, née Oakley, the mother of the liberal grandee Lord Roe of Derby. As he was a legatee of Mrs Roe, it is probable that they were kin, although the details of any relationship has yet to emerge. Yet the Roes, who ended up with a peerage, represent an extraordinary example of social mobility in the Derby of a century and a half ago and from them ran complex networks of kinship covering almost every level of contemporary society.

Further ramifications of the alliance between Ruth Redfern and Joseph Selvey arise from Ruth's sister's marriage to Charles Bennett, fish shop proprietor of 32 Loudon Street. The Bennetts were even then on the edge of the middle class, and their five sons and three daughters firmly established themselves as such. The elder son, T. Herbert Bennett (1870–1933), was organist of All Saints' before Dr Heath-Gracie and occupied the magnificent Georgian house at 99 Friar Gate. Three others were clerks, one, Alfred, with the railway, following a commission in the 5th Reserve Battalion, Wiltshire Regiment, in 1917. Another son, George Bennett, became a painter. Ernest married Mary, daughter of Alfred Brown, co-proprietor with his brother of another well-known local ironworks, Brown's. Her sister Florence married Herbert and another sister married E. Lilley, a mill-owner in the St Luke's area, their son being Garford Lilley, a most distinguished local cricketer.

SOCIAL MOBILITY – 2: THE ROES

Mrs Roe's origins were quite humble, her father Absalom Oakley having been a gardener who married the daughter of a Melbourne shopkeeper, possibly through employment at Melbourne Hall. There had been two Oakley brothers: Thomas, a partner of Alderman Roe in the timber business he founded on Siddals Road, and William, who, as a freelance steam-sawyer, must have also been closely bound up in the fortunes of the timber yard as well. It is, however, difficult to work out how Mrs Oakley came to own Gallows Fields (as the land on which the Vale Street houses were built was called) especially as

ownership passed on Mrs Roe's death to the second Mrs Roe, before passing on under a remainder. Mary Anne, Alderman Roe's second wife, had been the daughter and heiress of John Corden, 'licenced stamp distributor' and a descendant of the 17th-century tradesman who issued tokens. Through him ran inherited blood lines from several municipal families of that era.

The Roes' connections advanced hand in hand with their prosperity, the Alderman's sister Anne having been the second wife of Thomas Oakley. Their daughter married Gerard Llewellyn Hope, son of William, rector of St Peter's, scion of a most distinguished local dynasty and brother of the distinguished scholar Sir W.H. St John Hope (1854–1919). Yet William Oakley's daughters – the scholar's cousins by marriage – had married respectively a Gerard Street tailor and a simple weaver. Another cousin was James Oakley (1840–1910) a journeyman smith living cheek-by-jowl with his Selvey kinsmen at 53 Shaftesbury Crescent, in the shadow of Sir Francis Ley's Baseball Ground.

Of Alderman Roe's offspring, the eldest son, Alderman Sir Thomas Roe, was MP for the borough in 1883–1916 (with one gap), being knighted in 1894 and raised to the peerage in 1917. He was also thrice mayor of Derby and married a daughter of Matthew Kirtley, the

Sir Thomas Roe, later 1st Lord Roe of Derby. 131st mayor, who served three terms separated by 43 years; the only mayor to be made an (hereditary) peer. (M. Craven)

Vale Street, part of the Oakley-Roe property portfolio in the 1860s (2006). (M. Craven)

first locomotive superintendent of the Midland Railway. Unfortunately, the marriage was a late one for both and there was no heir to continue Roe's barony when he died aged 91 in 1923. His brother, Charles Fox Roe QC (1844–1905), died unmarried, but two of his sisters made the kind of marriages one might expect: Sarah married the founder, Rueben Eastwood, and Elizabeth married James Newbold, mayor of Derby in 1887, a union which extended the connections of these families considerably.

On the other hand, Lord Roe was uncle by marriage of Samuel Gray, a wheelwright (nevertheless, one employed at second hand, by Roe & Oakley's timber firm), but his brother, labourer Brian Gray, lived in considerable poverty at 7 Haarlem Street in Little City, dying there in 1897. His daughter Rachel, Mrs Kilburn, widowed in 1915, left an only child, also Rachel, who married the young Clerk to the Justices at the Shire Hall, Cecil Saunders, whose father Edward had come to Derby from Bedminster, Bristol, recruited by Sir Edwin Ann – also a Bristolian – to be a floor walker at the Midland Drapery.

This Edward had married a Vaughan Williams, a cousin of the great composer, thanks to whose mother, Margaret Wedgwood, this interesting complex of Derby families, ranging from labourer to the peer, comes within the ambit of the descendants of Erasmus Darwin and Josiah Wedgwood: social mobility indeed.

SOCIAL MOBILITY

Today, most of the locally-based descendants of this complex network of family relationships are owner-occupiers in professional jobs, retired or self-employed. Yet in the earlier generations there is one striking similarity between the Selvey-Redfern-Oakley-Roe-Bennett nexus and indeed the Denstone-Bridgart one of the previous era: the amazing range of social standing encapsulated in one extended family. In the latter it was possible to contrast a very opulent silk throwster, a Benedictine monk, a publican, a skilled plasterer, an architect, a builder and a starving framework knitter.

In the former we have chip-shop proprietors, nailers, millworkers, smiths and smallware dealers all close kin to a peer, a leading church organist, an internationally renowned composer, two solicitors, several mayors of Derby, mill-owners, ironfounders and the architect who wrote the definitive biography of Joseph Pickford. Yet Edward Saunders can recall his Derby great-grandmother sitting on the step of the family home in Grey Street, pulling on a clay pipe.

We have the testimony of at least one member of the Selvey dynasty that the stepmother of Lord Roe certainly did not shrink from entertaining her Selvey cousins at her grand Osmaston Road home in the 1870s. Likewise, in the mid-18th century, Sir Henry Every, 6th Bt., regularly entertained his ne'er-do-well second cousin, also Henry, at Egginton Hall during the latter's period as tenant of the Ship Inn, Full Street – a wise policy, as the mine host's grandson eventually succeeded as 8th Baronet!

Surely the underlying lesson in all of it – and there is no doubt that the ground rules are applicable not just in Derby – is that local society has always been fluid, class divisions permanently blurred by the ties and obligations of kinship and with limitless opportunities for self-betterment on offer to nearly anyone with energy, drive and vision, always helped by a measure of family support.

DERBEIANS IN AMERICA

Derby has always had close American ties. These go back to 1629, when Derby-born John Oldham, merchant, of Coleman Street, London, went to America to help found Plimoth (Plymouth) Plantation, Massachusetts. One of his sisters, Lucretia, accompanied him, marrying, soon after her arrival, Jonathan Brewster, a well-known pioneer American, as his second wife. In 1635 John and William Oldham, 'two little boys that were his kinsmen', went from Derby to join the elder John who was unfortunately killed by Indians at Block Island, Maine, a year later. Of these youngsters, the younger left descendants in America. Other members of the family remained in Derby, a branch settling in and around Alfreton at that time which still flourishes.

It may well be that the Oldhams went to America not just because they were Puritans (which they were) but

George and Hannah Hadley of Salt Lake City, formerly Derby, c.1900. (S.H. Palmer)

through the influence of the Pilgrim Father, Revd John Cotton (1584–1652), ejected minister of St Botolph, Boston, Lincolnshire, and who founded Boston, Massachusetts. Born in Bridge Gate to Derby attorney Rowland Cotton (d.1604), a member of the Cambridgeshire family from Cotton Hall, he was educated with the elder John Oldham at Derby School 1593–97 – the earliest pupils of the school actually on record – and it may well be that they kept in touch. His second wife, Sarah, Mrs Storey, was the daughter of Derby tailor Anthony Hawkridge, whose family were still tailor's in the borough into the 20th century. Once in America he became the leading spirit of the church in New England with living descendants.

During and after the civil war, other local families went to America, this time younger sons of Tory gentlemen, to Virginia and Carolina, like the Cokes, the Rodes, Abells and Sacheverells of Rearsby, nearly all with living posterity. Less fortunate ones were transported for assorted crimes, most managing to bob back up to the surface. Others went in the 19th century to better their work prospects like the sculptor William John Coffee (1773–1846), the theatrical impresario Richard Mansfield (1857–1907) and the hot-dog king Henry Stevens (1856–1934).

DERBY AND LOWELL

In 1773 another important migrant went to Boston, leaving his best friend, Joseph Wright's eldest brother John, behind, hesitating on the quay at Liverpool. This was Kirk Boott, second son of Francis, a Derby market gardener, born in Queen Street in 1755. He established an import/export business, which included introducing the US elite to Derby Porcelain, and became very wealthy, leaving at his death in 1817 five sons and four daughters.

The second son returned to London to run that end of the family business; the third son, Kirk Boott II (1790–1837), was sent to England to be educated, going to school in Ashbourne and then Rugby and making numerous visits to family in Derby. After three years at Harvard, he returned to Britain to join the army, seeing action in the Peninsular campaign in 1812–14 before being stationed in Sheffield as a captain in the 85th Regiment.

He visited Derby frequently at this time, staying at St Helen's House with William Strutt, with the Wrights and his aunt, Mrs John Horrocks. In 1818 he married Anne, a daughter of Thomas Haden, surgeon and protégé of Darwin who had been mayor in 1811 and 1819. Francis, a son of the Boott who had returned to London, later married Kirk Boott II's daughter, Eliza Haden Boott, and their daughter Mary married Charles Sydenham Haden, thus squaring the Derby circle yet again.

The younger Kirk Boott himself visited the Derby textile mills in 1817–18 and from 1821 was co-founder with Francis Cabot Lowell, Nathan Appleton and Patrick T. Jackson of a new settlement at East Chelmsford, on the confluence of the Merrimack and Pawtucket in Massachusetts. This was to be a cotton-spinning city, and Boott's role was to set it up and run it. He had hoped to call it Derby, but the sudden death of Lowell led to it being given his name instead. Lowell himself had been an aristocratic Boston merchant who had visited Britain and originated the idea of a model textile industry in New England to rival Samuel Slater's Pawtucket Mills, set up a little before, using ideas pirated from the Strutts at Belper, from whence he had come.

In 1824 Boott appointed Revd Theodore Edson as incumbent of his new settlement and personally designed St Anne's Church, which he based on St Michael's, Derby, in which he had been married, whereas the dedication was in honour of his wife. It will come as no surprise that the Edgeworths (offspring and sister of the Lunar Society maverick Irish landowner Richard Lovel Edgeworth, who had extensive American property) kept William Strutt fully informed of Boott's enterprise, for the entire project had Strutt's blessing.

Like Strutt, too, Boott was a competent architect, designing not only the church but workers' housing, mills and municipal buildings, some of which survive. In the end, the City of Lowell was a success and one of the entrepreneurs attracted to it by Boott was George Washington Whistler, who set up a works to construct railway locomotives there in 1832. His son was the eminent London-based impressionist painter James McNeil Whistler, later brother-in-law – and eventually,

as with most of his friends, sworn enemy – of Boott's nephew Sir Francis Seymour Haden, etcher and eminent surgeon. Boott himself was killed in a street accident in 1837, but his legacy – and posterity – continued.

Exactly how much of Strutt's own idealism and ingenuity went into Lowell and its extensive mills it is impossible to say, but the Derby intellectual revolution of the 18th century was a fundamental inspiration at Lowell, and if it should prove to have been international in its consequences no one should be surprised. After all, had Bostonian Benjamin Franklin not been a friend of Darwin's, a frequent guest of Whitehurst's and *eminence grise* of the Lunar Society?

The Bootts were in touch with the Duesburys, selling their wares in Boston well before 1800. Much later, the underrated William Duesbury III sold his interest in the china works in 1815 in order to set up a white paint factory at Bonsall using a new process of his own devising, omitting the toxic lead element. Indeed, Duesbury was a formidably talented chemist, but ahead of his time by about 150 years. The business failed, after which he went to America, following in the footsteps of his ne'er-do-well uncle, James Duesbury. Having known Boott from his Derby days, he settled in Lowell almost from its foundation as an industrial chemist. He was a convinced Universalist and designed the sect a fine chapel there. He married again in Lowell – perhaps bigamously, for we do not know the fate of his first family in Derby – having more children, before doing away with himself for reasons that remain obscure on 12 December 1845.

Lowell, Massachusetts, US. Panorama of some of Boott's mills, *c*.1830. (City of Lowell)

XIV

RECREATION AND RELAXATION

ENTERTAINMENT

From the mid-19th century onwards was the beginning of the first period in our history since the Romans when entertainment became available for more than the elite and ruling classes. Previously, about the only entertainment really universally available had been the fairs, which took place on the Morledge, which had become dominated by fun fairs by the later-19th century. These endured until 1924, when they were banished to Allenton. Fun fairs were also staged in the yard of the Swan Inn, St Peter's Street, in the period 1820–63. It was not until after World War Two, in 1948, that the council made the site of Bass's baths available and circuses also stand there to this day.

Circuses indeed had been held in a building to the north of Bag Lane, demolished in 1902 (now the site of the Co-operative Central Suite), from the 18th century. Visiting companies by 1879 included 'Lord' George Sanger's, whose waterproof marquee allegedly seated 12,000, and Keith's, although this was destroyed by fire on 24 March that year, with the loss not only of one (human) life, but also those of 20 horses, a donkey and a monkey to a total value of £4,000. The mayor launched a public subscription to make good Keith's losses and the company was re-established on The Holmes but soon went bankrupt, leaving Sanger for a while pre-eminent.

Another diversion which became formalised in the later 19th and early 20th centuries was ice-skating, previously enjoyed quite informally when the river or local ponds and lakes froze and was common before the 'litte ice age' ended in the 1880s. Indeed, it was that climatic change which probably served as the spur to this formalization. In Derby a skating rink was contrived at the Royal Drill Hall in Becket Street by 1874. Two years

Easter fair on the Morledge, 1913. (Derby Museum)

Elephants being led through the Cattle market for the circus held in conjunction with the Easter fair of 1913. (Derby Museum)

later the purpose-built Alexandra Skating Rink was opened on Uttoxeter New Road. The Alexandra moved in a decade or so to Normanton Road, where it was housed in an engagingly eccentric Neo-Classical revival building but closed in 1913 when the structure was converted into a cinema. The building almost came full circle when the cinema closed in 1950, for it was converted for skating again – roller skating, but it was demolished and replaced in 1953 as a dance hall, on which more below. Today roller skating is catered for at the Meteor Centre, an out-of-town shopping complex built in the northern portion of Little Chester in the 1980s; the nearest skating is at Nottingham.

Music-hall certainly represented the peoples' culture insofar as that term has any real meaning and much of such entertainment took place in small auditoria attached to public houses. The Barley Mow in East Street (closed to make way for Boot's, 1911) was renowned for having the Star music hall attached – founded in 1853, apparently – and even the rather more lowly Scarsdale Arms, Colyear Street, boasted a rather home-spun music hall from 1877, but which the landlord's widow put a stop to on his death in 1886.

The first purpose-built music-hall was on nearly the same site as Keith's Circus, but had also burnt down, due to the inefficient damping of an incendiary stage effect on 25 May 1873. From its initiation, however, the Corn Exchange had also housed the Palace Theatre of Varieties and this was prestigious enough to attract such lustrous names as that of Jenny Lind, the 'Swedish Nightingale'.

In March 1886 Andrew Melville opened the purpose-built Grand Theatre in Babington Lane, which was in direct rivalry with the Palace. Unfortunately, less than a month after its opening it too burnt down with the loss of two lives. Nevertheless, it was rebuilt and successfully reopened; Charlie Chaplin is reputed to have performed there as a child in support of his father's act. It struggled

on until 1950 when it closed and lay empty for a decade, before being bought by Mecca in 1960 and adapted into a ballroom as the Locarno, wrecking the façade in the process. It was Confetti's in 1988 and after several changes was up for sale in 2005 and its future is uncertain.

In the closing years of the 19th century, New Normanton, having grown vastly into a major inner suburb, also felt that music-hall type entertainment might be a viable proposition there, too. The south end of Upper Dale Road was, at the time, being built-up and, at a point where five roads met, a large public house – The Cavendish – was erected, being completed in 1898. The newly-electrified trams terminated there from 1904 and here too was built, in 1905, at first as a marquee, the Derby Pavilion, which catered for 'End-of-the-Pier' type shows. It was rebuilt largely in timber in 1909 and also showed films during the winter, but fire claimed this venue, too, in 1929. The site was claimed by a cinema 1937–60, which was replaced by a supermarket.

In 1914, too, another theatre, aimed at the music-hall style of entertainment, opened on Green Lane, at the corner of Macklin Street, called the Hippodrome and designed by the specialist London firm of Marshall & Tweedy. Whereas the Grand Theatre had been designed by Oliver Essex of Birmingham in a species of French Empire neo-classical: bland, grand and slightly over-dressed, like a tipsy aunt, the Hippodrome is a highly-successful adaptation of Queen Anne revival to such a use. It is said of the Hippodrome that while displaying the immortal talents of Bud Flanagan and Chesney Allen in 1926, the song *Underneath the Arches* had been written, committed to music by resident music director Noel Vincent, and given its first airing at Southport, shortly afterwards.

Dancing was catered for not only after World War One at the Palace, but in a ballroom at the lower end of St Peter's Street over a shop (still extant as a space within the structure) and another at The Spot, but converted

The Grand Theatre, as seen from Gower Street, at about the turn of the century. Conversion into a night club has deprived it of most of the detailing on its ornate façade including the loss of the pediment. (*Derby Evening Telegraph*)

The Corn Exchange redecorated as the Palais-de-Danse, 1921, by George Grey Wornum. (M. Craven)

into the Spot Cinema Theatre in 1910. The latter ended ignominiously in 1917, and the site today lies beneath the Eagle Centre. The Plaza ballroom was opened on the upper floor of Sanderson & Holmes's car showrooms, successor of Holmes's carriage works in 1935 by Sam Ramsden, scene of the debut of Ron Pountain ('Denny Dennis'). This was replaced by the former Alexandra Ice Rink, Normanton Road (at that time the Alex cinema), as the Trocadero dance hall, while the Plaza soldiered on until 1957, latterly as a discotheque until 1982. The 'Troc' was sold as a Bingo hall but burned down while being converted into a supermarket on 18 October 1982.

For the working man to make his own entertainment and hopefully to be one up on the brewers' prices, the Working Mens' Club was an essential institution, the first being established to provide some relief from life in Little City on Burton Road in January 1874. Previous to that one of the few free enjoyments had been the Promenade Concerts established in the open air in the Market Place and Friar Gate on summer evenings in 1869, although it is by no means clear for how many seasons this engaging idea endured, given the vagaries of English summer weather. In 1870, however, an 'American Bowling Saloon' was advertising in the *Mercury* at 28 Iron Gate; it does not appear to have lasted long.

CINEMA & ELECTRONIC ENTERTAINMENT

The cinema appeared in 1910, in which year three picture houses opened within four months of each other. Two, the Midland Electric Theatre in Babington Lane (with extravagant mock-Tudor interior, aping Haddon Hall, all by J. Eastham) and the Victoria Electric Theatre in Becket Well Lane (architect, J.H. Morton, partner of T.H. Thorpe of Derby) were purpose-built and both lasted exactly 50 years; the third was the ex-dance hall at The Spot.

Since 1910 there have been 20 cinemas in Derby, plus a further five in the suburbs, which later came into the orbit of the town, meticulously researched by Peter Good and expanded upon by Ashley Franklin. Four more had opened up by the outbreak of World War One. One, as we have seen, was in the former Alexandra Ice Rink on the corner of Normanton Road and genteel Hartington Street, originally founded in 1863 and converted in 1913 to the Alexandra Electric Theatre by T.H. Thorpe – latterly just the Alex – and lasted until acquired by Sam Ramsden in 1953 after a short period as a roller skating rink.

Gaumont Palace, London Road, by B.E. Jay, 1934. Since the photograph was taken in 1988, it has become a nightclub called Zanzibar. (*Derby Evening Telegraph*)

Two more cinemas opened in 1913 and another in 1914, before World War One called a temporary halt. Nevertheless, 10 new cinemas were opened between then and 1937, four in the suburbs. The best was without doubt the superb Art Deco Gaumont Palace, opened in London Road in 1934 with an unprecedented (for Derby) capacity of 2,400 seats. The interior was very rich, but less so later, having been simplified and made multi-screen by its new owners after becoming the Odeon in 1965, £10,000 worth of Compton organ being sold to St Philip's Catholic Church, Chaddesden. It is currently a nightclub called Zanzibar, but with its clean horizontals marred by a gigantic fibreglass representation of a palm tree and an Arab Sheikh leering over the parapet

After World War Two a supposed prestige hotel of 1966 – the Pennine, tucked away where no one could find it in Colyear Street, but mercifully so, in view of its uniquely ugly shuttered concrete façade – included a cinema, named the Superama and opened the following year. It became the Odeon Pennine after being taken over by Rank but became a disco in 1976. In 1981 the Metro cinema was founded in the former Art College, backed

Gloria Cinema, Chaddesden, built in 1938 and designed by A.J. Turner. Photographed 13 February 2001, just prior to demolition to make way for a supermarket. (Tony J. Griffin)

by the British Film institute, and subsequently two multi-screen cinemas have opened (both in 1988).

If the cinema was the first non-live entertainment available in Derby, the wireless was undoubtedly the second, a local station opening under the auspices of the BBC on St Helen's Street in 1971, followed by Ram FM in the 1990s. Yet experimental TV relays had been demonstrated by Victor Buckland (1898–1988), a radio retailer and engineer, from 1921, although his first really successful attempt came a decade later, a couple of years after the demonstration of a Baird television held in the Midland Railway Institute on 15 January 1929 by E.V.R. Martin of the Derby Wireless Club. Television as now understood, however, had to wait just over two further decades before it was available in Derby. The first BBC broadcast to be received was on 17 December 1949, when the Sutton Coldfield transmitter came on stream and, by the spring of 1953, 29 percent of Derbeians had television sets in their homes.

DERBY PLAYHOUSE

Another converted chapel, this time a Baptist one of 1830 in Sacheverel Street, became, in 1978, a cinema called the Ajanta, showing exclusively Asian films. In 1862–63 it had been converted into a Sunday school (Samuel Plimsoll, the Derby MP 1868–80 and sailors' friend, having laid the foundation stone), remaining as such until 1928, when it was sold to a Pentecostal sect.

On 1 November 1948, the Derby Little Theatre Club began in the modern gospel hall in Becket Street, built to replace the one in the former Theatre Royal by the trust set up by Alderman Wilkins, thus proving that whatever comes round, goes round. Among its leading lights was a youthful future theatre director, the acerbic John Dexter (1926–1990). On 1 October 1952 the old Sacheverel Street chapel was adapted as a repertory theatre by this company and opened as the Derby Playhouse. The auditorium caught fire and was burnt out on 26 March 1956, but by dint of hard work it reopened on 25 April 1957. A performance in May 1975 of *Tommy* marked its closure, after which it was transformed in 1978 into the Ajanta cinema, closed in 1980, the building lasting until 1988.

The Playhouse then transferred to a new building attached to the Eagle Centre shopping precinct, which opened in September in 1975 with *My Fair Lady*. To attest to its manifold shortcomings, nearly every newly-appointed Playhouse director announces without fail a desire to remove from the building as fast as possible. Furthermore, it faces the interior of a precinct which suffers persistent vandalism and has all the presence of a 1960s provincial airport terminal.

Centre of the Derby Society of Musicians, the Tiger, as designed by Joseph Pickford in 1764. (M. Craven)

MUSIC

The Derby Society of Musicians was founded in 1764 and met in a room in the then newly-completed Tiger Inn in the Corn Market, designed by Joseph Pickford. This lively society included an ensemble, which also met in some of its members' houses, which centred round Charles Denby, the son and protégé of William Denby, since 1743 the organist of All Saints'. This included the painter Joseph Wright (flute) and Peter Perez Burdett (cello). The younger Denby, who succeeded his father in 1771, was also a notable composer, publishing his Op.1 & 2, consisting of harpsichord sonatas, in 1792, followed by his Op. 3 (duets for forte piano and flute). In 1792 he was collecting subscriptions towards the publication of his first piano concerto.

Concerts in the 18th century were held mainly in All Saints' Church, and after 1773 at the Theatre Royal – Paganini played a concert there in October 1833. From 1793 a series of Music Festivals, Denby having initiated the first, were held again at All Saints', the soprano soloist being Eliza Salmon (née Mundy of the Markeaton family).

The organisation of these concerts – later held to support the Infirmary – were taken over on Denby's death by George Christopher Fritche (1769–1835), who succeeded him as All Saints' organist. Although his father

George (1726–1799) was successively landlord of the George & Dragon, Corn Market, and the Green Man, St Peter's Churchyard, when he married George Christopher's mother in 1765 he was described as 'trumpeter of the Blues' (the Royal Horse Guards), which certainly establishes the family's musical credentials. It is also a fact, as military historian Countess Tarnovski has pointed out, that '…a high proportion of these 18th-century regimental trumpeters and drummers were of African or Caribbean origin' holding out the intriguing possibility that George Fritche might have been the founder of Derby's first black family. Certainly he was not a Derby man in origin, but there were Fritches in Derby up to the Restoration period, and it is possible that George's father was brought into England as the black servant – then a fashionable 'must have', however distasteful the concept might seem to us today – of one of them. Against this is the lack of any contemporary record of the fact that he may have been black or partly so. Several generations of the family were prodigiously musical.

In 1817 the Derby Choral Society was founded by William Gover, son of the Master of the Militia Band, also running the Derby Philharmonic Society, 1835–40. The Choral Society gave an annual Christmas concert at the rebuilt Brookside Chapel for very many years, also in the Mechanics' Institute, from which one is forced to the conclusion that these buildings of William Mansfield Cooper must have had a fine acoustic.

Subscription concerts in the Assembly Rooms and Mechanics' Institute attracted national and international names, like Johann Strauss in 1838. This pattern, much diminished in favour of band concerts in the later 19th and earlier 20th centuries, continued until fairly recent times. After World War Two, concerts promoted by the Corporation were held in the Queen Street Baths. During the 1970s, a week long music festival studded with international names was run in the cathedral (where concerts had been banned as profane in 1873), sponsored by the Provost Beddoes with Philip Foulds, music shop proprietor, which was ended after 1978 by the opening of the present Assembly Rooms. An innovation of 1990 was the staging of a free classical concert in the open air in Darley Park, an event that has continued until the time of writing.

TWENTIETH-CENTURY SPORT

CRICKET

In the early 19th-century cricket matches seem to have been on Chaddesden Park, with the Wilmots as patrons. The local club was the South Derbyshire Cricket Club.

Derbyshire Cricket team c.1900, including Steve Bloomer and Rams star J.J. Bagshaw. (Bob Read)

There was then also a Derby Town Cricket Club, playing on The Holmes. Unfortunately, the construction of the new cattle market in 1861 caused the pitch to dry out and subside, making imperative a move to the racecourse in 1863. From it grew the Derbyshire County Cricket Club which was established with this ground as its base in 1870 and from which it still plays, with subsidiary grounds at Chesterfield, Buxton, Heanor and Ilkeston. Among the host of eminent players from Derby itself may be counted future mayor Alderman Unwin Sowter, William Mycroft, a very successful bowler whose son, Allen, was also mayor – in 1924, the borough's second Labour holder of that office – and Arthur Richardson (1907–1983).

BASEBALL

Beside Ley's foundry in Litchurch was a 12-acre amenity area called the Vulcan Sports Ground provided for employees of the works. In 1888 Sir Francis Ley, having become intoxicated with baseball during an 1881 visit to the US (during which he obtained the licence to manufacture the Ewart Chain Belt), founded a club at the foundry and invited two US teams to visit. In 1890 he hired US Baseball Coaches John Reidenbach and Sam Bullas from Cleveland, Ohio, to train his Derby team.

In 1889 a league of four teams had been formed, which Ley's Derby team duly won in 1890. The other clubs went on to fame as soccer clubs: Preston North End, Aston Villa and Stoke. In July that year the Baseball Association of Great Britain (from 1894 the National Baseball Association) was formed with 30 clubs which were expected to compete for the Spalding Cup, won by Derby in 1895, 1897 and 1899, the latter victory being over arch rivals Nottingham Forest. After 1898, however, baseball waned in public enthusiasm and the sport declined swiftly. Yet it was on this ground that the Derby County Football Club played for just over a century

from 1895, and it was known in consequence as the Baseball Ground, along with a stylish attendant public house, the Baseball Tavern, designed by E.R. Ridgeway and built in 1890.

The Derbyshire Baseball Association widened interest in the game locally. Up-and-coming players who entered the main team from the DBA and distinguished themselves included Black Country-born Steve Bloomer (1874–1938), who had come up as a soccer player via the Derby Swifts in the South Derbyshire Boys' League, founded in 1886. He came to notice by scoring the winning goal for the Swifts in a League final on the Arboretum playing fields on 7 April 1890. He subsequently played baseball and cricket too. Indeed, he had the honour, with teammate William Beresford, of holding gold medals for Derby cricket, baseball and football. But it was at the latter that Bloomer excelled most.

SOCCER

In 1884 the cricket club, some of its members stultified by the inertia of the winter season, spawned the Derby County Association Football Club, founder members of the Football League in 1888, their first game within its embrace having been played against Bolton Wanderers, which Derby County won 6–3. The team was universally known *ab initio* as The (Derby) Rams, from the anonymous and unlikely 18th-century *Ballad of the Derby Ram*, allegedly an animal of prodigious size and prowess and hero of a ditty of many variations, which in reality expresses the early 18th-century reliance of the borough on the wealth generated by sheep farming in the Peak.

Unfortunately, despite this promising start, they had the ignominy of finishing bottom and had to apply (successfully as it turned out) for re-election. The club's foundation came, incidentally, 14 years after an abortive attempt to revive the Shrovetide game in Derby on 1 March 1870. In all this, Steve Bloomer stands out as unique among the great players of Derby County, joining the club in April 1892 when Derby was barely five years in the League. He made his debut that September against Stoke and soon became popular with the crowd, not least because he was such a reliable goalscorer, being the team's leading scorer for 14 seasons. He was capped for England in 1895 and went on to represent his country 22 more times, including scoring twice in a 9–0 win over Ireland at the Baseball Ground in 1895. He rejoined Derby after four years in 1910, went to Germany, only to be interned for the duration in 1914, but returned as general assistant when the war ended. In 1966 a memorial to him was erected in Tiger Yard, after

Steve Bloomer memorial, Tiger Yard, photographed in July 1997. (M. Craven)

Pride Park Stadium, 2005. (M. Craven)

a campaign by his grandson Stephen Richards, set by the west door of the Market Hall.

Meanwhile, the Baseball Ground was purchased for £10,000 and the main stand was completed in 1926. Another move to a stadium designed by Modernist guru Maxwell Ayrton was let slip in 1947, and, indeed, the ground managed to pack in no less than 41,826 people in 1969 for a game against Spurs. Derby beat Charlton 4–1 in the FA Cup Final in 1946 on their fourth try, having been runners-up in 1898, 1899 and 1903, losing to Nottingham Forest, Sheffield Wednesday and Bury respectively. They also won the Football League Cham-

pionship in 1972 and 1975, the first time under the ever-popular Brian Clough (1935–2004), who remained a Derby resident until his death, less than a year after having been made the first Honorary Freeman of Derby since 1968.

After many subsequent vicissitudes, free newspaper magnate Lionel Pickering (1931–2006) rescued the club, but by 2003 debts had practically broken him and it was sold to a pair of Yorkshire investors who completely failed to turn things around. It was again sold in 2006 to a consortium of local millionaires. Derby County is notable for the remarkable fervour and enthusiasm of its supporters, which miraculously seems to survive even the most demoralising periods.

The greatest change effected under Lionel Pickering was the decision in 1994 to abandon the historic Baseball Ground for a new stadium in Pride Park. The new ground was ready for the start of the 1997 season and was opened by HM the Queen, with Pickering playing host; why precedent was not followed with the resultant bestowal of a knighthood is hard to fathom.

The Municipal Sports Ground, 1932–33, and Rams footballer Dally Duncan (1909–90) practising. He played for Derby County from 1932 to 1946. (Private Collection)

RUGBY

Derby has been no nurturer of Rugby League, as with so many towns further north. The first team to represent the town took the field on 21 November 1891 when they beat a Nottingham team 9–0. Derby won six out of seven matches the following year, playing on the Arboretum's new playing field. This club moved to the Municipal Sports Ground by 1926, when the game had found sufficient favour to have engendered a borough Police team. The 1930s saw the spread of the handling code throughout Derbyshire and new clubs were formed including Derby Tigers. Rolls-Royce spawned a club in 1943, probably as a result of the huge wartime increase in the workforce. Eventually, members of the Derby club and the Tigers amalgamated and moved to a new ground on

Kedleston Road, becoming the Derby Rugby Football Club. Since 2001, when that ground was bought for a hotly contested housing development, a new ground was acquired off Haslams Lane, Darley Abbey; the developer's shilling went towards a new club house of spacious dimensions.

ROWING

Rowing is another sport with a long local history which, in the 20th century, brought renown to Derby. Regattas were held regularly on the Derwent from the beginning of the 19th century but had stopped by 1846. In 1857, however, the Derwent Rowing Club was founded and revived the event, at first in conjunction with a cricket match, continuing until 1878, when the construction of Handyside's Great Northern Railway bridge over the Derwent and its attendant scaffolding and piling forced a change of course.

Derby School had a thriving club from 1863–89 and between 1879 and 1883 a master, J. Lowndes, won the diamond sculls at Henley five times. Another club was formed on 13 May 1879 by members of the Conservative Club called Derby Town Rowing Club. The 'Town' element of the name was dropped in 1906. They acquired one of the buildings from the recently-defunct Keith's Circus as a clubhouse and erected it on the Little Chester side of the river, close to the railway bridge, replaced in 1893.

The regatta was again revived after a false start in 1880, in 1903 and in 1931, the two surviving rowing clubs were again joined by Derby School and the sport was unaffected by the school going comprehensive and co-educational in 1972; indeed, girls' rowing was added in 1975, but in 1977 the school suddenly stopped its rowing in a fit of misplaced egalitarianism. Women had

A tranquil scene on the Derwent by Derby Rowing Club's buildings, c.1975.

been included in the Derby Rowing Club's crews from 1973, too, and both the Derwent and Derby Clubs now race crews of all types.

BOXING

We have already encountered Derby's place in the annals of prize fighting, but by the later 19th-century boxing, constrained by the rules codified under the name of the Marquis of Queensberry, was the coming thing. It enjoyed its real heyday in the 1930s and 1940s, in the open air at the Municipal Sports Ground, during World War Two at the Baseball Ground and subsequently at the King's Hall until a fall in popularity led to its replacement by professional wrestling at that venue, later itself transferred to the Assembly Rooms.

Much boxing went on in pubs or was organised through them. In 1938, for instance, Albert McLocklin and his wife Biff took over the Old Spa Inn on Abbey Street and combined with two other nearby landlords to promote quality amateur fights. The former brewhouse was converted into a gymnasium and young boxers of local repute fought under the resident management of Fred ('Bauble') Harrison (who ran a neighbouring chip shop) aided by Bob Kirkly, who had made a name for himself as a boxer as Bob Curley. Some of the lads nurtured here rose to national repute and memorable exhibition bouts were staged in the pub's back yard on Sunday mornings. The departure of the McLocklins to run the Marquis of Granby in Gerard Street led to this forcing house of pugilistic talent moving to premises in Agard Street where it became known as the Premier Boxing Club.

ATHLETICS

Athletics has a longer local pedigree. What may be termed as professional athletics continued in the 1820s, inspired by the prodigious performances of James Wantling, a China Works painter and the son of a potter there. He won purses of up to 200 guineas over longish distances, and was invariably heavily backed. He went to London in 1825, but inspired two poems in his praise and probably won his supporters more than he gained for himself.

After the abolition of Derby football, sports had been organised by the mayor as a substitute, and these occasions kept a form of athletics alive until at least the 1860s. In 1884, however, an athletics club was formed in the West End: St John's, later Derby Harriers, which in 1896 became the Derby County Athletics and Cycling Club. A leading light was Derby's most athletic mayor,

Osmaston, Osmaston Park Road, aerial view of the Municipal sports ground c.1925. (*Derby Evening Telegraph*)

Alderman Eggleston, from a family of confectioners of all things. This club still thrives and several members over the years have acquired international names for themselves.

BOWLS

Bowls were played on pub greens from the later 18th century and there was one on the north side of North Street, in Strutt's Park, until the site was appropriated for the construction of the Children's Hospital in 1883. In New Normanton the Mafeking, Porter Road, built, as one might expect, in 1900, had a popular crown bowling green of 824 square yards, which was the only surviving one attached to a pub in Derby until it closed in February 2007, the pub having been sold as a private house in November 2006. Indeed, bowling seems to have been in a long decline, many pub greens going as described above and even the venerable bowls club at the Arboretum, founded in 1862, had the misfortune of having to close in summer 2006 – a great loss. The Wheel in Friar Gate was long famous for its bowling green, too. It was laid out in 1726 by Francis Ward on a 1,078 square yard area and survived until the Bridgart family bought it to expand their yard. The (White) Swan in St Peter's Street also had a

fine green from the Regency period, which lasted some 50 years.

BALLOONING

It was from the White Swan's bowling green that the Derby ballooning pioneer and former silk throwster Emmanuel Jackson made a notable pioneering first ascent in 1850 before transferring his talents to the Arboretum later that year. He was not, however, quite the first, as this was claimed for 1813 in a narrative poem (but conceivably a later joke) entitled *Ralph Pitchfork's lamentable account of the Derby Air Balloon and his return Home to his Wife Joan* – unless the word lamentable in the title implies an abortive flight! Furthermore, Erasmus Darwin had sent an unmanned, silk-covered hydrogen balloon sailing across the Midlands on Boxing Day 1783 – the same year the Montgolfier brothers made their first hot air flight, which had thrilled him very much – which landed in the park at Pillaton Hall, Staffordshire, much to the surprise of his patient, Sir Edward Littleton! Jackson himself went on to give displays worldwide before murdering his wife and committing suicide at his home, 116 Burton Road, in 1883.

GREYHOUND RACING

It is worth mentioning, too, that the racing of greyhounds – derived from the now politically incorrect country sport of coursing – had a permanent home within the walls of Goodwin's County Gaol since 1928, although all structures within have long since gone. Luckily, the powerful Greek Doric façade still lowers down Vernon Street – its triumphal avenue from Friar Gate – its restoration in the 1990s being consequent upon the cessation of the dogs at the site, when it was bought and redeveloped for housing and offices under the name of Vernon Gate, the very latest use of the Norse street suffix!

SWIMMING

Finally, swimming has been covered in the multiplicity of its venues since 1828 and the city today still supports a vigorous club, housed in the Regional Pool, Moor Lane, built to less-than-exacting standards in 1974 and given a long overdue upgrading since 1988. In recent years several Derby swimmers have achieved international success, including at the 2004 Olympics and the 2006 Commonwealth Games.

EARLY PHOTOGRAPHY

It would, of course, be quite mistaken to assume that the citizens of Derby were obsessed by sport to the exclusion of all else. Their other interests were many and varied. A classic example of the diversity of talent available in the town lies in the genesis of the Derby Photographic Society. The first commercially active photographers in Derby had been Thomas Roberts – formerly a bookseller – operating Photographic Portrait Rooms in Victoria Street in 1849 and Samuel Brennen, who set up taking daguerreotypes in 1851, although no photograph by either from this era has yet been identified, although both men enjoyed long careers in the trade, Roberts's son only closing down in 1900, two years after Brennen. Yet a 'Photographic Operator' had been advertised as about to visit Derby in 1845.

Two of the very earliest datable and attributable are a view of Exeter House which was taken in early autumn 1853 by Richard Keene and a view of the west bank of the Derwent from Exeter Bridge of 1855 by W. Stretch. Keene, however, put Derby on the map photographically, although he always acknowledged the inspiration of Revd Canon Edward Abney of The Firs on Burton Road. Abney was vicar of St Alkmund's and was also a pioneer photographer, his inspiration being William Henry Fox-Talbot of Lacock Abbey, Britain's pioneer photographer, who, on 12 December 1832, had married 'French' Mundy's granddaughter Constance, being, as a result, a frequent visitor to Markeaton Hall. Constance's mother was an aunt of Abney's by marriage. Indeed, Fox-Talbot may have been able, through these associations, to have drawn some inspiration from the experiments in proto-photography of Josiah Wedgwood's son, Thomas, who managed, with the encouragement of Erasmus Darwin, to fix an image on sensitised paper as early as 1802, shortly before committing suicide, a tragic event which may have delayed the development of photography for a generation.

W. Stretch's photograph of the view north from Exeter Bridge, taken in 1855, from the original calotype. This is the earliest known view of the entire silk mill. There are still some riverside gardens left. (Derby Museum)

Richard Keene was born in 1825, the son of the manager of Peet's Mill in Brook Street, who had come up from London. He established himself in 1851 as a publisher and printer in Iron Gate, next to instrument maker John Davis, himself a keen amateur photographer. He also met John Alfred Warwick, Signals and Telegraph Superintendent of the Midland Railway and another keen photographer, who thereafter acted as Keene's photographic amanuensis. Both also worked closely with Thomas Scotton, who was appointed first full-time official photographer to the Railway Company in succession to Keene himself.

Keene soon added photography to his business activities, concentrating on views and scenes, selling the prints from a catalogue, as well as on special commissions for businesses and for local gentry families, rather than the more routine *cabinet* and *carte-de-visite* portraiture, although he did take portraits, notably one of his friend the philosopher Herbert Spencer posing with his father. Although it is customary to give Keene the credit for all the photographs emanating from his studio, he actually appears in many – usually as a bystander – and from this we may be certain that Warwick's hand was actually on the lens cap. Keene's pellucid views of the county and beyond comprised his

Portrait of Richard Keene c.1885. (John Keene)

commercial catalogue, and his views of Derby taken between 1854 and his death in 1894 form the core of a valuable archive of early photographs of the borough. Those taken before the widening of the streets show parts of Derby almost exactly at it would have appeared to Dr Johnson when he and Boswell visited in September 1777.

Ten years before his death, Keene had been a prime mover and co-founder of the Derby Photographic Society, a member of the Linked Ring and a founder member of the Photographic Convention of the United Kingdom, of which he was President elect at the time. Of his numerous sons, two had carried on the photographic tradition to 1936 and two others, William Caxton and A.J. (Jack) Keene, were artists. A homonymous great-grandson was mayor of Derby as recently as 1986. Richard Keene is a seriously underrated figure as a photographer, bearing in mind his introduction to the 'art-science', as he called it, the exceptional quality of his work and its early date.

This recording of the town was also taken up by W.W. Winter. In 1857 one E.N. Charles founded a studio on Midland Road, with the young Winter as his assistant. Charles died in 1864 and his widow, who carried on the business, subsequently married the wily Winter, hitherto the assistant. He rebuilt the studios into the form in which they survive today in 1867 to the designs of his friend (and another photographic enthusiast) H.I. Stevens. They are the earliest surviving purpose-built photographic studios in Britain, fortunately added to the Statutory List in 2000.

XV

THE EARLY 20TH CENTURY

THE CO-OPERATIVE MOVEMENT

In 1844 a co-operative store had been established in Rochdale, Lancashire, in which the profits of the shop were returned to the customers, who were members of the society which ran it. A similar society was set up in the North not long afterwards. This concept was swift to reach Derby, and in 1849 a group of men from William Mansfield Cooper's builder's yard – all members of the Union of Carpenters and Joiners – resolved to emulate their northern contemporaries. They set up a store in the yard behind the former George Inn and were initially 12 in number; the year by then was 1850. Their capital was at first £2 and their enlightened employer, the son of the last of the builder-architects, sent to Rochdale for information on their behalf. Their first transaction was to give to Mrs Leam – wife of Samuel, a sick member – a parcel of groceries gratis. Records were kept from 1854 and the Society survived a crisis in 1856 to become sufficiently well-found to be able to transfer to more spacious premises in Victoria Street in 1858 – right next door to W.M. Cooper's Brookside Chapel, which some of the older founder-members must have helped to build 20 years before.

In 1859 the Society broadened its membership from a strict Joiners' Union base, moved again – to 47 Full Street – and in 1860 there were 40 members. The store opened in response to working people's needs each evening from 7.00 to 9.30. Membership responded very quickly to a handbill campaign, however, and 1861 saw the opening of the first branch – in the West End (Parker Street) – and a Labour Hall, for meetings and hire. Two more shops opened in the West End by 1866, followed by one in Abbey Street. In 1870 a store was opened on Albert Street, designed and built by Robert Bridgart (and demolished in 1979), the first of five separate new buildings connecting the society's Albert Street premises with East Street to be erected by 1900, when the society celebrated its jubilee. At this stage there were 60 separate stores and departments running under the control of what by then had become the Derby Cooperative Provident & Industrial Society; later another dozen or more were added. The jubilee was also celebrated by the distribution of 14,000 earthenware teapots to members, made with blue, green or red patterning on cream by Brownfield's Pottery, Stoke. In 1877–89 the Society even developed five streets in New Normanton, each built up with small but well constructed terraced cottages for

renting by their members at reasonable rates. Each street bore a component of the name of the Society: Derby, Co-operative, Provident and Industrial streets and Society Place. Unfortunately in 1888, after parts of Normanton-by-Derby were absorbed by the borough, the existence of Derby Lane there caused the GPO to demand that Derby Street be renamed. For ease, one letter only was changed, producing Darby Street, Darby being the name of a prominent municipal family of the time.

The store on Albert Street was subsequently extended in 1913 when the magnificently Neo-Baroque Central Suite building by Alexander MacPherson was added, in 1924–26 in East Street and in 1937 in Exchange Street, the latter a fine *Moderne* building (page 242) which found a grander echo in the Co-operative Bakery building on Osmaston Park Road, designed in similar style but, thanks to the war, not completed until 1950. It replaced a CWS seed trail ground inaugurated in 1921, but was unceremoniously demolished in September 1993 for a new superstore, sold to Sainsbury's in 2004.

East Street Co-op buildings, Central Hall of 1913, by Alexander MacPherson. (M. Craven)

Derby Co-operative Society Women's Guild, Stenson Road branch, c.1914. (M. Craven)

A century or more before, the movement was suffused by the self help and proto-Socialist philosophies of John Stuart Mill and William Morris, and it moved in the 20th century towards the emergent Labour Party, whose first Derby MP was elected in 1900 in the person of Richard Bell, a Merthyr man in his third year as General Secretary of the Amalgamated Society of Railway Servants. Soon, the co-operative movement generally was to identify itself with the aims of the Labour Party, although it put up members of Parliament elsewhere on its own account and indeed until comparatively recent times.

By 1914 the society had formed a Womens' Guild, of a suffragist tendency, and Guild branches flourished,

Derby Co-operative Society, East Street/Exchange Street extension, completed in 1938, replacing a building of 1896, photographed in 2005. (M. Craven)

especially in the inter-war years, complete with colourful banners and some, at least, of the paraphernalia of the Friendly Society. They achieved much in helping to cement communities and in building on the independence many working-class women had briefly tasted during World War One, with their menfolk away – many for ever – they themselves replacing them in crucial roles in the factories and foundries of the borough

The Derby Society's first political council met in February 1918. The result was the initiation of good organisation throughout the borough's electoral wards and candidates were floated at the 1919 municipal elections. A.J. Tapping was in consequence elected the first Co-operative councillor in that year, in Dale (Normanton) Ward.

POLITICAL CHANGES

Nevertheless, the first ordinary Labour members had been elected before World War One and one of them, the railway employee and unionist who led the 1911 rail strike on the Midland Railway, A.E. Waterson, was elected in 1913 for Markeaton (thus, the West End) going on to become Co-operative MP for mid-Northamptonshire in 1918. He was a Derby Co-operative Society member and a Primitive Methodist. By the 1921 municipal elections the Labour and Co-operative movements had reached a joint agreement and the same year saw the appointment of the borough's first Labour mayor, Alderman W.R. (Will) Raynes (1871–1966), elected to the council in 1911. As with so many who followed him, he came from Lancashire and was also a Methodist. He became one of the two borough MPs in 1923, along with J.H. (Jimmy) Thomas, who had succeeded Bell in 1910. Will Raynes's career was short; he lost his seat in the 1924 election, whereas Jimmy Thomas went on to become a cabinet minister and later to party obloquy when he followed Ramsay Macdonald into the National Government in 1931, finally having to resign five years later over a pre-budget leak.

Mention of the political side of the Co-operative movement suggests that a pause might be made to consider the topic of the political climate. Since the Whig ascendancy in the 18th century, little changed in that following, and Whig, later Liberal, representation prevailed, with members serving lengthy periods. Between the Reform Act and Bell's election in 1900, only 12 men served in the two borough seats in that time, one for less than a year, being unseated for bribery. Of the remaining 11, four were Derby men and four others were county gentlemen or their close kin:

Samuel Plimsoll came, was elected, in time

contributed the one thing for which he will be ever remembered and went, unlamented. Geoffrey Drage, from Hatfield, stood – as a no-hope Tory – in 1895 and was unexpectedly elected with fellow Tory Sir Henry Bemrose, quite unexpectedly. He was replaced by Bell in 1900. From then until the present, one of the Derby seats (currently Derby South) has been held in unbroken succession by Labour: Jimmy Thomas in 1910 to Margaret Beckett today.

The other (Derby North from post-war) has changed hands frequently. It was taken by Sir William Collins (1859–1946) after Sir Thomas Roe resigned to take his peerage in 1916 – the just reward for a political makeweight long famous as 'Tommy Ditto', from his habit of capping others' speeches with '…and I say ditto to that, Mr Speaker…' Apart from being held by a Liberal in 1922–23, it has subsequently changed hands between the other two parties some six times, being currently held by former council leader and GPO worker Bob Laxton. Boundary changes for the two constituencies in 1968 deprived the Belper constituency (then held for Labour by George Brown) of Mickleover and parts of Derby to the north, and 1983 changes gave part of the town to the South Derbyshire seat, held then by Conservative Edwina Currie but since 1997 by Mark Todd.

LOCAL COUNCIL CONTROL

A similar trend has been apparent in the control of the borough (later city) council. In the 19th century control was largely with the Whigs and their successors, the Liberals, although control is an anachronistic term in this context, for the council then rarely split along party lines, the policies of the two main parties being separated by little in basic philosophy. Further, the council met but four times a year (although this increased later, as the complexities of local government snowballed from 1888) and there was vastly less legislative business.

In 1884 the Labour Co-partnership Association was founded, but it took until 1911 before a Labour candidate – Will Raynes – was returned in a local election. The next breakthrough was the election of the first woman councillor. This was a Conservative, Mrs E.J. Hulse, who had also stood for Parliament in the same year, 1918. Mrs Boden of The Friary had actually been proposed as a council candidate for the Liberals (on a temperance ticket) in 1909, but she had failed to get adopted – temperance had never been that popular. Oddly, one might have expected Mrs Hulse to attain the mayoralty, but in fact it was her husband – also a Conservative – who had attained this dizzy height – the year before his wife joined him on the council. In fact Derby's first female mayor was another Tory, Mrs Elizabeth Petty, elected in 1936, after which

there was a pause of 22 years until Labour's Alderman Mrs Florence Riggott was elected in 1958. The most recent and 12th was Cllr Ruth Skelton, a Liberal, in 2004 and the most youthful mayor at 35 since the younger Tommy Roe took office at the same age in 1867, although before the Municipal Corporations Act youthful mayors were quite common, the youngest of all being Hugh Bateman, who took office in 1720 at age 30.

The two seats won by Labour in 1911 were increased to seven by 1921, in which year Alderman Raynes was elected as first Labour mayor. In the 1920s there was a finely-balanced three party system in operation on the council, under the pressures of which a long-standing gentlemen's agreement that the mayoralty should alternate between Liberal and Conservative broke down. Alderman Raynes's term of office was in fact made possible by a chivalric gesture on the part of the Conservatives, based on the increasing strength of his representation. Nevertheless, in the October 1922 elections, Labour lost all its councillors, but followed this by a massive resurgence at the expense of the Liberals in 1925 when they gained 20 seats. Three years

Derby's first female mayor Mrs Elizabeth Petty JP (1875–1947), née Merryweather, originally from Southwell. She was also the first woman to win a contested council seat, at Dale ward. (M. Craven)

later they attained their first majority, lost it in 1930, but within a very few years had re-established it and entrenched it to such an extent that it has been overturned infrequently and only for short periods since: in 1968–71, 1976–78, 1988–94 and 2003–05, and even these were only made possible by the expansion of the city's boundaries in 1967 to include the outer suburbs.

With the extensions of the city's boundaries which occur from time to time – inexorable historical logic bringing today's Derby ever closer to the extent of pre-Conquest Northworthy – an increasing political balance may yet emerge. Nevertheless, the history of Derby over the last 50 or more years is essentially that of a borough (from 1977 city) shaped and created by one major national party, with its local origins traceable back through 105 years. Its rise in Derby was made at the expense of the Liberal Party, which locally went into almost total eclipse; they had no Mayor from 1930 to 2004, having briefly attained control of the council in 2003.

A Notorious Conspiracy

In 1917 Derby narrowly escaped international notoriety as the place which nurtured the murderers of Britain's prime minister.

This bid at assassinating Lloyd George (and Arthur Henderson, the Commons Labour leader and War Cabinet minister without portfolio), had something of an element of farce about it. The whole escapade puts one in mind of one of Dr Johnson's remarks: 'Sir, a woman preaching is like a dog's walking on his hinder legs. It is not done well; but you are surprised to find it done at all.' And so it was with Mrs Alice Wheeldon's assassination plot. It was certainly not done well: poison would seem to be a strange method for political murder; yet the fact that the matter was serious enough to merit subsequent trial and conviction nevertheless demonstrates that the plot was in earnest.

Mrs Wheeldon's son Willie was a conscientious objector and this had inevitably resulted in victimisation for the lad. Furthermore, she herself was an anarchist, outraged that the outbreak of the war had ended the ever more disruptive campaign for women's suffrage in which she had played a part 'of arson and sabotage', to quote William Rickards, one of two covert government agents who infiltrated her circle. The other, Herbert Booth, was known to the conspirators as 'comrade Bert'! At her second-hand clothes shop, over which she lived in Pear Tree Road, she hatched the conspiracy with her two daughters: unmarried Hetty, a schoolmistress of 'advanced revolutionary tendencies' and Winifred, married to Southampton chemist Alfred Mason. Hetty was a teacher at an Ilkeston school. Elaborate preparations were made,

in which the two agents took part, but on 29 January 1917 the police, acting on information received, arrested the conspirators in Derby, with the exception of Mrs Mason, who was picked up in Southampton the next day. They were remanded at the Guildhall and committed for trial. This was held in March 1917, F.E. Smith (Attorney General, later 1st Earl of Birkenhead) leading for the prosecution. Although the charge was tantamount to treason, Mrs Wheeldon avoided the supreme penalty, receiving but 10 years; Lloyd George sensibly allowed her release some months later. Mason, in charge of the actual poisoning, got seven years, his wife, five. Hetty was acquitted.

There is no doubt that the Wheeldons were a family of extreme left-wing kidney, closely involved in a local political cell and not averse to what such people like to term 'direct action' – a euphemism for violence. Indeed, papers released in the late 1990s in the Public Record Office reveal that Hetty admitted to 'Comrade Bert' that she and her mother had been part of a suffragist group that had set fire to Breadsall Church three years before, a charge levelled at the Suffragettes at the time and still emphatically denied, although 'Bert's' informant at the time had no motive for mendacity.

The question is, whether they were innocent left-sympathisers goaded into action by a pair of *agents provocateurs* or genuinely dangerous conspirators. The papers, which appear to be complete, do not conclusively settle the matter. However, of the two agents, one, Rickards, who used the alias Alex Gordon, was over a decade later admitted to a mental asylum, a fact used recently to impugn his evidence without serious justification. Yet they must have had an effect on the cell. Nevertheless, the transcripts show clearly that the two men did not actually suggest the plot but merely offered to assist once the matter had been broached. Indeed, any *agent provocateur* intending to frame the group would surely have evolved a more credible way of dispatching the Prime Minister than a poisoned air gun pellet delivered on a Surrey golf course!

The waters have subsequently become muddied by the ideological baggage of the 20th century, in that the romantic afterglow of Soviet Communism has tended to get mixed up with the capture, by the left, of the movement for women's rights. As so often, too, the standards of the present were applied indiscriminately to the *mores* of a past era without much ken being taken of the context. Consequently, Mrs Wheeldon has been seen variously as a martyr, an innocent dupe and as 'set up', whereas the things that come across most strongly are her extreme views, intemperate language and innate rage. Subsequent events serve as a telling coda to what occurred. Hetty (1890—1920) got married briefly to Arthur MacManus, shortly to become the first chairman of the British Communist Party and later a defector to Russia, where he became a Soviet citizen, while Alice's son, Willie, also went to Russia as a translator and was sufficiently integrated into the fabric of Soviet life as to be executed by the OGPU (forerunner of the KGB) in 1927.

The stark fact was that Mrs Wheeldon was a passionate anarchist whose family inclined to Communist activism. They were, understandably, seen as a threat to stable government in a nation at war which had already had to deal with a traumatic radical-inspired rebellion in Ireland and had to go forward in a world where Marxist communism was increasingly making itself felt as a political tenet; the Russian October Revolution was, after all, but nine months away. The case for infiltrating two agents must have been seen, in the context of late autumn 1916, as a sensible precaution. The only question remaining is whether they provoked the Wheeldon plot or merely played their part, the better to maintain cover. On any rational estimate, one has to give Lloyd George's government credit for keeping their finger on the pulse of various wartime dissidents. The pragmatism of Lloyd George, one of the supposed targets of the plot, in releasing Alice Wheeldon as soon as she decided on a hunger strike in prison, clearly demonstrates that the Government was not quite the luridly vengeful organisation that more radical commentators have repeatedly depicted it. When Alice Wheeldon died at 907 London Road, Derby, in February 1919 – a victim of the great influenza pandemic – Willie made a lengthy pro-Soviet peroration at her graveside before draping her coffin with a metre square red flag.

Which says it all, really.

ENLARGING THE BOROUGH

Derby, having taken over the Litchurch Local Board a decade before, became a county borough in 1888, assuming most of the functions which lesser towns at the same time surrendered to the new county councils. Its status was thus autonomous within Derbyshire and over the next few years it took over responsibility for education and welfare. In 1901 an Act of Parliament was obtained to enlarge the borough. This added the Alvaston & Boulton Local Board, further parts of Normanton, all of Osmaston and smaller portions of Chaddesden and Spondon. The Parliamentary committee which scrutinised the legislation deleted proposals to add portions of Darley Abbey and Littleover, however, after strong local protests. The Act also ended the preferential rating system granted to Litchurch which had been the bribe offered in 1877 to coerce the Local Board to throw its lot in with Derby. From this time too the number of wards returning elected members was increased from eight to 16.

A further Derby Corporation Act was obtained in 1927 (effective from 1928) which again enlarged the town. The extensions of the boundaries thus effected enabled the Derby Arterial Road – later known as the Ring Road – to be built from 1928–39, although it was never completed, the segment between the A6 at Broadway and the A52 at Nottingham Road Co-op Creamery, Chaddesden, being killed off by the war, after which the money to finish it was not at first forthcoming. When it was, the Inner Ring Road was projected instead. The idea of the original Ring Road was that it should be constructed well clear of the built up areas.

In April 1968, another extension was authorised. All the effective suburbs surrounding the town, constituting 'Greater Derby', but which were in the main administered by several different rural district councils, were included. This produced a council of 72 members, of whom 18 were Aldermen (previously 16), who served six years, and 54 were ordinary councillors (serving three years), as opposed to 48 before. The county borough was then run by 16 committees, six less than in 1935. This streamlining was aided by the removal of the borough police into the control of the County Police Authority a year before. In a sense, the 1968 extensions marked the apogee of the power and influence of local government of Derby for many were lost to the county council – then about to enter a particularly iconoclastic phase – in the reforms of 1974. It took 23 rather bleak years before reversion to the *status quo*.

WARTIME

The two World Wars made their mark on Derby. Great Britain is scattered with World War One memorials to the dead of communities from hamlets to great cities and Derby men were killed and wounded by the hundred and thousand; the official estimate put the number killed in action as 1,200, although the Midland Railway throughout its wider reach lost far more. They are commemorated by a large number of increasingly threatened memorials which were finally recorded by the Museum from 1992 at the suggestion of former Territorial soldier Cllr John Jennings, thereby anticipating a nationwide exercise of a similar nature by five years.

Derby's severe main memorial stands in the Market Place – having been moved on several occasions – designed by Percy Currey's partner C.C. Thompson and carved by A.G. Walker, unveiled in 1924. Another, rather more magnificent affair, executed in gleaming Portland stone, was erected by the Midland Railway beside the Midland Hotel in 1922 to commemorate all 2,833 of

C.C. Thompson's 1924 War Memorial (with sculpture by A.G. Walker) in the Market Place, photographed through the arch of the Guildhall portico when new. Note the market stalls – the area was then still being used as originally intended. (*Derby Evening Telegraph*)

their employees who fell. This spectacular affair is one of the few works by Sir Edwin Lutyens in Derbyshire.

The drain of manpower to the trenches was a severe blow to the foundries and factories of Derby and many women were recruited to fill their places, including in some of the heaviest work. This did much to emancipate women, to whom the government of Lloyd George rightly gave the vote in 1918, and encouraged the expansion of the Co-op Women's Guilds. From the end of the conflict, many women retained the places they had won in the nation's hour of need, and they have continually expanded their share of jobs ever since, despite a general setback during the lean years of 1931–36. One long-term effect has been to double the number of people able and available to work in the city.

The majority of those Derby men called up, or who volunteered, served with the Derbyshire Yeomanry or the Sherwood Foresters, a unit which had inherited the ram mascot which the old 95th Regiment had first acquired at Kotah, in the Indian Mutiny, whose current successor is Private Derby XXVII.

Other upheavals manifested themselves too. Belgian refugees streamed into the town; homes were requisitioned by the military authorities, petrol and food were modestly rationed and, most traumatic of all, in the small hours of 1 February 1916, Zeppelin L.14 bombed No.9 shed at the locomotive works, killing four men, C shop at the Carriage and Wagon Works (where there was long a plaque commemorating the event), Bateman Street, where there were further casualties, the gas works, Fletcher's lace mill, the test track at Royce's and at Burton-on-Trent; in all, 25 bombs were dropped, four people died and two were injured.

In the context of conflict, it is worth remembering that over the past 150 years six Derby men have been singled out for the Victoria Cross. Private Jacob Rivers of 1st Bn Sherwood Foresters fought valiantly at Neuve Chapelle on 12 March 1915 to become one of Derby's VCs of the conflict, albeit a posthumous one. Another was Gunner C.E. Stone RFA (21 March 1918 at Laponne) along with Brigadier Charles Hudson, 11th Bn, Sherwood Foresters (Asiago Plateau, 15 June 1918) and Capt Edward Unwin, CB, CMG, RN (Dardanelles, 1915). In previous wars only Private Robert Humpstone of the Rifle Brigade (22 April 1855 in Crimea) and Colonel Sir Henry Wilmot of Chaddesden, 5th Battalion, also of the Rifle Brigade (11 March 1858 in the Indian Mutiny), won this supreme honour. Rivers's mother was given the honorary freedom of the borough in 1923, an honour previously bestowed upon Wilmot as well.

Once victory had been obtained the celebrations were held on 21 July 1919, when athletic competitions were run, effigies of the Kaiser burnt, illuminated boats sailed down the Derwent and fireworks formed a climax to the

proceedings. Alderman W. Blews Robotham, a local solicitor and mayor in that year, paid for a white metal medallion to be struck to commemorate the event.

Nevertheless, it was World War Two which was felt much more acutely in Derby's everyday life, although the scale of personal loss was mercifully less. Again there was rationing, commencing in January 1940 and becoming more swingeing as the war went on (and even worse in some respects in the following peace). The first blackout anticipated Neville Chamberlain's fateful announcement on the wireless on Sunday 3 September 1939 by one day and continued for 2,061 consecutive nights. Despite the painting of white bands on street furniture and kerbstones, street accidents rocketed, 1,200 being killed on the roads in Derby alone in July 1941.

In 1937 the 200th Heavy Anti-Aircraft Battery was raised as the 249th Field Battery. It defended Derby from 1939 to 1941, stationed at Siddals Road, but the regimental HQ was at Kingsway. Its officers included 2nd Viscount Scarsdale. In 1941 it was posted to the Middle East, was at El Alamein the following year, and finished the war in Italy, being disbanded in 1945. During World War Two, the RAF controlled a number of barrage balloon units, the first balloon being flown from Bass's Recreation Ground as early as March 1939. One of these – designed to foil low-flying bombers –

Sir Edwin Lutyens's Midland Railway war memorial, Midland Road, built of Portland Stone in 1921. (M. Craven)

belonging to Unit No. 7 on Curzon Lane, Alvaston, broke loose and removed one of the four pinnacles of the cathedral tower by getting its hawser wrapped round it while still proceeding westwards!

Only a day after the outbreak of war came the first air-raid warning; those who had joined the Civil Defence or the ARP (Air Raid Precautions) had a chance to test their reactions, although, inevitably, it was a false alarm. The racecourse was the site for a battery of four 4.7 inch anti-aircraft guns which were manned by Royal Marines. They were backed up by barrage balloons and a searchlight unit. The lighter guns were at Markeaton Park, Normanton Barracks and Alvaston Camp. Drums of inflammable detritus were also positioned around the street, to foil bombing raids with smoke, but were never used in earnest.

Another swift result of the outbreak of war was the immediate evacuation of children; 9,700 in all trekked off, mainly to various locations in north and east Derbyshire. Derby school evacuated to Overton Hall. In July 1941 the Railway Operating Division of the Royal Engineers took over the newly-built and chastely handsome Railway College on London Road. There were lesser effects, too: football ceased for the duration at the beginning of 1940, although the stadium was used for other functions from time to time, including baseball once again, this time with US service teams playing scratch assemblages of local talent.

Restrictions on travel of any kind made holidays impossible and the council organised 'Holidays at Home' programmes, with plenty of activities – mainly centred on the borough's parks and the Assembly Rooms – to entertain potentially fractious children and bored adults, too. In the streets, the drive to accumulate scrap led to the destruction of most of the iron railings in front of various properties all over the town in 1941–42. Cast-iron and wrought-iron alike was taken, irrespective of utility, and irreplaceable examples of work by Robert Bakewell, to which the Yates family and the Haslams succumbed. Cast-iron railings had been placed before most houses, both palisaded terraces and the grander villas right up until the first decades of the present century, and nearly all was taken, wrecking the visual aspects of residential streets everywhere, especially as, after the war, each home owner replaced them as they saw fit.

Factories changed their roles, too. The railway works began making wings for Hurricane fighters and light tanks; later, in their vast Carriage and Wagon works, which once had produced 350 carriages and 10,000 wagons in one year, various other components were made. Several of the other foundries made various items of materiel: grenades, shells and gun turrets among them. Again, women were to the fore in replacing absent males at the factories, although all single women between the ages of 19 and 24 were called up, the WVS being prominent. A British Restaurant was established in Philipson's, in the office building on the corner of Market Place and Tenant Street.

Derby by this time had small elements of its population from all parts of the world. Certain of these were deemed to constitute a possible threat to national security and 350 of these loyal but foreign-born men and women were tactlessly rounded up and interned on the Isle of Man under the notorious clause 19b, the day of reckoning being 29 May 1940. They were joined by the head of a prominent local family with strong Derby ties: the British Union of Fascists' leader Sir Oswald Mosley Bt., and his wife Diana (née Mitford), whose sister Debo married the future 11th Duke of Devonshire. Also in May 1940, all signposts and road signs were removed from the town.

Thus, even if one could obtain petrol for one's car and manage to avoid hitting anyone in the blackout, one still had the problem of navigation without the aid of the traditional signposts.

Air raids during Hitler's War

The first air raid took place on 19 August 1940, the Baseball Ground being the only casualty on this occasion. There were about nine raids altogether, all targeted at Rolls-Royce. The fact that only one really achieved its objective is something in the order of a miracle.

A serious raid was on the night of 15 January 1941. Fifty high-explosive bombs fell on the borough, damaging 1,650 houses. It was on this occasion that the Arboretum bandstand and Florentine boar were destroyed. The worst single incident was a direct hit on the Railway Station, which destroyed much of the glass and iron roof, replaced after the conflict with present terrible reinforced concrete awnings. Four passengers and two members of the Railway's staff were killed and eight others were injured. Casualties in total were 20 killed and 48 injured. The worst raid was on 27 July 1942, when a bomb landed in the Rolls-Royce stores, killing 15. Sixteen others died, eight killed by bombs in Hawthorne and Abingdon Streets and 21 were seriously and 115 slightly injured. Had the aircraft not snagged a barrage balloon cable, the raid would have been much more effective; the two seconds gained would have delivered four bombs squarely on the main works and only one on the surrounding streets.

Rolls-Royce was camouflaged, the administration block to look like council houses, the water tower to look like a church tower and one workshop to resemble a chapel (by which name it has been known ever since) with the remainder resembling open ground. The presiding genius of this work was Ernest Townsend (1880–1944), probably the finest artist to emerge from Derby after Joseph Wright but, like so much else in Derby, greatly undervalued. Frequently, too, the enemy's radar homing devices were successfully jammed, leading the German navigational aids to suggest to the crews of the aircraft that they were bombing Derby when in fact their bombs were falling relatively harmlessly in countryside. The Germans maps were ineffective, many being some 40 years out of date. On 8 May 1941, for instance, 23 German aircraft raided the town, but their navigation beam was successfully jammed and the bombs fell well short. A successful raid on Rolls-Royce would have been disastrous on a national scale, and it reflects an enormous credit upon those involved that the main factories of the town escaped with only minor damage. Later in the war the enemy evolved the 'Nuisance' raid, in the course of one of which, on 27 March 1942, Rolls-Royce was actually bombed and strafed, as were pedestrians and a bus on Slack Lane: tragically, 22 lost their lives as a result.

Various other incidents occurred at Derby during hostilities, including the crash of a Hawker Hurricane I fighter of 46 Squadron from Digby, Lincs., on the railway embankment just beyond Normanton & Peartree Station on the old BDJR line on 24 July 1940 following engine failure. The pilot, P/O Maurice Cooper-Key – a member of a distinguished military family whose mother was killed in an air raid 15 months later – is thought to have been trying to reach open ground by the Barracks, having aborted a landing on Balfour Road playing field due to the presence of children. He was regrettably killed, due to the aircraft striking a signal gantry while sliding along the embankment, after which it burned.

In August 1944 some 8,000 V1-afflicted Londoners were evacuated to Derby; quite a few stayed on in the town and, of these, some are happily with us yet. Most people who were affected by bombing had Anderson shelters dug into their gardens; others had Morrison

Chester Green and City Road, Little Chester, excavating a public air raid shelter – no doubt right through the Roman layers! – November 1939. (*Derby Evening Telegraph*)

ones in their homes. The former are these days very thin on the ground, although as late as September 2006 one was extracted from a garden in Powell Street. Public shelters were widely advertised and a pedestrian in, say, The Wardwick, knew that in the event of the siren going, he or she could duck down into the Library basement, a designated shelter.

All in all, Derby got off remarkably lightly, despite the total of 74 killed and nearly 350 wounded in air raids by the end of the conflict. Quietly relieved crowds gathered in the Market Place at four o'clock on the afternoon of 8 May 1945 to mark the end of the war in Europe – VE day. Many streets were patriotically decorated but the atmosphere was muted. It was not until the end of the war in the Far East (VJ day) that the local people really let their hair down, on 15 August in the same year. As with the end of the previous conflict, however, life had changed irretrievably in the aftermath and the ambience of the borough with it.

THE SHERWOOD FORESTERS

As the local regiment, the Sherwood Foresters played a crucial part during World War Two. The lst/5th and 2nd/5th battalions for instance, newly raised, went to France in 1939 and were ultimately evacuated through Dunkirk in June 1940. After some time back in the United Kingdom, the former was sent to Singapore, arriving just in time to be surrendered to the Japanese in January 1942. Subsequently, they suffered terrible privations before ultimate liberation and their losses were severe. Lt. Col. Harold Lilly, OBE (1888–1954), of the Derby and Long Eaton mill-owning family, was the senior officer of the unit and much of the memorabilia acquired during this terrible period was given by his heirs to the Sherwood Foresters' section of Derby Museum, where it remains on display. The 2nd/5th were sent to North Africa and progressed thence to Italy. In 1944 they were transferred to Greece. The 6th Battalion had been redesignated the 40th Searchlight Regiment in 1936 and spent much of the war in the United Kingdom but in 1944 also went to Europe.

After the war, the regiment was granted the Freedom of Derby in 1946 but left Normanton Barracks for the last time in 1963, the buildings lingering on in various guises until demolished in 1981, being replaced by a leisure complex, opened in 1988. In 1970 the regiment amalgamated with the Worcestershires to form the 1st Bn, Worcestershire & Sherwood Foresters' Regiment (29th/45th Foot) usually known as the WoFors. The 5th/8th Territorial Battalion, raised in 1908 as the 5th from the old Derby 1st Volunteer Battalion, thereupon became the Sherwood Foresters (Territorial Force)

Normanton Barracks, Sinfin Lane, seen here on 14 March 1981, after their closure. After some years as a store for the Midland Railway Trust and the Museum, they were demolished to make way for a pub, super-cinema and bowling alley called Foresters' Park. (*Derby Evening Telegraph*)

which amalgamated with the 8th (Nottinghamshire) Bn, and in 1961 was further merged with the Mercian Volunteers. The 3rd Territorial Bn WoFors was reformed at Kingsway Barracks in 1971, moved to Sinfin Lane barracks in 1980 and continued until again being disbanded in June 1999.

Meanwhile, the 2nd Bn of the Foresters – the old 95th (Derbys) Regiment – merged with the 1st and was reactivated in 1952 to go to Korea, but in the event never went. The 6th Territorial Bn became the 575 (Sherwood Foresters) light anti-aircraft Regiment (TA) and in 1961 was redesignated 575 (Sherwood Foresters) Field Squadron, Royal Engineers (TA). Of the two centres of the Territorial Army in Derby in 1988, the one at Sinfin lost its unit in 1999, but the very dignified neo-classical centre of 1939 on Kingsway is currently due for redevelopment. The former establishment also for a time housed the short-lived Home Service Force, raised in 1980.

The WoFors served in Bosnia from November 1998 to April 1999, did two tours of Northern Ireland and from October 2004 until March 2005 served in Afghanistan. They exercised their Freedom of the city for the last time in August 2006, before being reformed yet again, this time as the 2nd Bn, the Mercian Regiment in September 2007.

ADOPTING AND TWINNING

World War Two introduced the practice of adopting military units, mainly with a view to concentrating interest over fundraising. Derby adopted HMS *Kenya* and also affiliated itself to 98 (City of Derby) Squadron RAF, a unit disbanded in 1976, a year before Derby was actually granted the status of a city. The use of the term 'city' by the RAF during the war was purely a misunderstanding and not part of a disinformation

campaign on the part of the borough! In 1972 Derby adopted the 9/12th Royal Lancers (Prince of Wales's), a unit which resulted from the amalgamation in 1960 of two regiments, both of which began in the early 19th century as Light Dragoons and had for many years recruited in the district. They exercised their Freedom of the city in May 1988 and are the major funders of the museum's military gallery, which they share with the yeomanry and the 95th. In 1975 HM Submarine *Sovereign* – powered by a nuclear reactor courtesy of Rolls-Royce and Associates – was also adopted.

Just as, in the aftermath of World War One (in 1922), Derby had 'twinned' itself with Fonquevilliers in France, associated with the Foresters' sector of the Western Front – Alderman Raynes becoming life mayor of the French town – so in the 1970s, the city twinned with Osnabrück in Germany, a link which, unlike the French one, still flourishes, although quite why it was chosen is not entirely clear.

A year after World War Two, Derby Rotary Club proposed the foundation of a War Memorial Village to accommodate disabled ex-servicemen and their families. The target sum was £100,000. The scheme was launched in 1947 at Shelton Lock, to be run by a co-operative of 24. It turned out to be a great success, being opened on 27 June 1949 by Princess Elizabeth (now HM The Queen) and by 1972 38 dwellings were operational. Today it is an integral part of the flourishing community of Shelton Lock.

MUNICIPAL HOUSING

The 20th century saw a great revolution in housing all over the kingdom and this was especially reflected in Derby. Municipalities acquired the power to build and let houses in 1919, and in 1929 a planning scheme was submitted to central government by the county borough wherein housing and industry were zoned, and not intermixed as heretofore. This represented what was then 'cutting edge' town planning theory, which was applied much more rigidly in Derby after World War Two when a clearly residential environment like Friar Gate and Vernon Street was 'zoned' for office development, thus strangling any sort of post-5pm life out of this most elegant and precious part of the city. Zoning is now largely old hat, although in planning, as in social theory, old beliefs die very hard, as witness the entirely non-residential nature of Pride Park. Fortunately, HRH the Prince of Wales, along with an increasing number of experts, do believe in it, only to be vilified by the braying members of an ageing architectural and planning establishment. Yet the success of the Prince's Poundbury near Dorchester does much to

Early municipal houses in brick and pebble-dashing, originally still with outside toilets, dating from 1927 and seen here in Plimsoll Street, New Zealand, named after Derby's 19th-century radical MP who contributed so much to safety at sea. The pretty, multi-paned windows are just beginning to be replaced in this 1970s view. (*Derby Evening Telegraph*)

prove what anyone living in a mixed economic area knew prior to 1945: that the admixture produces a much healthier social environment in which to live and is also replete with ecological gains resultant from the obviation of the need to commute.

Under the Municipal Housing Act, houses were to be grouped six, eight, 12 or 18 per acre, as opposed to the average 19th-century terrace of 25 to the acre. Private housing at that time stood at six to eight per acre, but the requirements laid upon councils by the Office of the Deputy Prime Minister (ODPM) in the Blair governments from 1997 has led to private and housing association schemes to increase densities close to the 19th-century working-class norm, achieved by building ever more apartments and cramming small detached houses in with precious little space between.

The Derby scheme was one of the first in the country to be approved, yet despite the 1919 show of zeal, only a niggardly 446 council houses were planned in that year. Pressure from the Government increased this to 1,000. Even so, the building rate fell behind schedule from the

first. In 1925 a delegation went to Sheffield to see the cast-iron houses being built there. It was possible to build these at a rate of five per week, and by 1927 Derby had built 500 in Crewton and Chaddesden. Thereafter, things rapidly improved, and by 1935 6,855 council houses had been built, and at Roe Farm, on the borders between Breadsall and Chaddesden, a further 1,668 were built by 1939. The standard varied, some housing being very basic and unlovely; many from the first phase still had outside privies, continuing the traditional pattern, although from 1929 this was eschewed in favour of inside plumbing. Some of the housing, designed by borough architect Herbert Aslin, such as those on Harvey Road, at the Alvaston end, was very elegant indeed, until their paned and casemented fenestration was replaced from the 1980s by uPVC, thus utterly ruining the basic refinement of his simple designs. However, compared with the very high standards of municipal housing achieved, for instance, in neighbouring Nottingham, most of Derby's provision was lacklustre. Indeed, one of the earliest estates, the

1920s Austin Estate, was considered something of a disaster. One interesting scheme was Exeter House, at first referred to as the Derwent Flats, overlooking the river and Long Bridge, although the entrance front, with its community-friendly *cour d'honneur*, faced Exeter Place. This complex of 45 units, was completed in brick and of a restrained three storeys in 1931, the first element of the Central Improvement Plan.

In the 20 years between the two wars, too, 5,000 private houses were built. Nevertheless, more than half of the borough's housing stock by 1954 was still pre-1900 in date, although on average in far better condition than in most English towns. By 1930, however, more than 1,200 houses had been condemned as unfit and cleared and half the remainder had gone by 1935. Many of the older houses, of course, lacked gardens; mostly they had only back yards. To enable the inhabitants to have somewhere to grow vegetables, however, 2,430 allotments were let, a trend which began in many towns very early in

The public clock erected by the parade of shops on the Mackworth estate, very much in the style influenced by the 1951 Festival of Britain. (*Derby Evening Telegraph*)

the 19th century and suggested by Dr Schama as the ultimate substitute for the cultivation strips the urban workforce had left behind in the country. This number of allotments has diminished sharply since with the great increase of houses with gardens, the increase in prosperity and the easy access to cheap foodstuffs, especially with the coming of the supermarket. Few, if any, working people now *need* to cultivate a plot to feed their families these days. Worse, the allotments themselves have been earmarked since 2000 as 'urban brownfield sites', upon which housing development is to be encouraged by the ODPM, and many have been cleared of the keen horticulturalists who rented them and sold to fuel the feeding frenzy of our developers.

After World War Two, a vast new estate was started at Mackworth. Whereas the pre-war estates had no real provision for amenities like shops, schools, places of worship or recreational facilities, Mackworth was planned to have all of these. Two thousand six hundred and sixty homes were built, housing some 10,000 people. Initially only 213 were privately owned, and most were on four streets of the development at Humbleton Farm, stalled by the outbreak of war. On the absurdly curvilinear and rather narrow roads were built an old folks' home (closed and demolished as 'uneconomic' in 2002), 30 shops (of which nine were private), three public houses, schools, two churches, a chapel and a filling station.

Yet to cope with the immediate post-war housing crisis Derby was obliged to erect a number of prefabricated homes and even temporarily used a converted army hutment. One hundred and three of the former survive on Bretton Avenue off Constable Lane, Littleover, built in 1946 and intended to last 10 years, but they survived and the council drastically upgraded them in 1986–89, 20 being subsequently sold off under 'right to buy' legislation. A grid of 10 numbered streets on Markeaton Park served housing provided using redundant military buildings and lasted some 15 years; the park is still cursed by the superfluity of decaying tarmac and house platforms. A further 3,340 homes had been built elsewhere by the municipality by 1958.

These were joined in 1963 by Derby's only high-rise block of flats, Rivermead House, near the river, below North Parade, by Thomas East (1906–1997), C.H. Aslin's successor in 1945 as borough architect. This unique structure is a manifestation of the architectural conservatism ever apparent in Derby and rather suggests that such a fault (if such it be) is to be applauded. Ironically, at its opening it was hailed as the future of housing by no less a savant than the chairman of the newly-formed Civic Society, the late Provost, Ron Beddoes, usually the most perceptive of men, demonstrating that even the wisest can get carried away by trendiness.

By the 1960s, too, more municipal housing had been built at Sinfin, Kingsway, Breadsall Hill Top, Sunny Hill, Priory Estate and Boulton Lane. In the decade following, Sinfin was vastly developed, mainly by private enterprise, rolling inexorably out over Stenson Fields towards the Trent and Mersey Canal. Subsequent construction of the A50 at this point between the canal and the river will probably be seen by those drawing up local plans as a natural boundary to which such development can be allowed, in the immediate future, to stretch.

In the 1980s, the emphasis was on improving existing houses rather than adding to the overall quantity, the latter role tending to be taken over by specialist housing associations. This trend was accelerated by the Thatcher Government's 'Right to Buy' policy, under which sitting tenants could acquire their council houses. At the same time, municipalities lost their remit to construct and rent housing to the housing associations.

Private building, however, continues at an ever-accelerating pace, encouraged by the ODPM and its successor. The first manifestation was the construction of a very large development – said at the time to have been the largest private housing development in the UK – on a piece of open but hilly ground between Chaddesden and Breadsall called Oakwood, being virtually completed by 1989 and comprising over 4,000 homes. Yet, nearly two decades on, this development is rather light on amenities and facilities and long lacked even such basic requirements as a school, for which its councillor to 2007, Mrs Derek Latham, spent years of lobbying to obtain.

EDUCATIONAL DEVELOPMENTS

Educating the children in these expanding areas of housing was, from 1902 until 1974 and again since 1997, Derby's concern. The 1928 Education Act, deriving from the Hadow Report of four years before, broadened the provision that could be made by towns like Derby. Eleven was established as the age of transition between primary and secondary education and the school leaving age was pushed to 14, rising further in 1944 to 15 and to 16 more recently. To cope with school leavers unable to find work in the depression of the 1930s, the borough also established a Junior Instruction Centre in the old Traffic Street (Castle) School. By this time, the Education Committee was the largest of the council with 28 members long under the expert chairmanship of H.H. Bemrose, competently and with pride running numerous schools containing 23,000 children and paying 762 teachers for educating them.

The example of Thomas Swanwick, Erasmus Darwin and the Spencers also kept a vigorous private sector

Percy Heylin Curney: St James's School, Reginald Street, 1913.

going in the 19th and 20th centuries. Apart from Derby School (brought under local authority control in 1905), establishments such as Friar Gate House School, founded as a preparatory school in 1883 in Jedediah Strutt's old home, still happily flourish.

The Sisters of the Convent of Mercy also opened St Philomena's school in the 19th century, which expanded into Highfield House, formerly home of Henry Evans of the Darley Abbey family, leaving the primary element in Bridge Gate until recent years. Unfortunately, the 40 acres of mature parkland surrounding Highfield House, which had, from the late 1990s, been designated by the council as part of its 'Green Wedge' policy of retaining strips of undeveloped land from the city boundaries towards the centre, were sold for housing redevelopment as a result of the ODPM's revised 'Brownfield' policy.

Derby High School for Girls is another long-established academy dating from the later 19th century, when it was in Osmaston Road, by 1935 in The Field there, a spectacular Regency villa which later became the Fire Service HQ. It moved after World War Two, to

Darley Hall, east front, in the 1950s, after attention by Joseph Pickford, first built in 1778. At this date, it was home to Central School, which moved to Breadsall Hill Top in 1959, the house (grade II listed) being demolished in 1962. (M. Craven)

Alexander MacPherson's superb south façade of Bemrose Boys' Grammar School of 1929–30, now a comprehensive; wartime photograph. (*Derby Evening Telegraph*)

another villa in Littleover, where it has much expanded and flourishes. A purpose-built primary school still stands in Stafford Street, dating from the 1880s, but the pretty building may not survive the construction of the last phases of the Inner Ring Road in 2007.

Many Local Authority Schools were returned to the new Unitary Derby Council in 1997 in less than perfect condition. It is only after 10 years inertia that they have

Homelands Girls' Grammar School; detail of Aslin's School hall (demolished 2005) photographed in 1999. (Carole Craven)

managed to obtain sufficient funding to repair some, replace others and make rationalisations, the latter leading to the closure of Homelands, the former Girls' Grammar School in Normanton. Herbert Aslin's fine building, with an excellent *Moderne* interior building, was demolished in 2006; its re-use would have been infinitely more constructive.

TWO VERY DIFFERENT NEW SCHOOLS

In 1991 the Conservative Government launched City Technology Colleges, educational centres of excellence sponsored privately but to recruit from a broad range of abilities, of which 15 were founded by 1997. This quickly led to the foundation of the Landau Forte College on the site of the former Co-op warehouse on Nottingham Road in 1992, sponsored, as the name suggests, by the charitable foundations set up respectively by developer Martin Landau and hotelier Lord Forte (died 2007), the latter being represented on the Governing Body by Hon. Sir Rocco Forte. Under two exceptionally able headmasters and the charismatic leadership of the first chairman of governors, Lady Brigstocke, the school has

Derby Grammar School for Boys, formely The Pastures, Littleover, from the lake in 2000. (Derby Grammar School for Boys)

flourished with year-on-year academic improvements and a major expansion in 2001–02, despite considerable coolness from the local education authority prior to 2003.

The same less restrictive educational climate of the late 1980s and early 1990s had also led a group of wealthy ex-Derby School boys to contemplate the founding of a new Boys' Grammar school to complement the High School, led by retired printing firm director John Blackton. Rebuffed by the NHS in an attempt to acquire the redundant Manor Hospital, Uttoxeter Road, in 1992, they instead acquired from the NHS the listed Rykneld Hospital, Littleover, built as The Pastures to the designs of Alderman Richard Leaper in 1806 for the Peel family of cotton spinners. This, then, with a 15-acre park – which may have been laid out by no less a figure than Revd Christopher Alderson, Queen Charlotte's Eckington-based landscape gardener, who was closely connected to the Peels – was acquired by Birch PLC to build houses. They then made available the house and about three acres to set up the intended school, which was sponsored from the outset by Derby venture capital company Williams Holdings and its Derby-born founder Sir Nigel Rudd. However, in 1995, under head Roger Waller, it got under way and has proved, like the Landau Forte College, an enormous success.

THE UNIVERSITY OF DERBY

The result of the 1970s merger between the Bishop Lonsdale College and the Technical College, the Derbyshire College of Higher Education, spent much of the following years lobbying to be made a polytechnic, only to be rebuffed. In 1989, however, the appointment of Roger Waterhouse as principal and a senior Derby accountant, Alan Woods, to the governors (rising to chairman in a year), began a transformation, both financial and academic, for the better, to meet the

Government's criteria for polytechnics. A further rebuttal was not contemplated. A third new arrival, Jonathan Powers, managed to engineer a vital grant of authority to validate research degrees. Yet the college was almost taken aback by the news in 1992 that it was to be designated a university instead of a polytechnic, thanks to a radical change of heart on the part of the Government, which unexpectedly decided to eliminate what was termed the 'binary divide' between universities and polytechnics. Thus the college had either to suffer yet another rebuttal or be designated a university. In the event, and probably clinched by the research degree validations, the latter course of action prevailed.

Thus in that year the University of Derby was born, its first vice-chancellor being Roger Waterhouse with Professor Powers as his deputy and underpinned by Mr Woods's sound fiscal control. Two new teaching blocks were soon completed, a 'learning centre' and a rather fine atrium, which both connects and softens the effect of the three ugly towers provided for the old Derby & District College of Art & Technology in 1956–66 by the Building Design Partnership.

Very early on, the university hit a serious accommodation problem when in 1994 over 200 students were recruited only to arrive to find that there was nowhere for them to live. The steep increase in numbers caught the country's newest university unawares, but it provoked an over-reaction.

In the light of these events, the administration of the university began property development on an almost reckless scale, erecting vast, barrack-like halls of residence along the Ashbourne Road and streets off, and planning to demolish and replace at least three of the fine middling-sized Regency villas lining Uttoxeter New Road. In the end, only two villas were actually demolished, one being Laverstoke Villa, built in 1868 for Edward du Sautoy by G.H. Sheffield, the first tile of which was ceremonially but unedifyingly removed from

Former Bishop Lonsdale College, Mickleover, built in 1962–64. It is due to be closed, cleared and redeveloped as housing in 2007. (M. Craven)

Devonshire Hospital, Buxton, built by John Carr as stables 1787–90 and adapted as a hospital by R.R. Duke in 1859. It was futher adapted as an outpost of the University of Derby in 2002–04. (University of Derby)

the roof in 1992 by du Sautoy's great-grandson, then chairman of planning. The other was architect William Giles's own house in Lonsdale Place nearby. Adjacent Lonsdale Hill, by T.C. Hine for William Bemrose, was saved through being spot-listed following an application to English Heritage. In all, the university built no less than seven halls of residence to accommodate some 2,500 students. To attain all this, one historic mill was lost, another nearly so.

The university also managed to establish itself at Buxton by merging with the High Peak College of Further Education and making up for any criticism of its lack of conservation in Derby by converting the Devonshire Royal Hospital as an outlying campus, which opened in 2006, a year after a multi-faith centre, of innovative design, was unveiled on the Derby campus after six years' gestation and at least one major redesign.

The university has since, despite appearing rather low down in the Government's university league tables on occasion, pioneered the recruitment of students from non-traditional backgrounds and forged closer links with the local further education colleges. Moreover, since its establishment, there has been a complete change at the top with the unexpectedly early retirement of

Derby University: multi-faith Centre completed in 2004. (M. Craven)

Professor Powers, followed by that of Mr Woods in 2003 and Professor Waterhouse in 2005, replaced as vice-chancellor by Professor John Coyne. The university's first chancellor, Sir Christopher Ball, also stepped down in 2004.

STREET TRANSPORT

Strangely to contemporary eyes, in 1954 only just over 1% of the population commuted out of the town to work. This rather startling statistic serves to remind us that the internal communications of the then borough had, as a consequence, to be of the best. With the constant expansion of the housing estates to points ever further from the centre, the rigidity and inflexibility of the tramway system had begun by 1930 to be apparent. Nevertheless, it was felt that electric traction was still the most efficacious mode of power and it was resolved to switch from trams to trolley-buses.

In 1930 there were 78 tramcars in service, yet no route had been extended since before the 1914–18 war. Indeed, this same year, the first service to be replaced by a motorbus, that along Nottingham Road, changed over. In 1932, however, the trolley-buses were introduced and the last tram ran from Victoria Street back to the depot on Abingdon Street on 2 July 1934. The first of these new vehicles were sizeable double-deckers with six wheels, although the first of the Daimler four-wheeled buses were introduced in 1938, and by the time the system was decommissioned in 1967 all the vehicles were of this

Derby Corporation tramcar no.68 outside the Spotted Horse (Post Office) Inn, Victoria Street, in the mid-1920s.

Trolley-buses advance up St Peter's Street, 1948. The
Whitehall Cinema is to the right and the Midland
Drapery is behind it. (*Derby Evening Telegraph*)

One of Derby Corporation's later trolley-buses (No.206, a Sunbeam F4 of 1949) at the turning circle, Kingscroft, Allestree, when new in 1949. (*Derby Evening Telegraph*)

same general type. In 1949 there were 100 trolley-buses and 68 diesel ones.

One of the reasons for the abandonment of the tramways had been the cost of replacing the worn out equipment. The same reason was advanced in the mid-1960s for the replacement of the trolley-buses: spares were becoming increasingly difficult to come by and vehicles almost impossible. Again, with the expansion of the town which continued vigorously, it was felt that the trolley-bus system, too, was not sufficiently flexible. In the light of the post-1973 oil crisis, there were many voices raised in Derby to say that they should have been retained and, indeed, they were quiet, pollution-free and very fast, although they had their disadvantages.

Despite the opening of new routes into the Mackworth Estate in 1953 and the acquisition of eight new vehicles in 1960, the last service ran on 10 September 1967, although one or two vehicles sallied forth in the ensuing few weeks to replace undelivered motor-buses and on works duties. The dismantling of the overhead wiring and the independence of the motor-buses enabled the planners to attain their own nirvana:

Derby's new bus station, photographed in 1934. (M. Craven)

the Derby One-Way Traffic System, introduced in 1970. This was remarkably successful in fact – if you were local and understood it.

The Corporation omnibus operation, from well before the war (protected as it was within the borough by a 1927 Act of Parliament) was in constant competition on longer routes with other operators, especially for traffic to the suburbs. After World War Two, the Trent Motor Traction Company and the smaller, Willington-based Blue Bus Company were the chief protagonists. However, in 1973 the Corporation undertaking absorbed the latter firm, but was itself privatised on 26 October 1986, when the buses came under the aegis of a wholly-owned subsidiary of the city council. Within a few years this had been disposed of under further legislation to a private operator, Arriva, eventually obtaining a near monopoly of all services within what was previously corporation territory.

OTHER TRANSPORT DEVELOPMENTS

THE CANAL

The canal closed after World War Two, lay derelict for a considerable time and was progressively filled in from the late 1960s. Part, towards the southern boundary of the city, was converted into a footpath, later adapted as a cycle path. The old basin behind the monumental ice factory was swiftly filled in, but the old grade II listed 1820 Bridgewater warehouse lingered on to 1977. The site of the White Bear Lock was covered in many feet of concrete to accommodate the Inner Ring Road. Indeed, modern developments have virtually obliterated all traces of the canal from the town centre. Even the weir by the towpath bridge across the Derwent has been drastically rebuilt.

All this, one might think, would act as a deterrent to any group wishing to undertake a restoration of the canal on the back of the vast revival of the popularity of inland waterways generally since the 1970s. Yet, incredibly, a group of local people decided that a restoration of the Derby Canal from Swarkestone to the Erewash via Derby was not only feasible but a practical proposition. Forming themselves into the Derby & Sandiacre Canal Society (and Trust) they issued a business plan, ran a feasibility study, worked out a way of restoring the canal without even attempting to regain the city centre and started drumming up recruits. Over rather more than a decade, they have restored significant stretches east of Derby, including at least one lock, and have managed to secure the support of the local authorities affected as well as to link in with potential developers of derelict sites adjacent to the line of the

Derby Canal in terminal decay alongside the silk mills on Siddals Road, 1948. (Derby Museum)

canal to good effect. In due time grant aid began to come in too, although the ultimate goal of a Heritage Lottery Fund grant to complete the job has proved elusive, possibly because of the practical problem – one that William Outram had experienced 210 years before – of getting craft and the canal across the Derwent, south of the railway complex.

Derby Canal: The long bridge, final decay, looking towards Derwent Row. (Derby City Council)

RAILWAYS

Fortunately, the railways of the town have fared somewhat better, being at least largely still running, although, as has been noted elsewhere, the Great Northern Railway line was closed in 1967 and much of its course has been infilled or demolished. The worst problem has been the site of its station and goods depot in Derby, immediately west of Friar Gate. This has lain derelict for 40 years, although the above ground buildings, except the colossal listed bonded warehouse, were cleared in the 1990s. Until 2006 uncertainty about the final course of the soon-to-be-completed Inner Ring Road seems to have hamstrung development of the site, along with the city's aspiration to put a high speed bus (or even tram) route through it to connect Mickleover via Mackworth using much of the old GNR trackbed.

The London Midland and Scottish Railway, which absorbed the Midland Railway (*inter alia*) as from 1 January 1923, was nationalised on 1 January 1948. Thirty-six years later, and only just after having been included in a conservation area, its historic station in Derby was demolished by nationalised railway undertaking, then calling itself British Rail, and replaced by a gimcrack structure aptly described by Professor

Gavin Stamp as a 'Hi-Tech style shack'. Behind a façade added by Charles Trubshaw in 1895 and earlier alterations by John Holloway Sanders in the 1870s, Francis Thompson's original and hugely long Trijunct station lurked more or less intact. By its demolition, an historic environment of national stature has been irretrievably flawed. It goes without saying that the old station was eminently susceptible to refurbishment and the extensive redundant office space therein would have been highly marketable in a restored state, a scheme favourably evaluated by the Derby Civic Society and the Derbyshire Historic Buildings Trust, the two bodies which also saved and restored the three streets of Thompson's delightfully-proportioned railway cottages opposite, again against strenuous opposition. The restored cottages won a Civic Trust award in 1984, the same year that the station was destroyed.

AVIATION

In the wake of Charles Rolls's enthusiasm for aviation and despite his untimely death, B.C. Hucks flew a Bleriot aircraft into Derby, landing on the racecourse on 11 July 1912. He was thus the first airman to overfly and land in the town, and he set an 80mph record speed on the same occasion. After World War One, flying had lost only some of its novelty, and on 10 October 1919, the mayor, Alderman W.B. Robotham, and his wife took a flight from the racecourse in an Avro aircraft.

By the mid-1930s, it had occurred to the borough council that the establishment of an airport might constitute a considerable benefit to trade in the town. Accordingly, the modest estate of Colonel Godfrey Mosley at Burnaston was purchased for this purpose. This suited Mosley, whose ancestor Ashton Mosley had built the elegant yet severe Soanian house on the site in 1824, as he had moved to Calke, which his wife had inherited from her father Sir Vauncey Harpur-Crewe, Bt., in 1924. The house became the terminal and the park before it, the grass airfield, with hangars erected thereon. It was opened by Sir Kingsley Wood in 1938 and was an auxiliary field for the RAF during World War Two.

Afterwards it became the base of Derby Airways (now British Midland), but having no hard runways, it became progressively less useful to increasingly sophisticated and large aircraft which the airline needed to stay in business. The most it could take was a Handley Page Marathon or a Douglas DC-3 Dakota. Ultimately, Derby joined in a consortium to build and run a new international standard airport at Castle Donington, which opened in the same year that Derby Airport, as Burnaston was known, closed.

The house was sold and decayed almost beyond repair,

1938: opening of Derby Airport, Burnaston. Police and Fire Officers take a flight in a De Haviland DH89 Dragon Rapide. (Derby Museum)

although the main area of the field itself and the hangars remained. The upsurge in private flying induced by the mid-1980s boom led to its reopening under private aegis for just this purpose in 1987. The house, by this time a shell with the south wall partly collapsed, had been grant aided for restoration as a nursing home. What in 1988 looked likely to have a happy ending, however, an unholy alliance of the radical Labour county and the Tory city councils combined to entice Toyota to the spot to make cars with government support.

All attempts to save the important and half-restored house, on a previous occasion strongly supported by the county's officers, came to nothing when such support was abruptly withdrawn and reversed; suddenly it wasn't worth saving any more.

In the end the building was, in a sense, rescued, for a Derby developer won the contract to demolish the house. He took it down with extreme care, having first recorded it thoroughly, and palleted it up for export, ironically, to a Tokyo golf club. Examples of the stair balustrade and ceiling plaster had already been rescued. The deal fell through on cost of transport. Subsequently, it was twice fruitlessly offered to Derby to be erected on the site of either Darley or Markeaton Halls but was refused and two attempts to build it on a new site for sale were frustrated by NIMBYism. Even the inspired suggestion that it could be rebuilt on the breathtakingly lovely site of the former Repton Park failed to impress the Calke Estate Trustees, and Burnaston House remains on pallets.

Meanwhile the club flying migrated from Burnaston to Tatenhill in Staffordshire, just beyond Burton-on-Trent. The East Midlands Airport, however, has been a great success.

FIRE SERVICE AND POLICE

An additional unit was needed for the borough fire brigade to cope with emergencies at the airport, although throughout its time Burnaston was never the scene of a major incident. Yet only three years before the airport was opened, the fire brigade had only four mobile appliances, one of which, replaced in 1934, had been the pioneering Daimler fire engine introduced in 1914. This, along with a twin of 1903 and a 60ft mobile ladder acquired in 1910, had been obtained to replace the horse-drawn Shand-Mason steam fire engine purchased in 1888, which replaced the manually operated *Niagara*, of which mention has already been made. Two Daimler engines had been added in 1920 and 1924. At that time the brigade was manned entirely by volunteers – it was called an 'Artizan Brigade' – and horses still had to be commandeered from the St Mary's Gate livery stables, or anywhere handy – even the cab rank in Victoria Street – in the event of a callout. Somewhat later, horses were hired from a livery stable in Curzon Street, and the fire station itself was a cramped building in Full Street opposite the Baths.

In 1892 the brigade was re-constituted as a professional one, having moved the year before into a new, purpose-built HQ beside the Corporation Stables on the corner of Willow Row and Lower St Mary's Gate, in front of the Gas Works. The new fire station had facilities for officers to be there on standby, whereas before they had lived in nearby streets with a board marked 'Fireman' attached to their houses and small boys were paid 6d (2p) to roust them out in the event of a fire. From 1893 24 alarm boxes were placed in various streets and automatic alarms began to be fitted to many mills and works. In 1926 the brigade consisted of two officers, a sergeant, four engineers and six firemen. It was taken under national control in the war in 1941 and returned to borough control in 1948; from 1939–45 a fire boat was kept moored by the Full Street Police Station.

To some extent, the fire brigade was inextricably linked to the borough police. Both were commanded by the town's Chief Constable and both units were frequently inter-dependant at the scenes of larger emergencies. Yet the borough police force was modest, too, for in 1928 there had been 159 men and a pool of 250 special constables, all split between two divisions: 'A' Division, based in an ex-chemist's shop in the Market Place (they had moved from the Guildhall in 1904), and 'B' Division, once the separate Litchurch force. There was a police station in the former King's Arms County Hotel in St Mary's Gate post war until 1989, another purpose-built as part of the Central Improvement Scheme's Magistrates' Courts of 1934 but closed in 2002 in favour of a huge new HQ on the site of the former Midland Railway Mansfield Road sidings, an area modestly named Prime Park after its developer. The old Litchurch-based police area is now served by a modern station in Cotton Lane.

The fire brigade remained under borough control until 1974, however, unlike the police. Yet the County

Fire Service established a new fire station in Ascot Drive in 1963, but when the Derby brigade was amalgamated with it, the Bold Lane depot was rebuilt as an ambulance station. Another fire station was built on Kingsway, Rowditch, at about the same period. Littleover Old Hall – a house built in 1890–91, replacing the old Harpur seat there – was bought from the bankrupt Rolls-Royce in 1971 and became the Fire Service Headquarters for the entire county, which it remains. The ambulance service, however, also long the preserve of the county council, has now become amalgamated with those of two neighbouring authorities and is run by a separate body, whereas the police are beholden to a county committee. A hugely unpopular attempt by the Blair government to combine the police force with those of several neighbouring counties – along the lines of the ambulance service – was cancelled in the nick of time.

Other functions lost by the town before reorganisation were electricity generation (nationalised in April 1948), health (regionalised in 1946), valuation and rating (to HM Inland Revenue in 1948) and the Gas, Light and Coke Company (nationalised shortly before). It is worth mentioning that by 1935, 42 years after their introduction, electric street lights outnumbered gas ones by 2,950 to 1,080; by nationalisation they were nearly all electric, except in some of the remoter and older residential streets, which lingered on with gas into the 1960s when North Sea Gas, which required all appliances to be extensively modified, caused their demise.

TOPOGRAPHICAL CHANGES

The Derby townscape has altered more radically in the 20th century than in any previous era in the history of the city.

One of the chief reasons for this is that prior to the mid-19th century old buildings were frequently taken down (or more frequently part-demolished only) and replaced on a piecemeal basis. With the redevelopment of Victoria Street in 1839, however, Derby saw its first redevelopment on an epic scale. Nevertheless, the architecture was of splendid quality and finish, with fine detailing; the materials were local ones and the scale was sympathetic. The same can largely be said for the St James's Street improvement and those of Irongate and St Peter's Street.

The three criteria by which one can legitimately judge the quality of urban new builds are materials, proportion and scale. It was only with the post-war developments in Derby that these three paramount concerns were increasingly ignored to the permanent detriment of the city, bestowing upon it monstrosities like the new Assembly Rooms, Heritage Gate, the DRI

The opening of the Derby Arterial Road – the present Ring Road – in 1939. The scene at the Chaddesden end of Raynesway. Herbert Aslin's bronze lamps and pylons (just visible, left) were swept away when the present A38 was built in the late 1970s to accommodate slip roads and widenings. (*Derby Evening Telegraph*)

are classic examples in the latter category. The destruction of the mediaeval Old Mayor's Parlour (1948), Darley, Markeaton and Osmaston Halls, the city's only Georgian Square along with its finest Victorian church at St Alkmund's (as well as the cradle of the settlement's evolution) and the Devonshire Hospital on Full Street are just some examples of the former. Further, the 2006 decision to allow the Quad building on the NE end of Tenant Street rather set the seal on the despoliation of the Market Place. Frequently, where an extensive development does seem appropriate, the opportunity is invariably missed and the replacement buildings were inevitably of very poor architectural quality.

Under the 1929 Derby Corporation Act, a planning remit was added to the powers of the council, strengthened by numerous subsequent pieces of national legislation allowing the compilation of the list of Buildings of Historic or Architectural Importance under the 1948 Town & Country Planning Act, its revision in 1969 and the power granted to the council to designate conservation areas. 'The people,' one local politician remarked five decades ago, 'Want bright new buildings,

nurses' home and so on. Another aspect was the increasing tendency to demolish buildings of the highest architectural quality, or ones with important historic associations. Herbert Spencer's birthplace, Exeter Street (1964), and his childhood home (1970), Erasmus Darwin's House (1933) and Whitehurst's House (1929),

The Spot photographed 13 November 1943 showing the *moderne* rebuilding on the inside of the curve designed by Sir Frederick Bennett in 1934. The high plain roof behind is that of the Gaumont Palace cinema. The 1906 statue of Queen Victoria was found to be too heavy for the new public lavatories and was unceremoniously removed to the gardens of the DRI. (*Derby Evening Telegraph*)

not shabby old ones' and this sort of thinking was very prevalent after the war and the long period of austerity. On being told the aims of the newly-formed Derby Civic Society in 1961, another aged savant remarked, 'There's nowt wrong wi' Durby.' So there may not be, indeed, but it is important to persuade the majority of the city's inhabitants that theirs is a distinguished historic settlement with a remarkable number of Georgian and earlier buildings surviving, and that it is all worth saving, will improve the quality of life of those who live here and will have – as Bristol showed in the 1980s – a beneficial economic impact in the longer term in terms of inward investment and tourism, especially as Derby has been, for most of the third millennium, the southern point of the Derwent Mills World Heritage Site.

An excellent example of small-scale redevelopment was the replacement in 1890 of a Restoration market inn called the *Royal Oak* set on the corner of Tenant Street and the Market Place. This had been refronted in the earlier 18th century in uninspiring fashion, but was finally replaced by a new inn of the same name in arts-and-crafts half-timbered style designed by James Wright. It closed in 1920 and was adapted as the town clerk's office in January the same year. The council moved out in 1948 when it was let as a solicitor's office but in 2005 was tactfully converted into a registry office and opened by HRH the Duke of Gloucester; one of the city council's most enlightened recent moves.

THE CENTRAL IMPROVEMENT PLAN

As early as 1919 a Town Planning Scheme was evolved, envisaging the enlargement of the Guildhall and the Assembly Rooms, although leaving both relatively unscathed. This did not proceed due to lack of resources. At about the same time the council had a notion to reconstruct the whole of the west bank of the Derwent as a 'War Memorial Garden', but this was stalled through the difficulty of acquiring the necessary freeholds and the lack of funds with which to do so. A further scheme of 1924–25 was far more extensive. It envisaged the building of the Ring Road, a new Civic Centre, various street widenings and extensions to the borough. In March 1925 an enquiry was held, but 'Economic considerations gradually whittled down the proposals until the scheme fell to pieces'. In fact, most of these considerations did go forward, a revised scheme gaining approval in 1929.

The centrepiece of the revised Town Planning Scheme was the Central Improvement Plan, approved in much revised form in January 1931 and in both cases the brain child of Herbert Aslin. There were four aims to the plan. The first was to rehouse under one roof the

C.H. Ashin: the first element of the Central Improvement Plan, Exeter House Flats, of 1931, seen from Exeter Place, September 2006. (M. Craven)

various and physically scattered departments of the council. The second was to improve the market which functioned partly along the Morledge, restricting traffic, and partly in the Market Place, where councillors considered it a nuisance. It may well be objected that the latter was the logical place for this, but the increase in traffic had persuaded the council that the Market Place should be made a merry-go-round for the municipal buses and with car parking in the middle. This was a most unfortunate aim, for its implementation led to the downgrading of the area, making it conceptually easier to take highly unfortunate decisions after the war regarding its further development. In 1988 a competition was launched for suggestions for the improvement of the Market Place, rendered visually sterile with the opening of the Assembly Rooms in 1977.

This resulted in minor changes all centred on a 'water feature' on the site of Rotten Row, designed by Walter Pye and built in 1990, but which few people seem to like, most preferring a traditional fountain. Plainly, in order to re-infuse the area with life and bustle, market stalls should be re-introduced without delay, and fortunately, over the last few years, occasional or specialised markets, at least, have been brought back and much appreciated (see page 265). In the first edition of this book it was suggested that, as a focus, something really stunning would be required, in the form of a large equestrian statue of Prince Charles Edward Stuart, or a new Conduit Head. In the event, the council of the day, when offered an equestrian statue of Bonnie Prince Charlie, caused this striking addition to Derby's public art – the only equestrian statue to be erected in the UK since the start of World War Two – to go instead on Cathedral Green, a much more isolated position, although close to the site of Exeter House, his whilom HQ in 1745.

The third aim of the plan was to improve traffic access to the centre of town and to relieve pressure on St Peter's Street. Finally, an improved crossing of the river at Exeter Bridge was considered a priority.

The basic cast concrete structure of the third Exeter Bridge, designed by C.A. Clews, pictured being tested for strength in 1929. It was completed to the designs of Herbert Aslin the following year. (*Derby Evening Telegraph*)

A plan was therefore drawn up under the aegis of Aslin, assisted by H.V. Lanchester. This envisaged continuing Full Street southwards on its main north–south axis to cross Derwent Street east of the Market Place and continuing as Corporation Street to Tenant Bridge to link with the Morledge, which, with Full Street, was to be widened, although this did not, in the event, happen until 1950. All the land, from the Power Station to Cattle Market Bridge, was to be cleared and filled in. It would then be developed with, from the north: fire station, police station and magistrates' court (Full Street), municipal offices, town hall, open market, bus station and car park (Corporation Street and Morledge), with gardens on the riparian side, much in the manner of the War Memorial idea of a decade before. The only development planned to the west of this artery

Aslin's new Police Station of 1934, attached to the rear of the Magistrates' Court in Full Street and latterly listed Grade II, seen on 27 November 1991. Vacated in 2002, its fate was unclear in 2006. (M. Craven)

was to be the extension of the Assembly Rooms to the east and south. Rightly, the rest of the area was to be omitted, the aim being merely to encourage its upgrading.

On the east side of the river, an area of foundries between Exeter Place and the Derwent was to be cleared and two blocks of flats built, under the provisions of the Housing Act, in 1930. In the event, only one was built, Exeter House Flats. The Town Hall was to go between the municipal offices and the open market (now the Council House car park) and was to be elliptical in plan. The Guildhall, following its two predecessors, and the Moot Hall, was to become redundant and would serve the purpose that it today happily fulfils as a place of entertainment.

The council put a bill through Parliament to acquire the 12 acres of river bank needed for the scheme and the land was cleared (including the removal of the shot tower in 1932 and the last river edge gazebo a year later) and the multifarious water courses and docks filled in, or, in the case of the Markeaton Brook, culverted. In 1928 work had begun on the bridge replacement by Aslin's predecessor, C.A. Clews, but only his understructure was suffered to survive, the remainder of the bridge being redesigned by Aslin with stone pylons bearing four plaques of Derby 'worthies': Darwin, Hutton, Strutt and Spencer, and opened in 1931. In July 1932 the remainder of the work got under way, starting with a new river wall south of the bridge. The following month the market was begun and the bus station, which was parabolic in plan due to the restricted nature of the site, and car park beyond in October.

In fact, the first things originally envisaged after work started on the bridge were the Municipal Buildings and the Town Hall. The former got under way piecemeal in 1938–41, but both were originally postponed in 1931 'during the period of financial uneasiness' as an official account so prosaically put it. All the buildings were, apparently, designed in consultation with the Royal Fine Arts Commission and were in Aslin's version of Classical Revival largely a beneficial facet of the scheme, since it resulted in buildings which, while perceived by some as unadventurous, were at least nicely proportioned, beautifully realised at the angles and along the exceedingly lengthy façades and to scale with those that surrounded them.

The bus station was the main innovation of this first phase, being advertised as 'quite a new departure with amenities even better than those usually associated with the largest Railway Stations and the architecture is wisely in keeping with the scheme'. In fact, it was one of the first in the country to have its facilities arranged with a platform layout and was important for that reason; it is also visually one of the most successful of the elements of the whole, the curved layout of the platforms, necessitated by the restricted site, making it the more coherent. Furthermore, here Aslin was in *Moderne* mode and the interior of his terminal rotunda was lavishly marbled and embellished with his typical wrought bronze work.

But in the end, Hitler intervened, with the Council House barely started. It was occupied by the army from 1941, completed in 1948 and opened by Princess Elizabeth (now HM the Queen) in 1949. Never built was the elliptical-plan town hall – now the car park – which was to contain elected members' offices and services along with the debating chamber. To make up for the loss of the latter, a curved, full height addition was plonked into the new council offices' central courtyard, which still serves. The Council House, too, was simplified, with Crittall windows instead of hardwood, the omission of a tapering light-topped tower rising from the entrance portico and much of the interior embellishment.

It might be added that in 2003 it became clear that the Council House was infested with poisonous asbestos, meaning that no repairs could be undertaken under health and safety rules without clearing the entire building for some three years. The decision was taken then to vacate the building in favour of new council offices, but little has happened since. The question arises as to the future use of the Council House once vacated and treated. Clearly the unlisted building could be demolished and this important site built over. Yet it is a fine building and should at all costs be preserved, and adaptation into the top-quality hotel Derby has long aspired to have would surely be the best solution, especially as the entrance front is bursting with fine quality public rooms essential for a prestige hotel. Moreover, the warren of offices on all three floors would convert with little trouble to bedrooms with en suite bathrooms also the debating chamber could be removed and the resulting courtyard glazed over as an atrium.

The aftermath of the war had a disastrous effect on the scheme. The island site on the east of Tenant Street had not had its intended facelift and was beginning to be an eyesore, especially from the mayoral suite, despite the fact that the creation of Corporation Street had at last revealed the Old Mayor's Parlour to public view. The result was that within three years it had been swept away, mourned by only a few and with little effective opposition, despite repeated offers from the Derbyshire Archaeological Society to buy it and re-erect it elsewhere. Thus passed the most important large timber-framed building of its date in an urban context in England then surviving. The loss was tragic and pointless, especially as the site remained largely unused until it was excavated for an abortive hotel scheme and eventually filled in to

Derby Market Place is once again used occasionally for specialist markets, as here in spring 2006. (M. Craven)

form the Sir Peter Hilton Memorial Garden, commemorating the fallen of the Korean War.

The failure to build a new Town Hall and to extend the Assembly Rooms also sounded the death-knell of the latter and cleared the way for the redevelopment of the site with the present Assembly Rooms and their unsightly car park. This was aided by a fire in the old Assembly Rooms in February 1963, which did relatively slight and eminently repairable damage, but, nevertheless, the entire building behind the façade – and all Robert Adam's plasterwork – was summarily demolished leaving the façade to be incorporated into a successor building. The New Assembly Rooms, designed in 1970 by Sir Hugh Casson, was oversized and brutallist and its construction involved the demolition of the entire north side of the Market Place, including Newcastle House, the 1713 County Assembly Rooms and the Horse & Trumpet Inn. But the Assembly Rooms are so vast and overpowering as to destroy the scale, harmony and proportion of the historic Market Place: a mistake C.H. Aslin would never have made; his plan was modest and in all a good one.

Derby Assembly Rooms by Sir Hugh Casson (built 1972–77). Ugly, brutalist and oversized for the mediaeval-scale Market Place – a typical Hugh Casson architectural ego-trip. The interior is good in parts but laid out confusingly. Photographed in 2003 after the Market Place was re-landscaped in 1992. (*Derby Evening Telegraph*)

XVI

POST-WAR DERBY

THE INNER RING ROAD

After the war, recovery was fairly slow and demolitions, like that of the Old Mayor's Parlour, were more the rule than any new schemes. In 1951 a new fire station was built, not beside Full Street Police Station, but on Nottingham Road, Chaddesden. A new bus depot was also provided on part of the old Osmaston estate at Ascot Drive, having facilities for both motor and trolley-buses.

In the mid-1960s, however, long maturing plans were laid to build an Inner Ring Road and at the same time to redevelop yet further the core of the city, to include high-level service roads. Littlewoods, built in 1969 on the site of most of Devonshire House, boasts a never-used car park on its roof, completely inaccessible, the result of this high-level scheme which would have seen pedestrians monopolising the historic streets, themselves in permanent shadow due to the access roads built over them at cornice level; such an arrangement would also have wrecked the appearance of almost every historic building in the city centre – a glance at the houses facing the A52 on the old Nottingham Road near the present Landau-Forte College gives something of the impression this scheme would have had. Mercifully, the City Fathers drew the line firmly at this, perhaps discouraged by the cost.

The Ring Road was the responsibility of the county council as Highway Authority, acting as agent for the Ministry of Transport. Complete, it was intended that it should run from a new motorway-standard arm of the A52 Nottingham Road, built along the old canal bed to bypass Spondon and Chaddesden, to a vast junction near the County Cricket Ground at the south end of the racecourse. This was to be called, from its shape on the ground, the Pentagon Island and the land infilled between

Derby's only Georgian Square, St Alkmund's Churchyard, pictured in February 1957 and already suffering from the shadow of the proposed Inner Ring Road. Apart from the church, no building was more modern than the 1790s; several went back to the 16th and 17th centuries and almost all were listed. (*Derby Evening Telegraph*)

the new road and the water meadows on the banks of the Derwent was to become the new, improved cattle market and there was to be a light industrial estate adjoining, accessed by a new road called Chequers Road, the water meadows having once included Chequers Close. The cattle market had to be moved, for an early stage of the road was to run from the Pentagon Island to another, equally enormous, on the old Cockpit Hill canal basin. From thence it was to run to Siddals Road by the 1863 Alexandra Inn which closed in 1988 in anticipation. Mercifully, when it became clear that this phase of the road was unlikely to be built, mainly through the listing of the Railway Cottages, the *Alexandra* – built by Sir John ('Brassy') Smith as an investment – reopened as an excellent real ale pub.

A new concrete bridge to be called Holmes Bridge would obliterate the old cattle market and the old 1861 bridge there would be removed. A series of curvilinear slip roads were then to cover most of Canary Island, obliterating all but Exeter Place and the Exeter Arms public house of 1817, to join a newly-aligned, high-level Nottingham Road which would leap the river on the Causey Bridge, passing about a yard from the south wall of the structurally vulnerable Bridge Chapel, before completely obliterating the whole of delightful and historic Bridge Gate, saving only Pugin's St Mary's Catholic church and the two Georgian houses, since 1863 the home of the Convent of Mercy. The entire stretch at this point was to be in a titanic cutting, which caused also the loss of the whole of St Alkmund's churchyard – a Georgian square with a mediaeval confectioner's shop on the corner of Bridge Gate, several of the 18th-century façades hiding 16th and 17th-century rearward fabrics, some of immense interest and importance – along with Stevens's Church of St Alkmund. The only silver lining to this cloud was the excavation of the church, an operation which yielded so much valuable information about the early borough and important artefacts, such as the stone interlace Anglo-Saxon sarcophagus now in the museum. Thence the road dived under King Street, removed the south side of St Helen's Street, and made a junction with Ford Street.

These earlier phases of the Inner Ring Road were completed in 1971, the A52 extension nearly a decade later. From the Siddals Road junction, the next phase was planned to swing south west right across the site of the Railway Cottages, but since the revitalisation of this area, the line has been altered slightly. Of this section only a short piece connecting London Road and Osmaston Road and widening Bradshaw Street has been completed, in 1964.

One of the most important links in the modern street pattern had been opened in 1982, called Sir Frank Whittle Way, running parallel with the old Stores Road from Pentagon Island to the A38 link at Little Eaton.

Building St Alkmund's Way; 1968 photograph looking from St Helen's Street towards King Street. (M. Craven)

Had this road been constructed as originally intended, as a dual carriageway (it was certainly cleared to that width), the destructive Phase IIIB of the Inner Ring Road, which is due to be built in 2007, would have been unnecessary, obviating the destruction of Richard Brown's marble works, the isolation of the 1680 vernacular Seven Stars Inn and compromising the setting of the incomparable St Helen's House. Thus, instead of channelling all north-bound traffic along the A6 to Five Lamps, where the roads would still be restrictively narrow, it would go east to Pentagon Island

Destroyed for the Inner Ring Road: St Alkmund's Churchyard, looking south in 1942. (NMR)

The Inner Ring Road still under construction in 1968. Note the site of the Eagle Centre, flattened but not yet built on. In the upper centre, the whole of much savaged Canary Island.

and then north along a dualled Sir Frank Whittle Way to Little Eaton and thence to the A38. It is this sort of complex interaction of powerful vested interests against the largely unheeded voices of conservationists that has caused certain writers to write critically of the city, such as Iain Nairn's *Derby is a mess* and Professor John Beckett's *Derby's architectural heritage has been all but destroyed by post-war development*. Hyperbole perhaps, but the point is made.

THE EAGLE CENTRE

In 1971 another great redevelopment scheme was initiated. Several streets south of East Street and north of Main Centre had been cleared of old housing, by no means all of it sub-standard as claimed, but mainly dating from the 1820s. Coal Industry Nominees, in partnership with the city council, started work on a new market to replace the open one in the Morledge, a vast shopping precinct and a new Playhouse. The whole was to be called the Eagle Centre, from the crest of the borough family, on whose Castlefields estate the land once lay: *an eagle rising proper grasping in the talons the shield of Pallas or*. It opened in 1976 and, apart from

being extremely unsightly, turned out to be impractical: hot in summer, cold in winter, vandal-prone, difficult to navigate around, unpopular and reputedly haunted.

The market portion, with interlocking hexagonal stalls was very difficult to find one's way around. Nor did the stall holders like it, as rents had risen alarmingly compared with the old open market, the site of which was thus freed up for redevelopment. With the benefit of hindsight, this would have been the ideal site for the prestige hotel the council was recommended to try and attract by consultants Hillier Parker, who were recruited in the 1980s to help advise on making the new Assembly Rooms pay. Unfortunately the land was grabbed by the Government for a new Crown Court Building – in the event an unremarkable structure – before the Hillier Parker report had even been commissioned. The result was that the only site left for any projected hotel was opposite, on Tenant Street. In the end this was just too small for a hotel with car parking large enough to be viable and the idea collapsed in the early 1990s, leaving a huge pit, dug by one aspirant hotel chain to accommodate the necessary underground car park, which rapidly filled with brackish water and detritus.

Nor were the pedestrian thoroughfares within the

The newly-built Eagle Centre in 1972 from across the Morledge, with the Castle and Falcon to the right. The covered market with its hexagonal stalls is to the left. (Derby City Council)

permanent part of the complex itself at all welcoming or easy to find one's way around, despite debouching onto the market, Albion Street, East Street and The Spot. Another exit was via an unsightly footbridge to the bus station terminal which it met at first-floor level, doing no favours to Aslin's rotunda, the damage to which was one of the reasons why English Heritage refused to list it in 1993 and in 2001. Furthermore, this bridge was prone to muggings and vandalism. The entire complex, including the Playhouse, set in a forbidding brick pile at the south-east angle of the complex, was serviced from above via a ramped access from Traffic Street, which was extended over East Street for many years on another rather ugly bridge, giving Derby a whole network of hidden streets at roof level, accessible only to authorised commercial vehicles.

The Eagle Centre also connected with the even less

The appalling Main Centre, photographed with Castlefields House – a block of Council offices – in the background when new on 3 July 1963. (Derby Evening Telegraph)

welcoming Main Centre of 1961–63, sandwiched between London Road and Traffic Street and overlooked by a large glass office block. The only thing the Main Centre had going for it was a decent bronze statue of a boy with a ram – very 1960s in style – by Wilfred Dudeney, a much worthier piece of public art than the tricky digital water clock that John Smith & Sons of Derby had been commissioned to place in one of the open spaces of the Eagle Centre. Both were serviced by intimidating and expensive subterranean car parks connecting via lifts and stairs.

The most serious problem these two very poorly designed shopping centres threw up was that they had the effect of shifting southwards the retail centre of gravity of the city from the shops gathered round its ancient core. Over the following decades, more and more outlets closed in the older part of the city and reopened either in the Eagle Centre itself or in St Peter's Street. The vacuum they left behind was harder to fill, most empty shops becoming estate agents, food outlets, insurance agencies or specialist retailers. In 1987 the north side of both Bradshaw Way and Traffic Street were developed with a hideous row of damagingly gimcrack prefabricated retail outlets, swiftly christened Lego Land, which effectively extended the Main Centre's facilities further. The effect on first time visitor coming from tree-lined and still elegant London Road can only be imagined; the whole development was a planning and visual disaster.

The multifarious problems of the Eagle Centre provoked its owners to undertake a facelift in the late 1980s, which was a minor improvement. The city council, in 1989–91, bit the bullet and entirely rebuilt its own portion, rebuilding the entrance onto East Street as a giant glass portico with escalators giving access to street level. All the hexagonal stalls were ripped out and replaced by rows of rectangular ones around a piazza, making shopping among them the pleasure it should have been all along. At the same time the bus station bridge was removed.

Yet this only seemed to ameliorate the problems of the Eagle Centre slightly. A vast and incomparably hideous brick multi-storey car park was built adjacent on Cockpit Hill and opened early in the new millennium. Not only was its massive bulk a real problem visually for an historic city to integrate, but the design was abysmal and its concept the more so, for it was placed on the inside of an extraordinarily busy traffic island, which made access and egress, especially on Saturdays, sales periods and Derby County home match days, virtually impossible. On the first weekend it was open it took some motorists over three hours to get out of it.

The Gordian Knot was cut by Australian firm

Modern national chain department store: Marks & Spencer, St Peter's Street, of 1936–37, designed by Robert Lutyans (1901–1972) son of the celebrated Sir Edwin. It is due to close in 2007. (M. Craven)

Westfield Shoppingtowns from 1999. They proposed replacing both Eagle and Main Centres with a new up-to-date and well worked out shopping complex, built to much higher overall standards. They subsequently acquired the two areas and began work in earnest in 2004, and by 2007 the southern part was nearing completion. The whole is due to be finished in 2008.

While Westfield's replacement will without doubt be extremely beneficial, it will exacerbate the problem of the retail flight from the old city core. Indeed, Westfield have announced that they have persuaded both Marks & Spencer and Debenhams to move, thus leaving empty three really quite large stores in Corn Market, St Peter's Street and Victoria Street and in the medium term at risk. As the Victoria Street Debenhams Store – which started off in 1962 as Ranby's – is an excellent building for its time and the purpose-built M & S in St Peter's Street is a restrained exercise in *Art-Deco* by Robert Lutyens, the town can ill afford to lose them.

THE DERBY PROMENADE

In 1989 the council unveiled a plan to pedestrianise the entire city centre from the cathedral to The Spot, where they devised a pseudo-*Bauhaus* style clock centerpiece where once Queen Victoria had stood – called by most Derbeians the 'gun-emplacement' – and intended to reflect the *Moderne* of Sir Frederick Bennett's curving façade of what had originally been Southern's on the inside of The Spot curve.

This was called 'The Derby Promenade' and opened by council leader Nick Brown in 1991. Despite the initial resistance of the retailers, it has worked quite well, although it was quite unnecessarily reordered in the

Pegler's 'Ram' statue of 1994, in East Street, photographed in 1995. (M. Craven)

The wrought steel 'Venetian portal' at the end of Corn Market, one of the more successful embellishments of the Derby Promenade, inexplicably removed in 2004 as part of 'Connecting Derby'. (M. Craven)

Centrepiece of the Derby Promenade is the so-called water feature designed by Walter Pye, to which few Derby people seem to have come to appreciate. For well-dressing purposes, it counts as a well, and is duly dressed and blessed by the cathedral each spring. Photographed on 27 November 1995. (M. Craven)

Corn Market sector in 2000 to include illuminated glass bricks bearing school children's designs and the removal of one of the three pieces of public art included in the Promenade, a large mild steel triple arch, consciously set near the arched gateway that adjoined the original County Gaol stood at this point up to 1755.

The other two creations are a vast millstone grit seated ram in East Street by Michael Pegler (1994), looking rather as if it had been carved from Lurpak rather than local stone, and a granite pillar topped by what looks like a wrecked helicopter in Iron Gate. This is to honour Derby's internationally renowned artist Joseph Wright by the site of his family home; the top is supposed to resemble an Orrery. The impetus for the latter was the museum's leading role in an international exhibition to honour Wright at the Tate Gallery, followed by periods in New York and at the Louvre, in 1990, which was a great success

An attempt, urged by the antiquities department of the museum as part of the Promenade, to honour John Whitehurst FRS in his bicentennial year (1988) misfired completely, resulting in a large bronze roundel being set in the pavement outside the house next door to Whitehurst's old home and looking for all the world like the lid of a London coal chute. Subsequent attempts have been made to get it re-sited, especially as the Derby Civic Society managed to get the house outside which the plaque should have gone added to the statutory list in 2004.

Art apart, the Promenade can be criticised for rather overdoing the faux-cobblestones and for being littered with a superfluity of luridly-coloured, French-made street furniture. Yet, as it turned out, the Derby Promenade did not materially affect – as had been feared – the trade of those honest-to-God retail outlets still surviving at this northerly end of the city.

THE PROBLEMS OF CONSERVATION

At the same time as the Eagle Centre, other schemes began. One, already reviewed, was to replace the old Assembly Rooms, in which context it is worthy of note that, in the end, the old façade, designed by Washington Shirley, 5th Earl Ferrers, and built by Joseph Pickford in 1763, was not included as originally proposed in the design of the new building, the idea being flatly rejected by the architect, Sir Hugh Casson, never one to allow anything of real merit to sully his creations. It was eventually consigned to the Crich Tramway Museum, where it stands as a piece of heritage window dressing; an object for architectural students to measure and little else.

Another scheme was to erect a vast amount of office space on Friar Gate, utilising what was left of the Friary garden. In 1967 this stunning Georgian Street had been declared Derby's first conservation area. Yet, as with that declared at the Midland Station in 1982, the integrity of the area so designated was soon compromised by inappropriate modern development. Friar Gate thus suffered two losses: the demolition of R.E. Ryley's monumental (but unlisted) Royal School for the Deaf of 1892–94, followed by the loss of five listed buildings either side of the Friary in 1971–73, including the 1696 Unitarian Chapel, one of the most important buildings of its kind in the Midlands, plus H.I. Stevens's chunky Neo-Greek Derby Savings Bank, later the TSB.

The Deaf School was replaced by banal flats, Friar Gate Court, and the rest made way for a series of four vast brick and concrete blocks called Heritage Gate, four-storey pastiche Georgian towards the road, but more uncompromising behind, facing Stafford Street and Friary

Derby Civic Society successfully persuaded the Borough Council to close Sadler Gate to all traffic after a decade of campaigning from 1962. This view looking towards the Old Bell Hotel on 8 September 1960 demonstrates why! (Derby Evening Telegraph)

Street which took a decade to let, due to economic downturns and lack of IT ducting.

In 1983 the then Secretary of State for the Environment, Lord Jenkin, said:

'We neglect at our peril...the disorientation which huge and abrupt changes in the environment in which people live can be extremely disruptive, not just to patterns of living and working but to the whole way in which people live and the view they have of themselves. The destruction of whole communities by well-meant but, in the end, disastrous comprehensive redevelopment has been widely chronicled and has now become part of the accepted wisdom. Continuity and familiarity are hugely important elements in life. The "Brave New World" may look very exciting on paper, but is often bitterly resented by those intended to benefit.'

This passage unfortunately sums up the entire problem in Derby since World War Two.

FUNDAMENTAL CHANGES

In 1938 Derby's industrial base was founded on a very few staple industries: railway engineering, motor-car and aero-engine manufacture, narrow tapes and artificial silk making. These, with the associated and component industries, mainly foundries, electrical and mechanical engineering, accounted for the employment of 48 percent of the registered workforce. Post-war, most notably between 1951 and 1961, Derby's growth rate was above the national average. Due to prosperity in these staple industries this situation began to seem to many like the natural order of things and likely to go on for the foreseeable future. Local unemployment averaged below 1 percent for each year from 1946 to 1952, with but two exceptions, in February 1947, when it rose to 5.5 percent due to the fuel crisis and from April 1952, when it rose to 13.3 percent due to a recession in the textile industry.

The sense of false security thus engendered meant that when the colder economic winds started to blow by the early 1970s Derby had not diversified its industrial structure as had Nottingham and had been much slower to build up service industries. Yet, even the perusal of a simple account of the city like this highlights the fact that no industry can go on forever unchanged. National circumstances, foreign competition, altering requirements of large-scale end users, the exhaustion of resources and many other factors cause decline in

industry. Yet, in a country like the United Kingdom, newer industries are invariably developing in response to changing needs. We have seen how framework knitting declined in the face of mechanisation and a decline in the industry generally; how the lead industry declined in the earlier part of the present century as new materials replaced what is in fact a highly toxic metal; how the fulling, combing and weaving of wool declined in the face of continental competition, and the similar decline of the silk industry. Thus, with the contraction of the railway industry, an unpalatable reality for decades (kept at bay by government subsidies), changes in household heating methods which killed the demand for stoves and grates, and other shifts in patterns, a whole sector of Derby's industrial base shrank quite rapidly.

The real impact of this was emphasised by the sudden collapse of Rolls-Royce in 1971. Thousands of people were pitched out of work from a firm which almost everyone believed would go on forever and in which they had assumed that their working futures lay. It was all horrifyingly traumatic. Nevertheless, both central and local government helped with redeployment programmes and many of the individual victims of the collapse were found alternative employment. One phenomenon noticed at the Bishop Lonsdale College, which had built a whole new campus at Mickleover in 1964, was the numbers of middle management people from Rolls-Royce who came along to be retrained as teachers. Within a decade at least one had made it to a headship!

Rolls-Royce was reconstituted in public ownership on slimmer lines as Rolls-Royce (1971) Limited. The RB-211 and the American airliner for which it was linked, the Lockheed Tri-Star, went on to great success and the former is still being successfully developed and sold round the world. More success has followed since, the workforce has built up again (although there have been further periods when minor recessions and the inroads of manufacturing technology have caused additional slimming-down of operations) and in the mid-1980s the firm was successfully re-floated as a public limited company and subsequently brought to full flower under the enlightened chairmanship of Sir Ralph Robbins.

The biggest shrinkage in jobs has been in the sphere of locomotive and rolling stock construction. Even under the nationalised phase from 1948 to 1996 the loco works in the UK were shrinking fast; domestic rail requirements had diminished and changed, and few works were geared to compete in overseas markets. British Rail Engineering Ltd was sold into private hands in 1994 to ABB Transportation and the research laboratories were divided among several enterprises, some extremely successful and innovative. A year after

Duckworth Square was Derby's second 'shopping centre' after the dire Main Centre, and was, if anything, even more oppressive and uninviting – certainly not worth losing the Becket Well and 1910 Black Prince cinema for. After almost a decade of dereliction, it was demolished in 2005, although no plans have been approved for a replacement at the time of writing. Photograph of February 1987. (*Derby Evening Telegraph*)

privatisation ABB employed 3,733 workers, a drop from 6,586 of 43 percent. That year, too, the order book fell empty and the future of the industry in Derby appeared to hang in the balance. This led to a further sale and further workforce-paring under the new owners, Adtranz, by which time the old rambling extent of the former LMS and Midland works had shrunk to one site off Litchurch Lane. New orders were won and things began to look up but, like the fortunes of the football club, the expectations of the industry in Derby fluctuated regularly. In 2001 Adtranz was sold to the Canadian firm Bombardier, for some reason pronounced 'bombardeeyay' in the French manner rather than the more correct British usage of the army; this could perhaps be due to the French-Canadian influence of the company's home base. They obtained a very impressive order for 700 electrostar trains in 2002 worth £856,000,000 but the company were facing another vacuum after the completion of this order in 2004. Eventually they were successful in winning further orders.

Likewise, Courtauld's at Spondon, formerly British Celanese, has suffered fluctuating fortunes, but again, has diversified and recovered, now being called Accordis.

Lesser textile firms have not been so lucky; some, like James Smith, the uniform manufacturers, set up by a jobbing tailor of Bridge Gate by an order for uniforms from the North Midland Railway in 1840, have closed. Often these closures have been in the wake of takeovers by other outside firms, who have subsequently 'rationalised' their manufacturing base. Derby's loss has frequently (as at Ley's foundry) been some other town's gain, just as Lambeth lost George Fletcher to Derby in 1863 when he wanted to expand his sugar-refining equipment manufacturing and as Manchester lost Rolls-Royce in 1907. In terms of textiles, however, many mills which have closed have reopened under the aegis of small, family-based Asian-owned firms and with the incentive of such a cellular organisation have flourished well.

The most far reaching changes have been in the upsurge in service industries, industries tied to the Information Technology revolution and financial services, too. Just as computer-generated Lara Croft was evolved in Derby in 1996 (and revived in 2006) and went on to conquer the hearts and minds of computer gamers, so plastic card banker Egg has come to Derby and brought employment opportunities.

273

AEA Building, Pride Park, by far the best building there, completed in 2002. (M. Craven)

PRIDE PARK

Egg set up its headquarters on Pride Park, a district of Derby that was previously a highly polluted industrial wasteland divided between Etches' Park gasworks and the Midland Railway's works. The 180-acre site was designated for economic renewal under the Major government's 'City Challenge' scheme, wherein public money would be released through a development company to make inner city land available for re-use and to involve the private sector for any subsequent development. Under this scheme Pride Park was launched in October 1992 and the first five years were spent detoxifying the area and resealing it against leaks of harmful material. The company set up to do the work for five years was Derby PRIDE Ltd, chaired by Sir Nigel Rudd.

The City Challenge area actually included much of Litchurch and New Normanton along with parts of Osmaston initially, and much government money was invested in improving these inner city suburbs and a great deal was done in urban renewal and economic development.

Derby simultaneously bid for a 'cutting edge science experience' and as a site for the government's millennium extravaganza. Amazingly, the city reached the final three in the race for the Dome but failed to get far on the science park idea. And at that time, it looked very much as if the Pride Park area would become a white elephant as well, as only the university showed any interest and even they, overstretched by building student residences, toying with Allestree Hall and Buxton's Devonshire Hospital, dropped out.

Furthermore, the site contained a group of important historic buildings: Britain's oldest – not just oldest surviving – railway locomotive round house, built by Francis Thompson for the North Midland Railway in 1839, a building that set the pattern of loco depots until the end of main line steam in 1968. Adjoining were the Midland Counties Railway carriage repair shed and locomotive depot, both of similar date and by William Parsons of Leicester. All had been derelict since BREL had walked away from them in the 1980s and, indeed, appeared to be due for demolition until top-level persuasion got them re-graded II*.

The problem from then on was end-use. The best scheme was a collaboration between the Derbyshire Historic Buildings Trust and popular music mogul Pete Waterman – head of an historic railway leasing firm, keen to migrate to Derby – to redevelop the site for active railway use, but wrecked mainly by the then still nationalised railway undertaking's mulish obstructionism in refusing a physical rail link to the site. There followed a decade of wrangling until September 2006 when Derby College obtained long-sought funding to restore the complex.

But this is to anticipate. After three years, there seemed to be no takers for Pride Park, despite the provision of roads with three points of access: from the A52 from Nottingham near another new retail centre built on the former MR sidings at Chaddesden and called the Wyvern Centre, from Station Approach and via Wilmorton. The Station Approach road crossed the main line via a flyover of horrendously inappropriate design by the then highways authority, the county council, bearing in mind that it cut across the end of the city's Railway Conservation Area, about 50 yards from the 1842 Brunswick Inn, a serious blemish on one of the gateways into the city.

The deadlock was broken by Lionel Pickering's brave decision in 1995 to move the football club there. From that point, the pump was primed, and although the government funding stopped in 1997, the area gradually took off, all the roads being completed in 2005 the same year that the last plot was sold, which is likely to become the UK Rail Centre.

THE NEW DERBEIANS

The availability of Asian businessmen to revitalize the textile industry has only been possible because of immigration from the Indian sub-continent, mainly during the 1950s and 1960s. The choice of Derby for these peoples, consisting of various sub-groups, was precisely because the principal industries were so stable in that period and employment prospects so good.

Another major influx came from the Caribbean Islands, and these two groups – occasionally mutually antagonistic regrettably – form the largest immigrant groups of non-European origin. Nevertheless, there were numerous other groups who were pleased to be able to settle in Derby in the immediate post-war period mainly as refugees from Communism and for precisely the same reasons. Of these, most were exiles from the aftermath of World War Two: people from all three Baltic states, especially Latvia; from the Ukraine, from Poland and from Serbia (then Yugoslavia). Nearer home, the Irish community, elements of which lived cheek-by-jowl with the young Thomas Mozley in the Wardwick in the 1820s, was swelled considerably since World War Two and the Scots element in Derby, tracing its residence in the town from at least the time of Boswell's kinsman, Dr Butter, was vastly boosted with the relocation of people from north of the border to help out at Rolls-Royce during the same conflict.

Since then a sizeable group of Vietnamese refugees have come into the town, there having been a reception centre for them set up by the county council at Breadsall in the late 1970s. Of all the groups, these were making the most profound cultural change and brought least with them, yet a decade after the arrival of the bulk of them, the majority have adapted well, and although many, having learnt English and 'converted' to English life, have gone elsewhere to seek their fortunes, others have settled successfully in Derby, adding to the increasing richness and diversity of life of the town.

Subsequently, Derby has seen the Blair government allocating large numbers of economic migrants and some illegal immigrants from troubled parts of the world: Albania, the former Yugoslavia, Kurds from Iraq, Somalis and so on. By and large, despite recent misgivings arising from terrorist attacks worldwide, and about the advisability of 'multi-culturalism' as against integration, Derby seems to be a tolerant sort of place to live. Indeed, the nearest analogy to present circumstances in the history of the city must be the mixture of formerly antagonistic strains dwelling together in the last years of the 11th century: Saxon, Danish and Norman, with – who knows? – the odd family of avowedly Celtic descent, too. We do not know what tribulations these early citizens of Derby underwent in a far less tolerant age, 'ethnic cleansing' and discrimination there must have been a-plenty at first, but the mixture ultimately produced a community united by a common ancestry and a fierce pride in their borough and the privileges they had acquired for it.

One cannot help but feel that the same strong admixture, similarly united by common descent, will ultimately take pride in the city in which chance landed them, as in the middle ages. Yet if this analogy has a flaw, it must be that with ever-increasing social mobility, few families, forged from such disparate elements, will remain sufficiently long within the boundaries of the local polity. It will be necessary to wait and see what happens.

The testing time for the labour force in Derby, still coming to terms with a social structure in flux, was the first half of the 1980s. Unemployment rose from 2.5 percent in 1979 to 10.6 percent in August 1982 and got even higher before beginning to fall again at the end of 1985, a trend which continued with 8.5 percent in August 1988 and lower still by 2006, albeit somewhat up from the 2000 figure, this in spite of the workforce being swelled by the addition of almost 50 percent of married women by 1979. Derby's industrial diversification, including the importation of long-overdue service and technologically sophisticated industries, is well established, and optimism seems justifiable.

THE DIOCESE OF DERBY AND ITS CATHEDRAL

Modern Derby may have lost the county borough status which it acquired in 1888, but purely in terms of status it received two great morale-boosters in the 20th century. The first was the creation of the Diocese of Derby, carved out of that of Southwell, itself a creation of 1883, prior to which date the whole of Derbyshire had been part of the Diocese of Lichfield. This came about on 7 July 1927 and added immensely to the prestige of the borough.

Derby Cathedral, as seen from Irongate, in 1993. (M. Craven)

At first, it was thought that the church authorities would select St Werburgh's as the new cathedral, and other places in Derbyshire were also canvassed. Eventually, Gibbs's All Saints' Church in Derby was selected, although at that time it was wanting as a cathedral in many respects. Nevertheless, it had triumphantly survived as one of England's finest Baroque parish churches with its 178ft late perpendicular tower, the highest in England after Boston Stump, despite a proposal to rebuild it in Gothic style by local architect John Wilkinson in October 1820.

The first Bishop was Dr Edmund Courtenay Pearce DD. To date the only armigerous holder of the office, his arms could, until its demolition in 1968, be seen impaled with those of the new diocese: *purpure a cross potent quadrate argent in chief three fountains*, over the entrance of the first Bishop's Palace, Breadsall Mount, a dignified Tudorbethan house on the ridge between Breadsall and Chaddesden and built in 1863 by H.I. Stevens. He had been preceded by two Bishops of Derby – Rt. Revd E.A. Were (in reality a suffregan in the Diocese of Southwell), whose 'palace', was really St Werburgh's vicarage, was also designed by Stevens, but was regrettably due to be completely dismantled for a housing development in 2006, despite being in a conservation area, and Bishop Abraham, who lived outside Derby.

Plans were drawn up by the first Provost of the new diocese's new cathedral, Herbert Ham, to extend the church, to designs by Sir Ninian Comper, to include a fine domed crossing. But little was done and any progress that was made was held up by the war and the want of a younger, more energetic provost. The changes came in the time of the fourth provost, Ronald Beddoes (1912–2000). By 1972 this energetic and far sighted man had tactfully extended Gibbs's edifice to Comper's design, as modified and scaled-down by his son Sebastian; had refurbished and added to Bakewell's profuse and filigree ironwork; supplemented the pioneering Hammond organ with a choir organ of traditional design; cleaned the grimy exterior of the building and installed new, startlingly contemporary stained glass in the old east end windows by the late Ceri Richards. All this was a colossal achievement for Beddoes and his able and quietly charismatic colleague throughout most of the period, Canon Paul Miller (1918–2000).

By the 1970s, too, the newly-cleaned and floodlit exterior housed a true cathedral, with a countywide role and a harmonious atmosphere. The sixth provost, Michael Perham, appointed in 1995 and since 2004 Bishop of Gloucester, had his title altered by decree of the General Synod to dean. He was the driving force behind the purchase of the former Clulow's bookshop – Derby's long-established specialist bookseller, put out of

business by the coming of Waterstones – and its conversion into cathedral offices, a restaurant, and cathedral treasury, all opened by HM the Queen on 14 November 2003.

City Status

For many years, and especially since World War Two, the council had been striving to gain the status of a city for Derby. The prerogative of the Crown, this is granted only sparingly but according to no specific criteria. As far back as 1927–28, Alderman Sturgess had visited the Home Secretary in an attempt to convince him to authorise such a move. Another attempt was made in 1935 to mark the centenary of the Municipal Corporations Act and again in 1954 to mark the eighth centenary of the granting of the borough's first charter.

It was widely believed, and in the light of these failures, that with the loss of county borough status in 1974 (yet another attempt to be granted city status having failed in 1968 when the boundary extensions were made) any further attempt was doomed to failure. One man refused to accept this: councillor G.T. Andrews, who strove remorselessly to keep the idea alive. When the form of the 1972 Act revealed that the future Derby District Council would have to apply to the government even to continue its 337-year-old mayoralty, he suggested that another application should be made, but the matter was turned down at local level. He then prepared his own submission, accompanied by a large petition, receiving the advice from the Home Office that, without the backing of the council, this would be unlikely to gain serious consideration. Andrews's aim was to argue for the application to be granted to coincide with the Queen's Silver Jubilee. However, the then Labour council, with the traumas of reorganisation still rocking them, turned him down flat. Notwithstanding, in May 1976 the council unexpectedly changed political complexion and the new leader, Ron Longdon, eagerly embraced Andrews's suggestion, and by virtue of council minute 1976/170 it was agreed on 9 June 1976 that an application should go ahead. Thus it was that on the day of the Silver Jubilee, 7 June 1977, the town was proclaimed a city under Royal Sign Manual, formally delivered by Her Majesty to Mayor Tillett on her visit to the new city on 28 July. This one act more than compensated for the blow sustained in the loss of powers to the county council in 1974, and has in many ways contributed to the optimism with which the city has progressed since. It is a great tribute to those who had the vision to persist with the concept when the cause seemed lost.

Following this triumph, the new city of Derby still

harboured two continuing aspirations: to regain its unitary, or independent status and to accord the mayor the prefix 'Lord', something the neighbouring city of Nottingham had fortuitously acquired when Edward VII mistakenly addressed the mayor there in a speech as 'My Lord Mayor' – setting a precedent which could not be overturned.

From 1988 both city and national governments were, unusually, Conservative and a concerted effort was made through the local MPs – including Greg Knight (Derby North), Philip Oppenheim (Amber Valley), Peter Rost (Erewash) and Edwina Currie (South Derbyshire) – to pressure the government into making further reforms that would reverse the more absurd results of those of 1974 and to ensure that Derby was given independence from the county council which had been stridently inimical to the government of the day since 1981. Ironically, by the time the concession had been secured, in 1996, the political complexion of the city had changed again. Nevertheless from April 1997, it was again an independent unitary authority.

A submission for a Lord Mayor was turned down in 2000.

ST HELEN'S HOUSE

The county council's legacy to the city in 1997 included a good deal of real estate, almost all including buildings with serious problems. One was Pickford's *chef d'oeuvre*, St Helen's House, built for John Gisborne in 1766–67 and later extended by William Strutt.

In 1974 the whole complex, in use as a WEA and teacher's centre, became the property of the county council, which neglected it. Once back in the ambit of the city, 23 years later, these problems had to wait their turn in a queue of leaking and inadequate school buildings. A new council grasped the nettle in panic in

St Helen's House, 'the finest Palladian town house outside London,' much abused but subject to bids to restore it in 2006. (M. Craven)

2003, closed the building in June 2004 on safety grounds and put it up for sale. After much huffing and puffing and unrealistic expectations that it had a viable future as an educational facility, it was finally sold to a restoring developer at the end of 2006, although its setting was about to be irrevocably compromised by the resumption of work on the Inner Ring Road.

'CONNECTING DERBY'

Quite the most problematical legacy left to the city by the county council in 1997 was the problem of the ring road. Against all the odds, this project was still in favour, despite numerous moves away from the rather dated concept. It almost seemed as if there was a potential loss of face involved in not completing it.

A revised scheme was drawn up forthwith and presented to the public through advertising for comment, although comment seemed superfluous. Whereas the county scheme envisaged running the unbuilt section west of Ford Street over the sensitive Friar Gate conservation area via the former GNR bridge made by Handyside's and sold to Derby Council by British Rail for £1 in 1989, the city, lacking adequate investment from the ODPM and various newly-hatched regional quangos, was forced to go for the cheaper option of crossing Friar Gate on the flat and beyond it, reducing the road to one carriageway in each direction.

This was dubbed 'Connecting Derby' and, being in parts exceedingly inimical to the city's heritage, was bitterly contested by conservation groups, albeit, in the end, to no avail. Vested interests proved too strong. Even an emphatic condemnation from English Heritage on its effect on the setting of St Helen's House was later watered down.

LOCAL GOVERNMENT IN THE 21ST CENTURY

In 1997 national government changed complexion and this was followed by two far-reaching changes, both emanating from the ODPM. The first was to fundamentally alter the way in which local government is run. Instead of a committee structure, with full participation from any councillor who might choose to make an intervention, led by more experienced members acting as chairmen, a 'cabinet structure' was adopted, more dependent on Whitehall and much less directly accountable. There are now a number of areas of responsibility, approximately reflecting those of the old

Thirty years before the Inner Ring Road was begun, plans were implemented to widen Ford Street, later an integral part of both the Inner Ring Road and 'Connecting Derby', to which end this magnificent William and Mary House in Friar Gate was demolished in March 1938 (the date of the photograph), the fabric having been allegedly sent to Williamsburg, Virginia, for re-erection. (*Derby Evening Telegraph*)

committees, each run by a 'cabinet member' but only accountable to the 'cabinet', occasional meetings of full council and a scrutiny committee of dubious partiality. Whether this has really 'streamlined' local government is arguable, and the public perception of it is to foster a sense of fatalism when it comes to trying to challenge decisions taken at cabinet level. Now, only the yearly elections of a third of the council affords any opportunity for effecting change. One suspects that it helps the officers of the council, and in this sense it probably has streamlined local government.

On top of this, there has been put in place a grant-giving quango called the East Midlands Development Association (EMDA), based in Nottingham, which funds all sorts of unexpected initiatives. Furthermore, 15 Urban Regeneration Corporations (URCs) have been set up nationwide, mostly with 'user friendly' names; Derby's is called Derby Cityscape and was launched in July 2003. URCs are set up to, '...address significant latent development opportunities by developing and managing implementation of a plan, agreed by the key stakeholders, following public consultation, to build business confidence and realise a collective vision for the future of the area.'

URCs have compulsory purchase powers, but no rate-raising ones, rendering them unaccountable. Derby Cityscape is underwritten by EMDA and by another Quango with powers to acquire and intervene nationally in the territory of divers local authorities (and with an especial remit concerning housing) called English Partnerships (EP) and both are represented on the Cityscape board along with the council, developers, and a handful of others designed to keep the lid on any friction. Most of the grandiose plans produced by Derby Cityscape are, by the admission of their officers, 'aspirational', the idea being to produce a blueprint that will attract major investment over a number of years to 'modernise' the city. Policy differences with the council have already occurred, notably in the Railway conservation area.

A particular problem is a long-standing project to build Riverlights, a retail and residential complex on the site of the River Gardens and bus station, lynch pins of the pre-war Central Improvement Plan, but frequent changes in basic specification suggested to many independent observers that it was basically flawed. The central problem seemed to be that the intervention of Westfield Shoppingtowns in revitalising the Eagle Centre has meant that most of the 'big name' retailers were whisked away. With other difficulties threatening, the developer duly folded at the end of 2005, having been allowed against ferocious but fruitless opposition to remove the bus station, forcing passengers to locate unsheltered new stops scattered across several streets.

Early in 2006 a new developer bought the entire site from the receiver and proposed to go ahead immediately with Riverlights. With the Eagle Centre nearing completion, it is difficult to see how Riverlights can hope to be any more viable than it was before.

Yet the concept of the URC is very close to that of the Improvement Commissions of 1768–1835, in that both acquired functions which normally lay with the Corporation and could think expansively. The difference was that the Improvement Commissions had rate-raising powers, although neither could be considered truly accountable. To complicate matters further for the hapless Derby citizen not in the know is the creation in the 1990s of the Derby City Partnership, operating under the byeline 'Derbyes!' claiming to be '…a Local Strategic Partnership delivering the National Strategy for Neighbourhood Renewal in Derby', also to deliver Derby's '2020 Vision' aimed at elevating Derby to the top 10 British cities by 2020. Additionally, yet another group, Derby City Growth, a self-funded private enterprise version, was set up, perhaps with a better chance of achieving something, united by self interest based on the common denominator of successful enterprise, which the organisation sees as likely to translate into an advance towards their goal of a 'new approach to economic development in the city'.

None of these, however, pay more than lip-service to the cultural development, history or heritage of the city, yet local quality of life and the vibrancy of tourism actually depend very heavily on them. It is hardly worth destroying great chunks of the historic city on the grounds of 'regeneration' and then wondering why tourists cold shoulder the result, as one or two other English cities have indeed discovered.

Cultural changes

The city council, belatedly acting upon a £10,000 legacy of 1945 from Alfred E. Goodey (who had previously left a collection of some 500 pictures of Derby views to the museum) built a modernist extension of Derby Museum in 1964, a decade prior to the creation of an industrial museum in the Silk Mill and the opening of a very stylish museum in Joseph Pickford's own house in Friar Gate in 1988. This represents a laudable expression of civic pride in the museums which can be laid at the feet of Labour leader of the council the late John Dilks, who was

the last prominent local politician to have a real feel for the importance of museums – the provision of which was never a statutory requirement of councils. Changes of funding of local authorities, the draining away of powers to allocate them as local politicians might wish and the increasing demands of Whitehall setting the agenda for local spending, have subsequently militated against expenditure on the museum subsequent to 1988, despite the welcome aid of Lottery funding.

Given the constraints upon local government, the only way forward has to be that adopted elsewhere in the UK – mainly with signal success – in setting up an independent trust to run and develop Derby's museums to the sort of standards expected in today's Europe. This would allow Joseph Wright to take his rightful place and enable such a trust to seek out ways of displaying Derby's other great asset properly – ceramics. There are presently two collections, that in Derby Museum and that owned and displayed by Royal Crown Derby. It defies logic, both culturally and economically, that these two should be kept apart; their unification is essential for Derby's cultural future.

A trust was indeed formed, but to promote exhibitions, take over the Metro cinema and promote some performing arts, mainly dance. From a temporary home in the Queen Street Baths complex, a purpose-built centre was thought appropriate, bringing all these elements together, pooling the eligible grant aid and reinvigorating the cultural life of the city along much more elite grounds than hitherto. Here, the coming of the university has been a significant factor, for among its student body there is the hard core of people most likely to foster patronage of what this body, Q-Arts, is seeking to bring about.

Q-Arts is at the time of writing starting work on the building to house its activities, called the Quad and to be sited in the south-east corner of the Market Place. The building, disliked by all but its sponsors, seems inappropriate for an historic Market Place, no attempt by its architects having been made to respect the grain of the historic square. Once built, it must be hoped that the Quad succeeds and that its two class-A exhibition galleries do not compete destructively with the three at the museum. A reservation is that the Quad appears to leave out in the cold the various very active local theatre and opera groups, long bereft of any permanent venue, which seems unfortunate, especially as they involve many ordinary people not otherwise involved in the increasingly elite-dominated 'arts'.

Finally, in 2003 the Derwent Valley from Cromford to Derby's Old Silk Mill was recognised – after a long and successful campaign, led by the Arkwright Society and backed by the county council in tandem with the other affected local authorities – as a World Heritage Site

(WHS). In Derby, however, opportunities have been lost and problem buildings within it, like Haslam's Union Foundry or Bath Street Mill, or in its buffer zone, notably St Helen's House and Brown's marble works, have not benefitted from the new perspectives.

In *Coriolanus* Sicinus asks 'What is a city, but people?' to which a chorus of citizens reply: 'True, the people are the city'. Yet mature Derby, with two millennia under its belt, is not youthful Rome, still sloughing off the crushing shadow of tyranny. The city of Derby is indeed its people through the ages and their remarkable achievements, which places those who live and work in the city today firmly in their tradition and with a responsibility to respond to the achievements of those who have gone before them, sung and unsung.

As yet, one cannot come to Derby and appreciate the almost global significance of the movements started by Whitehurst, Darwin and their friends. Furthermore, one sees little, apart from the splendour of the cathedral interior, largely uninterrupted, which represents in a tangible way the achievements of Bakewell, Lord Ferrers, Darwin, Whitehurst and Pickford, nor without aid appreciate the very positive links of these men and their tradition with Wright and their patrons among the intellectuals and the gentry of the region. Intellectual history is always the most problematic aspect of heritage to put across but, unless resources are put into making the effort, the contribution of these Derby men of national and indeed international renown will continue to languish. For this is the crux of Derby's problem: the continuing links with this movement, as represented by Kirk Boott, William Strutt, Richard Keene, Herbert Spencer and others who carried it into the 19th century and beyond, have been lost, obfuscated or severed in the inevitable changes in industrial patterns, through the lowbrow

corporatism of the 20th century and the consequent loss of inspiration and direction.

The one certain way to educate the elite, as well as the enthusiasts, is to attract visitors to the city from all over the world who themselves wish to steep their fingers in this rich tradition. John Whitehurst, for instance, was prominently celebrated in 2005 at an exhibition in The Hague celebrating Europe's contribution to Third World problems as the inventor of the hydraulic ram, now ubiquitous in irrigation schemes. Thus, as Derby gets deservedly known in an ever wider context, so the pride and self-confidence of local people in their city will soar. Likewise, in 2007, Derby ought to be at the centre of any event marking the bicentenary abolition of the Slave Trade with William Wilberforce's collaborator Thomas Gisborne being the owner of St Helen's House.

Both the promotion of visitors and the expansion of industry are absolutely vital, but with clear thinking and cool-headedness on the part of elected representatives, those who advise them, and the multiplicity of agencies that support them, the one must never be at the expense of the other.

The *genius loci* can have a civilising effect upon those who dwell in a place, and those who dwell in Derby are as fortunate as any in the United Kingdom. Among them flow strands of tradition as powerful as in any, whether it be the blood of the Allestreys, the traditions of the West End, the acquisition of a Whitehurst clock or a third or fourth generation employment at Royce's. For those who have come to the city more recently, from however far away, they will to an increasing extent – by common enjoyment of the environment, by marriage-ties made and to be made and by their own personal endeavour – come to be a part of that tradition too.

Derby in the 21st century has less to do with nostalgia, but everything to do with quality of life.

BIBLIOGRAPHY

Algar, R.A.M. *History of Derby and Derbyshire Affiliated Free Churches* London, 1901.

Allen, D.F. *Coins of the Coritani* in *Sylloge of Coins of the British Isles* London, 1963.

Allen, J.W. *Bygone Derby, Vol I Coaching Days* Derby, n.d. (*c.*1968).

Anderson, J. *William Duesbury, Father and Son: Men of Industry* Derby, 1987.

Andrews, G.T. *A Quest for Derby City Status* MS Derby, 1978.

Anon. *Letters from a Gentleman of London* Newcastle-upon-Tyne, 1757.

Anglo-Saxon Chronicle *The Anglo-Saxon Chronicle* ed. D. Whitelock, D.C. Douglas and S.I. Tucker, London, 1961.

Bagshaw, S. *A Directory of Derbyshire* London, 1846.

Barron, W. & Son *Catalogue* Derby, 1930.

Beauchamp, C.R. *Transportation and Chains* Smithfield, New South Wales, 1985.

Beaumont, R. *The Railway King* London, 2002.

Beckett, J.V. *The East Midlands from AD 1000* London, 1988.

Bede *Ecclesiastical History of the English People* ed. B. Colgrave and R.A.B. Maynors, Oxford, 1969.

Bell, C.S. *The First Hundred Years* Derby, 1979.

Bemrose, W. *Joseph Wright of Derby* Derby 1885.

Biddle, M. & B. Kjolbye-Biddle *Repton and the 'Great Heathen Army' 873–874* in J. Graham-Campbell, et al, *Vikings and the Danelaw* Oxford, 2001.

Biddle, M. & B. Kjolbye-Biddle *Repton 1986 An Interim Report* Oxford, 1987.

Billson, P. *Derby & the Midland Railway* Derby, 1996.

Birks, F.E. *History of the Derby Photographic Society 1884–1934* Derby, 1934.

Birley, A. *The People of Roman Britain* London, 1979.

Blaikie, W.B. *The Origins of the 'Forty-Five* London, 1916.

Blome, J. *Britannia* London, 1673.

Blunt, A.W.F. *The See of Derby* Derby, 1927.

Boswell, J. *The Life of Samuel Johnson* 2 vols., London, 1906.

Boydell, D. *Centenary Story* Manchester, 1950.

Boyes, M. *Allestree Hall* Derby, 1985.

Boyse, S. *An Impartial History of the Late Rebellion in 1745* London, 1747.

Bradbury, E. & R. Keene *All About Derby* 2nd Edn., Derby, 1884.

Bray, William *Sketch of a Tour into Derbyshire and Yorkshire* 2nd Rev. Edn, London, 1783.

Brighton, J.T. *Derby and the Civil War* Derby, 1971.

Brighton, J.T. *Royalists and Roundheads in Derbyshire* Bakewell, 1981.

Briscoe *Nottinghamshire and Derbyshire* London, n.d. (*c.*1908).

Bulmer's Directory of Derbyshire London, 1895.

Burke, Sir J.B. *Distinguished Families of the USA* London, 1937.

Burke, Sir J.B. *Landed Gentry* 2 Vols., London, 1898.

Burke, Sir J.B. *Landed Gentry* London, 1937.

Burke, Sir J.B. *Peerage and Baronetage* 1931, 1956, 1970.

Byng, Hon. J. *The Torrington Diaries* Ed., C. Andrews, London, 1935.

Calladine, M. *Lombe's Mill, an Exercise in Reconstruction* in *Industrial Archaeology Review* XVI No.1 (Autumn 1993), 87–99.

Calow, Marjorie *Homelands Remembered* Derby, 2002.

Camden, W. *Britannia* 6th Edition, London, 1607.

Cameron, K. *The Place Names of Derbyshire* 3 vols., *English Place Name Society* Vol. XXIX, Cambridge, 1959.

Campbell, B. *Horse Racing in Britain* London, 1977.

Cauter, & Downham, London, 1954.

Chambers, J. *The English House* London, 1985.

Chambers, R. *History of the Rebellion of 1745–1746* Edinburgh, 1869.

City Growth, Derby *Vision, Strategy & Ideas* Derby, 2005.

Clark, Richard *The Derby Town Chronicle 1513–1698* DAJ CXVIII (1998), 163–184.

Cobbing, B. & P. Priestland *Sir Thomas Stanhope of Shelford* Nottingham, 2003.

Colvin, H. *Biographical Dictionary of British Architects 1600–1840* London, 1978.

Cook, W.J. *Derby & District Directory* London, 1898.

Cox, J.C. *Notes on the Churches* of Derbyshire 4 vols, Derby 1879–1883.

Cox, J.C. *Three Centuries of Derbyshire Annals* 2 vols, London, 1890.

Cox, J.C. & W.H. St J. Hope *Chronicles of All Saints'* Derby, 1881.

Cox, T. *Magna Britannia et Hibernia Antiqua et Nova*, London, 1720–1731.

Coyne, A. *Sam's Plaza* Derby, 1986.

Cozens-Hardy, B. (ed) *The Diary of Sylas Neville 1767–1788* Oxford, 1950.

Craven, M.A.J.B. *The Derby Townhouse*, Derby, 1987.

Craven, M.A.J.B. & M.F. Stanley *The Derbyshire Country House* 2 Vols., Matlock, 1982, 1984.

Craven, M.A.J.B. *Derbeians of Distinction* Derby, 1998.

Craven, M.A.J.B. *Derby Street by Street* Derby, 2005.

Craven, M.A.J.B. *John Whitehurst, FRS, Scientist and Clockmaker* Mayfield, 1996.

Craven, M.A.J.B. *The Illustrated History of Derby's Pubs,* 2nd (revised) edition, Derby, 2002.

Cresy, E. *Report… into the Sewerage etc. and Sanitary Condition of the Inhabitants of Derby* London, 1849.

Cunliffe-Shaw *The Men of the North.*

Darlington, R.R. *The Cartulary* of *Darley Abbey, Derbyshire Record Series* Vol. I., Kendal, 1945.

Davies, D.P. *A View* of *Derbyshire* Belper, 1811.

Davison, A.W. *Derby, Its Rise and Progress* Derby, 1906.

Deanesley, M. (ed.) *The Burton Abbey Charters, in Collections for a History of Staffordshire, Staffordshire Record Society* Stafford, 1937.

Defoe, D. *A Journey Throughout the Whole Island of Great Britain 1724–1727*, London, 1907.

Derby City Council *Official Guides* Derby 1972, 1977, 1984.

Derby City Council *Charter Celebrations* Derby, 1978.

Derby City Partnership *Partnership Agreement* Derby, n.d. [*c.*2003].

Derby City Partnership *2020 Vision – Derby Community Strategy 2003–2006* Derby, 2006.

Derby Cityscape *Derby Cityscape Progress* Derby, 2005.

Derby Corporation *Your Derby: A Plan for Development* Derby, 1951.

Derby Corporation *Spotlight of Derby, various issues* Derby, 1957–1972.

Derby County Borough *Industries and Social Life Jubilee Souvenir, TUC 1918* Derby, 1918.

Derby County Borough *Electricity Department Extensions Opening Booklet* Derby, 1930.

Derby County Borough *Centenary of Local Government* Derby, 1935.

Derby County Borough *Derby, City of Vital Industries* Derby, n.d. (*c.*1935).

Derby County Borough *Official Opening of Derby Airport* Derby, 1939.

Derby County Borough *Derby Cavalcade* Cheltenham, 1954.

Derby Trader Derby '79 Derby, 1979.

Derbyshire Advertiser, Modern Mayors of *Derby 1835-1938 2* vols, 1909, 1935.

Derbyshire Archaeological Society's Journal 1879 to present.

Derbyshire Miscellany DAS Local History Section, 1967 to present.

Dickinson, M. *Seventeenth Century Tokens of the Bntish Isles* London, 1986.

Dobson, M. *The First Hundred Years of the Training College, Derby* Derby, 1951.

Dobson, M. *The First Hundred Years of the Diocesan Training College, Derby* London, 1951.

Doig, A.G. & M.A.J.B. Craven *Derby Trams and Buses* 2 Vols, Burton, 1986, 1987.

Dugdale W. *Monasticum Anglicanum* ed. J. Carley, H. Ellis and B. Badinel London, 1830.

Duke, W. *Lord George Murray and the 'Forty-Five.*

Eardley-Simpson, L.L. *Derby and the 'Forty-Five* London, 1983.

Edgeworth, M. and R.L. *Memoirs of Richard Lovell Edgeworth Esq. begun by Himself and Concluded by His Daughter Maria Edgeworth* 2 Vols., London, 1820.

Farey, J. *A General View of the Agriculture and Minerals of Derbyshire* 3 Vols., London, 1811–1817.

Farrington, J., R.A. (ed. J. Grieg) *Farrington Diary* London, 1925

Farmer, D.H. *The Oxford Dictionary of Saints* Oxford, 1979.

Farnsworth, D. *From Mearca to Clark-Maxwell* Derby, 1988.

Faull, M.L. *British Survival* ed. Ll. Lang, Oxford, 1977.

Fiennes, C. (ed. C. Morris) *Journeys* London, 1967.

Fitton, R.S. & A.P. Wadsworth *The Strutts and the Arkwrights* Manchester, 1958.

Finberg, H.P.R. *Roman and Saxon Withington, Leics, University Dept. of English Local History Occasional Paper No.8* Leicester, 1957.

Fowkes, D. et al (Eds.) *1852 Board of Health Map of Derby with Notes* Derby, 1980.

Fox, G. *Journal or Historical Account of the Life… of George Fox* London, 1694.

Fox-Davies, A.C. *Armorial Families* 2 vols, London, 1925.

Fraser, D. *Fields of Radiance: The Scientific and Industrial Scenes of Joseph Wright* in D. Cosgrove & S. Daniels (eds.) *The Iconography of Landscape* Cambridge, 1988.

Galbraith, G. (ed.) *The Journal of William Bagshaw Stevens* Oxford, 1965.

Garratt, H.J.H. & C. Rawcliffe *The Derbyshire Feet of Fines 1323–1546 Derbyshire Record Society XI* Chesterfield, 1985.

GEC (G.E.Cokayne) *The Complete Peerage* (14 Vols.) 2nd Edn, London, 1910–1959, 1982.

Girouard, M. *Robert Smythson and the Elizabethan Country House*, Rev. Edn, Yale, 1983.

Glover, S. *History and Directory of Derbyshire for 1827–1829* Derby, 1829.

Glover, S. *History and Gazeteer of the County of Derby* 2 Vols., 1st Edn, Derby, 1828–9; 2nd Edn., Derby, 1833.

Glover, S. *History of the borough of Derby as a Guide to Strangers Visiting the Town* Derby, 1843.

Glover, S. *History* and *Directory of Derby* Derby, 1849.

Goode, P. *Film Entertainment in Derby* Matlock, 1985.

Goodhead, E.E. *West End Story* Matlock, 1983.

Goodhead, E.E. *West End Tales* Derby, 1986.

Gough. J. *The Midland Railway, A Chronology* Leicester, 1986.

Grant, G.L. *Standard Catalogue of Provincial Banks and Banknotes* London, 1977.

Gunnis, R. *Biographical Dictionary of British Sculptors 1660–1851* London, 1953.

Hanbury, W.H. *Notes on the History of the County Borough of Derby* Derby, 1913.

Hardy, C. & R. Brown *Derby at War* Birmingham, 1979.

Harris, L. & G. Jackson-Stops *Robert Adam at Kedleston*, London, 1987.

Hart, C.R. (ed.) *Early Charters of Northern England and the North Midlands*, Leicester, 1975.

Heath, J. *Derby and District Motor Bus Proprietors and their Services Prior to 1930* Castle Donington, 1985.

Heath, J. & R. Christian *Yesterday's Town, Derby* Buckingham, 1985.

Heath-Gracie, G.H. *Organist? Why?* unpublished MS, 1980.

Hobson, W. *Queen Victoria's State Visit to Derby* Derby, 1891.

Holyoake, G.J. & A. Scotton *Jubilee History of the Derby Co-operative Provident Society* Manchester, 1900.

Hunter, J. *Familiae Minorum Gentium* 4 vols., Harleian Society Vols. XXXVII-XL, London, 1894–96.

Hunter, J. *Pedigrees* Harleian Society Vol. LXXXVIII, London, 1936.

Hutton, C. *A Memoir of Mr John Whitehurst FRS* London, 1792.

Hutton, W. *History and Antiquities of the Borough of Derby Down to 1791* Derby 1791.

Hutton, W. *Life of William Hutton and the History of the Hutton Family* Birmingham, 1816.

Innes-Smith, R.S. *The Chapel of St Mary-on-the-Bridge, Derby* Derby, 1988.

Jeayes, I.H. *Charters of the County Borough of Derby* London, 1904.

Jeayes, I.H. *Derbyshire Charters* London, 1906.

Jewitt, Ll. *The Ballads and Songs of Derbyshire* Derby, 1867.

Johnson, S. *Later Roman Britain* London, 1980.

Kelly's Directory of Derbyshire London, 1884–1941.

Kemp, H. *The History of Derby Charities* Derby, 1861.

Keys, J. *Sketches of Old Derby and Neighbourhood* London, 1895.

King-Hele, D. *Doctor of Revolution* London, 1977.

King-Hele, D. *Erasmus Darwin, A Life of Unequalled Achievement* London, 1999.

Kirk, P., P. Felix & G. Bartnik *The Bombing of Rolls-Royce at Derby* Derby, 2002.

Langley, R. & C. Drage *Roman Occupation at Little Chester, Derby: Salvage Excavation… 1986–1990* DAJ CXX (2000) 123–287.

Leahy, K. & C.M. Coutts *The Lost Kingdom – the Search for Anglo-Saxon Lindsey* Scunthorpe, 1987.

Leland, J. *Itinerary of a Tour Through England and Wales 1545* Oxford, 1760.

Leveaux, V.M. *The History of the Derbyshire General Infirmary 1810–1894* Cromford, 1999.

Lodge's Peerage London, 1911.

Lysons, S. & D. *Magna Britannia* Vol. V, Derbyshire, London, 1816.

Mackworth Townswomens' Guild *Mackworth Estate Jubilee – A Social History* Derby, 1982.

McLynn, F.J. *The Jacobite Army in England* Edinburgh, 1983.

Mallender, M. *The Great Church* Derby, 1981.

Margary, I.D. *Roman Roads in Britain* 3rd Edn, London, 1973.

Mavor, W. *The British Tourist* London, 1800.

Meaney, A. *A Gazetteer of Early Anglo-Saxon Burial Sites* London, 1964.

Meteyard, E. *The Life of Josiah Wedgwood* London, 1866.

Midland Railway *For King and Country 1914–1919* Derby, 1921.

Miller, P.W. *Derby Cathedral* Derby, 1972; Rev. Edn, 1981.

Morgan, P. (ed.) *Domesday Book* Phillimore Series Vol. XXVII, Derbyshire, Chichester, 1978.

Moritz, C.P. *Travels Chiefly on Foot through Several Parts of England, trans. A Lady* London, 1795.

Mozley, T. *Reminiscences* 2 Vols., London, 1889.

Mundy, E. *Varieties of Many Years* Derby, 1909.

Musson, B.B. *A Real Railway Child* Derby, 1996.

Myres, J.N.L. *Anglo-Saxon Pottery and the Settlement of England* Oxford, 1969.

Nash, G.C. *The LMS at War* London, 1946.

Nicolson, B. *Joseph Wright of Derby, Painter of Light* 2 vols. London, 1968.

Nixon, F. *The Industrial Archaeology of Derbyshire* Newton Abbot, 1969.

North, J.J. *English Hammered Coinage* 2 vols, London, 1963.

Ordnance Survey *Map of Britain in the Dark Ages* 2nd Edn, London, 1966.

Owen, A.E. *Parkfields Cedars – True to the End* Derby n.d. [1999].

Palmer, S.H. *Hadley Heritage* Provo, Utah, 1986.

Pattison, I.R. RCHM (E) *Report on Kingsway Hospital* York, 1995.

Payne, C.J. *Derby Churches Old and New* Derby, 1893.

Pevsner, Sir N. *The Buildings of England, Derbyshire* 1st Edn London, 1953; 2nd Edn London, 1978.

Phillips, Sir R. Bt *A Personal Tour Through the United Kingdom* London, 1828.

Pigot & Co. *Directories of Derbyshire* London, 1822, 1825, 1835.

Pilkington, J. *A View of the Present State of Derbyshire* 2 vols, Derby, 1789.

Poole, A.L. *Domesday to Magna Carta* 2nd Edn, Oxford, 1955.

Porter, L. *Shrovetide Football and the Ashbourne Game* Ashbourne, 2002.

Powell, K. *Cutting the Heart out of Derby, SAVE* London, 1983.

Reliquary 1st Series, 1860–1886.

Rice, D.G. *Derby Porcelain 1750–1770* Newton Abbot, 1983.

Ripley, D. *The Little Eaton Gangway and Derby Canal* 2nd revised edition, Oxford, 1993.

Rippon, A. *The Book of Derby* Buckingham, 1980.

Roberts, M. *Derbyshire Children's Hospital* Derby, n.d. [1977].

Robinson, J. *Derby Illustrated: Art, Trade and Commerce* London, n.d. (*c.*1891).

Roffe, D. *Derbyshire Domesday* Matlock, 1986.

Royal Commission on Historic Monuments *Inventory of Non-conformist Chapels and Meeting Houses in Central England*, London, 1986.

Rylands, J.P. (ed.) *Visitation of Cheshire 1580, Harleian Society XVIII* London, 1882.

Saltman, A. *Cartulary of the Wakebridge Chantries at Crich, Derbyshire Record Series VI* Kendal, 1971.

Saltman, A. *The Kniveton Leiger, Derbyshire Record Series VII* Kendal, 1977.

Saltman, A. *A Cartulary of Dale Abbey, Derbyshire Record Series II* Kendal, 1966.

Saunders, E.J. *Joseph Pickford of Derby* Stroud, 1993.

Saunders, E.J. *Biographical Dictionary of English Wrought Iron Smiths of the Seventeenth and Eighteenth Centuries* Walpole Society, 2005, 237–384.

Schofield, R.E. *The Lunar Society* of Birmingham Oxford, 1963.

Scott, A.B. *Littleover and Its Church* Derby, 1916.

Scott-Giles, W. *Civic Heraldry* London, 1933.

Seaby, P. & P.F. Purvey *Coins of England and the United Kingdom, Vol. I* London, 1988.

Seward, A. *Memoirs of the Life of Dr Darwin* London, 1804.

Shawcroft, J. *History of the Derbyshire County Cricket Club 1870–1970* Ripley, 1970.

Simcocks, J. (ed.) *Ruff's Guide to the Turf* London, 1979.

Simpson, R. *History and Antiquities of Derby* 3 vols, Derby, 1826.

Singleton, D. *A History of the Derwent Hospital* Derby, n.d. [*c.*1981].

Smith, M.E. *The Derby Canal* Ilkeston, 1979.

Stenton, Sir F. *Anglo-Saxon England* 3rd Edn, Oxford, 1971.

Stukeley, W. *Itinerarium Curiosum* London, 1724.

Sutherland, C.H.V. *English Coinage 600-1900* London, 1973.

Sylvester, C. *Domestic Economy* London, 1819.

Tait, J. *The Medieval English borough* Manchester, 1936.

Taylor, C. *Village and Farmstead: A History of Rural Settlement in England* London, 1983.

Taylor, F. (ed.) *Calendar of Crutchley MSS in the John Rylands Library* Manchester.

Todd, M. *The Coritani* London, 1973.

Turbutt, G. *A History of Derbyshire* 4 Vols. Cardiff, 1999.

Unsworth, W.L. *Seventy-Five Years' Co-operation in Derby* Manchester, 1927.

Victoria County History of Derbyshire 2 vols, London, 1905.

Vincent-Kemp, R. *George Stubbs and the Wedgwood Connection* Stoke, 1986.

Visitations: *Derbyshire*

    Flower, W. in 1569: Genealogist, New Series VII-V

    St George, R. in 1611: Genealogist, New Series VIII

    St George, R. in 1634: College of Arms MS C 33

    Dugdale, W. in 1662: London, 1879

    Dugdale, W. Nottinghamshire and Derbyshire Visitation Papers, ed. G.D. Squibb, trans. G. Ireland, Harleian Soc. NS.VI, London, 1987

Wacher, J. *The Towns* of Roman Britain London, 1974.

Wagner, Sir A.R. *English Genealogy* 3rd Edn, Chichester, 1983.

Ward, J. *Notes on the History of Derby Addressed to Mr Johnson* MS, 1893.

Walthall, W. *MS Annals of Local and National Events c.*1838.

Webbe, E.W. (ed.) *The Oddfellows' Companion and Guide to Derby* Derby, 1893.

Webster, G. *The Cornovii* London, 1975.

Weir, H. *More Odds and Ends About Derby and Derbyshire* Derby, 1910.

White, T. *Directory of Derbyshire* London, 1857.

White, W.D. *Derbyshire Clockmakers before 1850* Derby, 1958.

Whitwell, J.B. *The Coritani in BAR British Series* 99 Oxford, 1982.

Wigley, D.A. & I.T.P. Hassall *Quarndon* Derby, n.d. *c.*1962.

Williams, F.S. *The Midland Railway, Its Rise and Progress* London, 1875

Woodward, Sir L.I. *The Age of Reform* Oxford, 1962.

Woolley, W. *History of Derbyshire* (ed. C. Glover & P. Riden) Derbyshire Record Society, VI, Chesterfield, 1981.

INDEX